NIETZSCHE: THE BODY AND CULTURE

NIETZSCHE: THE BODY AND CULTURE

Philosophy as a Philological Genealogy

ERIC BLONDEL
Translated by Seán Hand

Stanford University Press
Stanford, California
1991

Stanford University Press
Stanford, California
© 1986 Presses Universitaires de France, Paris
English translation © 1991 The Athlone Press,
    London
Originally published 1986 in French by
    Presses Universitaires de France as
    Nietzsche le corps et la culture
Originating publisher of English edition:
    The Athlone Press, London
First published in the U.S.A. by
    Stanford University Press
Cloth ISBN 0-8047-1551-3
Paper ISBN 0-8047-1906-3
LC 89-51665

The man who seeks truth becomes a scholar; the man who wishes to act out his subjectivity can become a writer; but what must be done by the man who seeks that which lies between the two?

Robert Musil

Life does not act in a conceited way

Thomas Mann

Great men and rivers travel in a crooked path,
But move towards their goal.

Nietzsche

Contents

Abbreviations

An	The Antichrist
AOM	Assorted Opinions and Maxims
BGE	Beyond Good and Evil
BT	The Birth of Tragedy
CW	The Case of Wagner
D	Daybreak
DD	Dithyrambs of Dionysus
EH	Ecce Homo
GM	The Genealogy of Morals
GS	The Gay Science
HATH	Human, All Too Human
K	Kröner: Grossoktavausgabe
KGW	Nietzsche, Werke, Kritische Gesamtausgabe
LC	Lettres choisies
LPh	Le Livre du philosophe
Mus.	Nietzsche, Gesammelte Werke, Musarionausgabe
NPh	Naissance de la philosophie à l'époque de la tragédie grecque
NCW	Nietzsche contra Wagner
OP	Oeuvres posthumes
TSZ	Thus Spoke Zarathustra
UM	Untimely Meditations
VP	La volonté de puissance
WP	The Will to Power
WS	The Wanderer and His Shadow

Introduction

I am a nuance.
Nietzsche

Reading is always a risky business: we confront an enigma or run
the risk of roaming. But doesn't reading Nietzsche throw us into a
labyrinth from which no-one emerges unscathed, where even
Ariadne is absent, and which is to be recounted only through
symbols?

There is no need to have recourse to the famous cliché of
Nietzsche as someone who fell into the indefinable realms of
madness. Nietzsche, rather than becoming lost, is someone who
loses us: he is an enigma. And how can we fail to link him in our
minds with the disquieting interrogation carried out by that
dubious monster known as the Sphinx?

The Sphinx
There you crouch, inexorably
Like my curiosity,
Which pushes me towards you:
Yes, Sphinx, I am a questioner like you;
This abyss is common to us –
We might almost speak with the same mouth![1]

Reading is always a daring business: a *Wagnis*. This is precisely
the word Nietzsche uses to describe Oedipus, who is turned into a
symbol of his own genealogical decipherment of truth and examination of Life, here represented by the woman-Sphinx.[2] But is this
enigma just his object, or is it not also his text and its 'questionable
questions'? And in that case, 'which of us is Oedipus here? Which
of us Sphinx?'[3]

To confront the enigmatic monster, must one become a monstrous enigma? To read Nietzsche, must we have the 'fatal'
temerity of Oedipus?: 'the same man who solves the riddle of

nature – that Sphinx of two species – must also break the most sacred natural orders by murdering his father and marrying his mother'.[4] And Nietzsche recognizes in *Ecce Homo*: 'When I picture a perfect reader, I always picture a monster of courage and curiosity, also something supple, cunning, cautious, a born adventurer and discoverer'.[5]

So be it. But why not take Nietzsche at his word when he says: 'What strange, wicked, questionable questions! . . . Is it any wonder we should at last grow distrustful, lose our patience, turn impatiently away? That this Sphinx should teach us too to ask questions? *Who* really is it that here questions us?'[6] At the bottom of the 'common abyss' separating the Sphinx from Nietzsche, who can say whether there is not a hidden vacuity, like a mythical monster, to be demystified?

With Nietzsche, do we ever emerge from uncertainty? And is this deep or just phoney? Is it *Versuch*-type thought, which Nietzsche describes as a darkness criss-crossed by flashes of lightning, or is it just 'night, when every cow is black', as opposed to day when they are 'many colours'? Doesn't Nietzsche proclaim – and who has not been tempted to see this as an admission, and a regrettably belated one at that – in *Ecce Homo*: 'Perhaps I am a buffoon?'[7] Doesn't this 'canonize' him rather than make him into a genius? In other words, isn't Nietzsche the perfect example of someone who attracts the fantasies, projections and unquestioning acceptance of fanatical readers? Stendhal, whose principle, 'Be clear, precise and devoid of illusions' was quoted by Nietzsche, noted that 'the less intelligent your ultra, the more fanatical'.[8] Must we not *believe*, to the point of foolishness, if we are to see Nietzsche as someone guaranteed to raise the interpretative stakes, where he himself has denounced the dubious presumption of overestimating his perspicacity?[9] On the other hand, would we not be 'philistine' if, like a 'dull' Valenod or a 'stupid' Homais, we heeded Kant's warning:

> Everyone considers himself a lord to the extent to which he lets himself off work . . . one has only to listen to one's inner ear and profit by it to capture all the wisdom one can expect from philosophy. Moreover, the tone used here shows that such people see themselves not as scholars making a slow and careful progress . . . but rather as *geniuses* capable of attaining everything that assiduous work can bring them.[10]

In fact, the bias against taking Nietzsche seriously and a Nietzschean *Schwärmerei* are profoundly complicit: by acting as a foil for one another, they each put off confronting the text, to the point where we ask whether their apparent opposition does not, genealogically, conceal a desire to avoid that amounts to the resistance put up by a drive in the face of an enquiry that examines not only opinions, but also the 'body'. This Sphinx-like questioning is the genealogical question. No examination of Nietzsche can avoid the obligation to free itself from the mysteries of prejudice, the 'Ideal' or fashion.

Fashion has, in fact, decked out the Untimely in the garb of a gutter-press Punch, so that, as Hermann Broch has written: 'Nietzsche fanned the flames of twentieth-century middle-class irrationalism'.[11] Whereas Nietzsche himself, many of whose criticisms of the 'modern spirit' could be recalled here in their entirety'[12] had already written of his illustrious predecessor:

> Schopenhauer seems to belong to [our age] only by accident. . . . First, for a long time, . . . he had against him his lack of readers; then, when he acquired them, he had against him the inadequacy of his earliest advocates . . .; a new danger has gradually appeared in addition, deriving from the manifold attempts that have been made to adapt Schopenhauer to this feeble age or even to employ him as an exotic and stimulating spice, as it were a kind of metaphysical pepper.[13]

In this way 'around every profound spirit a mask is continually growing, thanks to the constantly false, that is to say *shallow* interpretation of every word he speaks, every step he takes, every sign of life he gives'.[14]

No doubt we could say that a mask is a useful way of hiding inconsistency. None the less Nietzsche was concerned enough about univocity to say regarding the *truth* of his work that 'I am frightened by the thought of what unqualified and unsuitable people may invoke my authority one day'.[15] Lying somewhere between a 'metaphysical' monolithism and an ideological explosion, sustaining a discourse that is more ambivalent than uncertain, and linking concepts to the workings of the imagination, Nietzsche presents his thoughts as a *philosophy*: this means that his thought risks less being handed over by some Judas or other to a metaphysic that scares some people off, than being taken over by *nihilism*, the reactive, spiteful thinking of nothingness.

What course do we adopt, then? In the case of Nietzsche it becomes almost a truism to say that we must preserve the irreducible originality of his revolt: 'Let us stand alone and not listen to others. . . . No more masters or models!'.[16] But what, then, is the hallmark of Nietzsche? It can only be his *text*. And what both contemporary reactions and tradition equally dread and obstinately avoid, by absorbing it into academic work, is first and foremost an open confrontation with the *enigma* of Nietzsche's text. To make this reading confrontation possible, we must discover a structure that governs the workings of Nietzsche's text, even if this emanates from a tension (between letter and body, or text and genealogical referent) that amounts to an impossibility. Failing this, any reading of Nietzsche will necessarily be condemned either to remain silent in the face of something presumably ineffable, or else to to what amounts to the same thing and give in to the arbitrary workings of an eclectic *Phantasieren*, a superior kind of gossip where it is difficult even to see on what grounds Nietzsche, in Laputa, can claim to have special rights.

Could this structural order be that of conceptual discourse? And, if so, must we equally presuppose a conceptual discourse peculiar to Nietzsche? No doubt, for if it were not so the commentator's discourse would reveal its own artifice and in addition would have to define the philosophical status and the use that it makes (or does not make) of those elements in the texts which lie outside discourse. To what extent is it therefore possible to assimilate Nietzsche's texts into a particular conceptual and discursive organization whose patterns we attempt to discern beneath the incontestable uncertainty of appearances? We can immediately perceive the resemblance between this approach and the dualist treatment that classical rationalist epistemology metes out to sense impressions. Can we conceptualize Nietzsche's texts without leaving something out, and are we not forced to do so by producing an occult logic that, however one sets about it, would fulfil the role of an essence or a hidden truth to the exclusion of appearances? If this happens we risk falsifying the originality of Nietzsche's, text and 'forgetting' especially the elements lying outside discourse which are raised by the genealogical question. Above all, this approach surreptitiously brings back to metaphysical rationalism an author who contests its methods.

Under these conditions, if reading consists in reordering a number of ambiguous, if not chaotic, elements, how is it possible to *read* Nietzsche without running away from him? Can we do it without abandoning ourselves to a giddy whim, or to the imperialism of a forced synthesis, that recalls the verbal violence with which Oedipus responded to the insinuations of that other Sphinx, Tiresias?

Can we hope for *Logos*? No doubt. The interpretations made by Jaspers, Heidegger and Fink, to mention only these, have paid homage to Nietzsche's thought and rescued him from a marginal position by relying on a rational philosophical discourse. But the logos effaces the uniqueness of Nietzsche's text. Not by unifying what on the immediate level presents itself as chaos: only a superficial approach could seize on this wonderful disorder simply to criticize or condemn it. More seriously, we can then only pay attention to whatever is a product of discursive thought, and have to write off everything else as picturesque or rhetorical, that is as belonging to the philosophically ambiguous status of art. If rationality, as a systematic collection of concepts, is not everything in Nietzsche, what is its relationship to the rest and the status of this 'rest'? This is our first question.

It is this reduction of Nietzsche's text to a discourse, which if not rational is at any rate 'metaphysical', that allows even Nietzsche's greatest commentator, Heidegger, to evade this philosophy of genealogical questioning by absorbing it into the process of subjectivation and increasing technicality which, in his opinion, characterizes metaphysics from Plato to Nietzsche. Blind to the interpretative, non-instrumental and anti-technical aspects of the body and genealogy in Nietzsche – which would make Nietzsche's thought something other than just an avatar of subjective technical manipulation – Heidegger can thus reduce Nietzsche's philosophy to a moment in the history of Being – or rather of the forgetting of Being. But the price paid is the effacement of the *Versuch*, the interpretative nature of the body and the genealogical question.[17] Reduced in this way to a few key *concepts*, Nietzsche's work becomes valuable only as an example of metaphysics and as such has to be superseded ... by the thought of Heidegger.

But if on the other hand we try to show how Nietzsche's thought escapes from metaphysics without falling into contradiction, by showing, like Karl Jaspers, the transcendental breaks and by having recourse to the existential leap,[18] or, like Granier, by thinking of truth as interpretation or Being as interpreted being,[19] we are none the less left with the problem of what status to accord this thought, which, as a consequence becomes necessarily relativized. Jaspers relativizes it, in fact, when he discerns in it an empty demand for transcendence, which permits him to refer it back to his own philosophy, while J. Granier, when he poses the inevitable problem of the status of Nietzsche's interpretation *of* interpretation, as a second discourse on interpretation, finds himself constrained to refer back to a metaphilosophy that is seen as a task, and so, in turn, to refer Nietzsche's thought back to something *outside* the text.[20]

Finally, even if, as in the case of P. Valadier, we expound the Nietzschean critique of Christianity as though it were a continuous doctrine by welding together different theses as one might do for Kant's religious philosophy, we reconstitute Nietzsche's thought in the order of reason and install him in a rationality that, however founded, neglects certain very specific aspects of Nietzsche's anti-Christian attacks: by its very objectivity, doesn't this approach lay itself open to the charge of having erased the texts' violence, their provocative nature, their drives, all of which are perhaps more fundamental?

So, who is the metaphysician: Nietzsche or his most celebrated, and righlty celebrated, commentators? If, as Nietzsche indicates in §2 of *Beyond Good and Evil*, metaphysics is characterized by dualism and reacts to the ambiguity of its object by setting up antinomies, conceptual discourse on Nietzsche falls back into what it criticizes along with Nietzsche. Through the very rigour of its concepts and its philosophical discourse, it sets in place a strange *dualism* which, like the logicist refusal and the prophetic *Schwärmerei*, evades the enigmatic ambiguity of the evolution of Nietzsche's text by separating what pertains to discourse from what partakes only of the irreducibly *perceptible* element: in this way metaphysics projects on to the text itself a not wholly unjustified will for discursive coherence, but, as in any projection, it does so at the price of the multiple and innocent nature of the object itself. Morevoer, this dualism cannot avoid relating Nietzsche's thought to something outside or beyond it which acts as the norm for discursive unity. From these heights Nietzsche's thought is judged *in absentia* to be relative, or considered a failure, either *in flagrante delicto* or subject to confirmation.

Whatever the cause, the inevitable result of such an undertaking is above all that the commentary itself is made relative. So before we can look for something speculative outside the text that can justify isolating the discursive elements of this thought, we must at least question the status of what *inside* Nietzsche's text remains *outside* discourse, whatever we call it, be it drives, rhetoric, breaks, incoherences, *Versuch*, music, comedy, solemnity, art, allusions, or language games. From this point of view, dualism puts a strain on reading itself. An often considerable distance separates Nietzsche's texts from the highly selective anthologies of explicatory discursive passages compiled by his commentators. No-one is in a position to give a complete account of all the workings or resonances of a text by Nietzsche, simply because they have read, for example, the voluminous work of Heidegger. In the plethora of literature that none the less exists on Nietzsche one looks in vain, even among his greatest commentators, for something that confronts the text itself in a way that allows us to link the discursive themes to those elements in him which resist discursive synthesis. To take just one example: commentators, foreign as well as German, leave to the reader's historical culture – or lack of it – the delicate task of deciphering Nietzsche's quarrels – such as the 'untimely' hit-and-runs in *Twilight of the Idols* – with the issues of his day, that are often pretty mysterious to a present-day non-German reader. And if we reply that this is of more interest to the historian than the philosopher, what should we think of a philosophical view of Nietzsche that neglects his particular attachment to and distance from his contemporary history? Is Nietzsche's period dead and gone now, and should we just think of it as a *caput mortuum* of Nietzsche's philosophizing, that ceases in time to be philosophical? This attitude, which is implicit in those great philosophical commentaries on Nietzsche which are linked to perennial problems surreptitiously transforms the *Unzeitgemässheit* into *Zeitlosigkeit*, untimely philosophy into *philosophia perennis*. And from then on, what could Nietzsche or, more generally, any philosopher have to say to *our* age apart from general pronouncements abstracted from our own age? And doesn't this even amount to saying that he has nothing essential to say in his own age about his own age? A sort of metaphysical eternity therefore hangs over many commentators who latch on to conceptual discourse to the detriment of whatever flouts it or even carries it. The discursive approach therefore leaves behind a pile of 'scoria' which are like pearls to Nietzsche and represent in this case the *Abfall* of the concept, as it were, here reduced to the same status as the perceptible world in Platonic dualism. Should we be content with forcing the philosopher in this way to confess – something done all too willingly and complacently in the case of Plato[21] – that his discourse cannot avoid letting art, that is rhetoric, images, style, escape into literary analysis or *philology*? It seems, then, that the dualist split permits work to be divided up in a way that satisfies both the philologist and the philosopher. If the former has never claimed exclusive rights to the study of Kant's or Spinoza's style, or the latter sought to deny that Goethe or Hölderlin are more than just metaphysicians, the same does not hold true for Nietzsche. The philologist will not find it surprising that the philosopher's discursive analysis misses out what it cannot understand: no commentary, however complete, can ever exhaust the work's (artistic) richness. And, in fact, the philosopher feels he must recognize that, although it is possible to get bogged down in fastidious details or fall into paraphrase, a commentary can only have a modestly didactic aim, that of reaching a better understanding of the relationships within the work which escape a first reading. It is true that no analysis of Kant's philosophy, for example, can ever replace direct contact with his work. But a knowledge of the primary Kantian concepts can help guide us through any text by Kant: the conceptual commentary and the work are *homogeneous*. This is not at all the case with Nietzsche: it is not the *detail* which escapes a *general* discursive study, but something that is *heterogeneous* to it. Suddenly the philologist can denounce the artifice of a philosophical study that not only represses aesthetic pleasure but also often interprets falsely or in an unwarranted way brings into the domain of philosophy what can be explained only by having recourse to history (whether literary, political or cultural) or structural analysis, or linguistics, or art history, or stylistics, for example. But in saying this, the philologist ratifies dualism even as he contests the philosophical point of view, since, in place of a 'truth' which he judges to be partial, he puts forward an art which, in the eyes of the philosopher, on the other hand, is part of the subordinate order of persuasion or which comes under the domain of history and therefore seems relative or suspect.[22] If we confine ourselves to deploring this dualism as a clumsy compromise, we remain blind to its essential aim, which is to mask the *conflict*, and avoid confronting the *enigma* or contradiction directly, in short to make *reading* Nietzsche impossible. But who can say that this conflict or enigma or reading is not precisely Nietzsche's specific contribution? The drawbacks of discursive dualism explain why Nietzsche turned to the essay, which is frequently a euphemistic term for empiricism or anything intellectually negligible. So we speak about 'perspectivism': but isn't Nietzsche merely used as an alibi here, in order to establish a kind of ideological 'tidy' that some would claim juxtaposes disparate elements without displaying too much concern for coherence? The eclectic essay lasted right up until Heidegger and Jaspers: Nietzsche was seen as a marginal dilettante of philosophy who was pleasant, unpleasant or just a joker, something that allowed the interpreter to dodge in and out of Nietzsche's contradictions, or his own, choosing only those bits of the work that confirmed a particular thesis. This was the primary reading of a work held to be secondary and marginal to serious things, but which was in fact as contemptuous as the idea of the warrior's repose, when the warrior is Cartesian or Kantian.

Once neo-Kantianism had been overturned, first, via Blücher, by Hegel, then by phenomenology, which we must remember introduced the readings of Nietzsche put forward by Jaspers, Heidegger and Fink to an ignorant ethnocentric French audience, and finally by structuralism, in the guise of Freud and Marx, we might have imagined that Nietzsche would no longer be forced to sit it out on the sidelines in France. But no 'structure' emerged to prohibit the appearance of an inverted form of eclecticism: instead, Nietzsche was disembowelled and turned into a bloodless example of how the text and meaning were to be emptied or evaded. There was a concentration only on those texts whose content apparently proved that a text has no content and that all meaning, which in reality is an epiphenomenon of drives or linguisitic structures, heralds metaphysics. Under the pretext of 'textuality' the text found itself desubstantialized or rather deprived of substance.[23] Conversely, another tendency gave the non–regulated affirmation of drives the positive value of a purely affirmative Nietzschean liberation. These two eclecticisms produced the same paradoxical result: the body dissolved into a signifier, the text into drives, both of these being avatars of dualism. Neither of these interpretations was founded on an order or structure or strategy of texts, and their meaning – full or empty – was reconstructed on the basis of a few theoretical *or* metaphorical quotations which were never given satisfactorily. If Nietzsche is anything more than a 'higher swindle', to use his own description of Plato, is he then dead, for want of a grounding for meaning and interpretation, or is he condemned to be suspended between two types of 'hemiplegia'[24]?

Bachelard has perhaps been the only one of Nietzsche's commentators[25] to propose principles of interpretation which bring out the coherence of Nietzsche's poetry and thought while challenging an 'intellectualist' dualism that recognizes images as being valuable only in so far as they illustrate ideas. He sets out to show that 'in Nietzsche, the poet in part explains the thinker',[26] as opposed to a tradition founded on an 'intellectualist psychology, that is always ready to read images as allegories': Nietzsche's images, therefore, have 'their own destiny', which is proof of the thesis, dear to the author, that 'the imagination, rather than reason, is the unifying force in the human soul'. What we have is no longer the philosopher 'saving' the poet by giving him, albeit somewhat stingily, a certain discursive coherence, but a philosophical politics in the making: 'Nietzsche's poetics . . . prepare the ground for Nietzschean morality'. Nietzsche is a 'master of moral imagery'.[27]

All the same, Bachelard placed too much confidence in the work of Desoille, and so was too hasty in giving the images a dynamism of their own; he hypostatized them independently of the 'body' in the Nietzschean sense and was not aware of the fact that they are sometimes literary allusions rather than a creation of the universal unconscious; finally, he assimilated them, without examining them, into metaphor. But in Nietzsche images are interpretations *of something*, metaphors *of the body*. Bachelard contented himself with privileging certain images as being mythic 'elements' that are constitutive of a Nietzschean 'cosmos', to the detriment of other metaphors that were no less insistent and definitely no less obviously 'poetic', and did not seek to reinscribe them in the labour and history that also determine them. Symptomatically, he did not integrate into his analysis Nietzsche's teaching on interpretation, the idea of culture as *Zeichensprache*, or, in Freudian terms, the laws of deformation (*Entstellung*). Finally, does the unique nature of Nietzsche's work lie exclusively in its images, which are quasi-substantialized by Bachelard, sometimes at the risk of endorsing the *kitsch* or lapses in taste of a *Zarathustra* whose aesthetics, far from being universal, are too marked by their period to be anything other than outmoded? Doesn't the work's uniqueness also lie in the figures, tropes, style, in other words its graphics, all of which attest to, and even constitute, a certain labour, not only of the collective imaginary, but also of the text itself? To attribute to the imaginary as such an autonomous power of structuration and coherence does not at all imply that we must confer upon it an abstract, quasi-metaphysical independence. This hypostasis of the imaginary, with its correlative disregard for the other non-conceptual elements which the text brings into play, replaces the old abstractions with a new, non-discursive one, namely the imaginary, which in spite of all Bachelard's finesse leads to an idealist reading of Nietzsche.[28]

Is it possible, in the wake of Bachelard, to discern a certain coherence in Nietzsche's texts without castrating or extirpating them, in every sense that Nietzsche maliciously gives to these words when he attributes them to moral idealism[29]?

1
Reading Nietzsche

If we contrast Nietzsche's text with the whole of classical rationalism's philosophical literature, we see straightaway one fundamental difference: there is a gap separating those discourses which try to establish (without success) a univocal correspondence between the signifier and the conceptual signified, a degree zero[1] held to be the norm, from those which attempt to link up concepts into a logically continuous system. If outside of formal logic we cannot find any text that succeeds – in so far as it is a question of success – in totally eliminating the polysemic charge of the terms it sets into play, if no text can therefore ever be completely suitable or link up terms in a perfectly systematic and demonstrative way, the tendency none the less to conform to such demands, which emanate from what we usually call the Logos, defines the text as a philosophical discourse. But it is precisely the impossibility of having such a pure Logos, and the inevitability of deviating from the path of logic which Nietzsche indicates and accentuates through his style, as though he wished to establish the fact that the gap, far from being an accident, corresponds to a deep *reality* and manifests the irrepressible emergence of such a reality in the face of the artificial demands, both rational and moral, of logic. If, as Nietzsche writes in an apt formula, 'the production of a logical phenomenon never conforms to what we find in books'[2] this is because ultimately '*nothing* in reality corresponds rigourously to logic'.[3]

In Nietzsche, therefore, the stylistic gap has not just an aesthetic value, but an ontological or, if you like, philosophical import, in several senses. First, his text is, in terms of form, discontinuous and aphoristic, in contrast to the architectonic project of the discourse of classical philosophy. On this point alone, we must ask ourselves what meaning is displayed by this distinctive characteristic, without seeking to efface it by postulating that beneath surface appearances there is some continuity that is supposedly more real for this approach, which would bring us back to dualism.

We can make the same remark about the conceptual tenor: not only does Nietzsche not seem to care much about not giving a strictly univocal definition of the value of the concepts implied in his text – for he seems to rely more on their 'value' than on their 'signified' – but he does not even try to link them up in a coherently demonstrative fashion, which can simply seem to lead to incompatible propositions. Is it the case, then, that in his text Nietzsche is being aphasiac in the two senses given to the term by Jakobson in his essay 'Two Aspects of Language and Two Types of Aphasia'?[4] Is he an aphasiac in terms of selection and combination, metaphor and metonymy, to the extent that the uses improper (metaphorical) terms and cannot combine signifiers in a chain that is at least coherent? We can obviously try to unravel the contradictions by isolating the various different levels on which Nietzsche's text successively operates, as Granier has done.[5] But the same problem remains concerning the articulation of these different levels. Does this articulation rely on rational logic or not, on what structure or law (historical, linguistic, logical, imaginary) do we construct it? Granier speaks of 'overdetermination',[6] but he suggests a movement of negation and sublation of a Hegelian kind, in which a given level is negated 'from an ontologically superior point of view', rather than an interpretative imaginary overdetermination of a Freudian or Nietzschean type. Therefore, the first question is to know whether or not the central terms of a text by Nietzsche (genealogy, *décadence*, nihilism, morality, the innocence of evolution, the dionysiac, eternal recurrence, force, weakness, etc.) really are concepts through which we can articulate or, on the basis of which, we can found, if not a systematic rationality of discourse, at least a unity (though of what order?) rather than being overdetermined terms, or tropes, that attest to a certain labour of meaning and imagination in the text.

Above all, Nietzsche's text often gives reading a proliferation, not only of images, but also of metaphors, and more generally of tropes, that is of figures which, as opposed to the discourse of classical philosophy, characterize the text as *substitutive*. In linguistic terms, the gap in Nietzsche's text seems to operate as much on the level of combination as on that of selection. We can read it without specifying the status of this deviation which is as much paradigmatic as syntagmatic, and in relation to which, in order to define its value, we must adopt what Fontanier called 'a simple expression':[7]

such that, if we admit the distinction between surface structure and deep structure, we must define the rules of transformation, to adopt Chomsky's terms,[8] and assign them a place, a structure and a source, which in this case are culture, interpretation and the body. For us, the questions raised by the text's 'deviation' crystallize in Nietzsche's metaphors, which give a privileged place to the problem of whether or not the body is the basis of interpretation. But Nietzsche's metaphors are not limited only to cosmic symbolism, though in fact, having read the sketches for *Philosophy in the Age of Greek Tragedy*, it is tempting to link them to the cosmologies attributed to the Greek. Their chain of interpretation relates them structurally to the body. Moreover, we must not forget other rhetorical tropes and stylistic 'deviations' (notably on the syntagmatic axis) which continue for the moment to question the method of interpretation necessary in order to *read* Nietzsche's text in its entirety.

Firstly, we can note the persistent return of a coherent set of metaphors (though we must discover the law linking them) which can either be original or taken by Nietzsche from some philosophical, literary, linguistic, or simply popular tradition, not counting the fact that it is very tempting to try to unravel what they reveal about Nietzsche's own unconscious heritage (or even to use them to project the reader's own fantasies), which at all events still obliges us to ask in what way they can tell us something about the body, culture and interpretation in general. It is thus possible to isolate a set of 'gynaecological' metaphors relating to the *vita femina*, which has an ontological import and is in turn related to metaphors of clothing (travesty, appearance, base) and sex (possession, violence, evanescence, seduction);[9] the metaphors of gastroenterology, applied, as we shall see, to the organization of the instincts and themselves linked to the metaphors of politics and thence to the metaphorical (or non-metaphorical) order of interpretation; metaphors that are medical or 'physiological' but equally philosophical (genealogical and philological) of the nose and ear; metaphors of surface and depth, light and dark; and finally, the metaphors of philology applied to culture, and thus to morality, religion and philosophy, which lead us to a metaphorical theory of interpretation.

But even more remarkably (and it is surprising that apart from a few brief references by a couple of commentators, among them Heidegger and Bertram no in-depth study has been undertaken in this field) most of the central notions in Nietzsche's thought themselves refer back to one or several sets of metaphors. And Nietzsche's use of these metaphors, which are often inherited from Germanic or Greek culture, displaces or overdetermines their accepted use. Let us take a few general examples. In accordance with the subtitle of *The Twilight of the Idols*, it is usual to present Nietzsche as someone who 'philosophizes with a hammer'. But it is equally normal to reduce this metaphor to designating a destructive philosophy which, wielding the critical hammer like a mace or felling-axe,[10] will end up, if we are not careful, blindly annihilating all moral, metaphysical or religious values. We can see the advanage that such a reduction holds for its authors: it allows them to assimilate Nietzsche's thought into what they take to be 'nihilism' – the destruction of all 'vital' values – a nihilism which must be resisted at all costs since their beliefs support their own weak faith. These assimilations, which are not carried out simply by non-specialists, arise when we neglect the surfeit in texts by Nietzsche, whom we go on reading as if he were Spinoza or Kant. But if it is incontestable that Nietzsche's hammer must 'break the old law-tables',[11] Nietzsche gives the hammer to the future legislator as if he were a sculptor or a blacksith, that he may 'write upon the will of millenia'.[12] The hammer is, moreover, one of the instruments used by the genealogist philosopher or doctor, since it must be used to 'sound out idols',[13] on this occasion acting simultaneously as a percussion mallet[14] and a tuning-fork, or the hammer in a *Hammerklavier* whose strings are struck when played or tuned.[15]

But this overdetermination also characterizes certain 'para-concepts' such as genealogy or *Übermensch*. The prefix or particule of this last expression, borrowed, in fact, from Herder and Goethe,[16] tends to suggest, in spatial terms, an overcoming that no longer works towards a transcendence, but operates instead on the level of immanence while, in temporal or historical terms, it brings a morally sick, decadent and feeble man towards a sort of human *Jenseits*.[17] As for genealogy, we know that it proposes to assess metaphysical concepts or moral evaluations by going back to their origins, their hidden drives, their 'conditions of existence', the body, all of which determine these values and make them possible.[18] But is this definition enough? Does it not also mask something? The essential part of our study will try to elucidate the idea or metaphor of genealogy. Nietzsche borrows the term from Greek antiquity, and evokes especially Hesiod's genealogy in the *Theogony*.[19] We may deduce from this on the one hand that the precise aim of genealogical analysis is to assign its origin to a universe of transcendent values, and on the other that it revolves around a birth and an evolution. Moreover, Nietzsche was able to read this term in Kant who, in the Preface to the third edition of the *Critique of Pure Reason* uses the word in order to characterize Locke's empiricist explanation of the concept of human understanding; and in Nietzsche as in Kant, 'genealogy' equally differs from 'dogmatism' such that, in spite of considerable differences, Nietzsche's genealogy, like Kant's *Critique*, tries to move to a sort of constitutive *a priori* and in some way has a 'transcendental' at stake. But above all, as is confirmed by the allusion to the sphinx and Oedipus in §1 of *Beyond Good and Evil*, genealogical research is an enquiry into the physiological and biological, or more precisely sexual, origins of concepts and knowledge, in other words of culture in general, origins which are normally hidden but which can be inferred through the simple medium of language, which justifies an enquiry into the relationships maintained in Nietzsche's text by genealogy and philology.

However, metaphor is not the only trope to which Nietzsche's text has recourse, a text full of *allusions* or *mythologisms* (to use Fontanier's technical terms) taken from various literary, artistic or philosophical sources. Examples include: the *Rattenfänger der Gewissen* or 'pied piper of consciences',[20] Dionysius, Ariadne, the Labyrinth, the Eternal Feminine, *Ecce Homo*, and so on. These allusions frequently combine with *paronomasia*, which Nietzsche uses to an almost crazy extent, exploiting first of all the rich morphological resources of the German language and then displaying a parodic intention that focuses, for example, on Wagner's dramas, or the Bible or Goethe. Sometimes these allusions take on a paronomastic value only by way of an implicit contrast: *Götzendämmerung* (*Götterdämmerung*); *Jenseits von Gut und Böse/*(*Jenseits von Raum und Zeit*). On other occasions the comparison is explicit: *heilig/langweilig;*[21] *Brecher, Verbrecher, Wortbrüchiger;*[22] *im Namen des Vaters, des Sohnes und des heiligen Meisters/*(*Geistes*);[23] *verlogen/verbogen;*[24] *Not, Wende/Notwendigkeit.*[25] But to this paronomasia we can add *metaplasia*, as in the apocope *panem et Circen . . . ;*[26] or the apenthesis 'monotonotheism',[27] which can be combined with paronomasia, such as *abwärts/abgrundwärts*;[28] *Veränderung/ Verichlichung*.[29] This is not only catachresis; it also produces a rhetorical effect whose status must be defined as either aesthetic or philosophical. Nietzsche's text teems with homonymic substitutions, metabolisms and syllepses, such as *Tarantel*,[30] *Ye-a/Ja*,[31] *gerächt/gerecht*,[32] *medicynisch/medizinisch*.[33] These tropes are defined as such by way of contrast to a 'simple' use of the German language, but equally in relation to the language of philosophical discourse,[34] or a particular literary, religious or popular language, which can make them seem parodies[35] but more fundamentally can be the index of an unstable situation in Nietzsche's text *vis-à-vis* any discourse, any language. We must therefore ask whether the gap produced by parody or rhetoric in Nietzsche's texts, and consequently the qualities defining this gap, have an ornamental or a philosophical value. To what extent can we distinguish between these values and in what sense do pleasure, drives and discursive reason share common characteristics, exclude each other or combine within the perspective of an imaginary attempting to conceive of genealogy and the body?

It would be fastidious to draw up an inventory of the figures characterizing Nietzsche's text from the point of view of syntax, semantics and logic, that is to say, style. But we cannot deny that they are related to Nietzsche's philosophical intentions, under the label of what he calls *Versuch* and 'great style'. Generally, Nietzsche's text displays neither unity of *tone* – burlesque, serious, ironic, tragic, grandiloquent and even theatrical tones constantly alternate, sometimes without transition – nor unity of *genre*. Nearly every genre is represented: proverbs, maxims, parables, philosophical demonstrations, dramatic dialogues, psalms, prayer, and so on. This diversity, bordering on disparity or even bad taste, at least in our eyes,[36] is something Nietzsche reproaches in Plato[37] but none the less defends in the name of a certain conception of style:

> To *communicate* a state, an inner tension of pathos through signs, including the tempo of these signs – that is the meaning of every style; and considering that that multiplicity of inner states is in my case extraordinary, there exists in my case the possibility of many styles – altogether the most manifold art of style any man has ever had at his disposal.[38]

In this way ellipsis, suspension, irony and litotes characterize Nietzsche's text, not only from the 'macroscopic' point of view, where he constructs the work from aphorisms and paragraphs, but also from the 'microscopic' point of view, where he constructs a phrase: numerous aphorisms break off into unfinished phrases, unanswered questions, a dash or a row of dots (*Gedankenstrich*), while even the white spaces separating them can be thought of as ellipses or anacolutha. The latter are also easily located thanks to the numerous dashes and dots that break up any syntactic unity,[39] and to the italics (the German *Sperrdruck*), one of whose effects is to give the text a syncopated rhythm. On this level of ideas, one characteristic stands out: instead of giving a logically ordered succession of demonstrative propositions, Nietzsche almost insolently offers a series of questions,[40] exclamations, apostrophes and dialogues.

This stylistic diversity is in turn superimposed by another, which can only be partially designated by the none the less striking use of inverted commas and italics (which in German typography have the same distinctive value): not only is the author or subject designated in the text not always the same, but he even speaks several languages, successively or simultaneously,[41] a procedure that was strange in its day and which has become fashionable only since Joyce. Nietzsche's text is, therefore, the locus of several different discourses, languages or lexicons. In addition, the text 'by Nietzsche' must not always be seen to be original. *Nietzsche contra Wagner*, for example, is a montage of earlier texts by Nietzsche, which have been reworked to a greater or lesser degree. Many other texts by Nietzsche are also partially made up of self-quotations. This would not be of any philosophical significance if the point was just to recall a passage in a similar context where texts had the same value, or to offer an apology, as in Rousseau or a publicity campaign, which also happens from time to time in Nietzsche. For Nietzsche the value of a given text cannot be summed up simply by its particular discursive tenor, but also depends on its strategic and polemic position with regard to a given historical or textual context. This remark can also be applied to quotations, both explicit and implict, with which the text is strewn. Thus 'all that is "intransitory" – that too has been only an "image"' ['*Alles "Unvergängliche" – das ist auch nur ein Gleichnis*'], in the chapter 'Of Poets' in *Zarathustra*,[42] is both a slightly modified self-quotation from the chapter entitled 'On the Blissful Islands' to be found in the same book: 'All that is intransitory – that is but an image!',[43] and a quotation from a poem in the Songs of Prince Vogelfrei: 'The indestructible is but your invention!' ['*Das Unvergängliche Ist nur dein Gleichnis!*'].[44] But this last text in its turn is a complete parody of the closing verses from Goethe's *Faust*, Part II: '*Alles Vergängliche ist nur ein Gleichnis*'.[45] The allusion changes the value: the movement from *vergänglich* to *unvergänglich* distorts the meaning of the word *Gleichnis* (symbol, image, figure, semblances, illusion . . .). Another example: in both the chapter entitled 'Among the Daughters of the Desert' in Part IV of *Zarathustra*[46] and in *Ecce Homo*'s 'Why I Write Such Excellent Books',[47] we find the same formula, not given in inverted commas, which everyone in Germany knows comes from Luther: '*Ich kann nicht anders, Gott helfe mir, Amen!*' ['I cannot do otherwise, so help me God! Amen!'] In the first case, this phrase contrasts the German Luther with a certain 'European' choice, and in the second, the quotation serves to 'justify' Nietzsche's conception of style – all of this relating to Luther's exclamation only in terms of opposition or substitution: the anti-Luther Nietzsche who is anti-German and the neo-Luther Nietzsche who is the founder of a new German language.

But this procedure is so frequent that we can state that, for a good part of the time, Nietzsche's text is not properly speaking 'by Nietzsche', but by the Bible, Goethe, Kant, Hölderlin, Mozart-Schikaneder, Novalis, Schiller, Wagner, Mörike, and so on. And beyond this, even if some immense culture, equal to Nietzsche's, were capable of tracking down every quotation in Nietzsche's text, we still could not legitimately attribute Nietzsche's text to a set of authors, including himself, since these quotations are parodically deformed, and detached from their context or authors, either in their morphology or their syntax or their value. The fact that the Nietzschean text cannot be unreservedly attributed to Nietzsche the author (*auctor*) and subject (*subjectum*), that is Nietzsche the guarantor of the productive unity of this text, can be linked to the critical analyses of the notions of subject, will and responsibility which we can read in *Twilight of the Idols*: 'one is a part of everything', 'no-one is responsible for what he is', which holds as much for a 'writer' as it does for 'will' in the world. This helps us to understand another gap that is the correlative to those already mentioned: Nietzsche's text questions assumptions about the univocal presence of the signified to the signifier. If re-transcription in a different context[48] already submits the text to a re-reading that alters its impact[49] (and obliges the reader to carry out such a task), the modified quotation obliges us to submit *Nietzsche contra Wagner*, for example, to a double reading that destroys the supposed semantic unity of the text, by placing it in a sense in a situation where the 'signified' escapes from a present understanding and becomes both present and past, itself and something other. This procedure is paradigmatic of the status of any text by Nietzsche. The same technique is therefore used in Nietzsche's frequent references to himself as 'Heraclitus',[50] 'Wagner',[51] 'Schopenhauer'[52], 'Caesar' or 'the Crucified Christ'.[53] We have to conclude that the process of rewriting, of which we find many examples in the course of reading unpublished material or correspondence,[54] as well as when we compare the published works to unpublished material (or even to other published works) not only bears witness to the intense 'stylistic' labour from which Nietzsche's definitive texts have emerged, but intrinsically concerns the textuality inherent in Nietzsche's works.

Once we have related Nietzsche's text back to several 'authors', and realized how it is made up of several levels, we finally see how it is literally 'polyglot' and belongs to several cultures. In the first place, it is peppered with expressions, whether quotations or original constructions, in Greek, Latin, French, English, Italian, Spanish, and even Sanskrit. But above all, many of the central concepts of Nietzsche's theory of the interpretation of culture are terms with foreign origins: French (*décadence, faitalisme*), Greek (the aesthetic ideal, genealogy, chaos), Latin (*amor fati*, nihilism), which in most cases are used in accordance with their multiple lexical or etymological origins – not to speak of such symbols or ciphers as Zarathustra (Persian), Dionysius, Apollo, Ariadne, Oedipus, the sphinx (Greek), Christ, Caesar, Borgia, Luther, Paul (Judeo-Christian), etc.

These brief analyses of the reading of Nietzsche will be expanded at the appropriate moments in order to isolate the philosophical stakes involved in the characteristics which they throw up. But already we can say that what we read by Nietzsche reveals a gap in which there are specific characteristics that, in contrast to discourse, we shall call *text*.

2
Discourse and Text: Nietzsche's Strategies

The *live* expression is what articulates the *live* existence.
Paul Ricoeur, *La métaphore vive*

Text is here defined as something that differs from discourse, where discourse is understood as a signifying whole that tends to create a fixed, established and univocal link between the signifier and the signified. This link is regulated by a code that, explicitly or implicitly, can find its bearings within the very discourse. In relation to text, therefore, *discourse* moves asymptotically in the direction of what we traditionally call the Logos, and its meaning is most closely tied to the skills language displays as a system, or differential logic. Nietzsche, who thinks of life as something extra-logical, through his style or text strives to exceed the limits of logical discourse, in order to enable the text, a meaning that is always constituted in a *said*, to be the *saying* of life, history, the body, to 'live',[1] in both the rhetorical and philosophical sense. How does he set about doing this, and what structure or schema controls the text as such? Nietzsche's text creates a *movement* of pluralization in relation to discourse, a movement produced by a *labour* whose law is the unifying and pluralizing imaginary order of the metaphor. As a scheme, this labour allows one to conceive of the plural unity of the tangible and the intelligible, of the body and the 'Spirit', and so to *say* life.

But going beyond logical univocity in this way assumes that, in contrast to discourse, a text is not controlled by a code which it contains and dominates, but by one or several possible codes which lie outside it. This implies that the text should be 'interpreted' rather than 'explained', to use Nietzsche's terminology. As such, Nietzsche's text is liable, not only for a *philosophical* analysis which, as a discourse, always reduces its movement to a series of signifieds, but also for a *philological* analysis, at least in so far as such an analysis tries essentially to isolate the text's economy. For the text goes beyond the limits of the said by referring to its other, which it does not entirely dominate, an area outside discourse that may be based on events or history, or drives, such that the appropriateness of the signifier for the signified becomes pluralized. But it also goes beyond logical continuity. How is it not then irremediably lost in plurality, in the signifier's drift away from any referent or signified, in the disappearance of meaning. The text belongs to an attempt on the part of a philological and philosophical reading to rediscover, as Freud had done for dreams, just what type of plurality and unity the text installs, to what univocal and plural referent it refers (the body, life as the principle of culture), and on what model of plural unity the text works (metaphor, in the last analysis) in order to help us to think and speak of life as a body and spirit.

This is therefore the problem: can we provide a law of production for Nietzsche's text that would not reconstitute the text in discourse and bring it back to the regulated game of systematic metaphysic, while on the other hand conceiving of its pluralization on the basis of a principle that allows us to set up the interpretation without ultimately and irremediably breaking the text up into nonsense? Nietzschean thoughts of interpretation, which Nietzsche's text puts into practice, just as much as the interpretation of Nietzsche's thought, depends on things which are impossible within a discursive dualism.

For the meaning of Nietzsche's philosophical enterprise, from one end of his work to the other, involves contesting a culture, the 'Christianity-Platonism' that ends up as 'modernity'. In other words, it contests a set of evaluations, both theoretical ('ideological') and practical, whose common structure is fixed as a morality and a metaphysics that are engendered by weakness and *décadence* to the point where they finally produce nihilism. As any culture[2] constitutes an attempt to master life, Nietzsche wishes to be the herald, beyond the death of God and nihilsm, of a new culture, that is to say, one that is not only a denial of life: a culture symbolized by the figure of an *Übermensch* projected beyond Good and Evil. Nitezsche's project is therefore executed as a genealogy, exposing the origins of the Ideal in the evaluating affects, and as a counter-proposition, in the face of the 'good man' of the moral Ideal, the proposition of a new type of humanity (*Mensch*):

The problem I raise here is not to know what ought to succeed mankind in the sequence of species (– the human being is an end –): but what type of human being one ought to *breed*, ought to *will*, as more valuable, more worthy of life, more certain of the future . . . out of fear the reverse type has been willed, bred, *achieved*: the domestic animal, the herd animal, the sick animal man – the Christian.[3]

The principal difficulty stems from the fact that Nietzsche speaks up against a metaphysics that retains the monopoly of discursive language, and so occupies the whole of the very field in which the new culture could be deployed. For Nietzsche, it is therefore a question of knowing if, through his own discourse, he can supplant on the same terrain as himself a metaphysical discourse that seems to him to be dwindling (by showing its non-fulfilment, for example), or if the only possibility does not involve speaking from outside, which then implies the 'risk' of a non-discourse that is perhaps derisory and, at its most extreme, impotent.

This attempt, which is played out on the level of the text, does not imply that we give up trying to discover a coherence to Nietzsche's work and that we should abandon it to what Hölderlin called poetic 'in-nocence'. Only fanaticism would contest the fact that there is first and foremost a discourse in Nietzsche, and to establish such a fact, we will state precisely that this discourse necessarily comes up against its own conditions of impossibility. At all events, it is not on this discourse that Nietzsche's enterprise bases itself, nor does it articulate its coherence according to the logic of discourse. Instead, it is based on the labour and the specific movement of the interpretative imaginary, the one thing that avoids the Scylla of a purely poeticizing counter-reaction to the Charybdis of discursive systematicity.

Nietzsche has provided sufficient reasons for those people who quite simply present him as someone who contrasts metaphysics with the ludic, the poetic with the meaning of the primary process, art with the vague meaning conceived of as the simple antithesis of reality and concept. But he himself understood, like Hume[4] before him, that this get-out *à la Célimène* risks being no more than an irrational gesture, another *Weglügen aus der Realität*, basically analogous with metaphysical deceit. For holding a pure and simple non-discourse, provided one can reach such a state, would simultaneously involve holding a contradictory 'discourse' and not holding any discourse at all. This would therefore rob one of the very means of opposing a metaphysical discourse, other than by making an irrelevant fuss. On the other hand, any discourse, even when it represents an opposition to metaphysical conceptuality, because of that very opposition and in spite of it returns to the dialectical movement, and soon seems to represent no more than a moment of that movement.

In a first phase, or rather at a first level, in fact, what we witness in Nietzsche's writings, which display the half-admitted, half-resisted influence of Schopenhauer, is an attempt to oppose philosophical and scientific discourse, theoretical knowledge, with life and art, which are models of a new culture. It is here that Nietzsche, without suspecting it, is closest to the spirit of the age, which is that of a post-romantic reaction to the intellectuality of the *Aufklärung*, 'soulless' science, the Hegelian system.[5] And we notice, as does Nietzsche himself, that his attempt, by the nature of its very ambiguity, offers two conclusions that create a dilemma: either it ultimately falls within the field of metaphysics, as in the case of Schopenhauer's philosophy, which is a second-degree metaphysics in so far as it goes beyond the limits assigned by Kantian transcendental philosophy, or else it is excluded from metaphysics, and ends up only as an *illusion*[6] that, for lack of a concept or word to designate it, remains a mute limit on the outer perimeter of thought:

The philosopher of tragic knowledge. He masters the frenzied instinct for knowledge, but not through a new metaphysics. He establishes no new belief. He feels tratically that the grounding of metaphysics has been taken away from him and yet he cannot be satisfied by the gaudy vortex of the sciences. He works at building a new life: he restores its right to art. . . . The tragic Philosopher sees a complete image of existence emerge, in which everything that falls under the province of metaphysics seems merely anthropomorphic. He is not *sceptical*. He must create here a concept: for scepticism is not the goal. When the instinct for knowledge reaches its limit, it turns back on itself and becomes a critique of knowledge. This is knowledge at the service of the best kind of life. We must even *want* illusion – that is what the tragic is.[7]

Let us look at this text. It presents itself, discretely, as an attempt at a critique of critical philosophy ('masters the frenzied instinct for knowledge'), but this non-transcendental 'critique' can only end up as dogmatism, as Kant had already predicted.[8] This is why this text insists on illusion, a term marked up by different uses to which it is put by Kant and Schopenhauer: illusion, here,[9] marks less a move beyond of a Schopenhaurian type then a regression in relation to Kant, towards pre-criticism, which explains why the text oscillates between 'concept' and 'scepticism'.[10] Sometimes, however, Nietzsche takes a further step, but one quickly sees the ambiguous nature of this move: 'Philosophising is still present as a work of art, even if it cannot be demonstrated as a philosophical construction ... The rarely demonstrated philosophy of Heraclitus has an art value that is superior to all of Aristotle's propositions'.[11] This text, which chooses art rather than truth, can seem on first reading to exclude itself quite plainly from metaphysics, since 'it does not establish any new belief'. But in reality, since it shows that philosophizing is present as a work of art and that 'art is true',[12] it confines itself to returning to the field of Schopenhaurian meta-physics, which is even more dogmatic,[13] since it does not define its right to hold the discourse that it does:

> The truest things in this world are love, religion and art. The first, through every distortion and masquerade, sees right into the core of the suffering individual and suffers with him, and the last, as a practical form of love, consoles grief by speaking of another order to the world and by teaching us to despise the latter. These are the three illogical powers that recognise them-selves as such.[14]

The return to metaphysics, beneath the appearance of a transgression, is more than evident: Nietzsche affirms that by 'recognizing itself' as an illusion and by positing itself as the artistic 'truth' of life, illusion becomes truth. In one sense it is so much so that it founds a meta-physics in the strict sense, which speaks of 'another order to the world' and posits itself *as* truth: 'Art therefore treats *appearance* as *appearance*, it does *not* want to trick, it is true'.[15] To say this is both to deny metaphysics, its *verum index sui* and, in speaking of a sort of *illusio index veritatis*, to reconstitute it furtively. In short, it involves a counter-discourse, which oscillates between the non-discursive ('art') and a discourse that is necessarily metaphysical ('truth').

From what position does one therefore speak in order to set the thought of a new culture against metaphysics? If 'poets lie'[16] or through their illusions can promote only an inoffensive 'truth' in the face of 'sacred deceit', the only resource left to destroy moral culture consists in placing onself *within* the metaphysical field. Only in this way, as Nietzsche says in *Le Livre du Philosophe*, can one conceive of 'the philosopher enmeshed in language',[17] a notion he repeats right up to the unpublished work of the late period: 'Language depends on the most naive prejudices. . . . We cease to think when we refuse to do so under the constraint of language. . . . Rational thought is interpretation according to a scheme that we cannot throw off'.[18] At this level, one's labour consists first of all in challenging metaphysics from within, seeking to show that its falsity lies in the way it denies the reality it claims to embrace. In this way a split text is born, in which a confrontation takes place between two discourses: on the one hand Nietzsche's discourse, a subject discourse that is essentially philological, and on the other hand, the discourse of metaphysics, an object discourse, that is held in order to deceive. The juxtaposition of these two discourses is signalled by the use of inverted commas and terms derived from metalogic, which contrast a language with a metalanguage.

But the difficulty remains: what is the grounding (reality, life, will to power, true interpretation, etc.) of Nietzsche's meta-discourse? Either there is a 'true' interpretation – Nietzsche's – that relativizes and eliminates the others (this is a conception that Nietzsche does not explicitly articulate, and which we must isolate in order to examine whether or not it makes thought return to the circle of systematic discourse while enlarging it); or else 'there are no facts, there are only interpretations', and we must ask ourselves how Nietzsche conceives of interpretation if he means to avoid the circular interpretation that mistrusts itself as interpretation. Nietzsche therefore has to be able to avoid offering proofs to the system while trying to supplant it with a more encompassing discourse. He therefore has to state in what new way he thinks through what metaphysics casts to one one side: the body, interpretation. For, in wishing to oppose metaphysics with this discourse that goes beyond it, Nietzsche still runs the risk of offering no more than a super-metaphysical discourse and thought.

Conscious of the difficulty, Nietzsche adopts an original path: within the metaphysical language he is constrained to speak, his

Versuch aims to inaugurate a para-discourse, a 'stand-in' discourse, that finds its coherence on the level of the metaphor, which is represented as the moving truth of life and the interpretation of the body. Nietzsche considers truth to be metaphorical: beneath the networks of concept and grammar, the metaphor follows what Nietzsche calls the *Leitfaden des Leibes* (the evidence of the body),[19] life's secret coherence. On the margins of his discursive analysis, Nietzsche therefore brings out images that have a metaphorical value. These images appear to be parasitic on the manifest discourse, but gradually find their own pertinence and movement: following a certain chain whose rule or scheme needs to be elucidated, these metaphorical elements undermine the discursive nature of thought. For example, to deny (*negieren*) that morality and metaphysics are the denegation (*Verneinung*) of life, Nietzsche presents his image of the *vita femina*.[20] The image, a return to literary content, edges a plural metaphorical insistence that forms almost a semiological system. Life is a woman, all appearance and make-up, a mask devoid of underlying reality or base, the innocence of becoming, a disconcerting game: this pure appearing is reified by the clumsy and unwholesome outlook of the theoretical man, a voyeur who perverts the innocence of becoming by assuming it has a *Grund*, a background, and several seductive ulterior motives. In addition, Nietzsche views this woman-life as an illogicality, a contradiction, the negation of a concocted essence: the so-called 'Eternal feminine', which is becoming and fecundity.

If there is a certain coherent continuity to Nietzsche's metaphors, is it not within this order that thought finds its foundation and a certain form of systematicity? But, assuming that one can reconstruct a semiological system in Nietzsche, as Bachelard has tried to do in his own way, would such a system not be a closed one, whose principle would make it homologous to a discursive system? Is it enough to replace a concept with metaphors if we wish to escape from the systematic structure of discourse? Unless we conceive of an order that is coherent while giving the reason, in an interpretative way, for its object outside the text: life as interpretation.

Nietzsche therefore tries his hand at a double discourse, which subverts itself through metaphor and loses on the one hand what it builds conceptually on the other: this is for him a way of managing not to fix what is both the principle and the object of his 'discourse', becoming, life, the body, and to retract the signified that necessarily is imposed when, from within the text, it directs itself towards a referent that it does not exhaust. And what do we do if, as is patent even in the last works, we want to have both an architectonics *and* bring out the 'chaos' or innocence of life? It is on this point that readings of Nietzsche must come to a decision: does Nietzsche represent a final, archimetaphysical philosophy, the subversion of all philosophy?

But perhaps there is a structure without system, in the order of the metaphorical thought of interpretation, through the way in which it helps to link up things and carry them forward. Perhaps the body and life can be grasped, less as signifieds than through an interpretative *signifying* whose locus is the text. In Nietzsche, the text is charged, not with designating signifieds (whose discourse has the task of reducing exteriority as much as possible), but with being the signifying process of the body and life, operating as the movement and labour of interpretation.

Nietzsche tries to promote what he calls the 'language of reality' which, as opposed to 'sacred deceit', presents itself as a *Ja-Sagen*. He affirms that all language is metaphysical in principle. If a *Ja-Sagen* is possible, therefore, a new language is needed: such is the meaning of having recourse to the *text* as the locus of a labour that both produces and sub-verts its signifieds.

Culture is analysed by Nietzsche in philological terms: it must be read as a language, wherein he shows that it is 'in reality' a false text, unsuited to its object, asemantic, a discourse unable to grasp life other than through denegation. But Nietzsche also presents the work of drives as a text, and, vice versa, the text is in the image of what it describes as a body, as life and as drives: both are interpretation. From this point on, we can apply to Nietzsche's text the statements he makes on the body, life and drives, of which his text is the *conversion*, and try to reveal the order of the work of interpretation in both cases. The hypothesis is, therefore, that Nietzsche's text *is* itself the affirmative culture, the affirmative interpretation expressed as *Ja-Sagen*, as mastery of life, if it is true that 'in truth interpretation is itself a way of mastering something':[21] the text is the 'language of reality'.[22] If language as discourse is metaphysical, a text, on the other hand, is *Versuch*, becoming, body, interpretation. No doubt any text is continually exposed to becoming a discourse again: 'rational thought is interpretation according to a scheme that we cannot throw off,[23] since in fact 'linguistic means of expression are useless for expressing "becoming"'.[24] So if Nietzsche's text can (and even must) fall back into discourse, it is because, 'we have not got away from the habit into which our senses and language seduce us . . . let us not forget that this is mere semeiotics and nothing real'.[25]

If a truth can be articulated about the body, life, reality, it can signify only through the text's saying (*le dire*), but also in the sense that it is a recanting, or unsaying (*un dédire*). If, for discourse, a text can be considered 'false', since it is plurivocal, for Nietzsche, on the contrary, it is discourse which, in the face of the text as they saying of becoming, is a fiction: a repression of textual movement, a degraded text.

> From the standpoint of morality, the world is *false*. But to the extent that morality itself is a part of this world, morality is false. Will to truth is a making firm, a making true and durable,[26] an abolition of the false character of things, a reinterpretation of it into beings. 'Truth' is therefore not something there, that might be found or discovered – but something *that must be created* and that *gives* a name to *a process*, or rather to a will to overcome that has in itself no end – introducing truth, as a *processus in infinitum*, an active determining – *not* a becoming-conscious of something that is 'in itself' firm and determined. It is a word for the 'will to power'.[27]

This typical fragment is first and foremost a discourse, but on a deep level it is also a text that implicitly marks its difference from philosophical discourse by a labour manifested in the italics and inverted commas, that are designed to take up again in one's very discourse what one is obliged to abandon to it – notably the term 'truth', a key concept of what in Nietzsche is metaphysical discourse. Nietzsche, who cannot contest a non-truth that would destroy his own saying, deports this word through the use of typographical signs that make it 'tremble'.[28] In addition, the active substantive verbs which replace passive abstract terms, the words forged by Nietzsche to mark his distance from the language of the grammatical 'herd', the key words 'production', 'process' and 'active determination' stress that only the text's movement and labour, unlike a necessarily inert discourse, can give an account of the world as a becoming and as life.[28] But one phrase, which risks becoming weighed down in a discursive formula and is therefore put in inverted commas by Nietzsche to mark it out, is all Nietzsche needs to characterize the text as an active determination: will to power.[29] As a style, that is to say where idiosyncrasy in the production of saying acts as a process of signifying, the text is a will to power: what is more, the text does not state the will to power, it *is* that will in the sense of being the structure of *Selbstüberwindung*, a going beyond of the *self* and the discursive *same*.[30] In relation to discourse, as a discovery of a signified that is supposedly already there, existing independently of the text's movement, the text is therefore an explosion, and one can even apply to it what Nietzsche attributes to the artist's art: 'ability to speak of oneself through a hundred speech media – an *explosive* condition'.[31] In this way the text, following the example of what it aims to signify, is a textual and corporal *polemos*.[32]

But we can then understand in what sense Nietzsche's very discourse *cannot be founded*. To do that, in fact, Nietzsche would have to be able, in the discourse, to signify an ἀρχή of which only the text as non-discursive movement can give an account. It is therefore remarkable that Nietzsche tirelessly pursues the project of giving his own thought a systematic foundation, by multiplying his plans in an almost architectonic way and by developing, above all in the unpublished fragments and drafts, a discourse that proliferates in proportion to its inability by definition to incorporate its extra-discursive foundation; but it is also remarkable that, at the same time, his text forever progresses increasingly towards a bodily signifying. But this progression is itself bound to 'failure', since bodily signifying is pertinent to the degree to which it effaces linguistic signifying and leads to the bodily signifying that lies outside the text, the blank of the text and, ultimately, madness.[33]

We also understand why commentators, by not taking the textual process into account, have managed, on the one hand, only to reduce the Nietzschean text to conceptual discourse, and, on the other hand, to misrepresent the Nietzschean text as an invertebrate gesticulation that destroys meaning, or to reduce it to the free play of *fetishized* signifiers (which allows ignorance to install a completely arbitrary 'commentary') under the pretext that some Nietzschean discourses refuse to treat becoming, the body and reality as signifieds that remain.[34] This is how a tradition operates, forever stubbornly trying to reduce the 'dangerous perhaps', and assimilate the text's *polemos*, or else drowning it in the inoffensive flimsiness of dilettantism.[35]

Our ambition is both more limited and more presumptious: without claiming to rely on Nietzsche so as to shoot off in the direction of a new thinking that would incidentally dispense with an antiquated fidelity to the text, this study intends to limit itself to Nietzsche's text. All the same, it would be hasty to accuse this study of academism: the latter consists precisely in avoiding a direct confrontation with the text, and in confining itself instead to a generally peripheral discourse which consists in pleading the work's prestige in order to use a system of rhapsodic quotation to avoid confronting, through *reading*, the text's labour and continual movement – an attitude that makes academism complicit with its apparent adversary, namely dilettantism. Our method, therefore, essentially aims to make the work of *reading* the text possible by bringing out, not so much a Nietzschean discourse, which is always suspected of being apocryphal,[36] as the processes that constitute the textuality of the text. Our discourse – for unless we risk taking a leap into poetic speech, or the realm of the unthought or the ineffable, our discourse can only be resolutely discursive – aims to account for the conditions prevailing for a *practice*, without replacing the text's *signifying* or, *a fortiori*, the text's *reading* (*lire*). We propose to use a *philological* method to the extent that it tries to isolate the material conditions of possibility (historical, linguistic, stylistic, etc.) but also the discursive conditions prevailing over the production and reading of the text.[37]

But our analysis also comes under the field of *philosophical* discourse to the extent that it uses philology as a means to interest itself in the semantic consequences of the text's labour. The basic moving force behind Nietzsche's philosophical enterprise is the problem of *meaning*: as much in terms of the possibility or the dissolution of meaning in the domain of culture as, more fundamentally, in terms of the ability of philosophical language to state and interpret the non-discursive reality of the body and life. No doubt Nietzsche challenges permanent, ready-made meaning and denounces 'morality' as a false meaning or mistranslation [*faux-sens ou contresens*]: but it is precisely this absence of meaning, namely nihilism, that sets his undertaking in motion, as he searches for one or several new meanings, a new culture, new philosophers. For Nietzsche, this is not simply a combinative system which just needs to have its productions codified: this dissolution of body and meaning, this idealism, is the moral and metaphysical reply that Nietzsche continues to oppose. The text subverts, not, as is thought by those people for whom philosophy is just a metaphysical form of antiquarianism, by tending towards the empty freedom of the pure signifier, but because it signifies by recanting a statement, or unsaying the said [*dédisant un dit*], a cultural idea that philology precisely strives to locate in the very text that is *derived* from it. If we abstract this content which Nietzsche's text works from, without forgetting the semantic consequences of the work of rewriting, the *Umwertung*, *Umdrehung* and *Umwerfung* to which he gives himself up, we rob ourselves of all chance of a reading that makes the text something other than a pretext or monument. The question of the problem of culture in general (*Kultur*) in Nietzsche passes through the location of culture as education (*Bildung*) in Nietzsche and his text. It is not just a question of 'trundling books' (*Bücher wälzen*),[38] but of isolating a *history* of the text, and so bringing out its labour. To neglect this is to offer the specific ideal of 'egypticism', which is dogmatic because it is anti-genealogical. This holds for the text as it does for culture in general: the metabolic is the metabolism of the text as a living body.

The reason is that philology is genealogical, that Nietzsche's text has a genealogy and that Nietzsche himself is a genealogist. Nietzsche's jests on this point accord with his conception of writing and reading, whether these are applied to the offshoots of affects, to 'psychology'[39] or to the text. Just as a non-genealogical, 'dogmatic'[40] interpretation, scorns the depth of drives which, at a slight remove, determines a cultural phenomenon, shortcircuiting meaning in the metaphysical mode, so a dogmatic reading of Nietzsche's text consists in suppressing its genealogical dimension, that is to say, its philological dimension. Thus, Nietzsche would have quickly revealed the dogmatism, without using a stronger word, in the racist interpretation of some of his own texts,[41] and we know what sarcasm he directs towards the sort of reader who has 'no finger for nuances',[42] distinguishing as he does between understanding and 'understanding'.[43] The reason is that language tends to efface the origin,[44] and consequently the genealogy of words and texts. When it is dogmatic, vulgar and common (*gemein*),[45] it effaces experience – needs, evaluations – that underlie the concept.

It must offend their pride, and also their taste, if their truth is supposed to be a truth for everyman, which has hitherto been the secret desire and hidden sense of all dogmatic endeavours. 'My judgement is my judgement: another cannot easily acquire a right to it' – such a philosopher of the future may perhaps say. One has to get rid of the bad taste of wanting to be in agreement with many. 'Good' is no longer good when your neighbour takes it into his mouth. And how could there exist a 'common good'! The expression is a self-contradiction: what can be common has ever but little value.[46]

Dogmatism cannot understand that the 'common' identity of Nietzsche's word and text covers an ocasionally contradictory multiplicity:

What ultimately is commonness? – Words are sounds designating concepts; concepts, however, are more or less definite images designating frequently recurring and associated sensations, groups of sensations. To understand one another it is not sufficient to employ the same words; we have also to employ the same words to designate the same species of inner experiences, we must ultimately have our experience *in common*. That is why the members of *one* people understand one another better than do members of differing peoples even when they use the same language; or rather, when human beings have lived together for a long time under similar conditions (of climate, soil, danger, needs, work), there *arises* from this a group who 'understand one another', a people. . . . One makes this same test even in the case of friendships or love-affairs: nothing of that sort can last once it is discovered that when one party uses words he connects them with feelings, intentions, perceptions, desires, fears different from those the other party connects them with. . . . Now supposing that need has at all times brought together only such human beings as could indicate similar requirements, similar experiences by means of similar signs, it follows that on the whole the easy *communicability* of need, that is to say ultimately the experiencing of only average and *common* experiences, must have been the most powerful of all the powerful forces which have disposed of mankind hitherto.[47]

We find ourselves in the midst of a rude fetishism when we call to mind the basic presuppositions of the metaphysics of language: – which is to say, of *reason*.'[48] We are being fetishists, even as we draw on Marx, Freud or Nietzsche – both the word and the concept are to be found in all three authors – if we regard the text as an evident or floating signifier, and pay no heed to the philologically assignable history of its production, or to its overdetermination and psychic elaboration (*Verarbeitung*), or to its genesis (genealogy). The word, when it becomes a fetish, is anti-genealogical: 'words dilute and brutalize; words depersonalize; words make the un-common common'.[49]

In fact:

'Inner experience' enters our consciousness only after it has found a language the individual understands – i.e., a translation of a condition into conditions familiar to him – 'to understand' means merely: to be able to express something new in the language of something old and familiar. ... The simple man always says: this or that makes me feel unwell – he makes up his mind about his feeling unwell only when he has seen a reason for feeling unwell. ... I call that a *lack of philology*..[50]

On the other hand, writing and speaking, for Nietzsche, must not be distinguished from physiological activities: 'being able to dance with the feet, with concepts, with words: do I still have to say that one has to be able to dance with the *pen* – that *writing* has to be learned?'[51] '*On ne peut penser et écrire qu'assis* [One can think and write only when sitting down] (Gustave Flaubert). – Now I have you, nihilist! Assiduity is the *sin* against the holy spirit. Only ideas *won by walking* have any value.'[52] Reading also comes under the province of physiology: 'even today one still hears with one's muscles, one even reads with one's muscles'.[53]

Philology, as the genealogy of the text, therefore has the task of bringing out the bodily origins of speaking and writing. Dealing with Nietzsche's text, genealogy, therefore, firstly passes through philological research. And conversely, philology is genealogy in that it aims to isolate the origin of the Nietzschean text on the level of affect, or *Erlebnis*. Our method, which was firstly called *philological*, must therefore, as such, be understood to be *genealogical*: and such is the philosophical meaning of our undertaking.

Our reading will therefore single out several levels:

A. Firstly, the Schopenhauerian stage, which marks the metaphysical ex-cess beyond rationalistic discourse. This is a dogmatic process, since it appeals to ideas such as intuition, genius and art, which are presented as means of access to the thing-in-itself. It is metaphysical, in the Kantian sense, that is to say 'pre-critical', in the style of Schopenhauer.[54]

B. At a second stage, the determination of the Nietzschean text becomes more tricky. The text appears as something that must be called a *para-discourse* whose instability can be explained by the ambiguous status accorded to metaphor. In fact, *as* metaphor: (a)   the text tends on the one hand towards conceptual systematicity, which makes it liable to the order Nietzsche calls metaphysical; (b)   on the other hand, it escapes in the direction of *anti-discourse*, the anti-conceptual retraction (*dédit*), the body's labour, the *Ja-Sagen* as the language of reality, which we have called *text*. For, as Paul Ricoeur shows in *La métaphore vive*,[55] metaphor institutes, through a 'semantic shock' which it constitutes, a 'demand in concept' which is 'not yet a knowledge through concept'.

If we admit that Nietzsche's texts try to articulate the body's saying (*dire*) as the conditions of possibility for *culture* in general, the text can only simultaneously set itself two contradictory aims. To say the body, we must enter the field of discourse *and* at the same time transgress it, so that both its other and its origins can show up. And if metaphor is, not determining, but paradigmatic of this movement of saying and unsaying (*dire-dédire*), it is to the extent that it imitates a textuality founded on the tension between identity and non-identity.[56] In fact, 'the metaphorical meaning of a word presupposes a contrast with a literal meaning which, in the position of predicate, offends against semantic pertinence'.[57] This tension in Nietzsche is found at a double level: between the metaphor and discourse (a contrast between a lexicalized literal meaning and a metaphorical meaning) and between discourse (which is eventually metaphorical) and text (a contrast between a stable signified and the process of signification that is textual labour).[58] And Nietzsche, who acts simultaneously as the bearer of a tradition and the 'aúthor' of a text, through the text as something beyond discourse and as something that refers to what lies beyond the text, linguistically and non-linguistically symbolizes the changes undergone by language as system.[59]

If Nietzsche's text is therefore μεταφόρα, this is obviously firstly in the sense that it seems, linguistically and stylistically, saturated with metaphors, without our being able all the same to reduce it to this unique principle; but subsequently and above all because the discursive and even metaphorical stages, or stases, to which one tries to tie it despite everything merely mask the oppositive *slippage* which, from discourse to metaphor and from discourse (even a metaphorical one) to text, oblige us to consider the text on several levels.

They are strata rather than chronologically ascribable stages. A serious diachronic study enables us to avoid unconscious or careless anachronisms[60] which lead us to view as isomorphs those texts which are anti-metaphysical because they are influenced by Schopenhauer, and those 1888 texts which are anti-metaphysical for totally opposite, genealogical reasons. It is important not to confuse a pre-critical moment,[61] for example the texts collected in *Le Livre du Philosophe*, with the textual, meta-critical work.

But the anisotopy of Nietzsche's text is rather of a synchronic order, above all in the texts after *Human, All Too Human*. Let us take an example. If one sticks to *discourse*, the title, which in this case can be translated without difficulty because it is isomorphic in the German original and in translation, of the *Fröhliche Wissenschaft* (*The Gay Science*) seems to announce merely an optimistic, liberating science, in the sense of *Aufklärung* (enlightenment).[62] But Nietzsche, long before *The Gay Science*, denied the conjunction affirmed by metaphysics between progress in science and the well-being of humanity.[63] Instead, he seems here to designate an anti-metaphysical science, *vogelfrei*, freed from morality, from fear (*Wir Furchtlosen*),[64] indeed from religion, a knowledge devoid of prejudice which is not, like that of the sages, based on unease and exorcism,[65] but reaches the peaks above the abyss, the depth beyond superficiality, the heaven beyond illness. 'Only great pain is the ultimate liberator of the spirit.'[66] This 'gay science' is therefore neither purely gay, nor properly a science, since it is suspicion and doubt.[67] If we envisage this title as a text, we must first of all doubt whether a science, as an objective knowledge (*Wissenschaft*), can be universally gay (*fröhlich*). The title is therefore a *metaphor*, the position of a contradiction: on the surface, on the level of concepts, there is isomorphism. But on the level of deep structure, the signifier contradicts its superficial unity.[68] This opposition is between a decadent science that is neither genealogical nor philological,[69] and a dionysiac science of the tragic abyss.[70] The title, on a *textual* level, brings in this opposition as the hollowed-out affirmation of a new 'gospel'[71] of knowledge, the 'good news' (*frohe Botschaft*) that would act as the antithesis to the Christian 'Dysangel' hostile to science.[72]

The anisotopic simultaneity of the discursive, metaphorical and textual strata therefore leads us to see a 'separation'[73] rather than a synthesis in Nietzsche's text.

Are we to call quits as regards Nietzsche's text? 'I prefer', he declares, 'to write something that deserves to be read in the way philologists read their writers rather than to squat (*hocken*) on top of an author. And at all events, the most mediocre production (*das Schaffen*) is superior to a discourse on works that have already been read (*über Geschaffenes*)'.[74]

This is certainly a commonplace. Any commentary on a writer of Nietzsche's dimensions is imprisoned in a dilemma: on the one hand the desire to be self-effacing in the face of the work's tangible splendours or conceptual force, an attitude that leads to paraphrase, but whose ultimate ideal is in reality silence; on the other hand, an attempt to explain, that is designed to evaluate the work's intellectual or formal qualities but ends up merely killing all life in the work by interminably detesting its *jouissance*.

But, in Nietzsche's case, this dilemma turns out to be more complex: in the first place, it creates a contrast between, on the one hand, an activist quasi-Cartesian 'resolution' that does not worry too much about nuances or fidelity to what is written and sees Nietzsche above all as the instigator of a conversion, an ethical, intellectual and spiritual itinerary, borne out as much by the work of Herman Hesse as by the summary poses of certain lightweight or steamrolling commentators;[75] and, on the other hand, a philological attitude that neglects incisive explanations in favour of the long path of method, trying to do justice to the *text*, sometimes successfully, sometimes, and more often, flattening it beneath the weight of an out-of-date tradition and method.[76] On the one hand, Nietzsche wants to be read by philologists, no mean ambition, and, on the other, he recommends: Go away from me and guard yourself against Zarathustra! . . . Take care that a falling statue does not strike you dead! . . . Of what importance is Zarathustra?[77] More precisely, this dilemma, accentuated by Nietzsche himself, makes us think less of the Cartesian contrast between will and understanding than the more subtle but irreducible[78] contrast, established by Hume, between a vulgar scepticism and a philosophical scepticism, between 'a false reason and none at all'.[79] This choice concerns, not a philosophical decision in which reason is the judge and party, but 'nature', that is, conditions of existence. And, says Nietzsche, 'one does not refuse conditions of existence; one can only have others'.[80]

On the other hand one can refute a second type of dilemma, touching this time on Nietzsche's intellectual, even 'spiritual' approach. Everything takes place as if a split were established among Nietzsche's commentators as to the Bergsonian schemes of intuition and intelligence. Sometimes we see that explaining Nietzsche as a philosopher and philologist amounts to playing down the sporting nature of his spiritual energy or, to put it in more contemporary terms, the creative spark of his contradictions. This attitude borders on a neo-Wagnerian neo-romanticism that is more anti-intellectual than anti-intellectualist; if the goal of reading Nietzsche should be knowledge, it is possible only on the basis of conditions that are, at the least, negative: philology, the Nietzschean critique of metaphysics and the philologial resumption by Nietzsche of the limits articulated by Kantian criticism. From this point on, the choice to be made here is not so much between respectful silence and dulling gloss, or between speculation and action, as between the reason and the non-reason of commentary.

But what can reason say about a Nietzsche who is not only a philosopher writer but also a musician and artist in the *irreducible* sense that he gives his reader *pleasure*? For Nietzsche creates a contrast between the philosophical effacement of the signifier in the face of the signified (which is similar to a single *reproduction* of the signifier and of pleasure) and his *style*. No doubt we should not, as has been the fashion for aeons, underestimate the *expressive* intentions of Nietzsche's style, that is to say, the attention he pays to the rigorous suitability of the signifier to the signified, his mistrust of grandiloquent and vague terms, and so of that one christens, apparently as a term of praise, 'floating signifiers'! But we should not forget the irrepressible insistence of the signifier to *several* points of view. For we often stress the polysemic charge of Nietzsche's texts, but without ever speaking of rhythm (short or long texts, interrupted phrases,[81] anacoluthons, dashes or blanks between aphorisms, syncopations, etc.) or melody (the choice of linking metaphors, hiatus and movements of a phrase, leitmotifs, alliterations, for example in *Zarathustra*) or harmony (several levels of writing, allusions, citations and parodies, the hierarchy of drives, etc.). All these aspects are linked through the text's *music*, to bodily references. Whether it is the case that we should dance, or that we should write and think only while walking, or that style should be alive, or that Nietzsche should invoke Dionysus as a symbol not only of tragedy but also of alcoholic and sexual intoxication, Nietzsche's text, in the body of its writing, claims to write the body and have the body write. If Nietzsche is a musician (with greater success in his language than in his instrumental compositions!) this means that his style is musical in so far as it is a body, and as music leaves the body, passes through instrumental physical bodies and ends up in the listener's body.[82] As *melody* (the improvement and phonic timbre of writing, the timbre's colour), *harmony* (the play of assonance, the text's polyphonic counterpoint) and *rhythm* (on the level of the accentuated phoneme, the word, the phrase, the aphorism, and the book),[83] Nietzsche's text *is* a body, and mimes the rhythm of *physiology*.

Unlike other philosophers and following the example of three exceptions to the artistic style, Plato, Rousseau and Schopenhauer, Nietzsche likes music and speaks of music and of composers, he speaks in music and through his music: 'Compared with music all communications by word is shameless'.[84] 'Formerly ... having "wax in one's ears" was then almost a condition of philosophizing; a real philosopher no longer listened to life in so far as life is music; he *denied* the music of life – it is an ancient philosopher's superstition that all music is sirens' music.'[85] 'I fear I am too much of a musician to be a romantic. Without music life would be a mistake.'[86] Thus, when Nietzsche concludes, 'Nor does it do any harm for you to treat me a little like a musician',[87] we must take this declaration literally: the attempt at music is an aspect of textual practice, in which Nietzsche is trying to 'express' what he cannot state through discourse.[88] For music (Nietzsche, unlike Schopenhauer, sees a danger in this) 'may dispense with words and concepts'.[89] The fact that music can participate in Nietzsche's plan to master the body through a textual and musical undertaking, is demonstrated, in a negative way, by the chief accusations launched against Wagner's music: that it is 'hypnotic',[90] 'narcotic'[91] or a morbid disease:

> I breathe with difficlty when this music begins to affect me; my *foot* becomes agitated and rebels against it: my foot needs a

cadence, a dance or march beat – not even the young emperor can march to the beat of Wagner's *Kaisersmarsch* – , my foot demands music, above all, the delights of a *good* movement, a step, a leap, a pirouette. But is protest not also registered by my stomach, my heart, the circulation of my blood? Aren't my entrails saddened? Do I unconsciously go hoarse? ... When I hear Wagner, I need a pastille ... I ask myself: what is it that my whole body is ultimately *demanding* from this music? For the soul is not involved. I thing it is asking for a little relief: as if all the animal functions should be accelerated by bold, light, wild and proud rhythms. ... My melancholy tries to find some rest in the hidden depths of perfection: that is why I need music. But Wagner makes me ill.[92]

The question to be put, then, is a brutal one: can we not accuse the philosophical option and the philological option (which is closer to music, moreover, than we think) of being deaf and of placing themselves on a plane from which art as pleasure, *and hence the body*, is repressed? Certainly. But the rigours of discourse, as Nietzsche and then Freud both said, are one of the forms of repression. Conversely, art and beauty, as shown by Thomas Mann in *Death in Venice* and Hermann Broch in *The Temptor*, and even earlier by Nietzsche, cannot either elude the temptation offered by the abyss, denegration, *décadence*, and also, as everything shows, by tyranny and death. Nietzsche, moreover, has not wished to choose between whatever is discursive and the text's art, both of which he suspected of being equally pernicious. Is it not for this reason that Nietzsche one day perhaps replaced his discourse and even his meta-phorical text with an impossible music, the blank-ness of what, for want of a better phrase, we call 'madness'? The enigma remains: is the rest silence – or music? It remains for us to have, like Thomas Mann, Hermann Hesse, Hermann Broch and Robert Musil, all the irony, human tenderness, measure, and *also* as Broch said of Musil, pitiless rigour and *messerscharf*[93] of great art, to be able to measure up to Nietzsche's art, to gauge the measure of his art, and to be in a position to pay him true homage. Infidelity to the writing is therefore forgotten and becomes insignificant when Nietzsche's multiple enigma, imprecise and distant, yet also frightening, rises up before us once more, thanks to an art that, in its faithful infidelity, is the only one than can still justify and evoke Nietzsche's words: 'Of what is great one must either be silent or speak with greatness. With greatness – that means cynically and with innocence'.[94]

3

The Problem of Culture in Nietzsche's Thought

The culture complex, as my chief interest.[1]

The relationship is no doubt not at all fortuitous: the central problem posed by Nietzsche's enigmatic thought concerns an obscure, polysemic and perhaps contestable notion, that of culture.[2] And yet both the unity and the contradictions of Nietzschean thinking boil down to this problem.

The first difficulty stems from an interlinguistic anisomorphism: *Kultur* is translated as 'culture' or 'civilization', but 'civilization' refers us to *Zivilisation* and 'culture' to *Bildung*. A difference and an overlapping exists between the respective semantic fields:[3]

$$
\text{culture}^4 \left\{ \begin{array}{l} \textit{Bildung}^5 \\ \textit{Kultur}^6 \end{array} \right.
$$
$$
\left. \begin{array}{c} \\ \textit{Zivilisation} \end{array} \right\} \text{civilization}
$$

Zivilisation designates the material experience of a civilization (*Kultur*), while *Kultur* refers to the ideological givens of a determined 'culture'.[7]

A few remarks can be made here: (1) *Kultur* and *Zivilisation* are opposites from the point of view of values: the former implies the 'noble' values of an intellectual or spiritual end, while the latter is linked to the pejorative appreciation of realizations considered 'simply' material. The two terms crystallize the *axiologically* opposed values of the cultivated man (or 'honest man') and the 'philistine') or 'bourgeois'), while absolutely they have only a *descriptive* value. (2) In German, one commonly uses *Bildung* to mean an individual's training, but it can also mean something collective,[8] while *Kultur*, in contrast to the French '*culture*', designates only a supra-individual level. (3) Finally, the opposition of culture and nature, which long ago became common in French, is used much less in German. It is *Bildung* and *Natur*, above all since Hegel,[9] which, in a specific situation, are used more absolutely as opposites.[10]

In what sense does culture introduce a problem? Paradoxically, theoretical questions, since their latin origins, have been structured by a metaphorical model,[11] whose logic, with its innocent appearance, disguises preconceived options and schemes of thought.

The resonances, in the word, of the Latin terms *cultura*, *cultus*, and *colere*, remind us that culture, in the figurative sense, evokes and transposes into 'human nature' the practices that concern physical nature: '*working* the earth, the collective term for the *operations* undertaken to obtain from the soil the vegetables that man and domestic animals need'.[12] Even in its abstract meanings, culture first of all represents, in Latin and in French, and implicitly in German, an *activity*, sustained by needs and therefore by lack. This given, whether physical (biological, botanical, chemical) or psychic (intellectual, spiritual) is always designated as nature: culture is seen as an act of transforming nature destined to force the latter, which is itself neutral, to serve properly human ends.

Such is at least the anthropomorphic legacy of the metaphorical equivalences. We can no longer conceive of nature in the same way as Cicero's metaphor of the *cultura animi*.[14] The latter: (1) presupposes 'chaos' or an unformed state in a fact, on the pretext that it does not correspond to a point of view that is in reality anthroponcentric; (2) above all contrasts the idea of 'nature' as a brute fact, which is a conceptually dubious idea, with the human subject of culture whose independence in relation to 'nature' is debatable. After Lucretius,[15] Spinoza (like Nietzsche at a later date) was already accusing the human 'subject', for example, as in Cartesian voluntarism, of mistakenly seeing itself 'as an empire within an empire'.[16] More recently, the natural sciences (physics, medicine, etc.) and the human sciences (anthropology, psychoanalysis, sociology, psychology, etc.) have obliged us to place this supposedly autonomous subject back within the system or systems of nature, and to stop thinking of the opposition between culture and nature in terms of activity and passivity, form and formlessness, creative man and sterile nature.

It scarcely appears possible any more for us to go on representing the concept of culture as a free activity, or even the concept of a 'realm' opposed to nature.[17] Culture, then, might well be no more than a word, a pseudo-concept referring only to the illusory perception that man, an unconscious natural being, would have of the gap that in him and around him separates nature from itself.

Whatever meaning has to be conferred on the concept of nature, whether it be scientific or a metaphysical or perhaps a poetic one, culture constitutes, in the Spinozist sense, one of its *modes*.

But to give up conceiving of culture as a 'realm' (Kant) or an autonomous 'empire' (Spinoza) implies that we no longer represent it as an *operation* independent of nature, that aims to transform human 'nature'. But is there a human 'nature', and can we legitimately separate this 'being' from an 'ought to be', one of whch is perhaps an illusion, while the other is merely an illusory perception of the 'lacks' of the first?[18] Whether we establish it as an artificial transformation[19], or, on the contrary, as the restoration of a human nature, in other words as a thought-out and reasoned fight against sensibility and drives or, on the contrary, as an effort to rediscover man's lost,[20] true (reasonable, pure, free, etc.) nature, culture, as a means of getting 'nature' to conform to certain norms, could well prove to be an illusion. Thus, Nietzsche identifies nature, the existence of drives, and the ideal:

> When we speak of *humanity*, we base our remarks on the idea that it might be what *separates* and distinguishes man from nature; but, in reality, this separation does not exist: 'natural' properties and those we speak of as properly 'human' are indissolubly intertwined. In his noblest and most elevated faculties, man is entirely natural and bears within himself the strangeness of this second natural character. His fearful aptitudes, which we take to be inhuman, are perhaps even the fertile ground from which some humanity or other can spring forth as much in the form of emotions as of actions and works.[21]

This text, dating from 1872, already heralds the later conceptions. One phrase from the later years: 'morality as the instinct to deny life'[22] indicates that morality, like the principle of culture, is in reality merely the instinct or drive themselves that reappear in a denegatory form 'behind the repressing force and take effect by means of it', to use the Freudian terminology.[23]

Therefore, 'it is *not* a matter of re-establishing natural feelings: for they never existed. Let us not be fooled by the words "natural" or "true"! They mean "popular", "ancient", "general" – they have nothing to do with truth'.[24] Culture cannot, then, be understood, according to Nietzsche, as something that aims to lead man back to a normative model called his 'true nature': that is just an ideal. Therefore, Nietzsche writes: '"Man's true nature": a forbidden turn of phrase!',[25] and he explains: 'What is good to a being? The achievement of his ends. What are a being's ends? The development of his nature ... that means that man's ends are the development of his nature. "To be man and not a horse". That is nothing. One copes by invoking one's "true nature", one's nature as it *ought* to be, and not as it is'.[26] Nietzsche in fact discovers that this 'true nature' is the expression of a desire, that is to say a necessary nature.[27] 'In the past, one would ask: is this thought true? Nowadays: how did we find it? What was its driving force?'[28] If, as Nietzsche repeats in the wake of Schopenhauer, 'we are led by our desires', if 'the world is desire',[29] the so-called 'true-nature' is merely a 'spiritualization'[30] of the body, a revelation of nature and of desire[31] as lacks. Is it Spinoza or Nietzsche who writes: 'this worthy verbal pomp ... belongs among the ancient false finery, lumber and gold-dust of unconscious human vanity ... under such flattering colours and varnish too the terrible basic text *homo natura* must again be discerned ... to translate man back into nature'?[32]

All at once, 'we need *new* appraisals of values, beginning with a critique and an elimination of the old'.[33] By nature, does Nietzsche mean a lack or gap separating the self from the self that promises illusions, or a full necessity that supplies us with certainties? Nature is opposed to the ideal as a necessity. But in that case does passing legislation in order to create '*new* appraisals of values' have any meaning, and is Nietzsche not tautologous when he offers the precept: '"retranslate" man into nature'? And if nature is a necessity, should we not recall Nietzsche's fine aphorism: 'Iron necessity is a thing which in the course of history men come to see as neither iron nor necessary'?[34]

The gap that, within nature itself, contrasts culture with nature might be precisely that of *desire*. But what nature? Might this lack of nature in the self not be specified as the opposition between *nature as desire* and *nature as necessity*, which would produce the illusion of an opposition between nature and culture? Culture would then be the name given to the task undertaken by nature as desire to assimilate nature as necessity to itself or assimilate itself to it. But who can prove that desire as nature is not an illusion in the face of necessity or that, on the contrary, the ultimate necessity of nature is not that of desire, that is to say, of *lack*? Should we speak of the necessity of lack or of a lack of necessity in nature?[35]

Culture designates the collection of activities, attitudes, forms of conduct and institutions adopted by human societies in the face of nature. It is a term of recent usage allowing us to embrace certain classic formulations of problems. Sticking to those formulations that are chronologically close to Nietzsche, for example those in Marx, but also in Hegel, this lack is explained as a negativity, the driving force of the dialectic, separating nature from itself: lack and negativity must be abolished, or only indefinitely cooped up, within nature (or, in Hegel, within substance), through labour, which is the progress of desire: labour is culture[36] (*Bildung*, but also *Kultur*). The Hegelian and Marxian dialectical presupposes, and returns us to, a lack or a gap separating nature from itself.

As for Freud, he defines culture as follows:

> Human civilization [*Kultur*] . . . includes on the one hand all the knowledge and capacity that men have acquired in order to control the forces of nature and extract its wealth for the satisfaction of human needs, and, on the other hand, all the regulations necessary in order to adjust the relations of men to one another and especially the distribution of the available wealth. The two trends of civilization are not independent of one another.[37]

And, in *Das Unbehagen in der Kultur* (*Civilization and its Discontents*), he specifies:

> The word 'civilization' [*Kultur*] describes the whole sum of the achievements and the regulations which distinguish our lives from those of our animal ancestors and which serve two purposes – namely to protect men against nature and to adjust their mutual relations.[38]

For Freud, then, culture envisages certain ends, based on a lack: this involves nature being in conflict with itself, where nature is understood as the nature of drives on the one hand, and as a physical, material and social nature, on the other. Culture ultimately designates the impossible task of settling the struggles of Eros and the destructive drives, other names for desire and necessity.

With regard to Nietzsche, finally, this gap, which he calls *tragic*, constitutes his most fundamental objection to metaphysics, which is guilty in his eyes of confusing the projections of human desires with the characters that make up reality. And, from another point of view, the fixing of nature as a will to power opens up, as is indicated in the *zur* of *Wille zur Macht* (*Will to Power*), an abyss that is always tragic, and in which what Nietzsche calls culture unfolds.[39] In paragraph 130 of *Daybreak*, in which he sketches the idea of the innocence of becoming[40] and that of eternal return,[41] Nietzsche speaks of getting culture to conform, by submitting man's drives, not to the false necessity of the 'true nature of men', but to the tragic necessity of reality as the innocence of becoming. Getting man to conform to chance and necessity cannot be taken for granted. Nietzsche tries to challenge the 'theoretical optimism' of a culture that does 'not go beyond the means of consolation',[42] and closes the tragic gap at the expense of a fantasmatic and 'idealist' negation of reality and necessity. For theoretical optimism, nature thus denied exists on a human scale in return for the suppression of its drives. On the contrary, tragic culture seeks to free itself from anthropomorphism. 'My task: the dehumanization of nature, followed by the naturalization of man, after which he will have acquired the pure concept of "nature"'.[43]

The conforming to reality that Nietzsche calls for does not amount to a conformist resignation. Confirmism signifies the removing of desire in the face of stability. Nietzsche wishes to submit desire to the innocent alterity and *inhuman* disorder of becoming, which robs this submission of all possibility of denying reality to the advantage of desire. It is the *décadent* who takes his desires to be realities, to which he can then easily submit himself. A *tension* thus appears between renunciation, *amor fati*, and dionysiac affirmation, a tension that defines culture as the effort to bring together tragic reality and desire: 'Not to admit false necessity – which would mean to submit uselessly and would be servile – consequently knowledge of nature! – But also not to *want* anything that goes against necessity!'[44]

In Freud also, the task of psychoanalysis consists in forcing the ἀναγκή on the libido without repressing it, by substituting resignation (the reality principle) for the neurotic defence mechanisms (the pleasure principle); in the same way, in Nietzsche, the will to power must be positively affirmed and the *amor fati*[45] substituted for the consoling illusions of the ideal. The problem of culture leads us first to distinguish between destiny and morality, between consolation and an affirmative tragic resignation.

It is the tragic gap between nature and itself *within man* that makes it possible to have the ideal and morality as well as resignation and *amor fati*. We must, therefore, determine the relationship that links the body to the ideal. If in fact 'spirit' and culture have a mechanical relationship with the system of the organism, which would be contrary to the tragic conception of culture, the task of introducing a new culture, and the *selection* itself would be deprived of meaning.[46] Certainly, we must maintain the link between the ideal and the organism or its drive, without which Nietzsche's philosophy would be brought back to a pure idealism. But this cultural link in which nature tries to close the gap within itself is *metaphorical*, semiological and interpretative. Nietzsche speaks in the event, not of cause and effect, but of 'symptoms', 'misunderstanding' and 'exegesis'.[47] The first task of the 'philosopher and doctor'[48] will therefore be to constitute this discipline which Nietzsche generally names psychology and which encapsulates genealogical analysis, in order to be able to define the status of 'spiritualization' represented by culture as a whole.

The problem of culture, as the gap between nature and itself, has been clearly perceived long before the modern age. For example, the goal of the Hobbesian 'artefact' is to reduce 'the war of all against all', a war presented by Hobbes as being the *necessary* consequence of *natural* law. As is borne out by the Hobbesian distinction between law and natural law, nature is the effort to 'preserve life' at the same time as being a threat of death. Even in Rousseau, where we would expect nature, contrary to Hobbes's views, to seem a flawless unity, it is 'perfectability', 'the faculty of natural man',[49] nature and anti-nature, that makes it possible to have culture as history, or as depravation in relation to natural stability. If there is no culture without a fall, lack or gap, according to Rousseau, this fall, lack or gap are things which nature gives itself.[50] And if the philosophy and human sciences of the century since 1860 present any originality, it is for having tried to show that the gap remains irreducible. 'Mankind is constantly caught between two contradictory processes, one of which tends towards unification, while the other aims to maintain or re-establish diversification',[51] writes Lévi-Strauss. Reading this, one cannot help thinking of the dubious contest evoked by Freud between the 'two Heavenly Powers', which are 'immortal adversaries'.[52] But does not Nietzsche's *tragic* thought also end up recognizing that *amor fati* represents the impossibility of any attempt to reduce the contradictions of becoming, to abolish the gap within the will to power? Culture therefore designates all of the processes by which nature, in itself, tries to overcome its inner gap, whether these are called desire, or will to power, and so on.[53] And we shall use this term to tackle, in Nietzsche's thought, his view of these phenomena.

But then is it not simply a question of the task an ethics sets itself? The Nietzschean view on culture would seem in that case to be the recasting of a classic problem, whose validity has been contested by Nietzsche.[54] Nietzsche can effectively be thought of as the heir to certain 'moralists', in the classic sense of the term. For him, the 'great problem' is that of morality:[55] an ambiguous affirmation to come from the pen of an 'immoralist', since one could not so obstinately, as Nietzsche does, challenge a system of values if it merely responded to a false problem. Nietzsche is one of the first to take as his theme, systematically on a collective level, the same problems that traditionally morality tackles within the framework of individual initiative.[56] A culture[57] is properly the way in which the problem of the *gap* is tackled by such and such a society or age or civilization. It is in this sense that we are accustomed to speak of 'Greek culture', Germanic or Oriental or Anglo-Saxon culture, or French or Chinese or Spanish or Hispanic culture, according to groupings that are occasionally arbitrary (nations, languages, literatures, empires, religions, philosophies, political systems, etc.), but are always collective. We even speak, absolutely, of culture, in order to signify the collection of modes of production, institutions, ideologies, techniques, arts, moral sciences, and religions of a given social and/or historical group, which is represented as 'civilized' as opposed to a mythic 'savage' or 'barbaric' state. In *reality*, the use of the word 'culture' is nearly always tacitly restricted to the ideological domain.[58] To speak of the 'culture' of a society or just of 'culture', is to privilege, under the influence of idealist and, just as frequently, ethnocentric,[59] assumptions, the importance of ideology and mentalities for the historical or ethnocentric characterization of a given socio-historical group or unit – in the majority of cases, only the West sees itself given the privilege of this supposed intellectual 'superiority' – even if we refer only to the monuments in which we think that these mentalities are elected to be laid down: works of art, philosophies, laws, religions, languages, etc. In this way we forget the material conditions for the possibility of these traces of the 'Spirit' of a civilization. Because of this, we only use the term 'cultivated' (which is always a term of praise) to describe the individual who bears witness to a knowledge, considered sufficiently large, of the monuments of culture, that is to say, as ethnocentrism obliges, the culture to which we belong like that individual.[60] The conception that we form of this personal culture obviously rests on the type of civilization to which we ourselves belong. The 'honest man', the 'cultivated' man of the nineteenth and twentieth centuries is supposed to attach more value to the knowledge of the supposedly spiritual remnants of a culture than to the knowledge of the processes, practices and modes of production that have made these same remnants possible. This man is once again said to have a 'culture' – which is general to the degree to which he can be rhetorically allusive – if he is equipped with the legacy of the 'humanities', what German calls 'Philology', and can quote or place Homer, Shakespeare, Racine, Goethe or Descartes, while one ordinarily hesitates to accord this distinction to someone who possesses an equivalent degree of competence in the realm of technology, science and the various empirical sciences. Such a choice obviously involves a discrepancy between 'culture' and *praxis*, which is made all the greater by the fact that no ideological consciousness evolves more slowly than practice.[61] It is this discrepancy proper to 'modern man' that Nietzsche was already denouncing within the framework of a philosophy that was still idealist, when he wrote in the second of his *Untimely Meditations*: 'modern man drags around with him a huge quantity of indigestible stones of knowledge, which then, as in the fairy tale, can sometimes be heard rumbling about inside him. . . . Knowledge, consumed for the greater part without hunger for it and even counter to one's needs, now no longer acts as an agent for transforming the outside world'.[62] This view of culture, which Nietzsche will call 'theoretical' or 'idealist', is symbolized by the *Kulturphilister*, who contrasts sadly with the Greek model of the complete man, the 'man who is truly a man'[63] whom Plato sought to promote.[64]

4

Problematics in Nietzsche and its Precedents

The problem of culture in Nietzsche has been underestimated,[1] and yet it forms the origin and centre of his thought.

Nietzsche poses this problem in a century that, after Hegel, tries to recapture what speculative, 'abstract' philosophy seemed in his eyes to have unjustly neglected: life, the concrete *Erlebnis*, singularity. Kierkegaard puts in a claim for subjectivity as against the 'general'; Stirner puts forward his individual notion; Feuerbach tries to recapture man's essence, alienated in the pseudo-transcendence of the religious; and the young Marx tries to put the feet of the dialectic back on the ground of 'real' human existence. The spiritualist idealism in vogue at the end of the nineteenth century and Bergson's vitalist intuition will mark, after Nietzsche, the ultimate manifestation of this anti-intellectualist and anti-systematic demand, in reality already moderated by some of the first to express it. This demand is similar to certain reactions on the part of German romanticism to the spirit of the *Aufklärung*: a refusal to regard politics as a rationalizable order, a mistrust of 'speculation' and 'pure' Reason, an insistence on the imaginary, the fantastic, art, the body a pre- or post-reflective existence, characterize several thinkers of this period. Although owing much to eighteenth-century rationalism and to Goethe's classicism, Schopenhauer, through his aggressive view of Hegelianism and his claim to have gone beyond Kantian critical rationalism, also adopts interpretations similar to the spirit of romanticism or which display a nostalgia for immediacy.[3]

It is indisputably from Schopenhauer that Nietzsche receives the shock that will determine the direction his questions will take. The initial question, naive perhaps in the eyes of 'theoreticians' is phrased as: what is life worth, 'what is the value of existence;'[4] why does one live? It is striking that our age, marked by 'scientificity', is the one that is most reluctant to recognize Nietzsche's debt to his 'educator', on the pretext of struggling against idealism. What it erases is, in fact, the brutally existential nature of this question. It is perhaps more composed, and finds these sorts of questions unworthy of 'its' Nietzsche, while it would taunt them with being puerile or false problems in someone else, reproaching them less for their ingenuity (a mark of a radical philosophical beginning!) than for their existential and referential nature, in brief, for their 'antiscientific' nature. But for Nietzsche, scientificity can be another name for an idealist denial of life, which Nietzsche tried to show is both the object and the origin of this interrogation. The specific gesture made by Nietzsche, in the wake of Schopenhauer, consists in putting himself on the side of existence in order to judge the theorists' view: he puts forward the foundations for a sort of *overturning* that is analogous but inverse to the one that Kant named Copernican: the spirit's judgement of life has to be substituted by a perspective whose criteria come under the jurisdiction of life, an irrefutable point of departure, in order to evaluate reason and spirit themselves. If the question of the value of life has more importance than speculative knowledge, it is because science, even while it abstracts itself from life and considers the latter to be confused or illusory, is still a product of life – which implies that it is precisely incapable of resolving a problem that goes beyond it because *the problem founds and conditions science*: the problem is that of life and its value. Nietzsche's *a priori*, inherited from the Schopenhauerian appropriateness of the will to live and the thing-in-itself, is no longer the theoretical principles of transcendental philosophy, nor even the *factum rationis* of moral law: it is Life. 'The philosopher in Germany has more and more to unlearn how to be "pure knowledge": and it is to precisely that end that Schopenhauer as a human being can serve as an example.'[5] It is life – but also a 'philosophy' conceived of as a philosophy of life – that has the job of judging life. From this moment on genealogy is heralded, genealogy being a discourse that brings all discourse back to life, its evaluative origins and the conditions governing its possibility. *Genealogy* wishes to promote *life* as the *transcendental* and the philosophy of *suspicion* wishes to supplant *critical* philosophy, the critical reason of reason.[6]

The problem of culture, in Nietzsche, is a genealogical and, properly speaking, existential one, since it bears on the existence of the thinker and the conditions governing the existence of all thought. The questions that it implies are therefore articulated in a referential way, querying the values of a given age, society or nation, which are constant referents in Nietzsche's discourse. Germans, Christians, philosophers, Jews, the revolution, women, Greeks, the English, etc., are all cultural phenomena that are endlessy analysed and questioned by Nietzsche, proving that Nietzsche never stopped bringing his questioning to bear on a reality outside the text, outside discourse, on a given 'world' that is as much the reality of drives serving as a background to genealogy as a network of ideological relationships operating between idols. The attempt to efface this given, as the reality to be discovered beneath the masks of the ideals, seems neo-idealist, even when it assumes the scientific principles of a structural reading – a reading which, it should be recalled, is essentially of use to the elements of a text and only then to given elements of a culture. Nietzsche's speculations have the particular quality, as the problem of culture as history above all shows, of never forgetting their goal: that of interpreting a reality, life, and cultures, and of being useful only to the extent that they are self-effacing when they finally come face to face with a body, an individual, a being, an existence, in short, Life. This reality is no doubt cut across by the ideal, if not controlled by it – 'there are more idols in the world than there are realities'[7] – and in this sense reality vainly tries to be *fragwürdig*, worthy of being questioned: it none the less always remains the origin of all thought. Therefore, reducing Nietzsche's thought to that of the play of signifiers, means forgetting that genealogy insistently reminds us of the bodily and vital ground from which all discourse speaks: even if we adopt the indirect backing of Marx and psychoanalysis (which are in turn themselves reduced to the play of concepts and signs) it means thinking that we can lose his shadow with impunity, like Peter Schlemihl. This is pure and simple idealism.

To evaluate, therefore, is first of all to put oneself forward as being life. 'To live is to evaluate', because a non-living person cannot, indeed, evaluate, that is to say articulate his or her 'conditions of existence'.[8] But as life is a collective history, Nietzsche straightaway poses the question of a supra-individual determination of the vital evaluations to be made on the level of collective schema, that is to say of a *typology* that structures what we call precisely a culture and differentiates specifically between such and such a particular culture.

Culture, for Nietzsche, is the more or less unified totality of
values that a society, age or civilization – as vital typological
totalities – offers itself in response to the question: why do we live?
'Warum lebe ich?', *'Wozu lebst du?'*. These are questions that
Nietzsche himself acknowledged to be 'strange'.[9] In the context of
Untimely Meditations, the *Warum* for Nietzsche refers back to an
ideal, in large part taken from Schopenhauer, who looks down
from a great height on the routines and compromises of philistine
existence. Later Nietzsche will understand that the *Warum* as an
ideal emanates from the same conditions of *tangible* and material life
as the existence that he condemns and that, as a result, the *Wozu* is
an evaluative interpretation that expresses the conditions governing
the existence of a being.

Nietzsche will therefore have to question, not only cultural
ideals, but also certain types of life: those of morality.[10] This
continuity in the challenging of present culture is borne out by
numerous texts, of which the following, dating from 1872 to 1887,
are a few:

> Where are we, scholars and unscholarly, high placed and low, to
> find the moral exemplars and models among our contemporaries,
> the visible epitome of morality for our time? What has become of
> any reflection on questions of morality – questions that have at all
> times engaged every more highly civilized society? There is no
> longer any model or any reflection of any kind . . . in our society
> one either remains silent about such things or speaks of them in a
> way that reveals an utter lack of acquaintance with or experience
> of them and that can only excite revulsion. Thus it has come
> about that our schools and teachers simply abstain from an
> education in morality or make do with mere formalities: and
> virtue is a word that no longer means anything to our teachers or
> pupils, an old-fashioned word that makes one smile.[11]

Speaking of 'the great man' in 1872, he writes:

> For now he will have to descend into the depths of existence with
> a string of curious questions on his lips. Why do I live? What
> lesson have I to learn from life? . . . He torments himself, and sees
> how no one else does as he does, but now the hands of his fellow
> men are, rather, passionately stretched out to the fantastic events
> portrayed in the theatre of politics. . . . To the question: 'To what

end do you live?', they would all quickly reply with pride: '*To become* a good citizen, or scholar, or statesman' – and yet they *are* something that can never become something else, and why are they precisely this? And not, alas, something better?[12]

Spring 1880:

> It is certain that our present culture is a lamentable thing, a soup that gives off a rotten stench. A few unappetising morsels float about in it, bits of Christianity, knowledge, and art. Even dogs could find no sustenance in it. But the means of challenging this culture with something are scarcely less lamentable – namely Christian fanaticism, or scientific fanaticism, or the artistic fanaticism of individuals who can barely stand; it is as if we were trying to cure a lack with a vice. But in reality, present culture seems to be lamentable because a great task has arisen before it on the horizon, namely the revision of every appreciation of value; but in order to do that, prior even to placing everything in the balance, we must first of all possess a balance – I mean that supreme equity of the supreme intelligence which sees fanaticism as the mortal enemy and our present 'universal culture' as being a performance from an itinerant actor and his monkey.[13]

Summer-Autumn 1887:

> The modern spirit's lack of discipline, dressed up in all sorts of moral fashions. – The showy words are: tolerance (for 'the incapacity for Yes and No'); *la largeur de sympathie* (= one-third indifference, one-third curiosity, one-third pathological irritability); 'objectivity' (lack of personality, lack of will, incapacity for 'love'); 'freedom' versus rules (romanticism); 'truth' versus forgery and lies (naturalism); being 'scientific' (the *document humain*:[14] in other words, the novel of colportage and addition in place of composition); 'passion' meaning disorder and immoderation; 'depth' meaning confusion, the profuse chaos of symbols.[15]

But is Nietzsche as 'unusual' as he pretends? The questions he puts to this 'modern culture' initially display the demands of a Schopenhauerian idealism in their scorn for a thoughtless immersion into tangible reality.[16] But Nietzsche goes beyond Schopenhauer and inherits a whole tradition.

First of all, he inherits Greece. Nietzsche never abandoned this

reference, whose content changes while remaining faithful to a
certain outline: struggle, the tragic, the meaning of the earth,
mastery, the value of becoming, the importance of the body, the
Selbstüberwindung. All of Nietzsche's work constitutes a discussion
with this culture. 'The rest of us moderns confront the Greeks with
our weak concept of humanity',[17] writes Nietzsche in 1872. But in
the Preface to the *Gay Science* of 1886 and in the Epilogue to
Nietzsche contra Wagner of 1888, Nietzsche repeats: 'Ah! those
Greeks! They understood one another in order to *live!*' Many
original views – or at all events views that were renewed after the
neo-Kantian view of Hellenism – on Greek culture and thought,
the role of the παιδεία and the irrational, for example,[18] merge with
Nietzche's intuitions. To form a certain type of man and constitute
a certain view of the world, maintaining a balance between tragic
destiny and man, between the πόλις and the individual was, as W.
Jaeger showed in the wake of Nietzsche, the specific task that
Hellenism assigned itself – and it is here that Nietzsche above all
sees himself. And if Nietzsche ends up opposing Plato, it is because
his educational project seems to him to be the symbol and the
betrayal of that ideal of educational culture. Plato's thought searches
for the καλοὶ κἀγαθοὶ who possess the ἀρετὴ and puts forward the
philosophical elaboration of the conditions governing their
promotion.[19] The goal of philosophy is therefore παιδεία, which is
viewed as something that educates or moulds a person, as witnessed
by the frequent use, in the *Republic*, for example, of the metaphor
of the πλάττειν – a distant precursor of Nietzsche's metaphor of
culture as *Züchtung*: Plato's philosopher as legislator, a master of
culture as πολιτεία aims to make souls 'manageable (εὐαγώγους)
for the person who knows how to train them (παιδεύειν) and
fashion them (πλάττειν)'.[20] εἶδος unifies the training that,
according to Plato, is practiced in sophistry in a haphazard way
(πλανεῖσθαι) which strangely coincides with the reproaches
Nietzsche addressed to the culture of our day. For Plato as for
Nietzsche, nature must be trained, if only by constraint, and
Nietzsche differs from Plato only in refusing to allow εἶδος, or
truth, as an end.[21]

To prefer Plato, in Greek thought, will be for Nietzsche the sign
par excellence of *décadence*, to give a false solution (idealism) to a true
problem (*Bildung*). But every one of Nietzsche's inspirers whose
views are to nurture his ambition to found a 'new culture' shows

their concern for a new culture and draws their inspiration from the Greek model: notably Goethe and Hölderlin.

Goethe is, in the eyes of Nietzsche, the person who, as a classic image of Olympian poise, undertakes an individual *Bildung*, an individual model of *Kultur*, drawing inspiration from what, according to him, forms the essence of Greek culture.[22] Even if, according to Nietzsche, it finally appears that 'Goethe did not understand the Greeks':[23] 'Goethe is exemplary (*vorbildlich*): an impetuous naturalism that progessively turns itself into a strict dignity. As a stylised human being, he reached a higher peak than any other German ever'.[24] 'Goethe, not only a good and great human being but a *culture* (*Kultur*).'[25] 'Our epic culture ultimately finds its full expression in Goethe.'[26] It is no doubt his own life that Goethe limits himself to trying to turn into a symbol of balance and culture. But outside philosophy, he is the person who pondered the most on the respective value of cultures,[27] independently of any pre-established moral criterion, and proposed, in his *Wilhelm Meister*, the educative model of the 'pedagogical province',[28] the only non-political, non-philosophical utopia, like those of Plato or Rousseau.[29] In comparison to these names, Nietzsche owes Goethe a vision of nature – and so of culture – that is less 'optimistic' and 'theoretical': 'Goethe's view of man's position in nature and the surrounding nature was more mysterious, more enigmatic and more demonic than that of his contemporaries'.[30]

Nevertheless, it is Hölderlin, the young Nietzsche's *Lieblings-dichter* (favourite writer), who instigates the move to regard culture as a problem. Through poetic reference to the Greeks, Hölderlin manifests a requirement, while the Goethe model is valuable for its almost idiosyncratic achievements. Hölderlin's hero, as a symbol of disparate incompletion for the whole of humanity, enjoins the Germans to recognize a new Greece, one that represents a way of organizing the state not based on diabolical oppression:

All the same, you concede a great deal of power to the State. It does not have the right to demand what it cannot obtain by force. ... By Heavens! the person who wants the State to be a school for morality has no idea how much he is sinning. None the less, by wanting the State to be his heaven, man has created a hell. The State is a rough walnut shell covering life, nothing more. It is the wall of the garden in which men grow flowers and fruit. But what use is the garden wall if the soil is dry? Only rain from the heavens is of any use. Oh rain! Oh enthusiasm! You will bring spring back to the people! And the State cannot order you to come. But if it refrains from worrying you, you will come in all your wonderful glory, enveloping us in golden clouds and raising us above mortal existence.[31]

And later Diotimes says to Hyperion: 'You will be the educator of our people, you will be a great man'.[32] Like Hölderlin's appeal, therefore, Nietzsche's call for a new culture, which is initally based on specifically German preoccupations,[33] expands to encompass the general problem of culture, notably in the wake of the 1870 war and the advent of the *Reich*, when the hopes he had placed in Wagner's project and in the renewal of German culture had been dashed: 'Our Hölderlin and Kleist, and who knows who else besides, were ruined by their uncommonness and could not endure the climate of so-called German culture; and only natures of iron, such as Beethoven, Goethe, Schopenhauer and Wagner are able to stand firm'.[34]

But what is this 'commonness' resisted by Nietzsche and those he invokes as his precursors? Reason. As Hölderlin says: 'Nothing of sense ever came out of simple common sense, and nothing reasonable ever emerged from simple reason'.[35] 'Simple reason' has 'limits'. This is the tension between, on the one hand, a philosophy of limits and of concept, like that of Kantian criticism, which tries to determine experience with the help of rules in order to form a knowable nature, and, on the other hand, a philosophy, or in Kantian terms a metaphysics, of intuition, which tries to go beyond these 'limits' because they seem pusillanimous, a fact that creates an *ambiguity* in Nietzsche that is inherent to his problem of culture.

In fact, culture is, on the one hand, viewed on the ultimate determining *agency* of forms of conduct and ideals that can be assigned to a given socio-historical totality: this is *Kultur* in the strict sense of the term. But, on the other hand, it is represented as a *norm*, a requirement, at all events a value that does not involve a simply *descriptive* analysis: this is more the significance that is attached to culture as *Bildung*.

At least in the initial stages, then, Nietzsche's questioning takes place within a domain that is to some degree para-philosophical. 'True' philosophy, that is to say, first of all, the metaphysics borrowed from Schopenhauer, must, in order to fulfil its authentic task, namely culture, 'go beyond', according to Nietzsche, traditional philosophies and sciences. Nietzsche will claim to be for Schopenhauer what Schopenhauer had wanted to be for Kant: someone who completes a legitimate attempt that was arrested along the way. But what does Schopenhauer's supposed progress represent in relation to Kant's criticism? Schopenhauer's metaphysics, like Hegel's represents, *in relation to Kant*, not progress but a regressive tendency: Schopenhauer and Hegel transgress the limits imposed on Kant's reasoning, the former by fixing the thing-in-itself as will,[36] the latter by affirming that the history of the Spirit, the substance-subject,[37] goes beyond the dualism of abstract understanding: but is this not achieved at the price of *dogmatism*? It allows Hegel to put forward history teleologically and to read it as a dialectical process that progresses through *Bildung* towards *Kultur*; it authorizes Schopenhauer to think of will as the thing-in-itself of phenomena. The constant repetition, in Nietzsche's texts, of terms like *Zweck*, *Ziel*, and, later, *wohin*, *wozu*, and *sollen*, within the actual problem of genealogy and the innocence of becoming, can testify to a preoccupation with *ends* that is consequently *axiological*.

The question of culture (*Kultur*), prior to Nietzsche, had been posed, particularly by Kant. But it was a problem to which, according to Kant, a reply could only be given within the extra-critical context of *reflexive* judgements. 'The finality of nature is . . . a particular *a priori* concept, which has its origin solely in the reflective judgement', writes Kant.[38] And he adds: 'only culture can be the ultimate *end* which we can reasonably attribute to nature in relation to the human species'.[39] To question nature's design concerning the human species and its history means to pose the problem of culture. But Kant who, in the wake of Herder, questions in this way whether nature has a 'plan' or an 'order' or a 'design', does not ignore the fact that, however necessary his questions are, they will only get a response – on the subject of unknowable human freedom – within the extra-critical domain in which Leibniz, speaking of the realm of grace and 'the ultimate reason of things', located his revelation of divine plans.[40] Kant's enquiries in the field of the philosophy of history constitute a continuation, within critical philosophy, or rather on the margins of it, of Leibniz's meditations on 'the ultimate reason of things', the 'harmony of all things', the 'universal perfection of the works of

God', in short on 'the sufficient reason of existence':[41] 'nature does
nothing in vain and is not extravagant in its use of means to attain
its ends'[42] is a proposition of the same nature as the Leibnizian idea
that 'there is always . . . in things a principle of determination . . .,
namely, that the greatest effect should be produced with . . . the
least expenditure'.[43] And if it is in Leibniz that we read: 'the reasons
of the world . . . lie in something',[44] it is Kant, a critic of the
physio-theological argument, who none the less declares: 'we have
too short a view to penetrate into the secret mechanism of the
organization [of nature]'.[45] Finally, nature, in Kant, 'needs a
perhaps interminable line of generations in which each one passes
on its knowledge to the next one in order ultimately to lead the
natural germs in our species to a degree of development that
conforms fully to its designs',[46] which corresponds to the Leibnizian
idea that 'there is a perpetual and a most free progress of the whole
universe in fulfilment of the universal beauty and perfection of the
works of God, so that it is always advancing towards a greater
development (*cultum*)'.[47]

However, Kant is permitted to speak only of a 'main thread' in
place of a 'dogmatic exposé', which guides reflexive judgements
concerning the 'ordered history'[48] of men, and he sticks to the
realm of the famous 'as if',[49] or analogy. On the other hand,
Nietzsche's meditations explicitly put themselves forward, nearly a
century after Kant, in terms of *ends*, within a pre-critical field.
Thus, Nietzsche writes in 1872:

> The problem of a *civilization* (*Kultur*) has rarely been correctly
> understood. Its *end* (*Ziel*) lies neither in the greatest possible
> *happiness* of a people not in the free development of all their
> talents: it shows, rather, in the just *measure* of the developments.
> Its end tends to go beyond earthly happiness: its goal is the
> production of great works.[50]

This helps us to understand the options he believed he could derive
from the Hegelian and Schopenhauerian problems, both of them
paradoxically reunited in the common undertaking to 'correct' or
perfect Kant's criticism in a theological and metaphysical way.[51]
There is scarcely a word that recurs more frequently in Hegel's and
Schopenhauer's texts than *Zweck*. This is what Nietzsche seems to
have retained of these two philosophies:

Hegel: 'The question as to whether, at the base of history and essentially the history of the world, there is a final goal (*Endzweck*), in itself and for itself, whether in history the Providential plan (*Plan*) is achieved, and achieved effectively, and whether there is any *reason* in history, is something that has to be decided for itself philosophically and hence as something necessary in itself and for itself.' 'A history without such a goal and without such a judgement would be merely an imbecile state of representation, not even a children's story, for even children demand that a story have some interest, that is: a given goal at least which one can sense, and link between events and actions and this goal.' Conclusion: every narrative must have a goal, and therefore the history of a people or the world must have one, too. That is to say: since there is a 'history of the world', a goal must also be found in the world process; that is to say: we only demand narratives that involve goals.[52]

But it is Schopenhauer that Nietzsche is thinking of when he writes that man 'can only justify his existence as a being who is destined in an absolute way to serve goals of which he is not conscious'.[53] Schopenhauer holds greatly to the notion of finality,[54] but he reserves it for phenomena, will being in itself devoid of a general goal:

> Man always possesses a goal and motives that regulate his actions; he can always account for his behaviour in each case. But ask him why he wants or does not want something in general, and he cannot reply. The absence of all goals and limits is, in fact, essential to will in itself, which is an effort without an end.[55]

If, therefore, during the period of the so-called Basel philological writings, Nietzsche assigns to culture the production of great works through genius – an extra-rational goal for history – it is because he borrows from Hegel the idea that culture is the goal and reason for history, but combines this with the Schopenhauerian idea of an extra-rational goal: genius. These considerations, the Hegelian one of a final totalization or the history of humanity's evolution, and the more Schopenhauerian one of a will whose very finality is irrational, mean that the problem of culture in Nietzsche creates a situation which overruns the limits assigned by criticism to philosophy, and brings us closer to a Leibnizian view of the world, the only difference being that God, that which changes everything, is here absent.[56] It is therefore difficult to ignore that the problem of culture in Nietzsche is initially put forward in terms that the Nietzsche of 1885, for example, would himself call idealist.[57]

The dubious state of this problem also sets into play the possibility of replies that are other than metaphysical to the question: '*Wozu das Leben?*', a question that is at least one of the radical ones put by Nietzsche. This question can only be answered by idealism – which is an ignorance of the factors leading him to speak – in an authoritarian and dogma-tic way: from Wagnerian 'idealists' (Malwida von Meysenbug) to open advocates of Pan-Germanism (like Elizabeth Förster) or crypto-Nazis (Bertram), including Stefan George's circle, Nietzsche's 'posterity' has been ' rich in prophets whose typically idealist language is marked by a peremptory authoritarianism that masks a lack of foundations.[58] But who will say that idealism does not still dictate the goals and illusions of our culture? Assigning new values without taking the trouble to designate the ground from which they have sprung is something that can be done by any old crank, just as destroying 'ancient values' can be done by any average nihilist. But shall we say that Nietzsche was able both to 'discover morality'[59] and to promote non–regressive values and ideals? Is Nietzsche still a metaphysician, a radical creator and destroyer, or just a marginal figure? The twentieth century, with the exception of Freud and a few other misunderstood authors, has not followed up these questions: it has let history take over, in its usual dogmatic way. It is indeed characteristic that Freud, in his problematics of culture,[60] tacks back and forth between science and philosophy, while the problem has been evoked, not by philosophers in the twentieth century, but by the great German-language novelists of the first half of the century: Mann, Musil, Hesse, and Broch, who develop their questions in a marginal field, the only one perhaps in which a hybrid question such as this could be given expression. Nietzsche's questions have been taken up in astonishingly faithful terms in *The Magic Mountain*, *The Man without Qualities*, *The Glass Bead Game*, *The Temptor* and *The Sleepwalkers*: a sign that perhaps such a question goes beyond, not only the competence of science,[61] which is itself a part of culture – Nietzsche takes away its independence – but also the strict field of traditional philosophy.

What replies does Nietzsche give? We must first show why this problem presses itself upon him as the centre of his reflections.

5
Nietzsche's Questioning and its Stages

'What is the value of existence?' or: 'Why is there life?' If metaphysics gave answers that were discussed and challenged by Schopenhauer, Nietzsche will only reject these answers later. But the question that Nietzsche relates back to the collective problems of culture is nothing out of the ordinary. Plato had already asked: ὄντινα χρὴ τρόπον ζῆν and πῶζ βιωτέον.[1] If Nietzsche is original at all, it is because he first of all asks this question within the context of the pedagogical preoccupations and ideological justifications related to the practice and teaching of philology, but equally within the larger historical context of the investigations made by a nation or age, in which economic, military, technical and political power admits to its weaknesses while seeking through its very success to offer itself justifications. 'Germanness', genius, and the Wagnerian hero, for example, play this model role for a civilization which has burst its limits through being flooded with its own power, at a cost it cannot ignore. What Adorno calls the 'grandiose weakness' of Wagner,[2] is symbolic of this context, in which force itself betrays fragility. Nietzsche, at one and the same time, quit his chair in philology at Basel, and broke off links with Wagner, along with the latter's musical aesthetics and religious and nationalist declarations: this allows us, negatively, to gauge the path that he would have covered. But from 1871 on, Nietzsche is aware that science, politics, economic and military victory, the State morality and religion, in particular in a Germany which up until then had been naively placed by him at the head of the *Kulturkampf*[3] in Europe, can offer no reply to a question that, although formulated by an individual, can none the less find the way to its solution only on a level that transcends individuality. So, what values can be proposed by the philologist, who represents both existing and potential culture, and who holds the model image of a possible type of complete man, in order to educate modern man and 'justify as such life'?[4] Nietzsche quickly realizes that this role can only be entrusted to the philosopher, since the philologist merely works with tradition, and is unable to keep going, in what he preserves, the force of creativity implied in a culture.

> Now, how does the philosopher view the culture of our time? Very differently, to be sure, from how it is viewed by those professors of philosophy who are so well contented with their state. ... He almost thinks that what he is seeing are the symptoms of a total extermination and uprooting of culture. ... Everything, contemporary art and science included, serves the coming barbarism. The cultured man has degenerated to the greatest enemy of culture, for he wants lyingly to deny the existence of the universal sickness and thus obstructs the physicians.[5]

An opposition is therefore born which is axiological in intention, between the given situation and the deep intelligible reality of culture, an opposition that suits Schopenhauer's dualist scheme:

> To the question: 'To what end do you live?' they would all quickly reply with pride: 'To *become* a good citizen, or scholar, or statesman' – and yet they *are* something that can never become something else, and why are they precisely this? And not, alas, something better? ... Man forgets himself. ... In becoming, everything is hollow, deceptive, shallow and worthy of our contempt; the enigma which man is to resolve he can resolve only in being, in being thus and not otherwise, in the imperishable.[6]

It is with this notion of *culture* as a guiding thread that the development of Nietzsche's questioning can emerge with the greatest necessity. It is against the background of his confrontation with the moralists' project and of an axiological philosophy, that we can see the meaning and the difficulties of Nietzsche's undertaking gradually emerging. At this point, his analysis begins to parallel that of a Marx, with the difference that Nietzsche establishes a typology of culture by finally referring culture back to the bodily idiosyncrasy of strength or weakness, whereas Marx opts for the view that ideologies and practices are, in the last instance, fixed by the economic factors that characterize a society. But the Nietzsche who analyses the problem of culture remains a moralist who, right up until the end, beyond *Umwertung aller Werte*, wants to create new values, and point the way to '*vorzuschreibende Wege der Kultur*' (prescribable paths of culture).[7] It is, in fact, difficult to repair the rift between the moralist project, which is *axiological*, and the *determinist* implications of a genealogical analyis. This is the problem that traverses Nietzsche's thoughts on culture.[8] To resolve this problem, can we really be content to evoke the *Umwertung*, an incantation which we imagine will allow us to fuse together the freedom of creation and the determined limits of the body?[9]

In a first phase, his 'Schopenhauerian' period, Nietzsche seems anxious to criticise and construct, and the antithesis of becoming and being is merely another way of designating this double process. In fact, he wishes to criticize 'defiantly'[10] the values of 'culture' in place (the 'becoming') and also attempts, with the same 'youthful courage',[11] and 'precocious, purely personal insights, all but in-communicable',[12] to build (in 'being') the foundations needed for a new culture. But Nietzsche's youth, like that evoked by Plato,[13] falls into the trap of metaphysics:[14] as Nietzsche himself says, quoting Talleyrand, it is good to 'distrust our first reactions: they are invariably much too favourable'.[15] Metaphysics, which arises earlier than we think, offers us a double-sided advantage: one side displays an enthusiasm for 'regeneration'; the other side displays inexhaustible resources in the critique of 'reality'. Nietzsche acknowledges this:

> Can deep hatred against 'the Now', against 'reality' and 'modern ideas' ' be pushed further than you pushed it in your artists' metaphysics – believing sooner in the Nothing, sooner in the devil than in 'the Now'?[16]

These early texts are *dogmatic*, and 'so sure of (their) message that (they dispense) with any kind of proof'.[17] This is *idealism*[18] in the strict sense: on the one hand Nietzsche contrasts supra-tangible ends to the reality of phenomena;[19] and on the other hand, a disregard for the origins of ideas[20] pushes him to overestimate their ability to force things to belong and work in a culture.

This creates a fundamental ambiguity that will continue to weigh on the problem of culture. Nietzsche is primarily a moralist in the sense that he replies to a state of things by demanding that it be transformed, and tries to isolate a set of principles for human conduct, judging this set according to various categories of values, and proposing various ends. But he is also a moralist in the sense that he is reluctant to put this problem of human conduct in strictly socio-political and univocally determinist terms. Compared to a Marxist analysis, Nietzsche's set of problems is striking for its insistence on axiological forms[21] and its recourse to a notion that does not come under the jurisdiction of a socio-economic perspective,[22] or a strictly individual perspective, since it places itself more on the level of what the eighteenth century called 'mores'.[23] To speak of *Trieb* (drive), as Nietzsche will do later, is to anchor the problem in organic individuality[24] and ignore the collective categories; while to speak of culture is both to posit *norms* and to affirm a drive-based determinism, to situate oneself on a supra-individual plane without trying to throw light on what determines conduct through the use of specifically sociological categories.[25] In short, culture and cultures, for Nietzsche, are not objects (in the sense that scientific sociology confers on this concept) or, as Durkheim would call them, *things*:[26] they are neither individual nor collective, but are collections of evaluations that are based on corporeity, as well as being, in the case of the Greeks or the tragic culture of the superhuman, normative models. This dualism can be seen once more in two schemes, that cannot easily be superimposed on one another: the 'economics' of the will to power and the superhuman as an end.[27]

Nietzsche writes in *Ecce Homo*:

> *Human, All Too Human* is the memorial of a crisis. It calls itself a book for *free* spirits: almost every sentence in it is the expression of a victory – with this book I liberated myself from that in my nature which *did not belong to me*. Idealism does not belong to me.[28]

This extension of his critique, which will transform idealist dualism into a critical dualism that is closer to Kant,[29] is the result of several instances of disillusionment which generated 'suspicion'[30]. Nietzsche resumes this shock in the *Attempt at Self-Criticism* of 1886.[31] Here he sees himself being led to give a *descriptive* and *critical* analysis of the different values represented by the great names and periods of history, above all Western history. This *analysis* is founded on the notion of culture (whose historical names or various realizations are just so many punctilious typical expressios) but Nietzsche is still looking for a criterion for his *critical* analysis and his propositions, a unique principle that governs the very thing he condemns. In this respect, *Human, All Too Human* is characteristic of a research – which is already a *Versuch* – that aims to fix the principle of history and culture as a *unity*, in particular since Socrates and Christianity. We can see this in the contrast between the free spirit and romanticism. By the latter Nietzsche means an irrational spirit or tradition, that is anti-historical, essentialist, mystical or, more generally, 'metaphysical', without yet conferring on the word its true genealogical unity.

Therefore, in *Human, All Too Human, Daybreak* and the first four books of *The Gay Science*, we read the meditations of a 'moralist' concerned to examine the value of 'mores' in an age or a people[32] or a barely defined order. Nietzsche advances by way of aphorisms grouped according to point of view, but is concerned to judge on the level of a socio-historical totality (nations, peoples, social groups, sexes, professions, ideas, religions, institutions, etc.), assembled ·into a unity that is as yet conceptually indeterminate: culture.[33]

The unity is something Nietzsche will only discover at a third stage, thanks to a method he became aware of when he presented himself as a 'historian',[34] 'psychologist' and 'philosopher of suspicion': the genealogical method. It is this method that organizes the principal notions of the final period: nihilism, *décadence*, morality, the superhuman, pessimism, psychology, bad conscience, resentment, etc. *Only* genealogical analysis can provide culture with a unity – one that is still superior to the unity Hegel attributed to historical cultures – or a status, and allow Nietzsche to assign this unity to the Western culture of Platonism and Christianity, so as to get us to look at Greek culture and the project of the superhuman.[35] In a general sense, culture is what expresses the '*wohin*' of an existence and determines, as the 'spirit of the age', the forms of behaviour, works and mentalities. But while there was idealism in the early Nietzsche, who overestimated the influence of representations, for Nietzsche the genealogist ideals now seem the 'encoded language' of the body (*Zeichensprache* or *Zeichenrede der Affekte*).[36] Geneaology, as 'semiotics',[37] that is to say as the allocation of a symptomatic phenomenon 'that does not know enough to "understand"'[38] its hidden determining drives, can now spare Nietzsche the first of the 'four great errors' that he denounces in

The Twilight of the Idols:[39] the confusion of cause and effect. For it is a confusion of cause and effect when one attributes to a culture, as a collection of values, a causal influence on the behaviour of individuals or groups:

> There are no spiritual causes at all! The whole of the alleged empiricism which affirmed them has gone to the devil! *That* is what follows!– And we had made a nice misuse of that 'empiricism', we had *created* the world on the basis of it as a world of causes, as a world of will, as a world of spirit.[40]

Genealogically, these representations are the mask donned by the 'body', which is the fundamental determining agency and uses ideal representations as disguised expressions of its desires. Culture is no longer 'merely' a collection of representations. It is all the *evaluation* of an age, a people or socio-historical grouping of some kind, the hidden face of the reality of a certain *bodily economy*, which Nietzsche sometimes calls 'idiosyncrasy' or 'metabolism' (*Stoffwechsel*).

Such a definition of culture as a body economy, a type of life, first of all makes it possible to discover a *synchronic* unity behind various human manifestations:[41] art, philosophy, politics, morality, religion, 'mores, the State, education and social relations',[42] whose genealogical solidarity can be grasped. But this definition makes it equally necessary (since it is possible) to ascertain a *history* behind culture, that is to say to fix a *diachronic* unity, where previously we had been content to record a succession of events which had no guiding principle. In this way, Nietzsche confirms and goes beyond certain analogous attempts on the part of his predecessors, while challenging their point of view: the Kantian transcendental subject is rediscovered in the body; Schopenhauerian will is transposed into a body, the in itself of culture; and Nietzsche pulls apart the Hegelian system and substitutes the genealogical ἱστορία of the ideal for the teleological history of the phenomenology of the Spirit. The body, by substitution, 'is' subject, will and Spirit.[43] In place of the figures of the Spirit, with genealogy one can determine types and stages (Platonism, Christianity, morality, the superhuman, the tragic age, theoretical, *décadent* and moral optimism, Socratism, the aescetic priest, resentment, bad conscience, etc.), and examine the value of values of this fundamental *unity* to Western culture: the Platonic and Christian morality that is deployed as metaphysics, ethic, science, political theory (socialism, for example), knowledge, aesthetics, etc. It is, therefore, an examination of culture, an evaluation of the evaluations of the *décadent* body as reason, which governs Nietzsche's enquiries into philosophy – enquiries that are no longer strictly *philosophical*, but are a *genealogical* appreciation of the philosophy that encompasses him. Thus Nietzsche, taking philosophy as an object, will place himself simultaneously inside and outside philosophy, by evoking 'new philosophers', judges of philosophy, who 'evaluate and create',[44] or by putting himself forward as a 'psychologist': revelatory terms for an extra-philosophical perspective, that regards philosophy as a particular case of its object: culture.

In this genealogical enquiry, culture is conceived as the collected *values* that govern the practice, ideals and mores of a given socio-historical totality (the Greeks, India, Christianity, the tragic vision of the world, the superhuman). But the major difference is that these values are evaluations: they are no longer just representations; they are also the collected means assumed by the *body*, according to a certain typological economy, within this totality, in order to make it master of life, obliquely (the 'weak' body) or openly (the 'strong' body). Culture, therefore, appears to be the expression of evaluations of (drive-based) nature *vis-à-vis* (physical) nature. The evaluations of life by itself *as will to power* – for the latter is none other than a reduplication on the part of a life that wishes to grow – are the manifest and latent aspects of life as an evaluating will to power. Practices and ideals, as things which make up the entity which we call culture are revelations and a travesty of the body and of life, according to an *idiosyncratic* 'economy'[45] that is expressed in Nietzsche's view by the relationship between the *affirmation* and *denegation* of life. In this way, tragic Greek culture uses illusion as an affirmation of life conceived as a tragic contradiction, while the Christian illusion masks, beneath the affirmation of a 'celestial nothingness' the body's denegation. The route followed by culture as a bodily vital idiosyncrasy, analysed genealogicaly, leads us to 'translate back into nature'[46] this culture which seemed to be separate from nature. Henceforth, culture therefore forms the object of a *Naturgeschichte*, to use the expression Nietzsche some-times takes to be synonymous with genealogy.

But a difficulty now presents itself: within the 'determinist' framework of genealogy, what can possibly act as the source of a *new* culture, represented necessarily as the norm of evaluations? Will it be the body, and how? Or will it be a selective idea, the Eternal Return ... of the *Same*? If culture is just a name for a nature that is trying to fill its own lack, what will be the source of the overcoming that Nietzsche continually demands, what will be the source of the *Übermensch*'s *transcendence*, even one that falls back on the imminent horizon of the Earth and the body? No doubt, the possibility of this overcoming is expressed by the will to power. But the latter merely expresses a possibility, whose meaning is determined by an idiosyncrasy, that is strong or weak. And surely it is only when we come to the idea of Eternal Return that we can conjure up, magically perhaps, the confrontation between a genea-logical necessity and a creative freedom?

But this problem arises in another way again: if the problems raised by Nietzsche remain on the margins of a moralist project, this is because he refers to concepts which are marginal in relation to the constituted scientific 'disciplines'. To speak of culture is to introduce the genealogical concept of *typology*. But in what sense can a type of bodily economy in its *idio*syncrasy be a causal determining factor in the construction of a socio-economic whole? A culture described on the typologocial level goes beyond the very individualities which it determines: but what status can a supra-individual body idiosyncrasy assume? Is its determination of origins ideal (an idealist temptation) or physiological (the risk of racism, which unfolds against a background of scientific uncertainty)? Is it, for example, Christianity that 'weakens' the body, or the 'weak' body that produces Christianity? Nietzsche's project can enter neither the field of a moralist *psycho*-logy nor the field of a *social* science.

But these questions reverberate: on what grounds can Nietzsche the individual present himself as being the '*froher Botschafter*' of new 'prescribable paths of culture',[47] break in half 'the history of mankind';[48] claim 'to hold the fate of humanity in (his) hands',[49] present himself as a 'destiny', a '*force majeure*',[50] that is to say as an *individuality* that determines the course of a *collective* history,[51] and feels responsible for the 'collective evolution of mankind'?[52] And on the other hand: how can Nietzsche the *philosopher*, or 'law-giver'[53] who creates new concepts,[54] be the initiator of *truth*'s 'battle with the lie of the millenia' and a 'war of spirits',[55] since 'one first has to convince the body'?[56]

This is a consequence of the uncertain status of the problem of culture, which cannot be a strictly philosophical one in the traditional sense of the term. But is this because metaphysics can only provide a culture of '*Wille zur Wahrheit*', or '*Wille zum Tode*', or is it because this problem goes beyond philosophy, as speculation, and involves *Erlebnis*? And yet, in §211 of *Beyond Good and Evil* and §409 of *The Will to Power*, the *Schaffen* and *Machen* demanded by the new philosopher concern not only life, the body, *Erlebnis*, but also *the concept*:

> They knock over the states and say: there is nothing elevated and worthy of adoration – because they themselves are incapable of creating (*shaffen*) states and gods. These people are my enemies: they want to knock things down and build nothing themselves. They say: 'all that is valueless' and do not wish themselves to create any value (*Keinen Wert schaffen*).[57]

To determine the goals of a *Bildung*, the memory of a culture, now seems to involve a sort of idealist voluntarism: one must *wish* to bring about the *idea* of a new type of man, as §3 of *The Antichrist* repeats:

> The problem I raise here is ... what type of human being one ought to *breed* (*man züchten* SOLL), ought to *will* (*wollen soll*). ... This more valuable type has existed often enough already: but as a lucky accident, as an exception, never as *willed* (*gewollt*). He has rather been the most feared ... and out of fear the reverse type has been willed (*wollen*).

The prophetic tone of a book entitled *Thus SPEAKS Zarathustra* rests on the same idealist voluntarism. Even though the 'fifth-gospel'[58] claims to challenge the Christian 'dysangel', the phrase could just as easily betray a continuity as announce a revival. But Nietzsche denied ideals all value since they were denials of reality. If Nietzsche's suspicions are therefore applied first and foremost to philosophy, if the primordial question is that of the value of philosophy for culture, which owns the *Gesetzgebung* (legislation) of the future – the body or the concepts?[59]

The reply may be that the reproach of idealism applies, as he himself recognized, to the Schopenhauerian Nietzsche. But is this imputation any less valid for the Nietzsche of *Beyond Good and Evil* and *Ecce Homo*? Nietzsche cannot ignore the fact that philosophy, like any ideal, has a grounding: life, from which it could not think of detaching itself without deluding itself as to its apparent independence. And because Nietzsche has shown that philosophy is 'a system of evaluations that partially coincides with the conditions of a creature's life',[60] 'a fruit, by which I recognize the soil from which it sprang',[61] he finds himself in a dilemma: whether to found 'true culture'[62] on the body, the '*Handeln*' (act), and to put it in the hands of life and practice; or else to count on the creation of new concepts and values by the new philosophical 'law givers'. We can see that this does not just involve a choice between theory and practice, since theory itself is conditioned by a practice, 'the judgement of muscles'. It is a dilemma, because the body already evaluates and because a concept is also a negation of life: 'Spirit is the life that itself strikes into life'.[63] This dilemma is resumed but not resolved in a posthumous fragment from 1888:

> Dangerous distinction between 'theoretical' and 'practical', e.g., in the case of Kant, but also in the case of the ancients: – they act as if pure spirituality presented them with the problems of knowledge and metaphysics; – they act as if practice must be judged by its own measure, whatever the answer of theory may be.
>
> Against the former I direct my *psychology of philosophers*: their most alienated calculations and their 'spirituality' are still only the last pallid impression of physiological fact; the voluntary is absolutely lacking, everything is instinct, everything has been directed along certain lines from the beginning –
>
> Against the latter I ask whether we know of any other method of acting well than always thinking well; the latter *is* an action, and the former presupposes thought. Have we a different method for judging the value of a way of life from judging the value of a theory?[64]

Nietzsche's thought, like Hume's,[65] oscillates between a philosophy that creates ideals and an insistence on the role of the body. 'We must create sovereign beings, which in terms of the whole are spectators (*zuschauen*) of the game of life who occasionally become actors (*mitspielen*) but without committing themselves too violently (*hineingerissen*)'.[66] 'Attempts to produce the ideal and later on to live the ideal'.[67] But, conversely, Nietzsche recalls: 'Character = organism';[68] 'what do I care for the errors of philosophers!'.[69] The balance between the two can be felt in this 1882 text:

For the 'treatment of the individual'

1. He must be separated from the nearest and the smallest to establish the complete independence in which he is born and raised up.

2. He must equally grasp the habitual rhythm of his thinking and feeling, the needs of his intellectual nourishment.

3. Then he must try all sorts of modifications, first of all in order to break habits (several changes of regime, with subtle observations).

4. He must sometimes rely intellectually on his adversaries, he must try to eat their food. He must *travel*, in every sense of the word. During this period he will be 'unstable and fugitive'. From time to time, he must rest from his lived experiences – and digest them.

5. Then there is the higher stage: the attempt to produce an ideal (ein Ideal zu *dichten*). This precedes the higher stage: actually living out this ideal.

6. He must pass through a whole series of ideals.[70]

What did Nietzsche in fact do himself? There was writing and thinking in order to isolate new ideals, not just living: 'My philosophy – draw the man out of experience, whatever the danger!'[71] This creates a precarious balance between aphoristic thought and blanks in which Nietzsche leaves 'words' to life and the body, lets them live – in silence. For, if thought can be only an ideal that ignores its *'pudenda origo'*,[72] and if *Erlebnis* remains nihilist, one must think and speak of life and at the same time live thought: 'I have always written with my whole body and my whole life: I do not know what is meant by a purely intellectual problem'.[73] 'Every truth is for me a blood truth'.[74] But surely every thought is a forgetting of the body? Is the thought body still a body?[75] And must we believe in the advent of another culture in which body and thought would not repress one another? 'Only later shall we adopt *philosophical* opinions as vital and existential questions.'[76] But how can we produce the advent of this culture itself?

We find the problem between the inside and the outside of metaphysics. Perhaps the idea of Eternal Return plays the same role of repeating and altering the identical as is played by inverted commas, which mark what is recanted or *unsaid* (*dédit*) when one must *say* (*dire*).

Our hypothesis is that Nietzsche's text, as a textual and bodily labour and movement has the job of signifying the *Ja-sagen* (and not the *Versagen*) that makes the body speak as grand reason: through the over determination of its central signs (genealogy, *Übermensch, Will to Power*, etc.), but its metaphorical movement and rhetorical procedures, which are those used by the play of drives: inverted commas, *Sperrdruck*, dots, dashes, anacoluthons, the world of aphorisms, alternating texts with blanks, the continual emergence of the body. The body becomes a text: Nietzsche's text is as much a practice as thinking.[77]

But does Nietzsche's text invite us to partake in an evaluating discourse or a bodily practice?

The last word – perhaps it is merely a word, or a silent *Erlebnis* – must be left to the mysterious 'thought of thoughts'. Just as the text must be and say the body, and the body make itself into a text, so thoughts must, through the Eternal Return of the identical, make themselves into a body. Nietzsche indicates that thought must be incorporated (*sich einverleiben*),[78] as the body is already a thinking unity, into an infinite[79] and circular movement of mutual influence in which cause and effect are constantly reversed: a circular movement that seems to be none other than the infinite and vicious circle of the Eternal Return, which unites – or founds – fate and voluntarism as it annuls them:[80]

But if everything is necessary, in what sense do I control my actions?' The thought (of Eternal Return) and a faith in it is a weight that, besides others, weighs on you more than they do. You say that nourishment, place, air, and society transform and determine you? But your opinions do this even more so, for they determine what food, place, air and society.– If you incorporate (*einverleibst*) the thought of thoughts, it will metamorphose you. The question for everything you want to do: 'is it true that I want to do it an incalculable number of times?' is the *heaviest* weight.[81]

Thought must be *incorporated*. If we abandon the morbid 'conversion' (*Konversion*), dealt with by Freud,[82] of the 'sick animal man',[83] which *endures* in its body the 'return of the repressed' (*Wiederkehr des Verdrängten*), is it not in order to commit ourselves – on the way to the *Übermensch* – to a 'conversion' (*Konvertierung*) to bodily thought: the thought of the Eternal Return of the identical (*ewige Wiederkehr des Gleichen*), of the identical as body and thought, of an identical body and thought, beyond the gap between the *Wille zur Macht* and the *Macht des Willens*?

6
Nietzsche and the Genealogy of Culture: The 'Versuch'

In proposing a genealogy of culture, Nietzsche attempts an impossible discourse. If we manage to grasp, in the functioning of texts, the reasons for the impossibility of Nietzsche's project, we can give ourselves the means of understanding Nietzsche's texts, not only by referring them back to the speculative content outside the text, but by following his actual *labour*. It is because Nietzsche's undertaking is impossible – in the sense that it cannot be referred back either to discourse or to non-discourse – that the text must be approached as a *labour*, a set of operations aiming precisely to overcome this dilemma without actually arriving at it.

It is only in this way that we can understand, conversely, why discursive statements on Nietzsche's thought necessarily fail to take account of their object, however all-encompassing they may be: there *is* no Nietzsche system. All the same, to bring Nietzsche back, on the other hand, to a 'perspectivism' that would be merely a euphemistic term for amateurism, is still to *reduce* him to insignificance. And the hope for an eventual *synthesis* between these two irreconcilable options has been reduced to nothing by the insanity that struck in January 1889.

And yet we see Nietzsche continue to hold out against this impossibility. This impossible undertaking of Nietzsche's is equally grandiose and derisory. Derisory? In trying to redeem Nietzsche, people sought to uphold his fatally metaphysical coherence. Grandiose? Nietzsche is swallowed up by a signifying machine, without any concern being shown for what Nietzsche calls 'reality',[1] and his texts are cut to ribbons. In both cases, resentment: the text is *nothing*. In both cases, whether small or large, we should simply like to remind the reader here that there must at least be *a* certain Nietzsche who wants to be read by philologists: which means that there are many discursive sequences in Nietzsche's texts, but that *at the same time* Nietzsche recants or unsays them (*s'en dédit*) – *and that he can only unsay what he has said*. Nietzsche does not say *nothing*; but he no longer says *something*. This is what *meaning* is, in Nietzsche. If Nietzsche can represent a truly new attempt to 'deny' metaphysics, it is to the extent that he does and undoes metaphysics *in the same movement*.

It is Nietzsche's very text that *assures* this *construction and destruction* of metaphysics, a systematic discourse of propositions bound to univocity leading to the negation of life, the body and becoming, and it is in his textual practice that we must find his operating rules. It would, therefore, be naive to catch Nietzsche red-handed at work on metaphysics: he has his *alibi*, since he is, *at the same time, somewhere else*; and it would be just as naive to imagine we could glorify him in an extra-discursive way since, in his text, it is *on the basis of the discursive* mode that the undoing and unsaying of discursiveness are practices, according to certain rules.

From this point on Nietzsche's 'contradictions', far from being a defect (in the eyes of the logicians of metaphysics) or praiseworthy (in the eyes of those who like to break things down)[2] are in fact surely the product of the impossibility that is structuring them?

This impossible discourse is genealogy, which is the key to the problem of culture.

The word does not cover a *concept*, except to define it very generally as a discourse (*logos*) on the production (genesis) of ideals and cultures by the body and life. For what is the body, what is life and in what sense should we understand production? The conceptual content that has been attributed to Nietzsche for a century begins to 'tremble', as Bachelard, following Nietzsche, puts it.[3] 'Content' is surely indicated rather by the processes of *writing* in Nietzsche. Or shall we say that Nietzsche paradoxically succeeded, when one day he fell silent, and let life speak or rather be? It remains to be asked whether or not insanity is indeed life's truth and if, in this pitiable assimilation, we do not have an illustration of a typically romantic reaction, vigorously criticized by Nietzsche, that consists in praising the dark night of the concept and of discourse, the ineffable point at which reflection vanishes, but not necessarily dualist metaphysics.

Only the text, as a genealogy of culture, can offer the possibility of access to life. The latter, if not a concept, is equally not a *thing* that is presented to a Bergsonian type of intuition. To contrast metaphysics with genea-*logy* is for Nietzsche to call discourse back to its extradiscursive origins, but at the same time to try to say, in the text, through language, what *all* language, *as metaphysics*, mutilates. The action of referring back to the origins or conditions governing the possibility of a discourse that is unaware of these conditions and is even founded on the occultation of these conditions in order to be what it is, the *same* as its origin and absolutely *other* than its origin, is how the conditions governing the impossibility of Nietzsche's genealogical discourse are presented. Genealogy must be a *heterology*, whereas any logos can only be sustained on a principle of homology.

Nietzsche, here, is on the wheel: split, literally, between *philology* and *misology*. We can understand, then, Nietzsche's fascination for Schopenhauer – the first metaphysician to subjugate the logos to its other: will – for philosophy as the metaphysics of the extra-rational, for art (music in particular, the direct expression of the will to live), and for literature (especially Greek literature, whose sense of tragedy fascinates a Nietzsche who is already anti-logical and anti-Socratic). More generally, we can understand the seductive power of the antinomic couple Apollo and Dionysus, the *mytho-logical* expression of polar opposites and their power to attract one another: Apollo is already the form, logic and discourse that dominates its other, Dionysus, which is life, drives, contradiction, outburst, and each repels and solicits its opposite, without any possible reconciliation or dichotomy. For Dionysus on its own is the abyss, while Apollo in isolation lies to itself. From this moment on, philosophy shows up as a misological philology. The result of this is the willingly ab-errant, a-logical and experimental medita-tions of Nietzsche the moralist in *Human, All Too Human*, or *Daybreak*, where he is astonishingly anxious to scatter the systematic, in short, the *logical* aspects of his general propositions.

But with the discovery, hesitant at first, of the guiding thread of genealogy, opposition is symbolized in the juxtaposition of *Thus Spoke Zarathustra* and the three dissertations of *The Genealogy of Morals*. Up until the end – and is 1889 a failure or a triumph, a symptom or a symbol? – the same dilemma will continue to structure Nietzsche's texts, indeed his life. Poetry, music, walking, writing, letters, insanity: these are as much evasions as they are expressions. Both wish to include in discourse the very thing that must be excluded from it: life, reality, the body. So *The Case of*

Wagner, a trial and a medical diagnosis, is subtitled: 'A letter written from Turin, May 1888'; the late works incorporate extracts from *Zarathustra* or poetic fragments; Nietzsche claims that 'only ideas won by walking have any value'[4] or that 'whatever is divine moves on tender feet';[5] *The Case of Wagner* carries at its frontispiece: 'A problem for musicians', wherein he declared that music must be adapted to the physiological rhythm of walking.

Nietzsche does not intend to stop speaking and writing in order to abandon himself, in silence, to the immediacy of the body and life.[6] Life is called 'unfathomable' by *Zarathustra*: life laughs at the label, which suggests an inaccessible profundity,[7] when, beneath its supposed naivety, life declares itself to be 'changeable and untamed and in everything a woman, and no virtuous one'.[8] The apparent immediacy of life does not hide a profound reality. This is again what is meant by the famous phrase: 'There are no facts, only interpretations'.[9] We read this as a relativist affirmation: Nietzsche wants above all to proclaim that there are no brute facts, for they are always already, in their mistaken factual ingenuousness, interpretations: reality and life *are* not, they are interpreted. This is the reason why Nietzsche writes, when he would have every reason to let life offer itself to him as it comes, and therefore to remain silent, following the example of Hume who fled metaphysical speculation and gave himself up to day-to-day living.

This is what Thomas Mann presents in a very Nietzschean way in his novella *Tonio Kröger*. He shows that, if life escapes the writer's intellectual analysis, deriding his analysis in his unconscious and his flimsy thought, it can none the less not be assimilated to the pure and simple brute health of a Hans Hansen or an Ingeborg Holm, narrow images of a life that 'disgust at knowledge'[10] tends too often to present as the antithesis of its own negativity. Life is neither Tonio Kröger nor Hans Hansen, it is offered neither in the bourgeois nor in the artist, not in conceptual knowledge, nor in stupidity, nor in sickness (Magdalena Vermehren), nor in health: but perhaps only to that sick monster who is yet nostalgic for health known as a 'bourgeois gone astray'.[11] Interpretation in Nietzsche will be precisely this discourse gone astray: but gone astray in the sense that not only does he challenge the truth of 'facts' or the 'concept', but he even lives off his own impossibility.

For if life, because it is interpretation, must be interpreted, *we will only get interpretations* of this life as interpretation. The dilemma becomes circular. In terms of perspective, interpretation interprets what interprets *itself* but does not speak itself, because every perspective is the very negation of life as a play of perspectives; every perspective, taking itself to be true, effaces the vast perspective outside discourse. Life is *broken*: and all knowledge, even perspectivist, of this rupture speaks simultaneously this life's truth (as a perspective) and falseness (as the unity and unilaterality of a perspective that excludes the others). Who will therefore express the play of perspectives, movement, practice, interpreting, anything other than a snapshot, a frozen or abstract moment?

Nietzsche's discourse is '*Verführer zum Leben*' (*Life's Tempter*), life in so far as 'it is founded to hold on to its foundation':[12] the life that hides as it offers itself up. And Nietzsche's text is precisely the first, in the philosophical order, to bear witness, through its *labour*, to the movement of this life.[13]

Where does it offer itself up, if not in *culture*? But what is culture in relation to life? It is for the sake of knowledge that Nietzsche examines the dominant culture of the West, Christian Platonism. But a culture can, itself, be considered a discourse, or a deforming expression, in the event, according to certain processes. Which ones? Those of *interpretation*, which masks and translates. But that reduplicates the difficulty: as a discourse on a discourse, an interpretation of an interpretation, Nietzsche's thought must *say* the unsayable origin of what is manifested *and* hidden, in culture: the body, which is, like life, an interpretation.

To reduce the heterogenity of his discourse and his object, Nietzsche will turn the latter into a *language*. Culture will be itself represented as a text. Nietzsche first of all presents himself, therefore, as a philologist of culture. For Nietzsche the philologist, culture as a text is a discourse wherein we must discover its method of functioning, its structures, and also its meaning, to the extent that this text refers back to what it does not contain: life, the body, as its principle and its referent.

This creates, in Nietzsche's work, as we shall see, the coexistence or intrication of two discourses: Nietzsche's discourse, and culture's discourse. Nietzsche, holding that all language is in principle metaphysical, has not the resources, like the Kant of the Analytic, to contrast the 'false' language of the culture he analyses with the truth that he would hold on to, even if it were that of a logic of truth, which expresses the conditions needed for experience to be constituted within knowledge; the truth, or rather the referential reality of his discourse is, in principle, outside of discourse. In the event, he should speak instead of texts, in the sense that a text is what is read: (1) as a process, a labour – and not only a system of differences that delimit a set of signifieds; (2) as something which refers us back to a referent or only to itself.

However, culture for Nietzsche is not an autonomous game of pure signifiers, but, as a law of perspectivism, a *heteronomous* collection and a process that finds its law only in relation to what lies *outside* of it, which it expresses and represses. As for Nietzsche's discourse *on* culture, it must be not only a *discourse*, in the sense of a dianoetic linking of univocal propositions, but a *text* that can say its object, and above all the origin of its object, only as the result of a *labour*. For discourse and text, in these senses, both belong to the order of language: as such, Nietzsche's discourse is homogeneous to culture as language. But the difficulty arose from the fact that the *logos* of *genesis*, the language on the origin that is genealogy proposes to refer the language of culture, the *text* that is culture for Nietzsche the philologist, to the body, while any language denies the body as such at the same time as it affirms it indirectly. Nietzsche the *philologist* must move away from philology towards physiology. This is a necessary and impossible undertaking. The philologist treats the text as an in-itself, as a structure, an autonomous object: literally idealist, it denies the body,[14] even if its labour is indispensable to the analysis of culture and text. And philology, as soon as it is extolled and practised, must at the same time be rejected in favour of *physiology* and the *philosopher as doctor*. This is the price paid to make 'possible' a genealogy that proposes to *read* and *evaluate*. But it can only read and evaluate if it precisely forgets to evaluate and it can only evaluate if it looks, beyond the reading of the text, to an origin that remains unsaid: an insoluble conflict, in Nietzsche, between a realist physiologism and a philological idealism.[15]

It is here that Nietzsche – whose extremely ambivalent remarks about philology can be explained in this way – tries a second course of action: the body will be presented by him as a play of forces analogous to the one at play within a text. Better again: medicine will be the art of *reading* the body's *text* and conversely the text will be studied as a sound or an echo from the body,[16] as a body that is not only readable but is also audible.

This creates an interminable text: genealogy, for we must say what the origin of every text is, while the origin is effaced as such by virtue of being expressed: to the point that we can in fact say, both that *there is* an origin – life –, without which genealogy gives way to idealism (a dogmatic forgetting of the extra-discursive origin), and that there is *not* an origin, since to express the origin is to repress it as an unsaid phenomenon that can be expressed only as process, a labour, a difference in perspective, and therefore as something that perhaps necessarily lies outside discourse.

This form of *labour* in Nietzsche's text is designated by him under the terms *Versuch* (attempt) or *Experiment*.[17] The first interpretation of these terms, which Nietzsche uses in order to qualify the manner *proper* to his philosophy, consists in saying that he uses it to designate a propaedeutic philosophical style, that insists more on research than on the completed system. This interpretation is not without truth, and the publication of an incredible number of posthumous notes, drafts and sketches can attest to the fact that Nietzsche, contrary to some of his affirmations, is not one of those who are capable of uncovering truths or *the* truth by the miraculous grace of an illumination. Heidegger recalls:

> It is a basic experience … that even the positing of the uppermost values does not take place at a single stroke, that eternal truth never blazes in the heavens overnight, and that no people in history has had its truth fall into its lap.[18]

For his part, Nietzsche insists on the rapture represented by his philosophical *Versuch*:

> Formerly … the small single questions and experiments were counted contemptible: one wanted the shortest route; one believed that, because everything in the world seemed to be *accommodated to man*, the knowability of things was also accommodated to a human time-span. To solve everything at a stroke, with a single word – that was the secret desire: the task was thought of in the image of the Gordian Knot or in that of the egg of Columbus; one did not doubt that in the domain of knowledge too it was possible to reach one's goal in the manner of Alexander or Columbus and to settle all questions with a *single* answer.[19]

Versuch signals the *genesis* or patient labour of a labyrinthine thought that recognizes it tackles the world as being an *enigma* and that tries to dispense with a God that guarantees external truths or with some Ariadne or other: 'Labyrinthine man never searches for truth, but only ever for his Ariadne – whatever he says'.[21] Moreover, the term *Versuch*, backed up by *Experiment*, refers back to the language of contemporary science and must remind the reader that the impatient claims of a metaphysics that is in too much of a hurry to check its truth contrast, in Nietzsche's day, with the impressively modest image of a science that ousts metaphysical 'truths' by a meticulous process of trial and error.[22] *Versuch* and *Experiment* therefore constitute the antithesis of the manifesto, which is soon to be opposed by the laborious underground labouring of the mole that 'tunnels and mines and undermines':[23] already genealogy is being announced, and its suspicion and uncertainty is eating away at 'convictions'.

This is a scepticism[24] that contests a false absolute, but it is also an attempt to inaugurate a *search* for the as yet unprospected unknown.[25] The dangerous wandering involved in searching (*Versuch*)[26] promises to uncover something new in relation to the narrow certainties of the past. Heidegger writes: 'Those who posit the uppermost values, the creators, the new philosophers at the forefront, must according to Nietzsche be experimenters; they must tread paths and break trails in the knowledge that they do not have *the* truth'.[27]

Therefore, the subtitle of *Beyond Good and Evil* is '*Vorspiel einer Philosphie der Zukunft*' (prelude to a philosophy of the future) not only in order to parody and deride Wagner's '*Musik der Zukunft*' (*Music of the Future*), scoffed at in *Nietzsche Contra Wagner* (in chapter 'A music without a future'), but in order to display a will to go beyond: 'There are so many experiments still to make! There are so many futures still to dawn!'.[28] Nietzsche sums this up in *Beyond Good and Evil*:

A new species of philosopher is appearing: I venture to baptize these philosophers with a name not without danger in it. As I divine them, as they let themselves be divined – for it pertains to their nature to *want* to remain a riddle in some respects – these philosophers of the future might rightly, but perhaps also wrongly, be described as *attempters* (*Versucher*). This name is in the end only an attempt (*Versuch*) and, if you will, a temptation (*Versuchung*).[29]

The genuine philosopher ... lives 'unphilosophically' and 'unwisely', above all *imprudently*, and bears the burden and duty of a hundred attempts and temptations of life – he risks *himself* constantly, he plays *the* dangerous game.[30]

But, as Heidegger and W.A. Kaufmann have too fleetingly remarked, *Versuch* has another meaning which is taken from the science of the day. *Versuch* and above all *Experiment* can be understood as a return to something 'concrete', in contrast to a systematically abstract style of *exposé*:

The solidity and binding quality of thought must undergo a grounding in the things themselves in a way that prior philosophy does not know.[31]

Viewed in this light, Nietzsche's aphoristic style appears as an interesting attempt to transcend the maze of concepts and opinions in order to get at the objects themselves. The key terms that Nietzsche uses time and again are now *Experiment* and now *Versuch*; but it is well to keep in mind that *Versuch*, too, need not mean merely 'attempt' but can have the characteristic scientific sense of 'experiment': it is quite proper in German to speak of a scientist as making a *Versuch*.[32]

More than this: Nietzsche is already concerned to take account of the given situation, and so returns to experiences left to one side by a systematic approach that neglects whatever is not 'philosophical':

So far, all that has given colour to existence still lacks a history. Where could you find a history of love, of avarice, of envy, or conscience, of pious respect for tradition, or of cruelty? ... What is known of the moral effects of different foods? Is there any philosophy of nutrition? ... If all these jobs were done ... then experimentation would be in order that would allow every kind of heroism to find satisfaction – centuries of experimentation.[33]

Above all, on the level of interpretative hypotheses, this introduces variations into certainties, and so questions the received principles of explanation in certain experiences wherein a scholar constructs artificial objects in order the better to grasp the hidden nature. This substitutes construction for the brute exposition of facts. Genealogy tries to question the apparent explanations of the given situation in order to reveal its driving principle. Experimentation is therefore risky and 'heroic', because it reveals the deliberately hidden forces of will. This is the value of the '*Wie wenn*'[34] (*and if*) which frequently occurs in Nietzsche's writing: what would happen, in reality, and in particular in a drive-based reality, if it suddenly occurred to us to think that ...? The consequences are not here purely theoretical: science then labours over its object by putting it in question, like the partner or victim of a power game. Truth, when it is experimented with, is no longer a mask – the mask of the 'will of truth',[35] it engages the *truth to will*: its power.[36] 'My philosophy: wrench man out of appearance, *whatever* the dangers! And do not be afraid, even if your life is in danger.'[37] *Versuch* is therefore dangerous, for it dares to claim that error is not only a defect in truth, but that truth is a form of error and that error is not 'only' error, but is weakness:

> Philosophy, as I have hitherto understood and lived it, is a voluntary living in ice and high mountains – a seeking after everything strange and questionable in existence, all that has hitherto been excommunicated by morality. ... How much truth can a spirit *bear*, how much truth can a spirit *dare*? that became for me more and more the real measure of value. Error (– belief in the ideal –) is not blindness, error is *cowardice* ... Every acquisition, every step forward in knowledge is the *result* of courage, of severity towards oneself, of cleanliness with respect to oneself ... I do not refute ideals, I merely draw on gloves in their presence ... *Nitimur in vetitum*: in this sign my philosophy will one day conquer, for what has hitherto been forbidden on principle has never been anything but the truth.[38]

For, as Nietzsche had already written in *Beyond Good and Evil*: 'Something might be true although at the same time harmful and dangerous in the highest degree; indeed, it could pertain to the fundamental nature of existence that a complete knowledge of it would destroy one'.[39] It is in this sense that we can understand a posthumous note dating from 1885: '"Nothing is true, everything is permitted!" ... We are conducting an experiment (*Versuch*) with truth. Perhaps truth will perish (*zugrunde gehen*) because of it! Fine!'[40] *Versuch* is dangerous, and questions the certainty of what is called truth, which is fundamentally an error: 'Truth is the kind of error without which a certain species of life could not live'.[41] For 'a belief can be a condition of life and none the less be false'.[42] If,

therefore, '"true" means nothing more than "useful to the preser-
vations of mankind"',[43] an objective that, in the light of knowledge,
has no absolute value, *Versuch* runs the mortal risk of expressing
both the 'true' and the 'false'. It assumes ultimately that there
cannot even be any living truth, for every truth is mortal: 'It is only
when adapted to living errors that truth, always dead in itself, can
be called to life'.[44] In a word, *Versuch*, which in this sense is the
image of life, is the mortal risk offered by a life that is alive only by
being false and true only by being dead. Which is true, then, asks
the *Versucher*, or experimenter, life as falsity, or truth as death?

> How many there are who still conclude: 'life could not be
> endured if there were no God!' (or, as it is put among the
> idealists: 'life could not be endured if its foundation lacked an
> ethical significance!') – therefore there *must* be a God (or existence
> *must* have an ethical significance)! The truth, however, is merely
> that he who is accustomed to these notions does not desire a life
> without them: that these notions may therefore be necessary to
> him and for his preservation – but what presumption it is to
> decree that whatever is necessary for my preservation must
> actually *exist*! As if my preservation were something necessary!
> How if others felt in the opposite way! if those two articles of
> faith were precisely the conditions under which they did not
> wish to live and under which they no longer found life worth
> living! – And that is how things are now![45]

Here we encounter the contrast between discourse and the life
which fixes discourse as a deceit. Genealogy can express the truth
about the origin of discourse (life) only on condition of expressing
what is the untrue truth of life.

Finally, *Versuch* questions every representation of truth as an
'already there'[46] and commits itself to conceiving of the truth of life
in terms of power, in which perspectives find their truth more as a
relationship to other perspectives than as scattered fragments of a
totality to be reconstituted. Nietzsche is already aware of this in
The Gay Science:

> A thinker is now that being in whom the impulse for truth and
> those life-preserving errors clash for their first fight, after the
> impulse for truth has proved to be also a life-preserving power.
> Compared to the significance of this fight, everything else is a

matter of indifference: the ultimate question about the conditions of life has been posed here, and we confront the first attempt to answer this question by experiment. To what extent can truth endure incorporation? That is the question; that is the experiment.[47]

Later, Nietzsche will prolong this analysis by revealing the idiosyncratic nature of perspectivist truth.[48] *Versuch* then shows the aphorism to be a complex of forces, in relation to which another aphorism represents another complex. The *Versuch*, or aphorism, is life polemically proclaiming its truth, which is to be or not to be graspable. Genealogy can only be a *Versuch*, an aphoristic and fragmentary game in which various forces confront one another which can only be expressed provided we acknowledge their *dynamic relativity*.[49]

It is for this reason that Nietzsche pays attention to distinguishing between levels and isolating perspectives, while knowing that suspicion must turn itself back on its own saying. The truth about life is only true provided there is an 'or else' followed by a row of dots (*Gedankenstrich*)[50] preceded by innumerable 'or else's[51] that mark the infinite plurality of living (genealogical) perspectives. The abyssal truth of life can be called 'frightening' by him; and that is why, when it comes to designating it, along with the adjective '*schrecklich*', the epithet '*fragwürdig*' keeps returning. Like the sphinx, this truth is a terrible questioning enigma[52] that one can only question. It is therefore not just coquettishness that makes Nietzsche say:

Alas, and yet what *are* you, my written and painted thoughts! . . . You have already taken off your novelty and some of you, I fear, are on the point ‚of becoming truths: they already look so immortal, so pathetically righteous, so boring! And has it ever been otherwise? For what things do we write and paint, we mandarins with Chinese brushes, we immortalizers of things which *let* themselves be written, what alone are we capable of painting? Alas, only that which is about to whither and is beginning to lose its fragrance! . . . Alas, only birds strayed and grown weary in flight who now let themselves be caught in the hand – our hand! We immortalize that which cannot live and fly much longer, weary and mellow things alone![53]

If genealogical discourse, like *Versuch*, is interminable, we can grasp its typical tactical methods. Genealogy is first of all practised as a philology and it is important to be able to grasp *in the texts* how it alternately puts itself into play and effaces itself. If we fail to do this, we shall have merely replaced the metaphysical *résumés* of Nietzsche's philosophy with a *résumé* that is just as dogmatic but is the 'negative' form, and which consists in saying that there is no Nietzsche philosophy.[54] Prior to being able to say (incisively) that Nietzsche's thought is the negation of all philosophy, all morality, all religion, all (metaphysical) discourse, etc., we must first grasp *how* and in relation to what content this thought operates these *negations*, which, moreover, are perhaps something other than negations. Surely it is necessary to be and to affirm in order to deny (even if we are denying nothingness)? What, therefore, is Nietzsche going to 'deny' in metaphysics, morality and Christianity? Let us read Nietzsche, and in the way he would have liked us to read him, as a philologist: 'a good reader will notice – a reader such as I deserve, who reads me as good old philologists read their Horace'.[55]

7
Nietzsche and Genealogical Philology

In the draft of a letter to Lou Salomé written in the autumn of 1882, Nietzsche plans to present himself as follows: 'I was *simultaneously* a philologist, a writer, a musician, a philosopher, a free-thinker, etc. (perhaps a poet? etc.)'.[1] No doubt, he is all of that at one and the same time, *et cetera*. But the first of these qualities is probably the one we forget the most often. And if it is true that Nietzsche quit his chair in philology at Basel, if he even remained harsh to the point of cruelty towards philologists, including the one he had been,[2] he still continues, *volens nolens*, and right up to the end, to claim inspiration from *philology*. The final struggle against Christianity in *The Antichrist* and the 1888 notes is led like a battle against an 'incapacity for philology'[3] and Nietzsche, in his published writings, often designates himself a philologist.[4]

That would not greatly matter if we were just dealing with 'Herr Nietzsche',[5] who, moreover, will continue to sign himself 'Prof. Dr. F. Nietzsche'. But it affects the text, the labour, the thought. Nietzsche's text can only be read by reference to philology.

The appeal to philology aims to attract the attention of Nietzsche's readers not only towards the speculative content of his works, but even more towards the text that offers itself up – or slips away: the text must be read and deciphered *as a text*, and not as such and such a discourse from traditional metaphysics, in which it is enjoined to play itself down in the face of its signified. As a text, that is to say, as something that, in its very *matter* (rhythm, semantic resonances, phonological assonances, rhetorical tropes, etc.) already offers elements of interpretation to the reader, but also brings to that reader a certain tangible *pleasure*. Nietzsche claims to write a text that is not only to be *understood*, but *read*: with pleasure, disgust, laughter or irritation:

As regards my *Zarathustra*, I think no one should claim to know it who has not been, by turns, deeply wounded and deeply delighted by what is says. Only such readers will have gained the right to participate in the halcyon element from which it sprang, with all its sunniness, sweep, and assurance.[6]

What is more, the text must be *interpreted*. The thickness of the signifier, the guarantee of emotional reactions to the text, also presents understanding with a shimmering signifier that distracts it and leads it astray in its labyrinthine search for meaning and *slow* decipherment that lingers over the text.[7] The term *lento* which Nietzsche uses almost always in order to characterize the type of reading that he wants for his texts, is perfectly suitable: its musicological colouring implies that we should be attentive to the text's musical 'colour' or 'timbre', in the phonological as well as semantic field; and the rhythm that he assigns to the labour of reading forces us to recognize the text's *resistance*, the difficulty there is in moving straight through it to a discourse, passing (*presto*) from the transparent signifier to the corresponding signified:

What a torment books written in German are for him who has a *third* ear! How disgustedly he stands beside the slowly turning swamp of sounds without resonance, of rhythms that do not dance, which the Germans call a 'book'! Not to mention the German who *reads* books! How lazily, how reluctantly, how badly he reads! How many Germans know, or think they ought to know, that there is *art* in every good sentence – art that must be grasped if the sentence is to be understood! A misunderstanding of its tempo, for example: and the sentence itself is misunderstood! That one must be in no doubt about the syllables that determine the rhythm, that one should feel the disruption of a too-severe symmetry as intentional and as something attractive, that one should lend a refined and patient ear to every *staccato*, every *rubato*, that one should divine the meaning in the sequence of vowels and diphthongs and how delicately and richly they can colour and recolour one another through the order in which they come: who among book-reading Germans has sufficient good will to acknowledge such demands and duties and to listen to so much art and intention in language? In the end one simply 'has no ear for it': and so the greatest contrasts in style go unheard and the subtlest artistry is *squandered* as if on the deaf.[8]

An author is always obliged to communicate movement to his words. . . . The moral: one must learn to read and teach one to read. . . . Look how quickly he reads, how he turns the pages – one after the other, within the exact same space of seconds. Check your watch. . . . The poor fool reads them *from end to end*, as though it were ever permissible to read a collection of thoughts like that.[9]

The philologist still reads words, whereas the rest of us moderns now read only thoughts. The person who finds language interesting in itself is another person from the one who sees it only as the medium for interesting thoughts.[10]

The time of reading, finally, presupposes that we allow ourselves the necessary delay in order to pass from one perspective to another, to '[spell] out forwards and backwards'[11] the text to be read: a task that is exactly the opposite of what philosophy has been asked to do from Plato to Schopenhauer, contrary to all 'intuition', to everything demanded of the διαλεκτικὸς συνοπτικὸς,[12] the dialectic ὁρμή. The *lento* tries to stop our charge towards the concept, the synoptic unity of philosophical knowledge:

Above all let us say it *slowly* . . . A book like this, a problem like this, is in no hurry; we both, I just as much as my book, are friends of *lento*. It is not for nothing that I have been a philologist, perhaps I am a philologist still, that is to say, a teacher of slow reading: – in the end I also write slowly. Nowadays it is not only my habit, it is also to my taste – a malicious taste, perhaps? – no longer to write anything which does not reduce to despair every sort of man who is 'in a hurry'. For philology is that venerable art which demands of its votaries one thing above all: to go aside, to take time, to become still, to become slow – it is a goldsmith's art and connoisseurship of the *word* which achieves nothing if it does not achieve it *lento*. But for precisely this reason it is more necessary than ever today, by precisely this means does it entice and enchant us the most, in the midst of an age of 'work', that is to say, of hurry, of indecent and perspiring haste, which wants to 'get everything done' at once, including every old or new book: – this art does not so easily get anything done, it teaches to read *well*, that is to say, to read slowly, deeply, looking cautiously before and aft, with reservations, with doors left open, with delicate eyes and fingers . . . My patient friends, this book desires for itself only perfect readers and philologists: *learn* to read me well![13]

One does not, therefore, skim through Nietzsche, one does not 'understand' him: one *learns to read him*,[14] and not to read Nietzsche as a philosopher:

> Nearly all philosophers . . . have not learned to *read* and interpret *concretely*, philosophers underestimate the difficulty of really understanding what another person has said, and do not pay attention. This is why Schopenhauer formed a completely false idea of Kant and Plato.[15]

This appeal by Nietzsche to philology is first and foremost an exhortation to draw inspiration from the philological method in order to read Nietzsche's texts in a way that is simultaneously conscientious, conceivable and new in relation to other philosophical texts. This is for us a lesson, and a principle. But above all, Nietzsche evokes philology because his text's style is closely linked to the practice of a method of philological reading that is applied to culture's 'text'. We must, therefore, question the reasons and consequences of this constitution of culture in a text. But from this moment philology is invoked not only as a reading technique but as a normative disciple. It involves reading culture like a text, but the text of Platonic and Christian culture is: (1) a hollow text bristling with improprieties; (2) a text that is already the work of *bad readers*, who, in interpreting reality, have revealed an incapacity for philology. Culture is an interpretation of reality, but Christian metaphysical culture is an erroneous interpretation, and so is a shady, slapdash reading of another text again, reality's text, and, on top of this, is also a philologically incorrect interpretation precisely because it confuses interpretation with the text.

A posthumous note is significant: 'I prefer to write something that deserves to be read in the way philologists read their writers rather than to squat on top of an author. And at all events, the most mediocre production is superior to a discourse on works that have already been read'.[16] If Nietzsche wants to be read 'well', it is because a 'good reader' like him is simultaneously a good 'author'. Reality, as a text, is worth more than all the texts *on* reality. But, in order to know what reality 'means' (*heisst*),[17] in all its enigma, we must simultaneously be a good philologist and reject philology, which becomes absorbed into the reality of the text, and so forgets the text of reality.

Philology is primarily the art of reading *lento*, in contrast to the impatience of a concept: the art of an indefinitely rebegun rumination, for the text to be read is enigmatic and 'heavy':

> Should this treatise seem unintelligible or jarring to some readers, I think the fault need not necessarily be laid at my door. It is plain enough, and it presumes only that the reader will have read my earlier works with some care – for they do, in fact, require careful reading. ... Also, the aphoristic form may present a stumbling block, the difficulty being that this form is no longer taken 'hard' enough. An aphorism that has been honestly struck cannot be deciphered simply by reading it off; this is only the beginning of the work of interpretation proper, which requires a whole science of hermeneutics. ... One skill is needed – lost today, unfortunately – for the practice of reading as an art: the skill to ruminate, which cows possess but modern man lacks. This is why my writings will, for some time yet, remain difficult to digest.[18]

One has therefore 'never finished' (*fertig sein*) with Nietzsche,[19] or with reality. Thus, 'philology, in an age in which we read too much, is the art of learning and teaching to read. Only the philologist reads slowly and meditates (*denkt nach*) for half an hour on six lines'.[20] But philology is also not only a love of language (*philo-logos*) but a respect for it that wishes to see the text kept free of the ill-treatment handed out by excessive haste: additions, deformations, distortion of meaning, misinterpretation, voluntary or involuntary flattenings: 'weakening or moderating metaphor'.[21] Respecting the text, first of all, for Nietzsche, involves not 'confusing it with the interpretation' given it,[22] and restoring or preserving what is the text's own property:

> The art of reading correctly (*richtig*) is so rare that virtually everyone is obliged to have a document or law or contract interpreted for him; much damage results from Christian preachers who, from the pulpit, offer us (*heimsuchen*) the Bible with the riskiest exegeses, and everywhere awaken a respect for this kind of artificial subtlety, when not actually arousing its imitation.[23]

Nietzsche, therefore, recommends philology as a way of returning to the text itself: 'We must read nothing *on* literature, and so we should write nothing on it, either. Therefore, I shall say *how* we should read. The task of philology. – To beware of the usual way of reading',[24] for, as Nietzsche goes on saying, from *Human, All Too Human* to *The Antichrist*, 'that is interpretation, not text'[25] and 'the text disappeared beneath the interpretation'.[26]

Philology is, therefore, a discipline that refines intelligence and probity,[27] and so there is no doubt that its valorization by Nietzsche is a legacy of his rigorous Protestant past in which he was an assiduous reader of the Bible.[28] Out of respect for the text, there is good reason to differentiate, if possible, between the *Deutung* or *Auslegung* (exegesis, interpretation in the strict sense) and *Interpretation*, a more or less free commentary or unfaithful gloss that is added to the text. Only respect for the text, as an autonomous object, which is all the more precious and exposed for being, as we know, since Plato, the helpless orphan whose 'father'[29] is absent, can lead to the truth through a patient labour on the part of the reader, coupled with an asceticism similar to humility:

> One must thus forgive the philologists too for being onesided. Production and preservation of texts, together with their elucidation, pursued in a guild for centuries, has now finally discovered the correct methods; the entire Middle Ages was profoundly incapable of a strict philological elucidation, that is to say of a simple desire to understand what the author is saying – to have discovered these methods was an achievement, let no one undervalue it! It was only when the art of correct reading, that is to say philology, arrived at its summit that science of any kind acquired continuity and constancy.[30]

More than a job or difficult task, philology is therefore raised to the level of virtue,[31] almost to the level of an ethics of knowledge. The novel colouring of the terms designating infractions of philology is not accidental. It is as if the text were this God whose name must not be abused; and the most enormous scandal is precisely that the priest 'abuses the name of God'[32] and, consequently, traffics in texts in the most brazenly dishonest way. Any text, in Nietzsche's eyes, must be treated as an exegete *ought to* treat Scripture or the Bible: any text is therefore *sacred*. Philology is not just a *realism* that insists on the text's materiality (much more so than on its semantic value), but is also a *morality* of the text and of language – the only morality Nietzsche has not managed to get rid of!

> We no longer endure it when a priest so much as utters the word 'truth'. Even with the most modest claim to integrity one *must* know today that a theologian, a priest, a pope does not merely err in every sentence he speaks, he *lies* – that he is no longer free to lie 'innocently', out of 'ignorance'. The priest knows as well as anyone that there is no longer any 'God', any 'sinner', any 'redeemer' – that 'free will', 'moral world-order' are lies – intellect, no longer *permits* anyone *not* to know about these things. ... We know, our *conscience* knows today – *what* those sinister inventions of priest and Church are worth.[33]

The philologist, along with the doctor, 'the two great opponents of all superstition',[34] see '*behind* the sacred books' and take it upon themselves to denounce them as 'fraud' (*Schwindel*).[35] Thus we must be armed philologically against Christian 'deception': 'One cannot read these Gospels too warily; there are difficulties behind every word',[36] for 'another mark of the theologian is his incapacity for philology'.[37] The philologist is meticulous, incorruptible and untimely':

> I do not know what meaning classical studies could have for our time if they were not untimely – that is to say, acting counter to our time and thereby acting on our time and, let us hope, for the benefit of a time to come.[38]

'I understand the word "philology" here in a very general sense', Nietzsche wrote in 1888: 'it means to be able to decipher (*ablesen*) facts without falsifying them through interpretation'.[39] But, in the same period, Nietzsche adds:

> The given fact is the death of Jesus. This has to be explained – That an explanation may be true or false has never entered the minds of such people as these: one day a sublime possibility comes into their heads: 'this death *could* mean such and such' – and at once it *does* mean such and such! ... None of these holy epileptics and seers of visions possessed a thousandth part of that integrity in self-criticism with which a philologist today reads a text or proves the truth of an historical event – Compared with us, they are moral cretins.[40]

Technical error here becomes stupidity or, more often, dishonesty. Thus, the expression '*Mangel an Philologie*' (incapacity for philology)[41] frequently returns in the published and posthumous writings of 1888: this defect is essentially translated as a *confusion* that leads to what Nietzsche calls 'arbitrary interpretation' (*arbiträre Auslegung*),[42] which he stigmatizes as 'an absolute lack of intellectual probity' (*absoluter Mangel an intellektueller Rechtschaffenheit*).[43] Confusion (*verwechseln*) is contrary to the very principle of philology, which is the art of distinction,[44] and consequently a school of respect for the differences in language and the text's specificity:[45]

> Our 'outside world' . . . is transposed (*versetzt*) . . ., we interpret it (*auslegen*) with the schematism of a 'thing'. . . . What I call the 'lack of philology': knowing how to read a text as a text (*einen Text als Text ablesen zu können*), is the most tardy form of 'inner experience' – perhaps a scarcely possible form.[46]

> The *lack of philology*: we endlessly confuse (*verwechseln*) the explanation (*Erklärung*) with the text – and what an explanation![47]

Philology is virtually a *pathos der Distanz*, with the presupposition, when faced with counterfeiting and amalgamation,[48] of a possible distinction between 'truth and error'.[49]

However, philology's honour is also its sterility. The philologist, as a reader, remains passive and non-creative, more of a bureaucrat than a genius. In the order of *Bildung*, the philosophical discipline has above all a negative and conservative value: the philologist, by refraining from interpreting or over-interpreting, confusing the rules of reading with the rules of creation, finds himself not only incapable of creating, but sometimes incapable of simply doing justice to the works he studies. Faced with whatever μανία there might be in a great work, philological meticulousness is just an obsession, when it is not hiding the resentment of someone who knows that he is only Sainte-Beuve because he could not be Stendhal, Balzac or Hugo:

> The history of philology is the history of a type of man who works hard but is not talented. This creates an extreme hostility and later on an excessive regard in place of a wiser and richer nature that *peters out* in a philologist. . . . The notion that a philologist is more able (for example than a doctor) to educate

the young is an assumption that is betrayed every day by experience. It is like a road-sweeper: nobody examines whether or not he is the best person for the job; it is enough that he is willing to do such a dirty job. In the same vein, each profession gets on with the task of educating the young, satisfied with the fact that philologists . . . do not educate them. . . . Antiquity has been discovered, in every essential matter, by artists, politicians and philosophers, not by philologists. . . . What the philologists are not willing to believe is that you could misunderstand Sophocles's tragedy in a hundred places, and not notice corrupt passages, and still understand and explain the tragedy better than the most meticulous philologist. . . . In general, anyone at all can understand an ancient author better than the philologist teaching a language. Why is this? It is because philologists are just aged schoolboys.[50]

If philologists are indeed 'destroyers of every faith that rests on books',[51] we can first of all ask if philology does not exert itself where it is best needed, something which is explained by the pusillanimity of philologists, who are respectful not only of texts, but of the conformity to be found in the traditionally received meaning of texts:

> What is the point of scientific education, criticism and hermeneutics if such a lunatic exposition of the Bible as is still cultivated by the church has not yet turned the blush of shame into a permanent skin colour?[52]

> The humour of European culture: one holds *this* to be true but does *that*. E.g., what is the point of the arts of reading and criticism as long as the ecclesiastical interpretation of the Bible, Protestant as well as Catholic, is cultivated as ever?[53]

The explanation for the philologist's effective conformism lies in the social exploration of its 'virtues' in a conservative sense:

> This is why the philologist has hitherto been the educator *as such*: because his activity provides the model of sublime monotony in action; under his banner the young man learns to 'grind': first prerequisite for future efficiency in the fulfilment of mechanical duties (as civil servant, husband, office slave, newspaper reader, and soldier). . . . The mechanical form of existence as the highest,

most venerable form of existence, worshipping itself (– type: Kant as a fanatic of the formal concept 'thou shalt').[54]

Nietzsche was a philologist and willingly ceased to be one; and he simultaneously and successfully honoured and vilified philology. Moreover, he was (and not only as an academic) a very good philologist and a very *weak* one,[55] 'a philologist, and why not a doctor?',[56] a philologist without being one. For, when he speaks (fairly *aggressively*) as 'a physiologist', or 'a doctor', Nietzsche does not rest at being a philologist: he is a reader of clinical signs, a decipherer of the body's text. If Nietzsche the 'philosopher doctor' consecrates himself to the affirmation of life, the philologist in him *devotes himself* to the *negative* task of genealogy: to flushing out negation, both in morality and in metaphysics. If the task of denying (*negieren*) denegation (*Verneinung*) is the job of the physiologist, the philologist is the person who *deciphers* denegation.

Nietzsche stretches the methods of philology to include what, in the strict sense, goes beyond its competence: the decipherment of culture, in so far as it presents itself not only in the form of texts, but also in other non-linguistic forms. We can view this as a sort of Nietzschean version of the 'Copernican revolution'[57]. Such an extension of the methods and abilities of philology for Nietzsche comes down to deciding that *all culture* (and even those things in it that do not present themselves in linguistic form) must be deciphered LIKE *a text*, constitutes a network of signs, and must be the object of *reading*. As such, culture refers no doubt to the things outside of itself at which it aims, but it remains none the less an object for a certain philology. Even more precisely, the genealogist is someone who unites the methods of the philologist and the physiologist: the philologist is the doctor's 'third ear',[58] and the latter has the task of reading and listening to the discourse of culture:

> Another form of recovery, in certain cases even more suited to me, to '*sound out idols*' . . . There are more idols in the world than there are realities: that is *my* 'evil eye' for this world, that is also my 'evil ear' . . . For once to *pose questions* here with a *hammer* and perhaps to receive for answer that famous hollow sound which speaks of inflated bowels – what a delight for one who has ears behind his ears – for an old psychologist and pied piper like me, in presence of whom precisely that which would like to stay silent *has to become audible*.[59]

Raised to the level of method, philology teaches the philosopher (even the doctor) to read culture like a text. We have spoken of a 'Copernican revolution'. Philology, even more than an epistemological model, provides genealogical analysis with its *transcendental*, in the proper sense of the Kantian term (forms and categories). The principles of philology are the conditions of possibility for the phenomena of culture as a text that forms the object of a reading and a deciphering. Nietzsche transforms culture into a set of *signs*, in the same way that the given experience is presented by Kant as the phenomenon of an in-itself that cannot be the object of a direct intellectual intuition and to which, in Nietzsche, the body's reality in itself corresponds. The body, which is the reality of culture, but unknowable as such, can only be approached as a set of signs: as a cultural phenomenon, it is a text, without being reduced, in the same way that the phenomenon cannot be dissociated from the unknowable noumenon which it represents for us.

Bringing things together in this way underlines a link between Kant and Nietzsche that touches on the conception of knowledge: in both cases, an *a priori* (the transcendental and philological reading) goes hand in hand with the impossibility of a direct apprehension of things-in-themselves. Such a comparison no longer seems reductionist or fantastical if we consider Schopenhauer the go-between: the will to life, the truth of the thing-in-itself according to Schopenhauer, is the link between the Kantian transcendental subject and the Nietzschean *Leib*: the latter justly qualifies as reality for Nietzsche, while Schopenhauer made it a phenomenon. This displacement allows us to perceive that Nietzsche proceeds, *vis-à-vis* Schopenhauer, as Schopenhauer does in relation to transcendental philosophy: Nietzsche gives a *reality*, as a thing 'in itself', to the *body*, and assigns, on the other hand, the status of illusion, deceptive in appearance or idolatrous in terms of morality, to culture, in the same way that Schopenhauer attributed the reality of the thing-in-itself to the will to life and transformed the reality of the Kantian phenomenon into an illusion.[60]

To decipher culture genealogically, is therefore to '*constitute*' it as a text. But in doing this, Nietzsche no doubt remains more Kantian than Schopenhauer: while affirming that there is something (in itself) behind the phenomenon standing as its 'cause', he maintains that this something is unknowable, if not through the philological categories, a discourse, a text, that is simultaneously latent, as a thing-in-itself, and manifest, as a phenomenon. The body is interpreted and is to be interpreted, it is deciphered, auscultated, read, and not at all intuited as such, without which genealogy as a discourse on latent things and semiology or symptomatology would have no meaning. The doctor and physiologist themselves treat the body in terms of the *reading* of a text. Culture is the body's text, but already the body itself is accessible only as a text. Nietzsche writes in *Daybreak*:

> Do I have to add that when we are awake our drives likewise do nothing but interpret nervous stimuli and, according to their requirements, posit their 'causes'? . . . that our moral judgements and evaluations too are only images and fantasies based on a physiological process unknown to us, a kind of acquired language for designating certain nervous stimuli? that all our so-called consciousness is a more or less fantastic commentary on an unknown, perhaps unknowable, but felt text?[61]

In order to insist on the constitution of *Erlebnis* as a philological phenomenon, in order to 'derealize' it, Nietzsche forces the accent on to *interpretation*, one prepared to state, in the form of the question-mark at the end of an aphorism, that *Erlebnis* 'is' nothing. By this he wishes to suggest that, like the thing-in-itself which is nothing to us, as an object of knowledge, *Erlebnis* as a body and as instincts only exists *for us* as something interpreted: a text *is* nothing until it is read and interpreted.

But is it the case then that Nietzsche falls back into an idealism that turns the body's reality into a phenomenon that is 'constituted' in a text by a transcendental[62] subject producing philological categories? Would culture and the body itself from that point on be just a text to be deciphered at the whim of interpretation? Certainly not. We must note, in this text from *Daybreak*, beside the philological concepts, Nietzsche's insistence on the physiological vocabulary of intuition, thirst, the satisfaction of instinct (*Trieb*). Nietzsche also assimilates 'interpretation' and commentary once again to an organic play of metabolisms, nutrition and waste.[63] Genealogy is only antimetaphysically operative if physiology and medicine reclaim for philology the body's reality outside the text (although this reality is masked and cannot be known directly). There is *nothing* behind the *Zeichensprache der Affekte*, behind the text: there is an outside-of-the-text that resists being reduced to 'words'.

Nietzsche, in his own way, maintains a more rigorously Kantian attitude, a *critique*, a transcendental idealism of a certain type,[64] that is equally opposed (as in the case of Kant in other equivalent terms) to the dreamy or dogmatic[65] idealism of word fetishists (philologism) who reduce all reality to language, and to the brute realism of biologism or, in some respects, of Schopenhauer.[66]

Philology is first and foremost a model for any analysis of culture. Nietzsche assigns it a noble role, but a role that is in large part due to its negative or cathartic virtues. As a philologist, who loves language, but is also its most implacable enemy, he says 'no' to culture's text, as an ideal that reads reality poorly. He therefore begins by criticizing the forms, the structure, the logic of discourse, the value and property of words. He operates a 'critique of pure discourse', a first form of genealogical 'suspicion': in this sense again, Nietzsche in his own way pursues an undertaking analogous to that of Kant. His philology is a 'science of the limits' of language, founded on the science of his true nature and raises itself into a language tribunal. This involves assessing which are the legitimate pretensions of such and such a discourse in culture, and which are illegitimate.[67]

Firstly, genealogical philology is a 'reading' and a 'listening'. In the very dense Foreword to *The Twilight of the Idols*, Nietzsche insists on the sonorous, almost phonological aspect of his method: his work is of an acoustic order. He proposes to sound out (*aushorchen*) idols:

> that is *my* 'evil eye' for this world, that is also my 'evil ear' . . .
> For once to *pose questions* here with a *hammer* and perhaps to receive for answer that famous hollow sound which speaks of inflated bowels – what a delight for one who has ears behind his ears – for an old psychologist and pied piper like me, in presence of whom precisely that which would like to stay silent *has to become audible.*[68]

But what is the nature of this listening? We need, says Nietzsche, a double hearing (*der Ohren noch hinter den Ohren hat*), in the sense in which one has the gift of double sight: a 'finer ear (*feinere Ohren*)'[69] or 'more subtle ears (*schärfste Ohren*)'.[70] Why are we given these comparatives or superlatives, which we find each time Nietzsche compares his philological hearing to the ordinary sort?[71] The reason is that common hearing is just a deafness:[72] for Nietzsche, hearing involves not only perceiving sounds but having 'an ear', being able to hear another sound, a resonance or a harmony *behind* the sound. The discourse that the philologist listens to is, in fact, a duplicity, like the distance between sound and its resonance or the muffling of resonance by the immediate sound. Thus, Wagner's power is described as follows:

> He is distinguished by every ambiguity, every double sense, everything quite generally that persuades those who are uncertain without making them aware *of what* they have been persuaded. Thus Wagner is a seducer on a large scale. . . . Open your ears: everything that ever grew on the soil of *impoverished* life, all of the counterfeiting of transcendence and beyond, has found its most sublime advocate in Wagner's art – *not* by means of formulas: Wagner is too shrewd for formulas – but by means of a persuasion of sensuousness which in turn makes the spirit weary and worn-out. Music as Circe.[73]

Consequently, the true philologist must not only be a reader, but above all be a 'fine ear', a musician.[74] The philologist has, as Nietzsche repeats, 'ears to hear',[75] cunning hearing.[76] Attentive, like a musicologist and a musician, to second resonances, the noises of the invisible, the secret tumult of our organs, he possesses a 'third ear'[77] that allows him to be sensitive to what can be heard behind words, as an accompaniment, echo or counterpoint – almost a *fugato*. He hears the unheard-of, and sometimes forces it, in a *Versuch*, to resonate:

> For one to pose questions here with a *hammer* and perhaps to receive for answer that famous hollow sound which speaks of inflated bowels – what a delight for one who has ears behind his ears.[78]

This faculty presupposes that we are sensitive to the word's musicality, its polyphony, everything that speech carries and expresses in the physical and physiological order, as shown *a contrario* by this text from *Beyond Good and Evil*:

> How little German style has to do with sound and the ears is shown by the fact that precisely our good musicians write badly. The German does not read aloud, does not read for the ear, but merely with his eyes: he has put his ears away in the drawer. In

antiquity, . . . the rules of written style were the same as those of spoken style . . . – *we* have really no right to the *grand* period, we moderns, we who are short of breath in every sense![79]

It is this form of hearing that is sensitive to the 'flesh' of speech that Nietzsche requires for his *Zarathustra*:

One has above all to *hear* correctly the tone that proceeds from this mouth, this halcyon tone, if one is not to do pitiable injustice to the meaning of its wisdom. . . . A tender slowness of pace is the *tempo* of these discourses.[80]

And Zarathustra will say: 'Yet the ear that listens to *me*, the *obeying* ear, is missing from them'.[81] To read well is to hear speech:

You Higher Men, midnight is coming on: so I will say something in your ears, as that old bell says it in my ear. . . . Soft! Soft! Then many a thing can be heard which may not speak by day; but now, in the cool air, when all the clamour of your hearts, too, has grown still, now it speaks, now it is heard, now it creeps into nocturnal, over-wakeful souls . . . do you not hear, how secretly, fearfully, warmly it speaks to you, the ancient, deep, deep midnight? *O Man! Attend!* . . . the hour approaches: O man, you Higher Man, attend! this discourse is for delicate ears, for your ears – *What does deep midnight's voice contend?*[82]

But that implies also that we know how to perceive unheard-of (*Unerhörtes*),[83] the almost inaudible, the *dull* rumbling that rises up from the depths of the world, the text and its music:

Our true experiences are not garrulous. They could not communicate themselves if they wanted to: they lack words. We have already grown beyond whatever we have words for. . . . – From a moral code for deaf-mutes and other philosophers.[84]

Attentive to the unique discourse in speech, the philosopher is deaf:

There are far more languages than we imagine; and man betrays himself more often than he would like. Everything speaks! But few know how to listen. As a result, man to some degree pours out his confession into a void; he squanders his 'truths' like the sun squanders light. Isn't it a pity that empty space has no ears?[85]

The new philosopher makes himself less attentive to the clamour of contemporary events so as to better perceive the thoughts that 'come on doves' feet', the 'stillest words',[86] for 'the earth revolves inaudibly'.[87] This is why we should 'watch and listen, you solitaries! From the future come winds with a stealthy flapping of wings; and good tidings go out to delicate ears'.[88] It is therefore useless to let oneself be deafened by 'events':

> As for the rest of life – so-called 'experience' – who among us is serious enough for that? Or has time enough? When it comes to such matters, our heart is simply not in it – we don't even lend our ear. Rather, as a man divinely abstracted and self-absorbed into whose ears the bell has just drummed the twelve strokes of noon will suddenly awake with a start and ask himself what hour has actually struck, we sometimes rub our ears after the event and ask ourselves, astonished and at a loss, 'What have we really experienced?'[89]

But:

> What one has no access to through experience one has no ear for. Now let us imagine ... that it is the *first* language for a new range of experiences. In this case simply nothing will be heard, with the acoustical illusion that where nothing is heard there *is* nothing.[90]

The philologist's fine hearing stems from the attention he pays as a genealogist to the reality of life, while the abstract metaphysician's superficial reading remains on the epidermis, according to *The Gay Science*'s formula:[91] for example, it attributes the search for knowledge to the apparent 'will to truth', while 'cocked ears'[92] perceive the hollow sound of the nihilist will:

> The zeal and subtlety, I might even say slyness, with which the problem 'of the real and apparent world' is set upon all over Europe today makes one think hard and prick up one's ears; and anyone who hears in the background only a 'will to truth' and nothing more, certainly does not enjoy the best of hearing.[93]

The manifest words secretly convey the rumbling deep within the body:

> 'But just a moment. ... Have you ever heard vengeance and hatred mentioned? Would you ever guess if you only listened to their words, that these are men bursting with hatred?' 'I see what

you mean. I'll open my ears gain – and stop my nose. Now I can make out what they seem to have been saying all along: 'We, the good ones, are also the just ones.'''.[94]

But an alert ear can discern what is said beneath the rowdy words – and Nietzsche's inverted commas separate the big words from what they in fact say:

'They call the thing they seek not retribution but the triumph of justice; the thing they hate is not their enemy, by no means – they hate injustice, ungodliness; the thing they hope for and believe in is not vengeance . . . but "the triumph of God, who is just, over the godless"; . . . Do I hear correctly? They call it Judgement Day, the coming of *their* kingdom, the "Kingdom of God." Meanwhile they live in "faith", in "love", in "hope"'. 'Stop! I've heard enough.'[95]

This passage recalls *Zarathustra*, which advocated lending an ear and, prior to accusing 'the just' of using falsifying designations, heard the word *gerächt* in the background of the word *gerecht*, just as he sensed that *Ja* contained *Ye-a*, the hee-haw of an ass. These revelatory resonances were perceptible only to Zarathustra's[96] ultra-fine ears:

To more fine and subtle ears all praise of virtue makes a ridiculous sound: such ears still do not perceive the virtue, for example, when someone is called 'modest' (when he rightly despises himself!), or when someone is called 'truthful' (when perhaps he does not want to be duped!), or 'merciful' (when he perhaps has a soft heart, that gives way easily) or 'chaste' (he is cold as a toad or does not like messy situations).[97]

The difference is always imperceptible, a murmur, a resonance, but its discovery is of capital importance.[98]

In addition: the gift of second hearing, in the sense in which Nietzsche speaks of a 'second consciousness'[99] is the gift of a philologist who knows how to listen as a physiologist and musicologist or phonologist, that is, above all as a 'physician'. What in fact is a sound? A sensation produced in the ear by the vibration of the air acting in accordance with the movements of a *material* body or milieu. The sound stems from a living body (tongue, larynx, palate, lips, etc.) when it is a voice; from an inanimate body when it is a noise or a sound, provoked by a shock or a movement: what the genealogist-philologist hears is always produced by a body and he can therefore only be a hearing philologist if at the same time he is a physiologist, or more generally a physician, listening to a body. For a (good) text 'renders' what the physical presence of the speaking subject offers immediately to the ear and eye, namely the body:

> The art of writing demands above all *substitutes* for the modes of expression available only to the speaker: that is to say, for gestures, emphases, tones of voice, glances. That is why written style is quite different from oral style and something much more difficult: it wants to make itself just as comprehensible as the latter but with fewer means.[100]

As a physician, the philologist must be able to situate and determine the nature of the sound in reference to its physical *origins*: the material of the emitting body, the type of shock or movement that produces the vibration. As an acoustics expert, he is capable of determining the state or nature of a distant or invisible body from the sounds it produces[101] or by himself provoking the shock and the movement that engenders the vibrations: he therefore hears the *physical* nature of the sound by referring that nature back to the material properties of its point of origin. This is *timbre*,[102] a specific quality of sound that is produced by a voice, an instrument or a struck object independently of its pitch, intensity or duration, or *sonority*, which musicians might call the sound's *body*.

This is the work of someone who 'philosophizes with a hammer': to 'hear', in the body of the sound, the nature or state of the body that is its origin. Depending on whether the sound is called *dumpf* (dull),[103] *hohl* (hollow) or *hart* (harsh),[104] and Nietzsche uses all the sumptuous resources of the German language to render the nuances of these timbres, we know if the body is healthy or sick, empty or full, wooden or metal, solid or cracked, etc. If the sound betrays the body's hidden interior, genealogy is therefore acoustic in the realms of phonology and physiology:

> For my part I have become accustomed to seeing in every moral judgement a kind of slapdash symbolic language, by means of which certain physiological facts relating to the body *wish* to be communicated; to those who have ears for such a thing. But who up until now has had ears for it! The proof is that in reality ears

up until now have been defective (or the ears were deceived and the interpretations false) and that consciousness has put itself out for thousands of years for nothing and *interpreted itself falsely*.[105]

It is the genealogist-philologist who philosophizes with a hammer. The least important use assigned by Nietzsche to the hammer is that of the destruction of mass.[106] Nietzsche more readily evokes the hammer used by the sculptor[107] or the blacksmith, the stone-cutter's bush hammer, the pick hammer or the mallet used on the cold chisel by the *Übermensch*. In reality, the hammer is used 'to pose questions ... and perhaps to receive (an) answer'.[108] *The hammer forces the silent body to speak:*

> Does nature not conceal most things from him, even in relation to his body, in order to keep him at a distance from his own entrails, his quick flowing blood, the complex vibrations of his fibres, imprisoned in a consciousness blinded by pride and illusion? Nature has thrown away the key.[109]

But the sound produced by the hammer discovers the body's idiosyncratic interior. On this level, the hammer is a musical instrument, comparable to the hammers in a piano, the percussionist's hammer, or even the *Stimmhammer*, the tuner's hammer, which Nietzsche mentions when he speaks of the tuning fork (*Stimmgabel*), a piece of metal one strikes like a hammer against a solid and fixed object to get the basic 'A' note.[110] A hammer is also used by a silversmith to preserve the quality and fineness of a precious alloy,[111] as well as by metallurgists who use an inspection hammer to detect flaws or cracks by striking a piece of steel, iron or cast iron and listening to the sound produced. Finally, the reflex hammer and the auscultation or chest hammer, supplement the stethoscope in allowing a doctor to make the patient's arteries 'speak', and so diagnose the state of certain organs, according to the sound produced.[112]

This sense comes under the domain of the acoustic: the shrewd ear. This is what 'sounding out the idols'[113] comes down to. Nietzsche, who uses the term *Götzen* (idols), whose semantic origins lie in Luther's German Bible,[114] recalls the Scriptures, which accuse the idols of being silent, as opposed to the God to whom Israel hearkens.[115] If the idols are silent, though, the silence itself (and even noisy 'silence' as opposed to 'background noise') is significant as a defence or resistance that can lead one to suspect the presence of an illness, or else as a symptom or misrepresentation.[116] Silence therefore speaks of an illness. Therefore, as Nietzsche repeats, 'all those given to silence are dyspetic'.[117] Only those who have 'new ears for new music'[118] hear what the silent person 'says', and what he does not wish to say – and many overtalkative people are silent. But here again Nietzsche recalls the Bible: it denounces idols fashioned from stone, wood, cast iron, silver, and gold. When these are struck by the hammer, they each give off a hollow sound, one that is stronger than it is full. When they are struck by the hammer, they sound empty (*leer*), hollow and silent (*stumm*); they 'say' how and of what matter they are made; they give out a sound (*Laut*) whose power is derived from the way in which they form a resonating chamber. Under the blows of the genealogical hammer (*mit dem Hammer Fragen stellen*), the idols speak (*reden*) of what they have in their intestines (*Eingeweide*):[119] namely, a void, nothing. A hollow (*hohl*) article, as with percussion instruments (the drum, snare drum, kettledrum, celeste), makes more noise than a full item, and the art of making every musical instrument rests on this knowledge. Idols-ideals speak of empty bodies: 'to sound out idols … that famous hollow sound which speaks of inflated bowels'.[120] The *Nichts*, the *nihil* of the Ideal, speaks in them. And this nothing, the resonant[121] words of the ideal, is the sign of an illness. Nietzsche demonstrates this on every page of his work, as, for example, in *The Gay Science*: 'Always big moral words. Always the rub-a-dub of justice, wisdom, holiness, virtue',[122] and in the *Genealogy*:

> the loud pharisaical gesture simulating noble indignation. The indignant barking of these sick dogs can be heard even in the sacred halls of science (I need only remind the reader once more of that Prussian apostle of vindictiveness and offensive use of moralistic claptrap. He stands out, even among his own crew of anti-Semites, by the vehemence of his moralistic drivel).[123]

In this way, the relationship between philology and physiology is revealed in the implications of the metaphorics of hearing. To sound out idols, the work of a genealogy that is an analysis of culture (which contains more idols than realities), is to pinpoint the origin of a sound, its nature (phonology), returning it to the body that emitted it (physics, acoustics, medicine), to be sensitive to its resonances (musicology, harmony), to read the hidden element (philology), to be sensitive to its *tempo*, rhythm, and style, that is to its tangible, physical and bodily idiosyncrasies.

For style is the thing that, in a discourse, best reveals the state of the articulating body: style is, in the philological order, genealogically the most pertinent aspect of a text: 'the teaching of style can on the one hand be the teaching that one ought to discover the means of expression by virtue of which every state of mind can be conveyed to the reader or auditor'.[124] 'The pace of his sentences shows whether the author is tired'.[125] And to whom does the study of style fall, if not to the philologist, who doubles up as a physiologist? For it is not only for stylistic reasons that Nietzsche declares:

> The first indispensable thing is life: style must *live*. . . . Rich living is revealed by a *richness* in *attitudes*. We must *learn* to consider everything, the length and conciseness of the phrase, the punctuation signs, the choice of words, pauses, the succession of arguments, as attitudes. Style must show that we *believe* in its thoughts, and that we do not just think them, but also *feel* them. The more the truth we want to teach is abstract, the more we must first seduce the *meanings* in its favour.[126]

> That which translates worst from one language into another is the *tempo* of its style, which has its origin in the character of the race, or, expressed more physiologically, in the average tempo of its 'metabolism'. There are honestly meant translations which, as involuntary vulgarizations of the original, are almost falsifications simply because it was not possible to translate also its brave and happy *tempo*, which leaps over and puts behind it all that is perilous in things and words. The German is virtually incapable of *presto* in his language: thus, it may be fairly concluded, also of many of the most daring and delightful nuances of free, free-spirited thought. Just as the *buffo* and the satyr is strange to him, in his body and in his conscience, so Aristophanes and Petronius are untranslatable for him. . . . What do all the swamps of the sick wicked world, even of the 'antique world', matter when one has, like him, the feet of a wind, the blast and breath, the liberating scorn of a wind that makes everything healthy by making everything *run*![127]

Style, for Nietzsche the genealogist, is the body speaking. A discourse, a man, an attitude, a literary text, a nation, a morality, a religion,[128] in short, a *culture* are all characterized by their *style*:

> To *communicate* a state, an inner tension of pathos through signs, including the *tempo* of these signs – that is the meaning of every style; and considering that the multiplicity of inner states is in my case extraordinary, there exists in my case the possibility of many styles – altogether the most manifold art of style any man has ever had at his disposal. Every style is *good* which actually communicates an inner state, which makes no mistakes as to the signs, the *tempo* of the signs, the *gestures* – ... The art of *grand* rhythm, the *grand style* of phrasing, as the expression of a tremendous rise and fall of sublime, of superhuman passion, was first discovered by me.[129]

In fact, style is to action and the text what timbre and colour are to sound, the body's second resonances. It is through their style that Nietzsche studies the great works that he evokes,[130] but also the individuals, ages and cultures:

> *One thing.* To 'give style' to one's character – a great and rare art! ... It will be the strong and domineering natures that enjoy their finest gaiety in such constraint and perfection under a law of their own; the passion of their tremendous will relents in the face of all stylized nature, of all conquered and serving nature. ... Conversely, it is the weak characters without power over themselves that *hate* the constraint of style. They feel that if this bitter and evil constraint were imposed upon them they would be demeaned; they become slaves as soon as they serve: they hate to serve.[131]

Style denotes the presence or absence of discipline, unity and hierarchy. And so 'to improve one's style – means to improve one's thoughts and nothing else! – If you do not straightaway agree with this it will be impossible to convince you of it',[132] for 'to write better ... means at the same time also to think better; continually to invent things more worth communicating and to be able actually to communicate them'.[133] To think well means to impose an order: 'grand style originates when the beautiful carries off the victory over the monstrous'.[134] Style is grand as an organizing force.[135] In these conditions, style is not only an outer form, but also the body of will:

One is an artist provided one treats everything the non-artists call 'form' as *content* or the 'very thing'. As a result, it is true, one belongs to a *world turned upside down*: far from this point on one regards content as something purely formal – including life.[136]

Decadent art is a decadent body, since style is the body's text and 'physio-logy' is the body's discourse:

> If anything in Wagner is interesting it is the logic with which a physiological defect makes move upon move and takes step upon step as practice and procedure, as innovation in principles, as a crisis in taste.

> For the present I merely dwell on the question of *style*. – What is the sign of every *literary décadence?* That life no longer dwells in the whole, ... the whole is no longer a whole. But this is the simile of every style of *décadence*: every time, the anarchy of atoms, disgregation of the will. ... Everywhere paralysis, arduousness, torpidity or hostility and chaos. ... The whole no longer lives at all: it is composite, calculated, artificial, and artifact.[137]

On the other hand, 'grand style' is a commandment: 'grand style follows on from grand passion. It does not deign to please, it forgets trying to convince. It commands. It *wills*'.[138] Nietzsche explains:

> Music and the grand style. The greatness of an artist cannot be measured by the 'beautiful feelings' he arouses. ... But according to the degree to which he approaches the grand style, to which he is capable of the grand style. ... To become master of the chaos one is; to compel one's chaos to become form: to become logical, simple, unambiguous, mathematics, *law* – that is the grand ambition here.[139]

From this point on Nietzsche contrasts *décadent* and ascendant in exactly the same way as 'romantic' and 'classic':

> *Décadence*. – This process is perceptible in the history of all art: the classical era is the one in which the difference between the ebb and the flow is very small and in which a delicious feeling of force constitutes the norm: what provokes the deepest disturbance always creates a *defeat*: only the period of *décadence* engenders them.[140]

The grand classical style:

> *Classic and romantic*. – Both those spirits of a classical and those of a romantic bent – these two species exist at all times – entertain a vision of the future: but the former do so out of a *strength* of their age, the latter out of its weakness.[141]

Romanticism is a *décadence* of style, because it is simply *décadence*: 'I admire Wagner wherever he puts *himself* into music'.[142] But, conversely:

> My objections to Wagner's music are physiological: why persist in dressing them up in aesthetics? Aesthetics, in fact, is just applied physiology. . . . I breathe with difficulty when this music begins to affect me; my *foot* becomes agitated and rebels against it. . . . But is protest not also registered by my stomach, my heart, the circulation of my blood? Aren't my entrails saddened? Do I not unconsciously go hoarse? . . . When I hear Wagner, I need a pastille . . . I ask myself: what is it that my whole body is ultimately *demanding* from this music? For the soul is not involved. I think it is asking for a little relief: as if all the animal functions should be accelerated by bold, light, wild and proud rhythms. . . . But Wagner makes me ill.[143]

Therefore, when a woman is 'wagnetized' (sic!), it is because she is 'ill', and 'something is not right with her sexuality, she lacks children or, in the most bearable case, men'.[144]

Nietzsche therefore wishes to be classical:[145] for him, all true greatness is measured in a 'grand style'. Style is what *can be heard* of the body, in so far as the latter is only accessible as a 'text'. Faced with a grand style, the physiologist must become a philologist:[146] this style 'speaks of itself',[147] it is the will to power turned into a text, it is 'the eloquence of power':

> here it is the mighty act of will, the will which moves mountains, the intoxication of the strong will, which demands artistic expression. . . . Pride, victory over weight and gravity, the will to power, seek to render themselves visible in a building; architecture is a kind of rhetoric of power, now persuasive, even cajoling in form, now bluntly imperious. The highest feeling of power and security finds expression in that which possesses *grand style*. Power which no longer requires proving; which disdains to

please; . . . which reposes in *itself*, fatalistic, a law among laws: *that* is what speaks of itself in the form of grand style.[148]

As an analysis of culture, genealogy must therefore become *a stylistics of the will to power and the body*. Thus, writers *are* the very text of culture as *physiology*:

Artists, if they are any good, are (physically as well) strong, full of surplus energy, powerful animals, sensual; without a certain overheating of the sexual system a Raphael is unthinkable – Making music is another way of making children; chastity is merely the economy of an artist – and in any event, even with artists fruitfulness ceases when potency ceases.[149]

Against the romanticism of great 'passion'. – To grasp that a quantum of coldness, lucidity, hardness is part of all 'classical' taste: logic above all, happiness in spirituality, 'three unities', concentration, hatred for feeling, heart, *esprit*, hatred for the manifold, un-certain, rambling, for intimations, as well as for the brief, pointed, pretty, good-natured. One should not play with artistic formulas: one should remodel life so that afterward it *has* to formulate itself. . . . Overwhelming through masses (Wagner, Victor Hugo, Zola, Taine).[150]

The essential and invaluable element in every morality is that it is a protracted constraint: to understand Stoicism or Port-Royal or Puritanism one should recall the constraint under which every language has hitherto attained strength and freedom – the metrical constraint, the tyranny of rhyme and rhythm . . . all there is or has been on earth of freedom, subtlety, boldness, dance and masterly certainty, whether in thinking itself, or in ruling, or in speaking and persuasion, in the arts as in morals, has evolved only by virtue of the 'tyranny of such arbitrary laws'; and, in all seriousness, there is no small probability that precisely this is 'nature' and 'natural' – and *not* that *laiser aller*! Every artist knows how far from the feeling of letting himself go his 'natural' condition is, the free ordering, placing, disposing, forming in the moment of 'inspiration'.[151]

Style, in other words the morality of a noble culture, is constraint, which gives a form to will and sharpens it by disciplining it.[152]

To read culture's text, is, moreover, to decrypt the hidden saying in what remains silent, and the latent meaning or posture (*Gebärde*) of the body in what speaks. 'The slightest constraint, the gloomy mien, any kind of harsh note in the throat are all objections to a man, how much more to his work! ... One must have no nerves.'[153]

Through this, Nietzsche affirms the break his method makes with the metaphysical tradition, or rather a tradition in the metaphorical order that constitutes it: that of vision (εἶδος, Θεωρία, evidence, a clear and distinct idea, *Wesensschau*, *Einsicht*, etc.). Whoever says method presupposes a certain relationship between 'reality' and the work of comprehension; Nietzsche challenges both the method and the constitution of reality in knowledge, such that he makes them appear as the metaphorical order of metaphysics. He contrasts vision with hearing. A method that rests on vision accepts the immediate presence of the object to true knowledge, the simplicity of a clear and distinct idea, and the ineluctability of the necessary evidence. For the genealogist, on the contrary, the sounds of the body get mixed up, subside and become suspect. The truth of the body is multiple and discrete.[154] Above all, it is not 'heliotropic', but is the vague darkness of a body closed to the light.[155] 'O Man! Attend!/What does deep midnight's voice contend?/... "The world is deep,/Deeper than day can comprehend."'.[156]

Nietzsche, aided by the metaphor of smell, confirms the implications of the sense of hearing. Genealogy is properly speaking *Otorhinology*, a listening to an olfactory perception of the distant or profound body. To understand the body's text means in some sense to smell it: 'Every word has its odour: there exists a harmony and disharmony of odours and thus of words'.[157]

Nietzsche uses the two metaphors together: 'I hear and smell it'.[158] 'One who smells not only with his nose but also with his eyes and ears will notice everywhere these days an air as of a lunatic asylum or sanatorium. ... Here the worms of vindictiveness and *arrière-pensée* teem, the air stinks of secretiveness and pent-up emotion.'[159] The two senses have in common a perception of something distant, a grasp of the properties of a bodily matter which it betrays of itself at a distance. Knowing a body involves sniffing its fragrance and hearing its resonances: 'And this *I* call knowledge: all that is deep shall rise up – to my height!'.[160] But the deep element is the Earth, the body, the entrails, which, though seemingly dark and silent,[161] make up the profound reality of culture: 'your entrails ... are the strongest part of you!'.[162] Although the entrails are hidden, they reveal themselves to one's hearing and sense of smell. The philologist knows how to inhale 'the odour of words'.[163]

> Yes, my fish-bones, shells, and prickly leaves shall – tickle hypocrites' noses! There is always bad air around you and around your feasts: for your lustful thoughts, your lies and secrets are in the air!
>
> Only dare to believe in yourselves – in yourselves and in your entrails! He who does not believe in himself always lies. ... Distance concealed from me the serpent-filth, and the evil odour.[164]

The olfactory sense allows us access to the depths of the living body, but also to its organic decomposition; in fact to its death:

> He who not only understands the word 'dionysian' but under-stands *himself* in the word 'dionysian' needs no refutation of Plato or of Christianity or of Schopenhauer – *he smells the decomposition.*[165]

The stench that is the specific manifestation of an organism, since only a living organism that is ill or dead can give off a stench, betrays morbidity:

> I am too hot and scorched by my own thought: it is often about to take my breath away. Then I have to get into the open air and away from all dusty rooms. ... When they give themselves out as wise, their little sayings and truths make me shiver: their wisdom often smells as if it came from the swamp: and indeed, I have heard the frog croak in it![166]

Swallowing one's words makes one ill:

> They have learned badly and the best things not at all, they have learned everything too early and too fast: they have *eaten* badly – that is how they got that stomach-ache – for their spirit is stomach-ache: *it* counsels death! For truly, my brothers, the spirit *is* a stomach! Life is a fountain of delight: but all wells are poisoned for him from whom an aching stomach, the father of affliction, speaks.[167]

If the body assimilates and digests badly, then it begins to swell and its breath is foul:

He who wants to understand all things among men has to touch all things. But my hands are too clean for that.

I even dislike to breathe in their breath; alas, that I lived so long among their noise and bad breath!

O blissful stillness around me! O pure odours around me! Oh, how this stillness draws pure breath from a deep breast! Oh, how it listens, this blissful stillness!

But down there – everything speaks, everything is unheard. ... I saw and scented in everybody what was *sufficient* spirit for him and what was *too much* spirit for him!

Their pedantic wise men: I called them wise, not pedantic – thus I learned to slur words. Their gravediggers: I called them investigators ...

Gravediggers dig diseases for themselves. Evil vapours repose beneath old rubble. One should not stir up the bog. One should live upon mountains.

With happy nostrils I breathe again mountain-freedom! At last my nose is delivered from the door of all humankind!

My soul, tickled by sharp breezes as with sparkling wine, *sneezes* – sneezes and cries to itself: Bless you![168]

Every illness stinks, and in particular the Ideal that is born from a body out of sorts: 'the ideal has hitherto been the actual force for disparaging the world and man, the poisonous vapour over reality, the great seduction to nothingness – '.[169]

One must guard against it:

I dwelt with stopped ears among peoples with a strange language: that the language of their bartering and their haggling for power might remain strange to me.

And I went ill-humouredly through all yesterdays and todays holding my nose: truly, all yesterdays and todays smell badly of the scribbling-rabble!

Like a cripple who has gone blind, deaf, and dumb: thus have I lived for a long time, that I might not live with the power-rabble, the scribbling-rabble, and the pleasure-rabble.[170]

Books for everybody are always malodorous books: the smell of petty people clings to them. Where the people eats and drinks, even where it worships, there is usually a stink. One should not go into churches if one wants to breathe *pure* air.[171]

I've had all I can stand. The smell is too much for me. This shop where they manufacture ideals seems to me to stink of lies. . . . I see what you mean. I'll open my ears again – and stop my nose.[172]

How Catholic, how un–German does August Comte's sociology smell to us with its Roman logic of the instincts![173]

According to Nietzsche, in the New Testament we find 'a musty odour of devotee and petty soul'.[174] And these different smells, all of them morbid, make us ill:

> my humanity consists, *not* in feeling for and with man, but in *enduring* that I do feel for and with him. My humanity is a continual self-overcoming. – But I have need of *solitude*, that is to say recovery, return to myself, the breadth of a free light playful air.[175]

> The 'German spirit' is *my* bad air: I find it hard to breathe in the proximity of this uncleanliness *in psychologicis* become instinct which every word, every gesture of a German betrays.[176]

> The genealogist must have *a sense of smell* (*Witterung*):
> It is my fate to have to be the first *decent* human being, to know myself in opposition to the mendaciousness of millenia . . . I was the first to discover the truth, in that I was the first to sense – *smell* – the lie as lie . . . My genius is in my nostrils.[177]

This involves not only 'smelling' (*sentir*) but also 'sniffing out' something (*pressentir*), pinpointing what had been hidden, managing to return to the origin of the stench:

> The entire history of the soul hitherto . . . is the predestined hunting-ground for a born psychologist. . . . He wishes he had a few hundred beaters and subtle well-instructed tracker dogs whom he could send into the history of the human soul and there round up *his* game. In vain. . . . The drawback in sending scholars out . . . is that they cease to be of any use precisely where the '*big* hunt'; but also the big danger, begins – precisely there do they lose their keenness of eye and keenness of nose. To divine and establish, for example, what sort of history the problem of *knowledge and conscience* has had in the soul of *homines religiosi* one would oneself perhaps have to be as profound, as wounded, as monstrous as Pascal's intellectual conscience was.[178]

The genealogist's sleuth must understand from what type of body the stench of the ideal comes: genealogy is *a history of origins*. To inhale the smell of the ideal, and sound out the idols, is to *read* the body's crypted secret which its resonance and its smell have been revealing since the beginning of the past, history, the unconscious, bodily intimacy.

All the same, we must not only flatter: we must live – and healthily, that is to say, breathe freely and get rid of miasma. Genealogy, as the other side of philology, is merely the negative aspect of a task that aims to encourage the body to live healthily. Genealogy, though, while detecting smells, does not suppress them. As well as diagnosis, we must establish a hygiene. Nietzsche therefore calls up 'the wind of a great freedom' which 'blows across everything',[179] the free and pure wind of the summits, free and fresh currents. 'Air! Air!'.[180]

> Exactly what it is that I, especially, find intolerable; that I am unable to cope with; that asphyxiates me? A bad smell. The smell of failure, of a soul that has gone stale.[181]

> I feel the urge to open the windows a little. Air! More Air![182]

> Air! Let in good air! Let Zarathustra in! You are making this cave sultry and poisonous, you evil old sorcerer![183]

> Oh books that release European air and not a nationalist nitrogen! They do the lungs good![184]

> Their idol, that cold monster, smells unpleasant to me: all of them, all these idolators, smells unpleasant to me. My brothers, do you then want to suffocate in the fume of their animal mouths and appetites? Better to break the window and leap into the open air. Avoid this bad odour! ... Many places – the odour of tranquil seas blowing about them – are still empty for solitaries and solitary couples.[185]

> I see you stung by poisonous flies. Flee to where the raw, rough breeze blows![186]

> Churches they call their sweet-smelling caves! Oh this counterfeit light! Oh this musty air! ... They thought to live as corpses, ... even in their speech I still smell the evil aroma of burial vaults.[187]

Many of the images (flies, breath, corpses, etc.) confirm that we are dealing here with organic smells, caused by the living person's illness or death: 'the man of today – I suffocate of his impure breath'.[188] But Nietzsche applies the metaphor of a foul-smelling organism to texts, including his own: '(*The Birth of Tragedy* smells offensively Hegelian, it is in only a few formulas infected with the cadaverous perfume of Schopenhauer'.[189] Hygiene, in this case, is initially left to the natural forms that must chase away the musty smells that are the products of *counter-nature*. This creates maxims and poems which have a practical as much as a metaphorical and philological value:

> *Keen air.* – The finest and healthiest element in science is, as in the mountains, the keen air wafts through it. – The spiritually delicate (such as the artists) avoid and slander science on account of this air.[190]

> *To the mistral.* – Mistral wind, you rain cloud leaper,/Let us whirl the dusty hazes/right into the sick men's noses,/flush the sick brood everywhere!/Let us free the coast together/from the wilted bosoms' blether,/from the eyes that never dare!/Let us chase the shadow lovers,/world defamers, rain-cloud shovers –/ let us brighten up the sky![191]

For, as Nietzsche writes:

> It was from this modernity that we were ill – from lazy peace, from cowardly compromise, from the whole virtuous unclean-liness of modern Yes and No. This tolerance and *largeur* of heart which 'forgives' everything because it 'understands' everything is sirocco to us. Better to live among ice than among modern virtues and other south winds![192]

Zarathustra, representing a healthy body, is a 'strong wind':[193]

> He who knows how to breathe the air of my writings knows that it is an air of the heights, a *robust* air. One has to be made for it, otherwise there is no small danger one will catch cold. The ice is near, the solitude is terrible – but how peacefully all things lie in the light! how freely one breathes! How much one feels *beneath* one! Philosophy, as I have hitherto understood and lived it, is a voluntary living in ice and high mountains.[194]

And as 'there are more idols in the world than there are realities',[195] Nietzsche's philology is 'a wandering in ice-fields and deserts'.[196] Precisely because he has 'a sense of smell', Nietzsche wants to avoid foul and musty smells, in the same way that his fine hearing drove him away from the irksome din of the public square.[197] Health, 'some indistinctive sense for what is harmful and dangerous',[198] allows you to smell any morbid threat and move away from it in the direction of the free, cold air that 'freezes the ideal'[199] and disinfects it, or else to leave nature the responsibility of purifying the atmosphere. The 'strong wind' chases away idols, and takes advantage of the situation to shake the fruit of the tree of truth:

> There is no reality, no 'ideality' which is not touched on in this writing (touched on: what a cautious euphemism! ...). Not merely *eternal* idols, also the youngest of all, consequently weakest with age. 'Modern ideas', for example. A great wind blows among the trees and everywhere fruits fall – truths. There is the prodigality of an all too abundant autumn in it: one trips over truths, one even treads some to death – there are too many of them ... But those one gets one's hands on are no longer anything questionable.[200]

The metaphor of smell, therefore, accords with Nietzsche's logic: to smell the ideal, to predict the ill body that it heralds, to chase away the noxious fumes, to be emptied out by nature, and then to breathe life into a new ideal:[201] 'I want to give oxygen to *a more robust ideal*',[202] writes Nietzsche, and he translates this non-metaphorically:

> I have declared war on the anaemic Christian ideal, ... not with the intention of annihilating it, but merely in order to put an end to its *tyranny* and install new and *more robust* ideals.[203]

But the metaphor is pursued, in his search for pleasing smells:

> It is to the *finished* being, who does my heart good, who is carved from a stout wood, that is tender and fragrant, and which pleases even my nose, that I dedicate this book.[204]

For Nietzsche, just as the unhealthy ideal stinks, so nature smells good: to be healthy is above all to be clean, while the ideal has muddy paws, and reeks of illness and the stuffy confinement of the 'whitened sepulchre'.[205]

> I have something which I call my inner nostrils. Every time I make contact with a human being, the first thing that is revealed to me is the degree of inner cleanliness – 'pure souls' are precisely

what smell particularly unclean ... for me, the idealist has a bad smell.[206]

Listen and smell: here, it is not the 'soul's eye' that perceives things, as in the Platonic tradition,[207] but the most material senses (as opposed to the privilege which Plato awarded to vision as the sense most distant from its object).

— And what subtle instruments for observation we possess in our senses! This nose, for example, of which no philosopher has hitherto spoken with respect and gratitude, is nonetheless the most delicate tool we have at our command: it can detect minimal differences in movement which even the spectroscope cannot detect. We possess scientific knowledge today to precisely the extent that we have decided to *accept* the evidence of the senses – to the extent that we have learned to sharpen and arm them and to think them through to their conclusions. The rest is abortion and not-yet-science: which is to say metaphysics, theology, psychology, epistemology. *Or* science of formulae, sign-systems.[208]

Smell and hearing seize the physics (acoustics) and the chemistry (organics) of the body itself, in its absence, depth or distance, through the 'emissions', sonorities or exhaltations that it projects itself, and not as the passive object of a light that confers life and clarity on it. Oedipus was as blind (before and after the revelation) as the blind Tiresias was a seer: Nietzsche credits him, as a genealogist, with senses of hearing and smell which are finer than the blind 'visions' of metaphysics, that are deaf and noseless. He demands 'the eyes of the senses and the ears of the spirit'.[209]

This method corresponds to a new 'constitution' of the object: if the genealogist listens, sounds out and smells, it is because his object, although it is named the 'Ideal', when all is said and done is more body, blood, entrails and matter, or sense and sensibility, than 'pure spirit'.[210]

This is the point at which to show how Bachelard's fine analyses of Nietzsche, even though they are founded on an adequate principle, remain idealist, in the Nietzschean sense of the term. Bachelard did see that Nietzsche's metaphors are 'coherent' in themselves.[211] But he curiously presents the body's economy as a principle of metaphorization, as the object and origin of a metaphorical transposition that encourages a genealogical and philological reading. He speaks of fundamental imagination, 'a dialectic of imaginary elements' – Imagination in itself. As it is not attached to a reality, this imaginary, in Bachelard's Nietzsche, can perform in a manner that is both coherent and overfree.

In Nietzsche's case, we are obliged to consider Bachelard's position, in which an imaginary is independent of a body, an idealist one. Bachelard has replaced a rationalist idealism with an 'imaginarist' idealism. He evokes 'those *direct and real* metaphors that constitute, for a doctrine of the imagination, certain immediate and elementary givens'. He is certain that in Nietzsche 'the poet explains the thinker', but who or what explains the poet, if it is no longer the concept that does so: is it the Imaginary (in itself) or the body, as a principle of metaphorical transposition, the 'grand reason' of the imaginary, that is to say as the object *and* origin of the imaginary?[212] Bachelard's method, as far as Nietzsche is concerned, must be pursued in the direction of looking into the imaginary structures of the physiological order, to the extent that the latter determines the metaphorical, or the imaginary – and here we must be prepared to conclude that the physiological imaginary in Nietzsche corresponds to an imaginary physiology, namely that what we have, is more of *a philosophy of metaphorical interpretation* than an objective physiology. For it is the (represented) order of the body, physiology, as *a metaphor of interpretation*, that structures Nietzsche's metaphorical order: the body, the object of the discipline that Nietzsche describes metaphorically, namely genealogy, is represented philosophically (metaphorically?) as an interpretation.

Leaning on the hypothesis of an imaginary that transcends the elements, Bachelard does not explain why Nietzsche breathes (*aspire*) and aspires to (*aspire à*) light air, and wishes for 'the nothingness of smells': it is because a bad smell reveals the warm, unhealthy underbelly of the plain's body and humanity, as opposed to 'the cold of the solitary peaks, the cold of the hills, glaciers, absolute winds'. It is precisely the genealogical perception of smells that makes Nietzsche and Zarathustra flee for the hills and long for the mistral, the pure air and the silence. Bachelard substituted an 'imaginarist' idealism. He evokes 'those *direct* and *real* metaphors that constitute, for a doctrine of the imagination, a number of immediate and elementary givens'. It is certain that Nietzsche 'the poet explains the thinker', but who or what explains the poet if it is no longer done by the concept: is it the Imaginary (in itself) or the body, as a principle of metaphorical transposition, as the 'great reason' of the imaginary, that is to say as the object *and* the origin of the imaginary?[212] Bachelard writes:

> Nietzsche wants air only to be bracing: cold and empty. For a true Nietzschean, the nose must experience the immense happiness or happy feeling of feeling nothing. It confirms an odour empty zone. *Smell*, on which Nietzsche so often prided himself, has the virtue of not *attracting* anything. The overman is given it so he can *stay away* from the slightest hint of an impunity. A Nietzschean cannot be content with a smell. . . . In contrast (to Baudelaire), Nietzsche writes:
>
>> Breathing the purest air,
>> nostrils wide as cups,
>> without future, without memory . . .
>
> The air is pure, dry, cold and empty.
>
>> I sit here, breathing the best air,
>> the air of paradise, in truth,
>> the clear, light, golden-streaked air,
>> as good as any to have
>> fallen from the moon.
>
> Nietzsche's imagination detects smells to the extent to which it frees itself from the past. Every pastism dreams of indestructible smells. To predict is the opposite of smell.

Bachelard, forgetting that the mouth of a man that *speaks* and *stinks* is evolved as the antithesis to the mouth of the cave, goes on:

> It is at the *mouth* of the cave – the strange cave at the mountain's *summit* . . . – that Zarathustra gives his lesson on the bracing effects of cold wind. . . . 'Have I ever found on earth a more pure air than you, the air in my cave? And yet I have seen many countries, my nose has learned to examine and evaluate many airs; but it is with you that my nose experiences its greatest joy'.

Bachelard does not bear in mind that the pure, silent air of the lonely mountain represents a flight from what Nietzsche discovered thanks to the *genealogical* sense of smell: the musty herd on the plain, the din of the public square, the flies, the body that has the foul smell of a secret body, one whose mouth simultaneously emits the morbid chatter and stinking breath of the body's illness. 'How can we resist the substantial synthesis of air, cold and silence? Through air and cold, it is silence that is breathed (*aspiré*).'[213] This whole metaphorical logic is structured by otorhinological genealogy, philology, physiology, while Bachelard dreams more of a purely '*spiritual*' imagination that produces its own rules.

'Ignorance of physiological matters' is 'damned idealism', writes Nietzsche, and he counterattacks: it is the hygrometric degree of air and the *tempo* (we note the term) of metabolisms that determine spirit, genius, and so imagination: 'the origin of the German spirit − disturbed intestines'.[214] This leads to several recommendations, beginning with Zarathustra:

Zarathustra was standing near the door of his cave as he spoke this discourse; with the final words, however, he escaped from his guests and fled for a short while into the open air.

'On pure odours around me,' he exclaimed, 'oh blissful stillness around me! . . .

'Tell me, my animals: all these Higher Men − do they perhaps not *smell* well? Oh pure odours around me!' . . . All three stood silently together in this attitude, and sniffed and breathed in the good air together. For the air here outside was better than with the Higher Men.[215]

'Stay with us, O Zarathustra! Here there is much hidden misery that wants to speak out, much evening, much cloud, much damp air! . . . You alone make the air around you robust and clear! Have I ever found on earth such good air as with you in your cave! . . . except . . . among the daughters of the desert − for with them there was the same good, clear, oriental air.' . . . With his nostrils, . . . he drew in the air slowly and inquiringly, like someone tasting strange air in strange lands.[216]

My man's fare, my succulent and strengthening discourse, is effective: and truly, I did not feed them with distending vegetables![217]

'And even you', said Zarathustra to the conscientious man of the spirit, 'just consider, and lay your finger on your nose! . . . Is your spirit not too pure for this praying and the exhalations of these devotees?'[218]

Careful, from his moralist writings like *Human, All Too Human* or *Daybreak* onwards, to insist on the little physiological, psychological and climactic details that seem to him to condition existence more than does speculation, Nietzsche, above all in his 1888 works, ends up expressly articulating, with a wealth of detail, the physiological principles of his philosophy and of his art of living which make him so 'wise': as he is always concerned about the purity of the air, he analyses the role the climate plays in relation to organic functions:

> Most clearly related to the question of nutriment is the question of *place* and *climate*. No one is free to live everywhere; and he who has great tasks to fulfil which challenge his entire strength has indeed in this matter a very narrow range of choice. The influence of climate on the *metabolism*, its slowing down, its speeding up, extends so far that a blunder in regard to place and climate can not only estrange anyone from his task but withhold it from him altogether: he never catches sight of it . . .
>
> Make a list of the places where there are and have been gifted men, where wit, refinement, malice are a part of happiness, where genius has almost necessarily made its home: they all possess an excellent dry air. Paris, Provence, Florence, Jerusalem, Athens – these names prove something: that genius is *conditioned* by dry air, clear sky – that is to say by rapid metabolism, by the possibility of again and again supplying oneself with great, even tremendous quantities of energy.[219]

This comes at the point where Nietzsche, in this same text, making 'ignorance *in physiologicis*' responsible for his ills, retrospectively accuses of idealism and of being 'a false step' 'that I became a philologist for example – why not at least a physician or something else that opens the eyes?'.[220] A philologist and a physician: Nietzsche wants to have been both, that is to say, he wants to be a genealogist. For him, in fact, the body deserves a 'spiritual diet (*geistige Diät*)'[221] and, if Nietzsche has managed to be healthy, leave the foul-smelling lowlands and climb up to the cold, clean air of the summits, it is, as he says, because 'it was only sickness that brought me to reason'.[222] Zarathustra 'speaks differently' because 'he also *is* different'.[223]

Here we can see the degree to which philology and physiology mutually implicate one another in metaphorical language.

But the philologist must abandon philological physiology for the 'active', experienced physiology of dietetics:

It became of a sudden terribly clear to me how useless, how capricious my whole philologist's existence appeared when compared with my task. I was ashamed of this *false* modesty. . . . Ten years behind me during which the *nourishment* of my spirit had quite literally been at a stop! . . . – I was moved to compassion when I saw myself quite thin, quite wasted away! . . . – A downright burning thirst siezed hold of me: thenceforward I pursued in fact nothing other than physiology, medicine and natural snience.[224]

Here the ill Nietzsche is a person who is ill *with* philology as an anti-corporal idealism with the contagion of *décadent* illness:

Sickness . . . bestowed on me that *compulsion* to lie still, to be idle, to wait and be patient. . . . But to do that means to think! . . . My eyes alone put an end to all bookwormishness, in plain terms philology: I was redeemed from the 'book', for years at a time I read nothing – the *greatest* favour I have ever done myself![225]

Therefore, one *must* be a philologist, says Nietzsche, and at the same time the 'opposite' of a philologist, 'both *décadent* and beginning', 'ascent and decline'.[226]

But why, then, does Nietzsche not abandon philology? Firstly because physiology cannot do without language. The body, in fact, is only accessible, in accordance with the Nietzschean philological 'transcendental', as a linguistic *phenomenon*, as part of a *semiotics*, never as a body-in-itself, as a non-linguistic *thing-in-itself*. In reality, the fact that Nietzsche offers himself up *as* a text signifies that he recognizes his depth, which is liable only to interpretation. The body and the world, as texts, are merely signs of themselves to a philological gaze that is not *in-tuitive*, but is a reading of an enigmatic meaning that does not offer itself up but is interpreted. Nietzsche wants to restore an enigmatic wandering to reality, as opposed to those who confuse objectivity with the in-itselfness of things.

In this respect, Nietzsche's thought remains closer to a Kantian, or Schopenhauerian model than to what we normally call 'structuralist' thought: he maintains a referential reality of the body outside the writing in which he enigmatically offers himself up to be deciphered. From this point on, if, on the one hand, the 'blanks' separating Nietzsche's notes and aphorisms, if the anacoluthons,

breaks and *Gedankenstriche* (dashes) interrupting the text's movement are significant as speaking silences, in the text they represent
moments during which the body lives with speaking, as a silent
jouissance or suffering: Nietzsche, the 'body' Nietzsche eats, sleeps,
drinks, walks, cooks, dreams, plays music, and makes tea or
skimmed cocoa.[227] If we ignore this body outside the text, treating
it as a 'poverty', we fall back into the furtive idealism of a
philologist or intellectual for whom the only reality is textual, and
every body is a signifier: what we call 'structuralism' would be
called neo-idealist *décadence*, by Nietzsche.[228] And he protests:

> I shall be asked why I have really narrated all these little things
> which according to the traditional judgement are matters of
> indifference. ... Answer: these little things – nutriment, place,
> climate, recreation, the whole casuistry of selfishness – are
> beyond all conception of greater importance than anything that
> has been considered of importance hitherto. It is precisely here
> that one has to begin to *learn anew*. ... Contempt has been taught
> for the 'little' things, which is to say for the fundamental affairs
> of life.[229]

However, if Nietzsche's reference to non-textual existence can be
(and has been) misinterpreted as the obscurantist promotion of
unthought, 'lived experience',[230] which is often just as 'ideal'
and ideological as its opposite, we must maintain, along with
Nietzsche, that any access to the body, all physiology, must pass
through philology: '*Zeichensprache der Affekte*'.[231]

But philology is not just (an exclusive) love of language, it is also
a *critique* of language, a mistrust,[232] even hatred of language: a
misology. '*Was redet nicht?*'[233] Philological mistrust is necessary:
language is encoded, everything that speaks of the body is
'*Zeichensprache*', semiotics or semiology. And as the spirit is the
body expressed according to certain modes of transposition whose
paradigm is language, culture as a whole is a language, but, as such,
is a coded transposition. Language, according to Nietzsche, does
not manifest, it transposes. This conception, which is not very
original,[234] opens up the way for a conception of culture and
morality as a second-degree transposition and deformation. This is
the founding affirmation of genealogy:

> *Die Moralen als Zeichensprache der Affekte! – die Affekte selber eine*
> *Zeichensprache der Funktionen alles Organischen*: morals viewed as

the coded language of the emotions! – but emotions viewed in their turn as the coded language of the functions of any organism.[235]

This leads to the proposition: 'We must maintain whatever belongs to the spirit as the coded language of the *body*!'[236]

What does this affirmation signify? That the real meaning of culture, and morality, as languages, is unconscious or hidden, and that, in order to 'discover' it (*entdecken*),[237] therefore, we need a 'philologist' and a 'psychologist' who are able to 'read *well*, that is to say, to read slowly, deeply, looking cautiously before and aft, with reservations, with doors left open, with delicate eyes and fingers'.[238] On the other hand, men of morality 'project their own honourable stupidity and goodness into the heart of things (the old God, *deus myops*, still lives among them!); we others – we read something else into the heart of things'.[239] So the psychologist is someone who, through this listening and reading, is capable of bringing to light 'the *hidden* history of philosophy (*die verborgene Geschichte der Philosophie*)',[240] and of 'understanding where this evaluation comes from (*woher diese Wertung stammt*)':[241] the psychologist, another name for a genealogist, knows how to ascribe to an individual's physiological idiosyncrasies the abstract qualities of the 'spirit' which the individual may articulate. '*WORAUS wird gehandelt? Das ist MEINE Frage*': what is the basis on which we act? That is *my* question. And Nietzsche specifies: '*Das Wozu? Wohin? ist etwas Zweites?*': the whys and the wherefores are secondary.[242] Thus, a psychologist is someone who refers a discourse to its hidden origins, while a philologist criticizes the same discourse *from the inside*, as a linguistic structure, and refers it only to another language: the language of reality, the correct language. Philology and psychology therefore designate the same taste, but the latter concentrates on the physiological origins (γένεσις) while the former concentrates on the discourse (λόγος). If 'the realm of the spirit must be maintained as the *Zeichensprache des Leibes*', philology deals firstly with the *Sprache* and the *Zeichensprache*, while psychology views *Sprache* in terms of '*des Leibes*', and so tends to efface language in favour of the body. Propositions such as: 'In every morality, we are concerned to discover higher states for the body',[243] or: '*Courage, shame, anger* have in themselves nothing to do with concepts – *physiological facts* whose name and moral concept (*seelisch*) are merely a symbol (*Symbol*)',[244] are of a *psychological* order, but are necessarily limited to *philological* considerations, something that becomes clearer when Nietzsche adds: 'What is affirmed by the language of the names for emotions? e.g. *ira*. What does it mean (*heisst*): to change a man through morality?'[245] Everywhere, in Nietzsche's genealogical analyses, the two disciplines are simultaneously applied:

> *Against Kant.* – Naturally, I am linked to something beautiful that pleases me *by interesting me*. But it is not naked (*nackt*). The expression of happiness, perfection, repose, even the fact that the work of art is silent, is open to judgement – all this speaks (*redet*) to our drives – ultimately I only experience something as 'beautiful' if it corresponds to an ideal of my own drives.[246]

This exemplary text posits a relationship between the ideal of the spirit and the physiological drive, translated psychologically into the idiosyncratic language (the text is in the first person singular) of emotions and sentiments ('interest', 'experience'), and it insists on the fact that these drives and emotions are not directly accessible ('naked') but can only become so through language ('*redet*', '*entspricht*', '*Ausdruck*': speaks, corresponds, expression). The word for an emotion is merely a 'symbol' to the physiologist and psychologist, but only language, in the philologist's view, can say what the emotion signifies. Finally, this text directed 'against Kant' reapplies to the Schopenhauerian concept of will and desire as a thing-in-itself certain limits inspired by Kant ('*es liegt nicht nackt vor*') which are transposed on to the philological plane: language is the phenomenon of the bodily thing-in-itself which cannot be known through *intuitus intellectualis*. The difference consists in the fact that Nietzsche substitutes the knowledge of phenomena (as opposed to the intellectual intuition in the in-itself) for an inter-pretation. We can at least deduce from this that Nietzsche is both Schopenhauerian when he substitutes the body's will to power for the inert and intellectual thing-in-itself, and Kantian in the way he recalls to its own Schopenhauerian tendencies the limits imposed by the philological 'transcendental'. Schopenhauerian *and* Kantian: it is this contradictory duality that determines both his originality and the impossibility of his task. In vain, Nietzsche reminds Kant that the Ideal's 'thing-in-itself' is the body.

At this point I cannot absolve myself from giving an account of the psychology of 'belief', of 'believers', for the use, as is only reasonable, of precisely the 'believers' themselves. If there is today still no lack of those who do not know how *indecent* it is to 'believe' – *or* a sign of *décadence*, of a broken will to live – well, they will know it tomorrow. My voice reaches even the hard-of-hearing.[247]

He is obliged, with Kant, to admit all psychology has to pass through the coded language of the body.[248]

So is Nietzsche not a philologist and idealist at the same time as being a psychologist, physiologist and realist? For Nietzsche, the psychologist represents the type Kant calls an 'empirical realist', someone who 'may admit the existence of matter without going outside his mere self-consciousness, or assuming anything more than the certainty of his representations, that is, the *cogito, ergo sum*'.[249] While Nietzsche uses the word 'hidden' to designate the genealogical order of an ideal,[250] Kant speaks of the unknowable character of the thing-in-itself: 'What the things-in-themselves may be I do not know, nor do I need to know, since a thing can never come before me except in appearance'.[251]

One might object that transcendental idealism establishes a necessary limit that is founded on the nature of the human spirit and the knowledge that wishes to present itself as a science:

> If by the complaints – *that we have no insight whatsoever into the inner [nature] of things* – it be meant that we cannot conceive by pure understanding what the things which appear to us may be in themselves, they are entirely illegitimate and unreasonable. For what is demanded is that we should be able to know things, and therefore to intuit them, without senses, and therefore that we should have a faculty of knowledge altogether different from the human, and this not only in degree but as regards intuition likewise in kind – in other words that we should be not men but beings of whom we are unable to say whether they are even possible, much less how they are constituted.[252]

It might seem on the other hand that for Nietzsche this limit is contingent, indeed to the denial of the body through morality. In reality, if it is true that the hidden body can be dis-covered (*entdekt*) by the genealogist, it can only be achieved *as a language*. Thus in Nietzsche it is still a question of genea*logy*, of physcho*logy*, of philo*logy*: we only have access to a body when it is transposed into a 'language' – that of culture. The break separating morality and *amor fati* does not, therefore, pass between language and the body, but between the language of denegation and the language of reality, which are both, *but to different degrees, Zeichensprache.* 'The emotions themselves in turn are a coded language of the functions of everything organic'.[253] The organic is thus undetectable as such. Morality, therefore, merely carries to a second degree (deceit,[254] unconsciousness, dissimulation) the transpository nature of language. For Nietzsche explains: 'the great philosophers are not conscious *that they are speaking of* themselves (*dass sie von sich reden*)' when they speak of 'truth, while at bottom it concerns them', such that 'the philosopher is merely a sort of opportunity and possibility for the drive, in spite of everything, *to accede to discourse* (*einmal zum Reden kommt*)'.[255] What is hidden in culture is spoken: '*Was redet nicht?*'.[256] Everything speaks – but this is why everything can lie, especially the Ideal:[257]

> With 'ends and means', we speak a coded language: but through it we designate merely the *incidentals* to *action* (its relationship to the *accompanying phenomena* of pleasure and pain.[258]

> For my part I have become accustomed to viewing every moral judgement as a botched form of coded language, through which certain of the body's physiological facts *wish* to communicate themselves to those who have ears to hear them. But who up until now has had ears![259]

> *To communicate oneself* is therefore from the beginning *to extend one's power over others*: at the base of this drive we find an ancient coded language.[260]

All of this is resumed in the text from *The Twilight of the Idols*, in which Nietzsche strongly expresses his philological principle:

> there are no moral facts whatever. .... Morality is only an interpretation of certain phenomena, more precisely a *mis*interpretation. ... To this extent moral judgement is never to be taken literally: as such it never contains anything but nonsense. But as *semeiotics* it remains of incalculable value. ... Morality is merely sign-language, merely symptomatology: one must already know *what* it is about to derive profit from it.[261]

This is the doctrine that Nietzsche applies, for example in *The Antichrist*:

Chance, to be sure, determines the environment, the language, the preparatory schooling of a particular configuration of concepts: primitive Christianity employs *only* Judeo–Semitic concepts. . . . But one must be careful not to see in this anything but a sign-language, a semeiotic, an occasion for metaphors. It is precisely on condition that nothing he says is taken literally that this antirealist can speak at all.[262]

Nietzsche's philologism allows him to give a rigorous grounding to a theory of philosophers, to a critique of visual illusions, while psychology allows him to escape from linguistic idealism, linking this deceit to the denial of the *body*, and therefore fixing it as a *physiological error*, replacing *Fehlgreifen* with *Irrtum* or *Schein*. Here it is no longer a question of an error of the spirit committed against the body, an inadequate vision (which comes under the domain of dualism), but of an error *of* the body committed against itself, where the genitive makes the body both subject and object. The conditions for the possibility of this error *are, essentially, language,* as the body's absence to itself.

Genealogy is a double science. Although it is unitary, given Nietzsche's monism,[263] it is a *divergent* unity: reduced to the text, the body is merely an ideal, whereas Nietzsche tries to give back to philosophy the body's *Erlebnis*, its lived experience. So psychology must, under pain of remaining dumbly silent or speculative, appeal to philology, which abolishes it. Genealogy develops both: (a) as a referential discourse, that refers to the other: the body, life (in psychology); and (b) as a systematic, idealist discourse (in philology).

This opposition can be found even in the 'style' of Nietzsche's commentaries, whether 'existential' or naively referential, or thingist, or 'realist', or ultra-speculative, or idealist, or 'double-Dutch' or 'structuralist'. No *Umwertung*,[264] or *Umlernen*,[265] or *Umwerfen*[266] or *Umdeuten*[267] can change any of this: if there must be or can be a discourse on the body's origin of discourse, namely genealogy, this genealogy, as a discourse can only be idealist. In Kant, the thing-in-itself is *unknowable*; in Nietzsche, the body and life as language are not *lived*.[268] To institute genealogy, Nietzsche must *simultaneously* proclaim the lived exteriority of the body in relation to language *and* consider the body and culture as languages that are homogeneous to his own philological discourse, something which is incompatible. This is a point of real 'inversion' for Nietzschean *discourse*, if not in evaluating (in so far as they come from the body): it can only be resolved in a *practice* that 'experiences' the body without reflecting on it and therefore risks conceiving of it in an 'idealist' way. For 'men act differently from the way they speak'[269] and all life is a falsification.

The formulations of this inversion of evaluations do not escape this antinomy. Firstly because the evaluation itself comes from the body, and a new evaluation presupposes what is in question: the healthy body – and where will this health come from?[270] Next because the terms whose order are to be inverted reveal or betray the antinomy of philology and psychology which lays the foundation for the possibility and impossibility of genealogy: surface/depth, motives/hidden origin, words/actions, conscious/unconscious, ideal of desire/fact of reality, or, in the terms evolved above, structure/reference.

Nietzsche always sets two terms in opposition in order: (1) to invert the primacy of the one over the other; (2) more fundamentally, to destroy the illusory autonomy by showing that the second includes the first.

In the gap or interval, life laughs at what Zarathustra says about it, because it is *Wille ZUR Macht*, self-overcoming (*Selbstüberwindung*).[271] Like wisdom, life is 'perfidious', 'an unfathomable abyss', 'deceptive' and when 'she speaks ill of herself, then precisely is she most seductive'.[272] Philology sticks to the surface, whereas psychology, which is concerned with the living body, tries to evoke its depths. But from the bottom one sees only the surface: for a sounded depth can be no deeper, like 'the unexhaustible well' that the bucket of words, even when full, will not empty.[273] To be a living body is to be other than what is said about it, a fraction of the word that freezes the living into a corpse-like stiffness:

> We must interpret every movement as a gesture, as a sort of language thanks to which forces are understood. There is no trace of misunderstanding in the inorganic world, the understanding there seems perfect. It is in the organic world that error begins. . . . The contradiction is not between what is 'false' and what is 'true', but between the 'abbreviations of signs' and the signs themselves. The essential thing is the construction of forms that represent numerous movements, the invention of signs that

resume entire varieties of signs. ... Thought is not yet the internal phenomenon itself, but another coded language that expresses a compromise of power between the emotions.[274]

To make a body into a simple discourse is to kill it: idealism, of which Nietzsche writes in *The Twilight of the Idols* that it is always attracted by the slight stench of carrion.[275] The body's life is language, a death perpetually reported; it is *dissimilation, dis-assimilation*. It is, therefore, in the precarious play of structure and reference, between surface and depth, word and action that the impossible task of genealogy is acted out and thwarted. The truth of this genealogy is to be an illusion, whose reality is a surpassing, whose hold is a lack. Genealogy is a *negative* theology: a theology of the completely other, confiding and defying with regard to a god whose transcendence is silence: Life.

Philology studies the culture of the interior, as a linguistic structure, but its task is more *negative* than positive: it wishes to refuse (*negieren*) denegation (*Verneinung*) of the body and of life in the discourse of culture. Psychology confines itself to referring to the reality of the living body. But it can only do so through the para-linguistic device of the metaphor.

8

The Critique of Metaphysical Discourse: Philological Genealogy and Misology

> Language depends on the most naive prejudices of grand *concepts* ... we read disharmonies and problems into things because we think *only* in the form of language. ... *We cease to think when we refuse to do so under the constraint of language. ... Rational thought is interpretation according to a scheme that we cannot throw off.*[1]

This text exposes, in an almost Kantian spirit, what we have called the 'philological revolution'. To think, here, is to speak: more precisely, we can only think according to the forms (*Formen*) and limits (*Grenzen*) of language. For Nietzsche, what we grasp are things, which exist not in themselves, but are linked to one another according to concepts isolated in them by language. Language is therefore the *a priori* of all thought.[2] This is so much so that we are no longer even aware of the limits between thought and language. ('*Hier eine Grenze als Grenze zu sehen*'): it is 'a scheme that we cannot reject', almost as necessary and universal as the Kantian *a priori*.[3]

But it is just as important to note Nietzsche's '*nur*', the expression of a *limit* and *a condition of possibility*: 'we can only (*nur*) think in the form of language'. But 'language is built on the most naive prejudices among us': Nietzsche wishes to move to a critique of language as a metaphysical prejudice and a critique of metaphysics as a language. To unmask the prejudices in metaphysics: but in relation to what truth? That of reality. But, as he affirms that we cannot reject the forms of language, even supposing that there is a language that is proper to reality (which is debatable), reality will only ever be thought and read like a language, that is to say falsely. Nietzsche proceeds like a philological Kant who would claim simultaneously that things are knowable only as a phenomenon (language) *and* that phenomenal forms are illusory in relation to the in-itself (language is prejudiced). This claim turns Nietzsche into a mixture of Kant and Schopenhauer. Nietzsche falls into the *petitio principii* of which he accuses Kant: the presupposition of an in-itself, that allows him merely to speak to a language illusion. From two things we derive one: either Nietzsche denounces metaphysics as a linguistic illusion – and then has to posit a reality or truth that is 'in-itself'; or else he rejects the in-itselfness of any thing, and he cannot criticize metaphysics and language – unless he turns illusion into an ontological principle, like Schopenhauer, in the form of metaphysics as interpretation.

But Nietzsche does not renounce either of the terms in the alternative: when he criticizes the linguistic illusion of metaphysics, he contrasts it with the in-itselfness of things[4] which, following the example of Kant, he evokes negatively in regard to the illusion or the phenomena.[5] But that does not prevent him from going on to criticize this in-itself, even if it has been posited as the unknowable correlate of illusion. And equally he feels the necessity of leaning his critique against a 'positive' conception of reality. He will turn to metaphors taken from physiology, psychology, medicine and politics – as if this philologist thought he had a better chance of reaching the body and reality through the discourses on the body. Looking for reality in this way, he merely accentuates his interpretative character, rather than his objectivity. For these disciplines will be presented by Nietzsche not as sciences revealing reality, but as semiotic systems.

Nietzsche is therefore aware: (1) that genealogy implies philology; (2) that genealogy requires the abolition of philology in physiology; (3) that physiology itself is not a direct science of the real body, but a metaphor of the language of bodily reality, an inadequate scheme. If language is metaphysical or metaphorical, it is perhaps because there is *only* a *metaphorical* reality for us. In culture, there is only a *language* on reality, a *metaphor of reality*. Nietzsche wishes to pass from the discourse (critique) on moral language (philology) to the discourse on reality and the body (physiology), but in vain: he can express reality only through his language and the means of the philologist: metaphor. So Nietzsche's physiological metaphors above all will be *metaphors of the body as a philological object*, of a body that is not given, but read, not physiological, but philological, perhaps because he is the principle of interpretation.

Nietzsche therefore firstly denounces the rhetorical illusions of morality and metaphysics: philology.

Then he uses physiological metaphors, which are still a rhetoric: physiology.

Finally he returns to philology, proposing physiology as a certain philological art of reading, while reabsorbing all the preceding metaphors into the metaphorical system of the art of interpretation: the metaphors used in interpretation and the reading of the body.

To use philology presupposes: (1) that the object of analysis is (or is represented as) a text; (2) that our job is to read this text; (3) that the task incumbent on the philologist, namely reading, consists, ideally, in grasping, on the basis of the materiality of the text as a group of signs, everything to which these signs 'refer'. As the signifying material is not univocal, the philologist must *decipher*. Firstly the genre of texts which the philologist is dealing with is not a discursive system founded on a unique code that axiomatically regulates the correspondence between signifier and signified. For Nietzsche, God, as a nomothete, is dead. In addition, the philological practice and idealogy which Nietzsche claims for himself present the text as a group of signs that have a *referential* value.

Philology is therefore caught between the apparently univocal materiality of the text as a set of differences and the wandering infinity of the interpretative task that results from the equivocal nature of the text's referentiality. The entire art of interpretation (*Kunst der Interpretation*) rests on this gap and is inscribed in the imprecisely demarcated space separating *semiotics* (*language*) from *semantics* (the text as *speech*).

We can understand Nietzsche's attitude to philology, an unstable discipline by virtue of his task: *to interpret* the text, isolate its meaning, and *respect* the words, the semiological matter of the text. There two indissociable aspects stand in opposition to one another. Nietzsche congratulates philologists for gaining respect for the text in the face of abusive interpretations; but he jeers at philologists for their myopia, which confines them to the narrow world of words and books. Philology surpasses itself; it is a discipline: the text has value only if it refers to what lies outside it, but it is also a corpus, a network of differences that can be spotted. The text is a structure and a reference, the possibility of overcoming at the same time as being a closed system: it is the 'antinomy of philology'.[6]

So what does it mean, for Nietzsche, to say that culture, indeed the world, is a text?

— It is a group of *signs*, which are distinctive and arranged according to a certain syntax or style.

— This signifying group is also a group of signs that refers to one (or several) meanings, and to certain referents. It is a group whose code (or codes) is external to it, contrary to the 'abstract' and formal temptations of the philologist. To say that culture is a text, is for Nietzsche to underline its semantic and referential value: the text is a structure, but also a sign, it organizes itself for its *other*.

— This culture, as a text, is therefore to be deciphered: it is the thing whose meaning or value is not exhausted by the internal play of signifiers, but rests on the alterity of material elements in relation to themselves resulting from an interminable extrinsic relationship which makes *signs* out of things and *alters* them in relation to their own identity. Interpretation or deciphering are played out between this identity and this alterity of signs in relation to themselves and the closed group that they constitute.

— In these conditions, the text emerges from univocity and it is a bid for power if one claims that it is univocal, either by isolating it from the history, drives or idiosyncracies of the interpreter, or by deciding, just as arbitrarily, that, as a 'structure', it contains its own code. For the philologist, there is no unique truth in the text, to the extent that the text does not only depend on itself and does not specify its code: to interpret is to study the always uncertain compatibility of the virtual codes and internal value of signs. But this compatibility can scarcely be objectively determined, since the text can be a symptom of the referentially assignable power that invests it and cannot be abstract, like an object of reading, from the reader's codes, or the drives which the reader invests, without which it would not exist as a sign, but only as a simple object. If it is to be read, the text *makes a sign* to the reader, who must not only know the text, but interpret it. The task, therefore, consists in reducing plurivocity by referring to the text's signifying materiality,[7] after having first, conversely, sought to develop the plurivocal semantic charge: an antinomical labour of reduction and surpassing.

Charles Andler, recalling that philology is, in the strict sense of the German usage, 'the science of classical antiquity', proposes to translate 'philologist' as 'humanist',[8] an allusion to the Renaissance attempt to establish a link between antiquity and modern times. But he took good care not to forget that philology is also, even for Nietzsche, a science, that is both historical and linguistic (underlined by the French meaning of the word): he concludes that, for Nietzsche, 'humanism understood in the sense of philology should be both the science and the art of living',[9] a discipline that is torn between science and the search for meaning, technique and philosophy. It is in accordance with one of the demands of philology that Nietzsche quit philology for philosophy, and remained a philologist while ceasing to be one. It really is being 'tortured on the wheel'.[10]

None the less, to the extent that the philologist is not or not yet the philosopher also demanded by his task, he is first and foremost a *sage*: when faced with risking interpretations, he must adopt a negative task of *preservation*, which his scientific training allows him to adopt, and he must first of all struggle to determine structurally the differences within the text itself prior to referring it to something other than him. Philology is a *Wissenschaft*: a group of different forms of knowledge. Knowledge of what?

Philology is primarily founded on a knowledge our age would call *linguistic*. But Nietzsche is above all located in a critical philological position *vis-à-vis* modern culture when it is considered a language to be deciphered and demystified. He intends: (1) to show, through *deciphering*, that morality and metaphysics are *masked* discourses of the body, and operate according to roles of deformation that can be seen philologically; (2) to *criticize* linguistically the relationship between the word and the body or reality as illustrated by metaphysics and morality: philology then becomes a critique of a *false* interpretation of reality.

Such is the meaning of the remark that closes the First Essay of the *Genealogy of Morals*, in which Nietzsche speaks of physiology and medicine as complementary to one another:[11]

The philosophy department of some leading university might offer a series of prizes for essays on the evolution of moral ideas. Perhaps my present book will help to encourage such a plan. I would propose the following question, which deserves the attention of philologists, historians, and philosophers alike, *What light does the science of linguistics, especially the study of etymology, throw on the evolution of moral ideas?* However, it would also be necessary for that purpose to enlist the assistance of physiologists and medical men. This can be most fittingly accomplished by the professional philosophers who as a body have shown such remarkable skill in the past in bringing about amicable and productive relations between philosophy, on the one hand, and physiology and medicine, on the other. It should be stressed that all tables of values, all moral injunctions, with which history and anthropology concern themselves, require first and foremost a physiological investigation and interpretation and next a critique on the part of medical science. The question 'What is this or that table of values really worth?' must be viewed under a variety of perspectives, for the question 'valuable to what end?' is one of extraordinary complexity.[12]

When he gives the programme of his 'critique of moral values', Nietzsche refers the evaluation of the value of these values back to *genealogy*, while he reserves the task of the *interpretation* and unmasking for *philological* reading:

> We need a critique of all moral values; the intrinsic worth of these values must, first of all, be called to question. To this end we need to know the conditions from which those values have sprung and how they have developed and changed: morality as consequence, symptom, mask, *tartufferie*, sickness, misunderstanding; but also, morality as cause, remedy, stimulant, inhibition, poison. Hitherto such knowledge has neither been forthcoming nor considered a desideratum.[13]
>
> It should be obvious that all that matters to a psychologist of morals is what has really existed and is attested by documents, the endless hieroglyphic record, so difficult to decipher, of our moral past.[14]

The body 'causes' the text, forces it to 'be born'; it is the soil on which the text 'grows' – but it can only be *read* there.[15]

Let us note: (1) that the genealogist's typological evaluation is always preceded by a reading that deciphers; (2) that Nietzsche substitutes terms taken from philology's vocabulary (reading, interpreting, deciphering, meaning, etc.) for terms that are generally used in scientific, historic and philosophical explanations (judging, understanding, examining, estimating, determining, explaining, knowing, reasons, etc.). Nietzsche presents his point of view as an interpretative perspective:

> A kind of sturdy peasant simplicity ... believes even today that everything is in good hands, namely in 'the hands of God'. ... They project their own honourable stupidity and goodness into the heart of things ...; we others – we read something else into the heart of things.[16]

This erroneous interpretative refraction is a *reading* of a text: 'we read disharmonies and problems into things because we think *only* in the form of language'.[17] Thus three levels can be distinguished:

(a) *level I*: Nietzsche reads a text, culture, morality;
(b) *level II*: morality is an interpretative discourse (false, defective, inexact, abusive);
(c) *level III*: this moral discourse is the interpretation of *reality* which itself is still a *text*.

And the whole of Nietzsche's philological struggle aims to denounce the falseness or the arbitrary nature of the interpretations as well as the *confusion* of these different levels, of interpretation with explanation, of interpretation with text.[18]

It is this that is shown by the text-programme in which Nietzsche denounces morality as an interpretation (level I), one that is, moreover, defective, confusing its interpretation (level II) with the text of nature (level III) which it is reading:

> You must pardon me as an old philologist (I) who cannot refrain from the maliciousness of putting his finger on bad arts of interpretation (II and III); but 'nature's conformity to law' of which you physicists speak so proudly (II), as though (III) – it exists only thanks to your interpretation (II) and bad 'philology' (III) – it is not a fact, not a 'text', (III) but rather only a naïve humanitarian (II) adjustment and distortion of meaning (III). ... But, as aforesaid, that is interpretation (II), not text ...; and someone could come along who, with an opposite intention and art of interpretation (I), knew how to read (I and II) out of the same nature and with regard to the same phenomena the tyrannically ruthless and inexorable enforcement of power-demands – an interpreter (I and III) who could bring before your eyes the universality and unconditionality of all 'will to power'

(III) in such a way that almost any word (II) and even the word 'tyranny' (II) would finally seem unsuitable (I and III) or as a weakening and moderating metaphor (I and III) – as too human – and who (I and III) none the less ended by asserting of this world (III) the same as you assert of it (II), namely that it . . . is the only interpretation (III and I) – and you will be eager enough to raise this objection? (III or I) – well, so much the better (III and I instead of II).[19]

This paradigmatic text treats certain phenomena of modern culture, not as deformations or errors of *language* in relation to the *facts* of reality, but as an erroneous *interpretation* of a *text*: an interpretative gloss in relation to a faithful interpretative discourse. From this point on what we are substituting is not the so-called objective reality of natural laws – naive realism – but another interpretation that is faithful to the text. Reality is not what we try to *see* behind the interpretation, but what is necessarily offered up to the *interpretative wondering* of reading. There is no 'true world' hidden beneath the text's appearance: there is only an enigmatic text to be interpreted.[20] Thus, Nietzsche declares in *Ecce Homo* that he has 'spelt out' (*buchstabiert*) *décadence* from one end to the other and in both senses.[21]

As philologist one sees *behind* the 'sacred books', as physician *behind* the physiological depravity of the typical Christian. The physician says 'incurable', the philologist 'fraud'.[22]

One cannot read these Gospels too warily: there are difficulties[23] behind every word. (They are the) false-coinage of word and attitude as an *art*, . . . the art of holy lying.[24]

In nearly every philosopher, the use of a precursor and the struggle undertaken with him is unrigorous and unjust. They have not learned to *read* and interpret *correctly*. Philosophers underestimate the difficulty of really understanding what someone else has said and do not pay attention. This is why Schopenhauer formed a completely false idea of Kant and Plato. Usually, artists also read badly, with their penchant for allegorical and inflated explanation.[25]

And more generally:

Linguistics helps to prove that man has completely and falsely named nature: but we have inherited these terms, and the human

spirit has grown from these mistakes, which have nourished it
and given it strength.[26]

This is why 'morality consists of words'.[27] Also:

> Honesty demands that instead of the vague high-sounding moral
> vocabulary we normally use, we call by their names only those
> elements that are recognizable and dominate in a mixture of
> things, even if these dominating elements have up until now had
> a bad reputation.[28]

In *Beyond Good and Evil*, §20, Nietzsche shows how the philosophical order is structured by grammar and linguistic relations,
which are themselves founded on physiological evaluations,
such that we can propose the formula: physiology → grammar
(language) → philosophy.[29] This leads to the following:

> The clue to the correct explanation was furnished me by the
> question 'What does the etymology of the terms for good in
> various languages tell us?' ... Here we have an important clue to
> the actual genealogy of morals.[30]

Nietzsche substitutes hearing for vision:

> 'Your eyes must grow accustomed to the fickle light. ... All
> right, tell me what's going on in there, audacious fellow; now I
> am the one who is listening.'
>   'I can't see a thing, but I hear all the more. There's a low
> cautious whispering in every nook and corner. I have a notion
> these people are lying. All the sounds are sugary and soft. No
> doubt you were right; they are transmuting weakness into
> merit.'
>   'Go on.'
>   'Impotence, which cannot retaliate, into kindness; pusillanimity
> into humility; submission before those one hates into obedience
> to One of whom they say that he has commanded this submission –
> they call him God.'[31]

This text marks the return of words that present the moral ideal as a
language to analyse: *heissen, sagen, lügen, reden, Worte*, etc., and the
inverted commas indicate a discourse. Nietzsche does not ask:
'What is morality, virtue, etc.?', but 'what is the meaning (*was
bedeuten*) of ascetic ideals?', something repeated by the first paragraphs of the Third Essay of the *Genealogy*, which deals with the

'meaning' of such and such a phenomenon (Wagner, Schopenhauer, Luther).[32] The reason is that morality is a certain way of speaking, of naming in order to evaluate,[33] of interpreting:

> *There are no moral facts whatever.* ... Morality is only an interpretation of certain phenomena, more precisely a *mis*interpretation. ... To this extent moral judgement is never to be taken literally: as such it never contains anything but nonsense. But as *semiotics* it remains of incalculable value. ... Morality is merely sign-language, merely symptomatology: one must already know *what* it is about to derive profit from it.

Morality is a language, with its 'formulae',[34] which have to be deciphered, interpreted, and 'translated':

> As soon as their instincts begin to speak, as soon as they moralize.[35]
>
> He is unknown to himself, so he interprets himself in this way. – Morality is the only scheme of interpretation by which man can endure himself.[36]

Nietzsche resumes his undertaking as follows:

> My attempt to understand moral judgments as symptoms and sign languages which betray the processes of physiological prosperity or failure, likewise the consciousness of the conditions for preservation and growth – a mode of interpretations of the same worth as astrology, prejudices prompted by the instincts (of races, communities, of the various stages of life, as youth or decay, etc.). Applied to the specific Christian-European morality: our moral judgments are signs of decline, of disbelief in life, a preparation for pessimism. *My chief proposition: there are no moral phenomena, there is only a moral interpretation of these phenomena. This interpretation itself is of extra-moral origin.*[37]

For:

> What is the meaning of the act of evaluation itself? Does it point back or down to another metaphysical world? (As Kant still believed, ... moral evaluation is an *exegesis*, a way of interpreting. The exegesis itself is a symptom of certain physiological conditions, likewise of a particular spiritual level of prevalent judgments: Who interprets? – Our affects.). ... I understand by

'morality' a system of evaluations that partially coincides with the condition of a creature's life.[38]

Whosoever articulates an exegesis, articulates a distortion: here between physiology and intellect. The moral is that it is our drives and the physiological aspect of our nature that speak, while masking themselves as such: '"Inner experience" enters our consciousness only after it has found a language the individual understands'.[39] The consequence of the fact that our relationship to reality passes through language is that our relationship to reality is falsified, *in a sense that Nietzsche assimilates to morality*:

> Against positivism, which halts at phenomena – 'There are only *facts*' – I would say: No, facts is precisely what there is not, only interpretations. We cannot establish any fact 'in itself'. . . . In so far as the word 'knowledge' has any meaning, the world is knowable; but it is *interpretable* otherwise, it has no meaning behind it, but countless meanings. – 'Perspectivism'. It is our needs that interpret the world; our drives and their For and Against.[40]

> Our values are interpreted *into* things. Is there then any *meaning* in the in–itself?! Is meaning not necessarily relative meaning and perspective?[41]

Significance, which seeks to isolate interpretation, therefore pre-supposes a hiatus between word and will, between text and 'body', between culture and what culture is a sign of. To the point that 'we set up a word at the point at which our ignorance begins, at which we can see no further, e.g. the word "I", the word "do", the word "suffer": – these are perhaps the horizon of our knowledge, but not "truths"'.[42] This leads to the general proposition:

> The will to power *interprets*: . . . it defines limits, determines degrees, variations of power. Mere variations of power could not feel themselves to be such: there must be present something that wants to grow and interprets the value of whatever else wants to grow. . . . In fact, interpretation is itself a means of becoming master of something.[43]

We can now understand Nietzsche's reading of morality:

> It assumes that man feels free and bad, which can only be due to a false, unscientific interpretation of his acts and feelings. It

introduces the notion of sin into one part of his acts, and the notion of the effects of divine grace into another. False psychology and the fanciful interpretation of motivation is the essence of Christianity.[44]

This is a fundamental remark:[45] Christianity is an error of interpretation and rests, as a historical movement, on a false interpretation by Paul of Jesus' message. Christianity teaches in principle 'a deceitful interpretation'.[46] 'Christians have unlearned how to *read*, and yet, what efforts Antiquity had made, with its philologists, to learn to do so! But the Bible!'[47] Nietzsche the philologist expresses his whole self in this criticism:

> Why did the Greeks exist? Why the Romans? – Every prerequisite for an erudite culture, all the scientific *methods* were already there, the great, the incomparable art of reading well, . . . the whole *integrity* of knowledge – was already there! . . . *All in vain!*[48]

This deformation of reality is possible because reality transcends itself as a sign. Firstly because there is no brute 'real' given for man. Humanity as the sum of evaluations, such as tradition, language, morality, etc., is always already there:

> To realize that what things *are called* is incomparably more important than what they are. . . . What at first was appearance becomes in the end, almost invariably, the essence and is effective as such. . . . But let us not forget this either: it is enough to create new names and estimations and probabilities in order to create in the long run new 'things'.[49]

For Nietzsche, there is no direct access to the in-itself and no rational essence to the world, the latter being merely the thought but non-totalizable totality of our perspectives and interpretations.[50] Being is will to power. The world is an enigma because it offers itself up to interpretation to a will to power that, subjectively and objectively,[51] is multiple, in the process of becoming. Because of this, any text can only refer to what lies outside it in order to find its codes of decipherment: there is no closed system, or text implying its own code. Perspectivism implies the referential character that gives the text (a closed corpus) its opening and its infinite possible interpretative plurality. From this point on, there is no 'true world' that a unique and 'reasoning' 'subject' might explain: 'Interpretation, and *not* explanation'.[52]

The world's text: a will to power for wills to power, a group of signs of one or several wills for other wills of the reading body. For all that it is not a pure appearance, *Schein*, but a sign, *Erscheinung*.[53] For Nietzsche the philologist the text is located between the impossible unique code that is axiomatically univocal (pure idealist thingism) and total undifferentiated wandering. To interpret is to read dangerously. If we must have what Nietzsche calls a '*ephexis* in interpretation', the text must be 'deciphered' and not 'falsified'.[54]

The text creates a sign equivocally but resists: '[It] cannot be deciphered simply by reading it off; this is only the beginning of the work of interpretation proper. . . . One skill is needed – *lost* today, unfortunately – for the practice of reading as an art: the skill to ruminate'.[55] To read reality is never to have finished (*fertig werden*) with the text, to be 'slow'.[56] We search slowly for what is not *nothing*, and we slowly seek only what is never *given* to immediate intuition. The philologist's slowness is the same as Ariadne's in the labyrinth: we can get lost,[57] but there are paths.

The art (*kunst*) of interpretation, or the art of reading[58] is not a simple technique. The corollary to this is that there is a difference between interpretation and text, without which reading would be a simple mechanical activity. We will establish a contrast, not between true interpretation and false interpretation, but between: (1) plural interpretation and dogmatic interpretation (the type that does not recognize itself to be an interpretation made against the backdrop of a plurality, but presents itself as the unique and absolute truth of the text); (2) strong interpretations and weak interpretations, quick and patient interpretations, poor and rich interpretations, superficial and genealogical interpretations, naive and profound interpretations. If there is no single true interpretation, there are none the less 'abusive' interpretations: '*schlechte Interpretationskünste*', '*Sinnverdrehung*'.[59] We can read (*herauslesen*) in nature something other than what is read in it by a 'defective philology'.

Not that all interpretations are arbitrary, but nature is not, as the science of physicians would have it, liable for a single explanation that coincides with its object: nature. It therefore enlarges the possibility of apprehension while limiting their status: '*nur Interpretation*'. Therefore Nietzsche concludes: 'Granted this too is only interpretation – and you will be eager enough to raise this objection? – well, so much the better'. He means that the wandering of interpretation, including his own, the gap between reading and the text, in so far as they multiply perspectives, are preferable, in their very precariousness, to the dogmatic reabsorption of the enigmatic text of nature into an 'explanation'. There is no truth in itself for nature as a text, not even a 'subjective' truth which this text has for a 'subject', there are only readings, perspectives, a poetic *fantasizing* approach to the text. Here Nietzsche is very Kantian, with the difference that he substitutes *Dichtung* for *a priori* concepts and forms. He begins, for example, by criticizing the concept of free will exactly as Kant excluded the phenomenal knowledge of noumenal freedom, as being *Missbrauch*,[60] and he concludes:

> One ought not to make 'effect' *into material things*, as natural scientists do (and those who, like them, naturalize in their thinking), in accordance with the prevailing mechanistic stupidity . . . one ought to employ 'cause' and 'effect' only as pure *concepts*, that is to say as conventional fictions for the purpose of designation, mutual understanding, *not* explanation. In the 'in itself' there is nothing of 'causal connection', of 'necessity', of 'psychological unfreedom'; there 'the effect' *does not* 'follow the cause', there is no 'law' rules. It is *we* alone who have fabricated causes, succession, reciprocity, relativity, compulsion, number, law, freedom, motive, purpose; and when we falsely introduce this world of symbols into things and mingle it with them as though this symbol-world were an 'in itself', we once more behave as we have always behaved, namely *mythologically*.[61]

An interpretation is only a truth for a reader, because it is founded on signs,[62] and cannot coincide with the text, in the same way that the phenomenon does not become confused with the thing-in-itself.[63] 'If phenomena are things in themselves, there is no place left for freedom',[64] and in the same way, in Nietzsche, if interpretation is confused with the text, reality escapes the will to power, through its univocity, and interpretation no longer points to signs, but only to things. In this domain one must 'abolish knowledge' (of the text) 'in order to secure a place for belief' (as interpretation), for the risks of interpretation.[65]

And yet, while freeing the text's plurivocity, Nietzsche maintains the opposition between 'arbitrary' interpretations and philologically correct interpretations, and even demands that we refer interpretations back to 'the primitive texts':

> This worthy verbal pomp too belongs among the ancient false finery, lumber and gold-dust of unconscious human vanity, and that under such flattering colours and varnish too the terrible basic text *homo natura* must again be discerned. For to translate man back into nature; to master the many vain and fanciful interpretations and secondary meanings which have been hitherto scribbled and daubed over that eternal basic text *homo natura*.[66]

The responsibility for this falls on philology (genealogical and philosophical). If the goal of this science is semantic, Nietzsche's philology relies first of all on an objective approach to language.

This is the heart of the problem of culture for Nietzsche: the critique of morality. What does Nietzsche understand by this term? It is the ultimate principle of what constitutes metaphysics as a weak and illusory interpretation of reality. But morality (and with it metaphysics) is a language that is ill constructed, demented or impertinent. Not only does it not refer back to what it wishes to designate but, more profoundly, its signifiers are deprived of any referent: the moral signified is a nothingness that is put in place of reality. Nietzsche affirms that morality is a negation of reality (life), and, vice versa, that the signifiers (concepts, notions) of morality are forms of nothingness (*nihil*, fictions, illusions). Morality is an 'imaginary' discourse.[67] Such an affirmation presupposes, on the one hand, a reality against which we should have to measure the pertinence of moral language and, on the other hand, a language that already exists or is to be invented, which would act as a yardstick.

But we have seen that reality can only be deciphered via a language. And this language, which is supposed to be more suitable, had to be invented. Moreover, it turns out that *any* language is suited to reality, in other words, is moral and metaphysical. Nietzsche is therefore led to a critique of language as such: language, as something seductive (*verführend*), creates fictions that wipe out the reality of becoming, relations of force and the will to power. Nietzsche, therefore, would either have to forge a new extra-moral language, which is to attempt the impossible, or else refer to a reality outside language, which is an admission of

philosophical failure and, moreover, would contradict his philological apriorism. Caught between mystifying life and placing an
exclusive confidence in the power of language to reveal the reality
of life, or between the Schopenhauerian or 'nihilist' problem of the
illusion of phenomena and the idolatry of the word that characterizes the moral ideal, Nietzsche can only choose a 'Kantian' kind
of way out. But this implies: (a) that he must produce a new type
of language that is forever threatened by silence or inanity of sound;
(b) that he ultimately denies language any ontological significance.

In this 'impossible discourse', the use of inverted commas
illustrates Nietzsche's ambiguous position. It occurs too frequently
for us not to consider it a significant constant in an author who
wrote on the march. It has two different merits.

Firstly, for Nietzsche, it indicates that he is quoting reported
words or passages, above all in order to mark the difference
between his own discourse and a foreign discourse, between metalanguage and language. And while it is rare for Nietzsche to use
inverted commas to designate well-known expressions or quotations from famous authors,[68] he uses them very frequently for the
key terms relating to morality. He wishes to stress that these
expressions are improper, if not vulgar, slang, obscene or incorrect:
he knows that they 'set the wrong tone' and that the 'fault' is not
his. In the cases of lexical impropriety, Nietzsche supplements the
inverted commas with terms like '*nennen*', '*heissen*', '*sagen*', ('*named*',
'*called*', '*said*') in order to distance himself from a common designation: 'Finally, humanity called his despair and impotence "God"'.[69]
'It is a *falsification* of the facts to say: the subject "I" is the condition
of the predicate "think"'.[70] '"God", "beyond", "self-denial" – all
of them negations (*lauter Negationen*).'[71] 'These words "altruistic
instinct" sound to my ears like "wooden iron".'[72] 'It is an
unexampled misuse of words when such manifestations of decay
and abortions as "Christian church", "Christian faith" and
"Christian life" label themselves with that holy name.'[73] 'Perhaps
Luther's greatest merit was to have had the courage of his sen-
suality (in those days one spoke, delicately enough, of "evangelical
freedom").'[74] 'The honourable term for *mediocre* is, of course, the
word "liberal".'[75] 'The tartuffery called "morality".'[76] '"Innocence":
that is their name for the ideal state of stupefaction; "blessedness":
the ideal state of sloth; "love": the ideal state of the herd animal that
no longer wants to have enemies.'[77] 'Let us not forget those

auditory hallucinations which, as "Socrates' demon", have been interpreted in a religious sense.'[78] 'Those things which mankind has hitherto pondered seriously are not even realities, merely imaginings, more strictly speaking *lies* from the bad instincts of sick, in the profoundest sense injurious natures – all the concepts "God", "soul", "virtue", "sin", "the Beyond", "truth", "eternal life".'[79] '"*A drive (Antrieb) at best*" – a phrase used for "resigning" (*Abtritt*).'[80]

It is, in fact, *the whole of language* that, according to Nietzsche, has to be placed within inverted commas:

Language depends on the most naive prejudices (. . .) and thus (we) believe in the 'eternal truth' of 'reason' (e.g. subject, attribute, etc.).[81]

The mechanistic concept of 'motion' is already a translation of the original process into the sign language of sight and touch. The concept 'atom', the distinction between the 'seat of a driving force and the force itself', is a sign language derived from our logical-psychical world. We cannot change our means of expression at will: it is possible to understand to what extent they are mere signs. The demand for an adequate mode of expression is senseless: it is of the essence of a language, a means of expression, to express a mere relationship. – The concept 'truth' is nonsensical. The entire domain of 'true-false' applies only to relations, not to an 'in-itself'. – There is no 'essence-in-itself' (it is only relations that constitute an essence –), just as there can be no 'knowledge-in-itself'.[82]

Nietzsche provides several examples:

'Attraction' and 'repulsion' in a purely mechanistic sense are complete fictions: a word.[83]

We set up a word at the point at which our ignorance begins, at which we can see no further, e.g. the word 'I', the 'do', the word 'suffer': – these are perhaps the horizon of our knowledge, but not 'truths'.'[84]

'Immediate certainty', like 'absolute knowledge' and 'thing in itself', contains a *contradictio in adjecto*: we really ought to get free from the seduction of words.[85]

Are we not permitted to be a little ironical now about the subject as we are about the predicate and object? Ought the philosopher not to rise above the belief in grammar? All due respect to governesses: but is it not time that philosophy renounced the beliefs of governesses?[86]

Through words and concepts we are still continually misled into imagining things as being simpler than they are, separate from one another, indivisible, each existing in and for itself. A philosophical mythology lies concealed in *language* which breaks out again every moment, however careful one may be otherwise. Belief in freedom of will – that is to say in *identical* facts and in *isolated* facts – has in language its constant evangelist and advocate.[87]

Every word is a prejudice.[88]

Language belongs in its origin to the age of the most rudimentary form of psychology: we find ourselves in the midst of a rude fetishism when we call to mind the basic presuppositions of the metaphysics of language which is to say, of *reason*.[89]

Speech, it seems, was devised only for the average, medium, communicable.[90]

How many ills have for example been caused by the mummified error covered by the word 'abstraction'![91]

The 'miracle' only an eror of interpretation? A lack of philology?[92]

Can Nietzsche get reality to speak without falsifying it? Inverted commas point up the fact.

Secondly, Nietzsche uses inverted commas to show the gap that exists between language in general and his own language. He has recourse to the language accepted, one that is to his eyes the most metaphysical of all: German. This leads to the frequent use of words borrowed from other languages. In doing this, Nietzsche re-speaks a moral language: because new words are lacking, he uses the old ones *in inverted commas*, which is a silent way of carving out a gulf between himself and metaphysics on his own ground. With these inverted commas, Nietzsche tries to break the charm (*Verführung*) of his own 'anti'-metaphysical discourse. If for example 'true' and 'false' are metaphysical, unusable notions, Nietzsche cannot use them against metaphysics:

From the standpoint of morality, the world is false. But to the extent that morality itself is a part of this world, morality is false.

... 'Truth' is therefore not something there, that might be found or discovered – but something that must be created and that gives a name to a process.[93]

Through using inverted commas, Nietzsche brings forward two uses of the concepts of truth which he wants to show as being different. So here again, Nietzsche forbids us to speak of 'world' in general, but writes: 'Do you know what "the world" is for me?'[94] He criticizes the notions of being and identity: '*In a general sense, we can admit nothing of being*, because then becoming loses its value. . . . This hypothesis of being is the source of every calumny as regards the world',[95] but he writes: 'Do you want a *name* for this world? . . . *This world is the will to power – and nothing besides!*'.[96] And we can quite clearly spot this double game of saying and unsaying in this text from 1887–8:

> There are no ultimate durable unities, no atoms, no monads: here again 'being' has been first of all introduced by us. . . . It is our *irreducible need for conservation* that leads us constantly to posit a less refined single world from what remains, 'things', etc.[97]

Or again in these texts:

> That which is called *idol* on the title-page is quite simply that which has hitherto been called truth.[98]

> One trips over truths. . . . Only I have the standard for 'truths' in my hand. . . . The *oblique* path – it was called the 'path to truth'.[99]

Finally, we can observe how Nietzsche tries to confer another meaning on an expression used in accepted philosophical language when he challenges Rousseau in this way:

> *Progress in my sense.* – I too speak of a 'return to nature', although it is not really a going-back but a *going-up* . . .: Napoleon was a piece of 'return to nature' as I understand it. . . . – But Rousseau – where did *he* really want to return to? . . . Even this abortion recumbent on the threshold of the new age wanted a 'return to nature'.[100]

However, the critique of moral language by Nietzsche is necessarily double: (a) It is philological (or linguistic), but it is primarily formal (or 'structural'), though it cannot be only this. (b) But in the genealogical project, in so far as Nietzsche tries to 'deabsolutize' moral language and unveil the semantics of morality, this critique becomes the referential or 'semiotic' deciphering of morality. From this point on, the latter is no longer the closed system of a language studied as such, but a 'symptomatology':[101] it is no longer a system of internal differences, but the reported text of its pseudo-autarky to the body of which it is the symptom. It is here that philology comes within a hair's breadth of physiology and dispossesses itself of its prerogatives: the *critique* of language makes way for the *deciphering of a relationship* to the body.

As a philologist, Nietzsche has recourse to the linguistic disciplines (rhetoric, stylistics, grammar, lexicography, phonology). But, as a genealogist and physiologist, he must invent a new type of research, and reorient the meaning of existing disciplines. It is here that Nietzsche offers the most original contribution, that of a series of mixed disciplines: the etymology and history of the language, the semantics of translation and transposition, the theory of the rhetoric of the will to power. For reasons of clarity, we shall follow successively these two aspects of a psychophysiophilology.

Nietzsche's goal is to show how, far from presenting pure Ideas that are useful as *models* of conduct, morality presents only signs, and therefore that moral discourse does not correspond to a 'natural language' which alone has 'true' words at its disposal.

His goal, therefore, challenges the thesis presented by Cratylus in Plato's dialogue: 'An original soundness in naming things exists, which belongs by nature to each reality'.[102] 'The thing that tends to characterize soundness is the aptitude for revealing the nature of each reality.'[103] He maintains, like Hermogenes, the 'conventional'[104] or arbitrary nature of 'names'. This is what he repeats in his works, where we find only one reference to the problem outlined in *Cratylus*:

> In the past, it seemed that, in comparison with language, we could not deduce it from the nature of things. The arbitrary (*willkürliche*) attribution of the names already in Plato's *Cratylus*: this point of view in fact presupposes a language prior to language.[105]

If there is no natural language, morality as a language system will be just one language among others. Nietzsche therefore studies its linguistic structure first of all, then launches himself into a comparative study of 'moral language' and what it designates, under different labels, as correct language. But by placing himself in a philosophical perspective, Nietzsche adopts less the descriptive position of the linguist than the *normative* position of the 'grammarian', the lexicographer, the rhetorician, and the stylist – in short, the Professor – which, in a more or less openly semantic move, aims to hold on to moral language, less for a dialect than for a parasitic language, a linguistic deviation. He therefore corrects the grammatical exercises of morality, but with the difference that 'true' grammar remains to be defined.[106]

This deviation would be merely an accident, analogous to a mistake in pronunciation or a lapse or grammatical 'fault', if it were not for the fact that its universality can be attested: morality is more than a deviation in dialect, or a chance fault, it is a language, a definite corpus used by a definite group. It is in this sense that Nietzsche isolates it as an object of study for the philologist. But, contrary to the properly linguistic objective point of view, Nietzsche isolates its pertinent characteristics in order to bring out their anomaly: the attitude of the *evaluating* philosopher or philologist. It is important not to erase this trait, which in Nietzsche complements the critique of values, even if there is a tendency to forget Nietzsche's normative will and concentrate on his critique of norms (including grammatical and semantic norms), and even if this appeal to the philological norm is surprising: for it is as if Nietzsche were describing a writer's idiosyncratic language, a dialect[107] or a slang in relating them back, in a way that seems incongruous to us, to an assignable scientific 'truth' or a correct expression.[108]

'Morality exists only in words.'[109] The whole of moral discourse is imaginary and its elements, functioning and structure reflect this flaw: 'What, then, is this struggle of the Christian "against nature"? Do not let us be deceived by his words and explanations!'.[110] And Nietzsche adds, in order to give a 'psychological' explanation of this Christianity, that the terms in question are founded on the denegation (*verleugnen*) and repression (*vernichten*) of desire, which permits the (false) interpretation of nature and desires.

> I rebel against the translation of reality into a morality: therefore I abhor Christianity with a deadly hatred, because it created sublime words and gestures to throw over a horrible reality the cloak of justice, virtue and divinity.[111]

Therefore:

> The church believes in things that do not exist, in 'souls'; it believes in effects that do not exist, in sin, in redemption, in the salvation of the soul: it stays everywhere on the surface, at signs, gestures, words to which it gives an arbitrary meaning.[112]

> The [good man] invents (*erfindet*) actions *that do not exist*: altruistic, holy acts; faculties *that do not exist*: 'the soul', 'the spirit', 'free will'; beings *that do not exist*: 'saints', 'God', 'angels'.[113]

There is a flaw of integrity in the interpretation of reality:

> All these epileptic saints and visionaries did not possess a thousandth of the rigorous attitude towards oneself displayed by today's philologist in order to read a text or examine the truth of an historic event. ... Compared to us, they are moral cretins.[114]

Here are some examples evoked by Nietzsche:

> 'Causality' eludes us; to suppose a direct causal link between thoughts, as logic does – that is the consequence of the crudent and clumsiest observation. ... 'Thinking', as epistemologists conceive it, simply does not occur: it is a quite arbitrary fiction. ... The 'spirit', something that thinks: where possible even 'absolute, pure spirit' – this conception is a second derivative of that false introspection which believes in 'thinking': first an act is imagined which simply does not occur, 'thinking'.[115]

> 'Mechanical necessity' is not a fact: it is we who first interpreted it into events. ... Only because we have introduced subjects, 'doers', into things does it appear that all events are the consequences of compulsion exerted upon subjects – exerted by whom? again by a 'doer'.[116]

> Nature ... measures the world according to magnitudes posited by itself – such fundamental fictions as 'the unconditional', 'ends and means', 'things', 'substances', logical laws, numbers and forms.[117]

> My basic idea: the 'unconditioned' is a regulating fiction to which we can attribute no existence ... Like 'being', 'substance', every thing that does not have to be drawn from experience, but that in fact have been extracted from it by an erroneous *interpretation* of that experience.[118]

The places of origin of the notion of 'another world': the philosopher, who invents a world of reason, where reason and logical functions are adequate: this is the origin of the 'true' world; the religious man, who invents a 'divine world': this is the origin of the 'denaturalized, anti-natural' world; the moral man, who invents a 'free world': this is the origin of the 'good, perfect, just, holy' world.[119]

We have not got away from the habit into which our senses and language seduce us. Subject, object, a doer added to the doing, the doer separated from that which it does: let us not forget that this is mere semeiotics and nothing real.[120]

First proposition: There are no moral actions whatsoever: they are completely imaginary. ... Through a psychological misunderstanding, one has invented an *antithesis* to the motivating forces. ... According to the valuation that evolved the antithesis 'moral' and 'immoral' in general, one has to say: there are only immoral intentions and actions. ... The psychological error out of which the antithetical concepts 'moral' and 'immoral' arose is: 'selfless', 'unegoistic', 'self-denying' – all unreal, imaginary.[121]

By way of résumé, to use a hypothesis that was very early on coined by Nietzsche, 'morality is an *interpretation* of physical instincts',[122] but an interpretation whose terms covers 'pipe dreams' (*Einbildungen*).[123]

Here, then, is a language that is stripped in the main (its key words) of real correlate. We could compare it to a poetic language, if its distinctions were not 'harmful', or to the empty workings of a formal language, like mathematics, if Nietzsche did not add (a) that this language is badly constructed, (b) that the imaginary nature of its signifieds can be deduced from certain qualities on the part of its speakers (as opposed to logic or mathematics, where they are abstract) or from the instincts of the group producing the language: a genealogical and psychological analysis articulates what makes it *displaced* in relation to reality. 'Displaced' rather than 'badly constructed' for, as a corpus corresponding to a typology, moral language, a truly formal and stereotyped language, is in certain respects well constructed, like any language: it says what it wants to say, does not say what it does not want to say and, through its connotation, indicates that it belongs to a 'physiological' group and type that deny reality. It is genealogy in the proper sense.

The fact that this language is displaced in relation to reality is indicated in several convergent remarks made by Nietzsche. They are of several types: stylistic, rhetorical, grammatical (syntactical), phonological, lexical.

From lapses in 'taste' to characterized misinterpretations, Nietzsche hunts down examples of non-sense and stylistic failings. Prior even to retranslating them back into a 'suitable' language, that of physiology, Nietzsche picks out tropes and deviations, and on each occasion more or less implicitly contrasts them with a concrete expression: 'We know well enough how offensive it sounds when someone says plainly and without metaphor that man is an animal'.[124]

Here are some examples of his denunciation of stylistic flaws or improper rhetorical figures:

Event and necessary event is a tautology.[125]

Transcription of the proposition, 'I, Plato, *am* the truth'.[126] People like to call Brahms the *heir* of Beethoven: I know no more cautious euphemism.[127]

All names of good and evil are images: they do not speak out, they only hint. He is a fool who seeks knowledge from them.[128]

One does not say 'nothingness': one says 'the Beyond'; or 'God'; or '*true* life'; or 'Nirvana', 'redemption', 'blessedness'. . . . This innocent rhetoric from the domain of religio-moral idiosyncrasy at once appears *much less innocent* when one grasps *which* tendency is here draping the mantle of sublime words about itself.[129]

Love is the state in which man sees things most of all as they are *not*. The illusion-creating force is there at its height, likewise the sweetening and *transforming* force.[130]

Evil according to the code of rancour . . . is precisely the good one of the opposite code, that is the noble, the powerful – only coloured, reinterpreted, reenvisaged.[131]

By which means does a virtue come to power? – By exactly the same means as a political party: the slandering, inculpation, undermining of virtues that oppose it and are already in power, by rebaptizing them, by systematic persecution and mockery. Therefore: through sheer 'immorality'. What does a desire do with itself to become a virtue? – Rebaptism; systematic denial of its objectives; practice in self-misunderstanding; alliance with existing and recognized virtues; ostentatious hostility against their opponents. Where possible it purchases the protection of sanctifying powers; it intoxicates, it inspires; the tartuffery of idealism.[132]

Moral rhetoric is determined by desires, which try to *euphemize* what is felt to be a forbidden aggression and to *slander* the thing against which aggression shoves desire. Rhetoric expresses the speaking subject's *affectivity*. Toning something down means evaluating it positively in order to impose one's own desire in spite of the internal or external interdictions; blackening something means slandering in order to acquire power. Rhetoric always comes under the domain of 'psychology' (or genealogy). This is why, for Nietzsche, language, as a closed system, does not exist: it expresses and hides what lies outside of it. Morality, on the other hand, pretends to essentialize words and concepts.

Any formal analysis of language in Nietzsche is provisional. 'The spell of definite grammatical functions is in the last resort the spell of *physiological* value judgements.'[133] To speak is to signify affects, and the study of language allows the philologist-psychologist to rediscover them:

> *The things people call love.* – Avarice and love: what different feelings these two terms evoke! Nevertheless it could be the same instinct that has two names – once deprecated. . . . and the other time seen from the point of view of those who are not satisfied but still thirsty. . . . Our pleasure in ourselves tries to maintain itself by again and again changing something new into *ourselves*; that is what possession means. . . . One can also suffer of an excess – the lust to throw away or to distribute can also assume the honorary name of 'love'. When we see somebody suffer, we like to exploit this opportunity to take possession of him; those who become his benefactors and pity him, for example, do this and call the lust for a new possession that he awakens in them 'love'.[134]

The link between 'words' and 'desire', 'naming', and 'pleasure' or 'need' is explicit in two posthumous fragments:

> Everyone desires that no doctrine or valuation of things should come into favor but that through which he himself prospers. The basic tendency of the weak and mediocre of all ages is,

consequently, to weaken and pull down the stronger: chief means, the moral judgment. The attitude of the stronger toward the weaker is branded; the higher states of the stronger acquire an evil name.[135]

In the new Testament, and specifically in the Gospels, I hear absolutely nothing 'divine' speaking: much rather an indirect form of the most abysmal rage for defamation and destruction – one of the most dishonourable forms of hatred. ... Clumsy abuse of all kinds of philistinism; the entire treasury of proverbs is laid claim to and fully utilized.[136]

And Nietzsche adds:

This was the most fatal kind of megalomania there has ever been on earth: when these lying little abortions of bigots began to lay claim to the words 'God', 'Last Judgment', 'truth', 'love', 'wisdom', 'Holy Spirit' and with them made a boundary between themselves and 'the world'; when this species of man began to reverse values according to his own image, as if *he* were the meaning, the salt, the measure, and the standard of all the rest – one should have built madhouses for them and nothing more.[137]

Rhetoric is not innocent:

The *firmness* of your moral judgment could be evidence of your personal abjectness, of impersonality; your 'moral strength' might have its source in your stubbornness – or in your inability to envisage new ideals. And, briefly, if you had thought more subtly, observed better, and learned more, you certainly would not go on calling this 'duty' of yours and this 'conscience' of yours duty and conscience. Your understanding of *the manner in which moral judgments have originated* would spoil these grand words for you, just as other grand words, like 'sin' and 'salvation of the soul' and 'redemption' have been spoiled for you.[138]

Among these little accidents and 'matches' I include so-called 'purposes' as well as the even much more so-called 'vocations': they are relatively random, arbitrary, almost indifferent. ... Is the 'goal', the 'purpose' not often enough a beautifying pretext, a self-deception of vanity after the event that does not want to acknowledge that the ship is *following* the current into which it has sailed accidentally? that it 'wills' to go that way because it – must?[139]

We can therefore understand the 'grand style': style is related to affects and is supposed to translate them without any turgid rhetoric: 'Compact, severe, with as much substance as possible, a cold malice towards 'fine words', also towards 'fine feelings'.[140] This is a constant refrain in Nietzsche:

> I am full of defiance and malice towards what is called the 'Ideal': my pessimism consists in having recognized the way in which 'sublime feelings' are a source of misery, that is to say of man's belittlement and abasement. We deceive ourselves whenever we hope for 'progress' in an ideal: up until now, an ideal's victory has always been a regressive movement. Christianity, revolution, the abolition of slavery, philanthropy, a love of peace, justice, truth: all these big words are valuable only as banners to be waved in a struggle: certainly not as realities, but only as terms of pomp for something else altogether (if not the opposite!).[141]

> *Critique of grand words.* – 'Freedom' for *will to power*, 'Justice', 'Equal rights', 'Fraternity', 'Truth' (in sects, etc.).[142]

It is not at all surprising, then, that Nietzsche's opposition to Christianity is translated into a critique of the New Testament's *style*: whether posthumous or published, these texts are innumerable.[143] Nietzsche reads the New Testament (or Wagner, who is also attacked for his style, or lack of style[144]) as a text in which only effect is aimed at, whose style is pompous, vulgar, and a reflection of the 'washouts' who wrote it: 'bad taste', 'rococo', 'verbosity' (*GM*,III, §22) as opposed to the heroic 'grandeur' ('judeo-heroic': *NCW*, Music without a future) of the Old Testament. 'Rhetoric', viewed as an excess or seduction (*Verführung: WP*, §210) in relation to pure simplicity and a vigorous style therefore indicates a sickness 'of the soul' or of 'improper' desires.[145]

Lack of skill is only one feature: morality moves easily from a general turgid style to the specific negative cases of it, such as slander and deceit which, philologically, are misinterpretations or a grammatical form of error:

> The idealist: a creature that has good reasons to be in the dark about itself and is prudent enough to be in the dark about these reasons too.[146]

> *Christ's error.* – The founder of Christianity thought that there was nothing of which men suffered more than their sins. That

was his error. ... But the Christians have found a way of vindicating their master since then and of sanctifying his error by making it 'come true'.[147]

Words trick you, but most often they do so in a favourable way: in this context, Nietzsche therefore uses the related terms *Verführung* and *heiligen*:

> *Morality as a means of seduction.* – Compare the related logic of *Luther*. A pretext is sought to introduce an insatiable thirst for revenge as a moral-religious duty. Hatred for the ruling order seeks to sanctify itself – (the 'sinfulness of Israel': foundation of the power of the priest). Compare the related logic of *Paul*. It is always God's cause in which these reactions come forth, the cause of right, of humanity, etc. Even in the case of the *anti-Semites* it is still the same artifice: to visit condemnatory judgments upon one's opponent and to reserve to oneself the role of *retributive justice*.[148]

This *Verführung* is directed towards a positive or negative dissimulation (sanctification and transfiguration or defamation):

> An ideal that wants to prevail or assert itself seeks to support itself (a) by a spurious origin, (b) by a pretended relationship with powerful ideals already existing, (c) by the thrill of mystery, as if a power that cannot be questioned spoke through it, (d) by defamation of ideals that oppose it, (e) by a mendacious doctrine of the advantages it brings with it, e.g. happiness, repose of soul, peace or the assistance of a powerful God, etc.[149]

> To say that what matters is not whether a thing is true or not but how it acts shows an absolute lack of intellectual probity. Anything is good, deceit, slander, the most brazen travesty, if it serves to raise the level of the moral temperature to the point where one 'believes'. There is a real school of *means of seduction* that win you over to belief. ... We must note: (1) the passionate heat of 'love' (based on ardent sensuality); (2) the absolute *vulgarity* of Christianity: its endless exaggerations and prattling; its lack of cold intellect and irony; its total lack of martial bearing in every instinct; its priestly bias against virile pride, sensuality, the sciences, the arts.[150]

> A collective defamation of whatever is not themselves.[151]

Masterstroke: to deny and condemn the drive whose expression one is, continually to display, by word and deed, the antithesis of this drive.[152]

Natural inclinations *are* satisfied, but under a new form of interpretation, e.g. as 'justification before God', 'the feeling of redemption through grace' (– every undeniable pleasant feeling is interpreted thus! –), pride, voluptuousness, etc. General problem: what will become of the man who defames the natural, and denies and degrades it in practice? In fact, the Christian proves himself to be an exaggerated form of self-control: in order to restrain his desires he seems to find it necessary to extirpate or crucify them.[153]

Do not let us be deceived by his words and explanations.[154]

The relation between word and drive is one of denial. But, on the grammatical level, negation is seen by Nietzsche as a *semantic* error. This is an interesting criticism to note, and one that parallels Nietzsche's accusation that morality improperly fixes *meaning*, by means of language. If the text does not have a single meaning: 'the same text allows us to make innumerable interpretations: there is no "just" interpretation',[155] all meaning (*sens*) is not dissolved away into the fluence of arbitrariness, since Nietzsche's examination of morality uncovers a number of misinterpretations (*contresens*: literally, counter meanings). 'Morality is only an interpretation of certain phenomena, more precisely a *mis*interpretation'.[156] This is why the moral judgement 'as such . . . never contains anything but nonsense'.[157]

What kind of misinterpretation are we dealing with? As if it were not from the first an utterly fruitless undertaking to try to unite 'classical' and 'German' in one concept![158]

'German spirit': for eighteen years a *contradictio in adjecto*.[159]

Philosophers have had from the first a wonderful capacity for the *contradictio in adjecto*.[160]

Modern ideas, false ideas. 'Freedom', 'equal rights', 'humanity', 'compassion', 'genius'. A democratic misinterpretation (*Missverständnis*) (a consequence of *milieu*; the spirit of the times). A pessimistic misinterpretation (an *impoverished* life, detachment from 'will'). A *décadent* misinterpretation (neurosis), 'the people', 'the race', 'the nation', 'democracy', 'tolerance', 'the *milieu*', 'utilitarianism', 'civilization', 'the emancipation of women', 'popular culture', 'progress', 'sociology'.[161]

Morality is only an interpretation of certain phenomena, more precisely a *mis*interpretation.[162]

What are we dealing with? Religious misunderstanding. Moral misunderstanding. Philosophical misunderstanding. Aesthetic misunderstanding.[163]

I have already defined the *modern* as physiological self-contradiction.[164]

Now everything is false through and through, mere 'words', chaotic, weak or extravagant.[165]

Everything of Christianity I have seen seems to me a contemptible verbal ambiguity.[166]

Whoever has theologian blood in his veins has a wrong and dishonest attitude towards all things from the very first. . . . Out of this erroneous perspective on all things one makes a morality, a virtue, a holiness for oneself, one unites the good conscience with seeing *falsely* – one demands that no *other* kind of perspective shall be accorded any value after one has rendered one's own sacrosanct with the names 'God', 'redemption', 'eternity'. . . . Wherever the influence of the theologian extends *value judgement* is stood on its head, the concepts 'true' and 'false' are necessarily reversed: that which is most harmful to life is here called 'true', that which enhances, intensifies, affirms, justifies it and causes it to triumph is called 'false'.[167]

Is moral language a load of twaddle? No: Nietzsche isolates it as a unit by allotting it to a certain regulated operation and to a designated group of speakers who understand one another. Moral language has a certain syntax, that of popular grammar, but it is strange to the extent that it joins together imaginary notions. The difficulty that exists linguistically in conceiving of an *erroneous grammar* brings to the fore the referential and semantic conception that Nietzsche has of grammar and philology.

What poverty there is among all the earlier philosophies, once language or at least grammar and the whole of what they retain of their 'people' no longer whispers their words to them! Words harbour truths, or at least certain presentiments of the truth: that is the reason for their stubborn belief. This creates the tenacity they display in hanging on to notions like 'subject', 'body', 'soul', 'spirit'.[168]

(To say) that when there is thought there has to be something 'that thinks' is simply a formulation of our grammatical custom that adds a doer to every deed.[169]

Except for governesses who even today still think of grammar as a *veritas aeterna*, and consequently look on the subject, the attribute and the complement in the same way, there is no-one innocent enough to go along with Descartes in positing the subject 'I' as being the condition of the verb 'think'.[170]

Our oldest metaphysical grounding is the one we shall get rid of last of all, always supposing that we succeed in getting rid of it. This find is one that was incorporated into language and grammatical categories and became so indispensable that it seemed we should have to stop thinking, if we were to renounce such a metaphysics.[171]

I fear we are not getting rid of God because we still believe in grammar.[172]

The snares of grammar (the metaphysics of the people).[173]

Morality relies on the structure of grammar more than the meaning, and that is why it can handle fictions, which Nietzsche calls 'a religious–moral nomenclature'.[174] Naming is an abstraction constructed from a *referential* illusion, which we shall study later, and can be viewed as a lexical confusion. This is the principle of moral language: consequently 'name' and 'call' (*heissen, nennen*) are some of the most frequently used terms in Nietzsche's language when he is evoking morality as a language. But to the erroneous (correctable) designation is added the 'creation' of a word that serves to ontologize the nothingness. In these two respects, naming supports desire. It is therefore as much a Babel (in the eyes of Nietzsche who makes himself the representative of an exact language and a precise lexicality) as a creation *ex nihilo*, through which the *nihil* of nihilism imposes its imaginary.

To the extent that everything big and strong has been conceived by man as *superhuman, strange,* man has grown smaller. He has separated two faces from one another, one of them pitiful and weak, the other strong and astonishing, and created two distinct spheres, the first of which he calls 'man', the second 'God'. And he has continued with this, in the period of moral idiosyncrasy, he has not interpreted his elevated and sublime moral states as being 'willed', as the 'work' of his person. The Christian equally decomposes his own personality into one petty and feeble fiction which he names 'man' and another which he names 'God' (Saviour, Messiah).[175]

It is misleading to call the *Leid* (suffering) we may experience at such a sight, and which can be of very varying kinds, *Mit-Leid* (pity) . . .: how coarsely does language assault with its one word so polyphonous a being! . . . They are a *different* kind of egoists from the men of pity; – but to call them in an exceptional sense evil, and men of pity good, is nothing but a moral fashion which is having its day.[176]

When an instinct *intellectualizes itself*, it takes on a new name, a new charm, a new price. We often contrast it with the instinct that was its first degree, as if it were the opposite.[177]

The world of appearances and the world *invented by deceit*: it is antithesis: the latter was up until present named the 'true world', the 'truth', 'God'. It is the *former* we must abolish.[178]

As for denouncing confusion, we read such denunciations on every page: 'what is familiar is known'.[179] 'Scientifically in your sense (you really mean, mechanistically?).'[180] 'The so-called "good conscience", a physiological condition sometimes so like a sound digestion as to be mistaken for it.'[181] Deaf (*dumpf*) desires, what others call the "ideal".'[182] '"God" is today no more than a pale (*verblichen*) word, not even a concept.'[183] 'Following the same emotional logic, all pessimistic religions bestow upon nothingness the title of God.'[184] '"Wanting to urinate" means first of all that there is oppression and constraint, then a means to free oneself from constraint, then a normal way of using this means once reason has suggested it. In themselves this oppression and constraint have nothing to do with relieving the bladder: they do not say "I want", only "I am in pain".'[185] 'This abominable exasperation of the pathological egoism of peoples and races, which lays claim these days to the term "grand politics".'[186] 'Up until now truth was called *deceit*.'[187] 'The notion of *free will* has little meaning: one says "yes" to what one *is*, one says "no" to what one is not.'[188]

We say people are good when they follow their heart, but also when they obey only duty; people are good when they are mild, conciliatory, but also when they are courageous, inflexible and harsh; people are good when they do not consider themselves, but also when they surpass themselves as heroes; when they are the unconditioned friend of truth, but also when they are pious, and glorify things; when they obey themselves, but also when they are dutiful; when they are people of noble quality, but also when they do not scorn and do not look up; when they are good-natured and avoid conflict, but also when they wish for war and victory; when they always want to be first, but also when they do not want to push ahead of anyone else.[189]

Nietzsche, who was fond of word-games and was a metrician philologist, pays great attention to the phonological aspects of these confusions, which often rest, according to him, on a pun or homonymous relationship between signifiers. He thus anticipates certain linguistic analyses made by Freud in *The Interpretation of Dreams* and *Jokes and their Relation to the Unconscious*. Only, far from reducing the unconscious to the phonic play of the signifier, he always refers phonological play back to moral man's search for an end, one in fact founded on drives. It is in this way that he speaks of the 'jangle of moral expressions',[190] and the 'rub-a-dub of justice, wisdom, holiness, virtue'.[191] For 'the person for whom current prejudices do not begin to emit a paradoxical sound (*Klingen*) has not yet stopped to think'.[192] It is this phonological category of confusion that contains certain famous examples of ambiguity that cover a confusion in one's drives, examples such as '*Ja/Ye-a*',[193] '*gerecht/gerächt*'[194] or again '*lieben/leben*',[195] '*Brecher/Verbrecher*',[196] or '*Schleiermacher*'.[197]

In the event, these would only be gratuitous verbal games if Nietzsche did not bring to the fore what he calls the

machiavellianism of power (*unconscious* machiavellianism): the *will to power* appears; (a) to the oppressed, slaves of all sorts, as a will to '*freedom*': the act of *freeing oneself* seems the only goal (from a moral and religious point of view: 'responsible to one's own conscience', 'evangelical freedom', etc.); (b) to a stronger species that grows in power, as a will to supremacy; if initially without success, then by restricting themselves to the will to '*justice*' . . .; (c) to the strongest, richest, most independent and brave, as a '*love* of humanity', the 'people', the Gospels.[198]

It would therefore be naive to lay the blame for verbal confusion on 'stupidity' or 'dullwittedness'. This is a deliberate 'ruse' on the part of drives which, beneath the ideal, aim for power. The play on words is a sign of the (underhand) game played by desires: naming, designation and the verbal hypostasis of fictions are ways in which one can reach a *goal* by confusing understanding: '*essential view*: "good" and "bad" qualities are at bottom *the same* – they rest on the same instincts of conservation, appropriation, choice, desire to reproduce, etc.'[199] To have something is to acquire power:

> Reality has been deprived of its value, its meaning, its veracity to the same degree as an ideal world has been fabricated. . . . The 'real world' and the 'apparent world' – in plain terms: the *fabricated* world and reality.[200]

> Fear is the mother of morality. . . . Everything that raises the individual above the herd and makes his neighbour quail is henceforth called *evil*; the fair, modest, obedient, self-effacing disposition, the *mean and average* in desires, acquires moral names and honours. . . . 'We wish that there will one day *no longer be anything to fear!*' One day – everywhere in Europe the will and way to *that* day is now called 'progress'.[201]

> [Language covers] crimes in psychology: (1) all *sadness* and all *unhappiness* have been falsified by an idea of wrong (of fault) . . .; (2) all *intense joys* . . . have been stigmatised as guilty, dangerous and suspicious; (3) everything great in man has been falsely interpreted as abnegation . . .; (4) *love* has been travestied as devotion (and altruism), when it is a conquest or a gift that results from the overabundant richness of the personality.[202]

Every appearance exists for morality. Such is the meaning of the frequent (and spicy!) use that Nietzsche makes of the verb 'to baptize' (*taufen*). And, as if to indicate the dialectical appearance, in the Kantian sense, that is carried over by a morality that confuses word and thing, he adds the (also Kantian) use of '*als*' or the conjunction '*als ob*'.

> It is on account of this their 'faith' that they concern themselves with their 'knowledge', with something that is at last solemnly baptized 'the truth'.[203]

Have all gods hitherto not been such devils grown holy and been rebaptized?[204]

Education means learning to rebaptize or to feel differently.[205]

Schelling baptized (a faculty for the 'supra-sensible') intellectual intuition, and therewith satisfied the most heartfelt longings of his Germans, which longings were fundamentally pious.[206]

All he has to do [is] exercise a little art of name changing in order to make them see as blessings things which hitherto they had abominated.[207]

The little rebellious movement which is baptized with the name of Jesus of Nazareth.[208]

What does *covetousness* do in order to become a *virtue*? It debaptizes itself; disavowing its intentions; practising misunderstanding on itself; allying itself with existing and recognized virtues; displaying hostility towards the enemies of such virtues.[209]

The Jewish priesthood had managed to present *everything* it claimed *for itself* as being a divine order or obedience to a divine law. . . . Everything that helped to preserve Israel and *facilitate* its existence . . . was seen not as natural but as coming from 'God' himself.[210]

Unfitness for power: one's *hypocrisy* and *prudence*: as (*als*) obedience (subordination, sense of duty, morality); as docileness, devotion, love . . .; as fatalism, resignation; 'objectivity'; self-tyranny . . .; as criticism, pessimism, indignation, teasing; as a 'saintly soul', 'virtue', 'self-deification', 'beyond', 'purity towards the world', etc.[211]

The three great naiveties: knowledge, the means to happiness (as if . . .); the means to virtue (as if . . .); the means to 'denying life' – to the extent that knowledge serves to disillusion us (as if . . .).[212]

The superior values . . ., these *social values* have been raised into a law above man, to give them more importance, as if they were God's commandment, 'realities', the 'true' world.[213]

As if the puny little soul, the virtuous average animal that is the gregarious form of man not only had pre-eminence over the stronger and more wicked type . . ., but also, in a general way, properly speaking represented for man the goal, the medium and supreme desirability.[214]

No signifier is obviously univocal, for Nietzsche, but this is precisely because it can be reinscribed within various configurations based on drives.[215] You have to be a metaphysician, says Nietzsche, to believe, while disguising the fact, in the absolutely arbitrary nature of the sign, which is useful only *in abstracto* to morality and science, both of which are complicit in the way they bracket off concrete temporality. A signifer, whether linked to a single and unique signified, as in morality, or isolated in abstract from any signified, can only be pure if it is abstracted from historical temporality and the *living* body.[216]

Nietzsche's analysis, above all from 1885 on, will unfold by having recourse to philological-type disciplines that are simultaneously *synchronic* (translation, the rhetorical theory of naming, denegation) and *diachronic* (etymology, the history of languages). But it will always involve referring back to the body outside the text.

Nietzsche can then put out hypotheses, on the basis of how language operates, about the laws governing how the 'body' operate, and the play of drives. But these intuitions will remain conjectural, since attributing a rhetoric to the body will amount to confusing sign with signified, and moralizing the body, a Schopenhauerian intuitive realism. So we see Nietzsche take note of this realism: the will to power is for him just 'a phrase to designate'[217] a process, and not the very essence of reality. Finally, the *semiotic* nature of moral language leads Nietzsche to avoid a vulgar physiological realism by using categories taken from philological deciphering in order to describe physio-logy. Nietzsche knows that it is just a *metaphor*, a working *a priori*, which he takes care not to confuse with the thing to which it applies. We can even wonder whether the basic problem for Nietzsche's philosophy is not the heterogeneity of language and the body, something Nietzsche the sick intellectual spent his whole life trying to resolve, using complex circuits that, as long as he wrote, could only belong to *language*.

Therefore, to attribute to Nietzsche, retrospectively, a 'rhetoric of the unconscious', in the event of the *Selbst*, is to go back towards the thing *in* language that reveals language's dependence on the body's reality.[218]

Etymology, translation and history are disciplines through which Nietzsche tries, in the field of morality, to link language to a bodily origin, a historical origin, the past or extra-linguistic referent.

Nietzsche fastens on to the general project of decoding terms. These designations are first of all pinpointed, so he can give the rules by which they operate and consequently translate them exactly into a proper language or, failing that, bring them back to reality by way of a referential gesture.

But the reality that Nietzsche sets up against morality is first and foremost the origin (*Ursprung*), history: that is why Nietszchean genealogy will be formulated along the lines of etymological research, the equivalent of 'the natural history of morals'.[219] And reality is also the body, the affects, the drives (psychology, physiology) acting as a foundation or source or origin (*Ursache, Grund, Herkunft, Abstammung*). For want of being able to reveal the body, Nietzsche will give a reading of it that essentially slips into the metaphorical vocabulary of filtration and engendering. Philological genealogy therefore ends up using physiological-type metaphors in order to *reach an origin*, and through these Nietzsche tries to pinpoint the meaning (but also to avoid the metaphysical value) of notions like those of cause, origin, foundation and derivation.

Freeing oneself from the *Verführung der Sprache*[220] essentially involves denouncing terms of designation in order to show how moral language deforms reality.

A. Nietzsche uses several *processes*. Firstly, inverted commas (*Gänsefüsschen*). As soon as Nietzsche theorizes the notion of morality in relation to language, his use of inverted commas becomes systematic. They are used[221] to signal: (1) a reported discourse; (2) an improper discourse (one that is asemantic, alexical, incorrect, vulgar or 'contemptible', or even 'imaginary'). The inverted commas indicate an other language, the language of the other: and this separation indicates less a difference in linguistic structure than a difference in drive-based typology. With inverted commas, we want to say *who* speaks: they are the badge of a certain *type* of person, the *cross* with which Nietzsche pinpoints the Christian moralist:

> Words are sounds, designating concepts; concepts, however, are more or less definite images designating frequently recurring and associated sensations, groups of sensations. To understand one

another it is not sufficient to employ the same words to designate the same species of inner experiences, we must ultimately have our experience *in common.* That is why the members of *one* people understand one another better than do members of differing peoples even when they use the same language; ... there *arises* from this a group who 'understand one another', a people ... the history of language is the history of a process of abbreviation [Abkürzung]. ... Exactly which groups of sensations are awakened, begin to speak, issue commands most quickly within a soul, is decisive for the whole order of rank of its values and ultimately determines its table of desiderata. A human being's evaluations betray something of the *structure* of his soul and where it sees its conditions of life, its real needs.[222]

To pinpoint *how* one speaks is to be able to say *who* is speaking. If inverted commas isolate a typology whose language betrays a structure, then Nietzsche bases the contrast between what is proper and what is improper (inverted commas) on the contrast between strong and weak, real and illusory. Moral language is an instrument used by the weak to gain power and consequently to reject reality. And it is because the weak person talks a great deal more than he acts that the dominant language is that of the weak, who in Nietzsche's eyes, are the ones who triumph. This creates the link between the struggles against weakness, morality and language.

Inverted commas, therefore, indicate that moral language is a discourse that has been *stripped of integrity*, because it is fashioned and spoken by weak people whose designations vary in Nietzsche according to the different examples (but also examples taken from one genre) that he evokes: the Christian, the metaphysician, the German, the priest, the scholar, etc. We can therefore understand very well why Nietzsche takes it out specifically on the Germans: it is both because they have in common certain sensations and value judgements (a cultural and physiological entity) and because they speak the same language. If Nietzsche insists on 'the arbitrary nature of interpretation'[223] in morality, it is in order to insist all the more – in contrast to the structural point of view that *isolates* the language of physiology, and so rigorously separates culture from 'nature' – on the *link* between the body and language in general that constitutes a language as a *cultural* phenomenon in the Nietzschean sense, as a mixture of nature (drives, sensations) and culture (signs).

For Nietzsche the physiologist, the arbitrary nature of the sign exists in an idealist abstraction, but on each occasion the necessity of meaning exists in relation to physiology.

'"German philosophy" – I hope you understand its right to inverted commas'.[224] 'The worst *mutilation* of man that one can imagine, being made out to be (*angeblich als*) a "good man".'[225] 'The domestication ("the culture") (*Kultur*) of man does not go very deep. ... Where it is deep, it immediately represents degeneracy (type: the Christian). "Savage" man (or, in moral terms, a *bad* man) represents a return to nature, and in a certain sense, the re-establishment of man, *cured* of "culture".'[226] 'The criminal use up until now of the word "truth".'[227] 'And an ideal of this type, raised above humanity in the form of a "God"!'[228] 'No trace of intellectual integrity – nothing but the "love of good".'[229] 'Nothing is more rare among philosophers than *intellectual integrity* ...: they know in advance what they have to demonstrate, one could say that they recognize one another as philosophers because of the way they agree about these "truths".'[230] 'Luther and his peers ... managed to put up with existence only by turning away from themselves, throwing themselves into their *opposite*, and living in *illusion* ("faith").'[231]

A lack of integrity is always accompanied by the invention of *imaginary* notions: §15 of *The Antichrist* gives a veritable anthology of these creations, and is peppered with vengeful inverted commas. But denunciations are not only applied to Christianity:

> 'Progress' is merely a modern idea, that is to say a false idea.[232]

> The concept of guilt and punishment, the entire 'moral world-order', was invented *in opposition* to science – *in opposition* to the detaching of man from the priest. ... When the natural consequences of an act are no longer 'natural' but thought of as effected by the conceptual ghosts of superstition, by 'God', by 'spirits', by 'souls', as merely 'moral' consequences, ... then the precondition for knowledge has been destroyed – *then one has committed the greatest crime against humanity.*[233]

> I traverse the madhouse-world of entire millenia, be it called 'Christianity', 'Christian faith', 'Christian Church', with a gloomy circumspection ...: there is no longer a word left of what was formerly called 'truth'. .... The priest knows as well as anyone that there is no longer any 'God', any 'sinner', any

'redeemer' – that 'free will', 'moral world-order' are lies. . . . We know, our *conscience* knows today – *what* those sinister inventions of priest and Church are worth, *what end they serve*, with which that state of human self-violation has been brought about . . . – concepts 'Beyond', 'Last Judgement', 'immortality of the soul', the 'soul' itself.[234]

The 'apparent' world is the only one: the 'real' world has only been *lyingly added*.[235]

A psychological error from which is born the idea of this *antinomy*: 'moral', 'immoral'; 'disinterested', 'altruist', 'devoted' – and all of that *unreal*, imaginary.[236]

However, the invention of the imaginary can only be accomplished by dissimulating reality. It is once again naming that, according to the logic of Nietzsche's metaphorical discourse, plays the role of travesty. Nietzsche puts word (naming) and dress together as a mask or pre-text and, conversely, compares philological suspicion and the demystification of designation to an unveiling, or 'discovery' (*Entdeckung*).[237] 'Luther's Reformation: coarsest form of moral mendaciousness under the guise of "evangelical freedom".'[238] This metaphor would merely reintroduce the metaphysical game of appearance versus reality were Nietzsche sometimes not to invert the classic relationship of the one to the other, by showing that it is not appearance that fails to be, but that it is reality of drives that is basically 'lacking' and has 'failed', and so needs a mask of words in order to give itself an essence: 'Where a man's inadequacies are to be found, there is an opportunity for imaginary ideals to appear'.[239] The word, like clothes, is the real lure in the lack attested to in the *zur* of *Wille zur Macht* (*Will to Power*). It is, therefore, a weak will that thinks it can fill this lack with the false fullness of a word; and a strong one that recognizes and perhaps even accentuates this lack of being and has no need, in order to 'be' (that is in order to become) for words to appear. This ambiguity in the use of language as a fiction (a fiction of being and a being in the mode of fiction) confirms the ambiguity of language itself (in Nietzsche's eyes) which can serve a weak, ontologizing will, or a strong will that tends towards accentuating appearance:

What do you suppose [a human being who has turned out badly] finds necessary, absolutely necessary, to give himself in his own eyes the appearance of superiority over more spiritual people and to attain the pleasure of an *accomplished revenge* at least in his imagination? Always *morality*; you can bet on that. Always big moral words. Always the rub-a-dub of justice, wisdom, holiness, virtue. Always the Stoicism of gesture. . . . Always the cloak of prudent silence, of affability, of mildness, and whatever may be the names of all the other idealistic cloaks in which incurable self-despisers, as well as the incurably vain, strut about. . . . And a confidential question: Even the claim that (philosophers) possessed *wisdom*, . . . has it not always been . . . *a screen above all?*[240]

But Nietzsche has underlined that if this is a need for 'reality that is lacking something',[241] it is a gratuitous game for a noble: 'Nobles, εσθλοί, people who are truthful, who do not need to disguise themselves'.[242]

Inverted commas indicate that appearances are deceptive. '"*Deus nudus est*", says Seneca. I'm afraid he is well wrapped up! Better still: "clothes maketh a man" applies to gods as well!'.[243] One of Nietzsche's favourite tasks consists in making a list of standard terms:

Impotence, which cannot retaliate, into kindness; pusillanimity into humility; submission before those one hates into obedience to One of whom they say that he has commanded this submission – they call him God. The inoffensiveness of the weak . . . given honorific titles such as patience; to be *unable* to avenge oneself is called to be *unwilling* to avenge oneself – even forgiveness (for they know not what *they* do – we alone know what *they* do). Also there's some talk of loving one's enemy – accompanied by much sweat.[244]

The whole of morality is therefore a verbal disguise,[245] and moral language a 'mascarade', a 'wardrobe'.[246] But when 'the European disguises himself *with morality*',[247] what does he travesty? Acts of feebleness, 'mediocrity', and ultimately a 'will' or 'drives' ('*weakness*, whether that weakness be called vice or virtue'[248]) that remain silent and hidden, for a priest, 'forbids any part of reality whatever to be . . . spoken of'.[249] Thus, 'the states . . . designated by the highest names are epileptoid states'.[250]

A relation must be established between the *denegatory* value of terms and *negative* drives, such as vengeance, hatred, contempt, condemnation, so that moral language is condemned to affirm a *euphemistic* fiction.[251] And Nietzsche is as sensitive to the falsity of affirming reality as he is to the falsity of denying it. Morality, for him, is a huge euphemism. And this is why Nietzsche not only attacks it as 'a lack of realism' but also as a hypo-critical dishonesty that blurs the categories of affirmation and negation, as a disappearance of rules that turns reality into a confused hustle and bustle:

> The hybrid European ... definitely requires a costume: he needs history as his storeroom for costumes. He realizes, to be sure, that none of them fits him properly – he changes and changes. ... Again and again another piece of the past and of foreignness is tried out, tried on, taken off, packed away, above all *studied* – we are the first studious age *in puncto* of 'costumes', I mean those of morality, articles of faith, artistic tastes and religions, prepared as no other age has been for the carnival in the grand style, for the most spiritual Shrovetide laughter and wild spirits, for the transcendental heights of the most absolute nonsense and Aristophanic universal mockery.[252]

> *Histrionics.* The colourfulness of modern man and its charm. Essentially concealment and satiety.[253]

> Moralistic verbal tinsel and valences of this sort ... are beautiful, glittering, jingling, festive words: (but) this worthy verbal pomp ... belongs among the ancient false finery, lumber and gold-dust of unconscious human vanity.[254]

> The modern spirit's lack of discipline, dressed up in all sorts of moral fashions. ... Confusion, the profuse chaos of symbols.[255]

Nietzsche therefore sets his heart on distinguishing between affirmation and negation, which is why he systematically removes the *tissues* of deceit represented by big words:[256]

> One should bring to light and honour the names of the instincts that are really at work here after they have been hidden for so long beneath hypocritical names of virtue.[257]

> We wish to saturate nature with humanity and save it from divine mumbo-jumbo.[258]

> Paralysis of will: where does one not find this cripple sitting today! And frequently so dressed up. ... There is the loveliest false finery available for this disease; and that most of that which appears in the shop windows today as 'objectivity', 'scientificality',

... merely scepticism and will-paralysis dressed up ... 'the barbarian' still – or again – asserts his rights under the loose-fitting garment of Western culture.[259]

Diligent in business – but indolent in spirit, content with your inadequacy, and with the cloak of duty hung over this contentment.[260]

Hatred of evil is the ceremonial cloak with which Pharisees travesty their personal antipathies.[261]

Courage confronted with one's own nature: dressing up in 'moral' costumes. – That one has no need of moral formulas in order to welcome an affect.[262]

The aesthetics of 'disinterested contemplation' through which the emasculation of art today tries, seductively enough, to give itself a good conscience.[263]

Your most secret tyrant-appetite disguises itself in words of virtue.[264]

The magnificent Sunday clothes of morality.[265]

It is the philosophy of disappointment that wraps itself so humanely in pity and looks sweet. ... They call it *l'art pour l'art*, 'objectivity'.[266]

We, too, associate with 'people'; we, too, modestly don the dress in which (*as* which) others know us, respect us, look for us – and then we appear in company, meaning among people who are disguised without wanting to admit it. We, too, do what all prudent masks do, and in response to every curiosity that does not concern our 'dress' we politely place a chair against the door.[267]

'Not to seek *one's own* advantage' – that is merely a moral figleaf for a quite different, namely physiological fact.[268]

I want to strip your masked values. Let me simply repay you for having wrenched off the cloak of your secrets. To tell the truth, I have seen you naked.[269]

On the other hand, Dionysus does not need words:

[I should like] to follow the human custom of applying to him beautiful, solemn titles of pomp and virtue. ... But such a god has nothing to do with all this venerable lumber and pomp.

'Keep that', he would say, 'for yourself and your like and for anyone else who needs it! I – have no reason to cover my nakedness!'[270]

This task is completed by undertaking to translate moral language. This undertaking is designed to restore meanings to moral confusion, and is the opposite of the task of naming, with the difference that it does not link together a name and a reality, but two signifiers, according to the order of genealogy. We shall see this later on. But how does naming work?

B. The *linguistic* modalities of naming are linked to its *genealogical* role. Nietzsche uses every mode of attribution: prepositions (*zu*, *als*), verbs (*nennen*, *heissen* and their derivatives or synonyms, such as *taufen*, *heiligen*, etc.):

> That your virtue is your Self and not something alien, a skin, a covering: . . . with others, their vices grow lazy and they call that virtue; . . . their brake they call virtue! And there are others who are like household clocks wound up; they repeat their tick-tock and want people to call tick-tock – virtue. . . . Truly, I have taken a hundred maxims . . . away from you.[271]

> The philosopher . . . knows how to discredit his opponents as 'seducers' and 'underminers': then he goes hand in hand with power. The philosopher in a struggle with other philosophers – he tries to compel them to appear as anarchists, unbelievers, opponents of authority.[272]

> *A sovereign instinct, a fixed hierarchy.* This is what we call a 'truth'.[273]

Attribution, like judgement, is the site of error;: but, if naming is false in relation to the 'nature' of its object, it is 'true' in relation to a will: 'We call something "good" or "bad" *in relation to ourselves*, and not in relation to the thing we are judging! The basis of "good" and "bad" is egoist!'[274] It is in this way we must understand the following terms:

> They do *not* call themselves the weak, they call themselves 'the good'.[275]

> 'Sin', the priestly version of that animal 'bad conscience' . . .; the patient has been transformed into a 'sinner'.[276]

The organization and concentration of the sick ... (the word *church* is the popular term for this grouping).[277]

Profound depression is how I generally describe what is commonly called 'religion'.[278]

To dignify vengeance by the name of justice.[279]

Mechanical activity. ... Nowadays it is spoken of rather dishonestly as 'the blessing of labour'. All [the priest] has had to do ... has been to exercise a little art of name changing in order to make (sufferers) see as blessings things which hitherto they had abominated.[280]

It is in *Zarathustra* that Nietzsche most often enters into the game of denouncing names, profiting, like the prophetic texts that inspire him, from ambiguities:

Weeds want to be called wheat![281]

Especially those who call themselves 'the good' did I discover to be the most poisonous flies: they sting in all innocence.[282]

Most of the terms used by Nietzsche to designate modes of naming and distorting are compound words preceded by particles that indicate the overturning, twisting and perversion of meaning, under the common rubric of what Nietzsche names the '*Verführung der Sprache*': *um-* and *ver-*, as well as the prefixes that designate rejection: *ab-*, or *weg-*.

Moral intolerance is an expression of weakness in a man: he is afraid of his own 'immortality', he must deny his strongest drives because he does not yet know how to employ them.[283]

The beyond as the will to deny reality of every kind.[284]

Morality as instinctive denial (*Verneinung*) of life.[285] A good man, who dodges reality through deceit (*Weglügner der Realität*).[286]

The ideal ...: one denies (*negiert*), destroys (*vernichtet*) ...: anti-nature ideal (*wider-natürlich*). ... *The three ideals*: (A) which *fortifies* (*Verstärkung*) life (pagan), (B) which *weakens* it (*Verdünnung*) (anaemic), (C)   which *denies* it (*Verleugnung*) (anti-nature). The 'divine state' manifested: in its supreme plenitude – in the subtlest choice – in the destruction and scorn (*Verachtung*) directed against life.[287]

The strength of a spirit could be measured by how much 'truth' it could take, more clearly, to what degree it *needed* it accentuated, veiled, sweetened, blunted and falsified.[288]

Who [is it] that is really evil according to the code of rancour[?] The answer is: precisely the good one of the opposite code, that is the noble, the powerful – only coloured, reinterpreted, reenvisaged.[289]

If German offers more opportunity to compose words from particles, it is in any case significant that Nietzsche uses or creates terms involving *ver*- which he especially intends for morality: *Verneiner, Verleumder, Vergifter* (D §8), *verhübscht, verrationalisiert* (KGW, VIII, 2, 9 (182)), *Selbstverstellung ins 'Heilige'* (D, §44), *Verlästern, verleugnen, vernichten* (WP, §228),[290] *Verleumdung, Verdächtigung, Verfolgung, Verhöhnung, Umtaufung* (WP, §311), *verfälschen, verdünnen, verjenseitigen, vergöttlichen, verschönen* (BGE, §59), *Veredlung, Verklärung, Verschönerung, Verfeinen* (BGE, §61), *vergessen, verstecken, verklären* (BGE, §187), *vergolden, vergöttlichen* (GS, §139). All these terms describe the processes of morality and 'Christian' metaphysics.[291] In the same sense, we find *umwerten* (WP, §226),[292] *umgestalten*,[293] *umtaufen, Umdrehung* (WP, §265).

The general law governing all three deformations is given by the word *Verneinung*. It is so systematically used, and in a sense that is so close to that of psychoanalysis, that it is tempting to link it to its use in Freud. The logic of the German language authorizes the analogy. Morality is a *denegation* of drives, disavowing the very thing it practises by a sort of denial or verbal transformation and deformation, confirming through this refutation the emergence of the desire that makes it exist and speak. Its language is thus constantly *negative* and *negating*, as shown in the overlapping use, in Freud and Nietzsche, of *Verneinung* and *Verleugnung*. The definition in *The Dictionary of Psychoanalysis* by Laplanche and Pontalis: 'Procedure whereby the subject, while formulating one of his wishes, thoughts or feelings which has been repressed hitherto, contrives, by disowning it, to continue to defend himself against it'.[294] can be juxtaposed with these analyses by Nietzsche:

Masterstroke: to deny and condemn the drive whose expression one is, continually to display, by word and deed, the antithesis of this drive.[295]

All the drives and powers that morality praises seem to me to be essentially the same as those it defames and rejects.[296]

Everywhere the real origin of morality is denied.[297]

And here are two examples of an application of this principle:

> Cruelty has been refined to tragic pity, so that it is denied the
> name of cruelty. In the same way sexual love has been refined to
> *amour-passion*; the slavish disposition to Christian obedience;
> wretchedness to humility; a pathological condition of the *nervus
> sympathicus*, e.g. to pessimism, Pascalism, or Carlylism, etc.[298]

> One had placed a prohibition upon all the strongest, most
> natural, indeed the only real drives – henceforth, in order to find
> an action praiseworthy, one had to deny the presence in it of such
> drives.[299]

Finally, Nietzsche distinguishes, like Freud, between denial and
denegation (*Verleugnung* and *Verneinung*) in this formula through
which he stigmatizes the deceit of 'faith' as an institutionalized
neurosis: 'I call a lie: wanting *not* to see something one does see,
wanting not to see something *as* one sees it'.[300]

Nietzsche thus re-enters the tradition by which moral philosophy
offers a critique of error and illusion, but he applies it to philosophy
and morality, on the basis of a Schopenhauerian metaphysics of
illusion. If he criticizes this illusion (which he extols, moreover, as
being a condition of life, this time following Schopenhauer in a
negative way), it is as negation that he criticizes it. But negation, as
a rejection, wears down the fundamental principle of life, which
Nietzsche substitutes for God in his imminent 'theodicy', and, as
denegation, offers the semblance of being affirmative. It is an *idol*.
We have elsewhere sketched a genealogy of this critique of idolatry:[301]
if Nietzsche's Hellenism goads him into valorizing appearance, it is
biblical Christianity that leads him to overturn idols and shams,
including those belonging to 'Christianity'. Finally, for Nietzsche,
morality is a nothingness. Nietzsche condemns it because this non-
being acts (negatively) on reality, and harms being, which implies a
positive causality: it *is*, while *not being*. Has Nietzsche read Plato's
Sophist? *Dubitandum*.

The philological denunciation of philology at all events presupposes a whole philosophy, which in truth has been barely
sketched, of reality and culture. Culture – morality, through its
linguistic qualities, being an exemplary case – is founded on a *verbal
illusion*, and is a 'mask', a 'coating', a 'skin': this supposes that

reality must be so hard[302] that it is *necessary* to mask it. This does not apply only in the case of weakness or falsity, in which case we may ask whether they are not as universal, as anthropological categories, as their theological equivalent, sin, which is conceived of as a creature's intrinsic incapacity to know the reality of good and evil. The same holds for the hypothetical *strong* man, for whom reality is '*schrecklich*' and '*fragwürdig*'.[303] The goal of morality is *consolation* and *justification*: it is the job of idols to furnish the moral 'truth' and the support of which man has been deprived. Like a biblical prophet, Nietzsche denounces these two functions. What motive, if not moral integrity, inspires him? If philology is not an absolute, but an instrument, what principle can justify this criticism, if not life which, taken as an absolute, can only play the role of a theological principle? By what right can one deny man (even moral man) justification or consolation, whether on the psychological level of health or the metaphysical level of theodicy? If the second interdiction evokes tragedy and its Hellenic symbols, the first seems to suggest a link with Nietzsche's Lutheran legacy. In both cases, as a comparison with Freud would confirm, Nietzsche is battling here, in the name of reality, against a pleasure principle, a primary process.[304]

It is not only *décadent* culture, but *all culture* that demands a delay or mask: 'Social custom demands that we put up with the displeasure of an unsatisfied need, and that desire knows how to *wait*. To be immoral, therefore, here means not to be able to put up with displeasure in spite of the thought of power laying down the law'.[305] In relation to this reality of social custom, morality is, at a second degree, what allows us to attain a certain satisfaction *in spite of* the obstacles. Morality is fundamentally a consolation, for Nietzsche,[306] an indirect way of expressing forbidden drives: 'Moral judgement brought to bear on men and things constitutes a consolation for the oppressed, the wretched, the victims of inner torment: a way of wreaking vengeance'.[307] It is once again in the posthumous fragments of *Daybreak* that we find one of Nietzsche's most penetrating propositions: 'The spirit men show in combating evil is lacking in their invention of joy; so it is that humanity as a whole has up until now never moved beyond the means of consolation'.[308]

Denegation, which is in this sense *paradigmatic of all culture*, is one of the privileged means of consolation: 'To refuse to see a bad thing, not to admit that it exists (*ableugnen*), to change its significance (*umdeuten*), to place one's intellectual honour in negation – a means of consolation (*Trostmittel*).[309] As Freud profoundly puts it, we must *defend ourselves* against reality: if denegation is not merely of a rhetorical nature, but is a defence mechanism in our drives, it is because reality is an enigma, a terror; in a word, *tragic*. From the Greeks, the Old Testament (above all Job), and Schopenhauer, Nietzsche retains the fact that reality wounds, and *he does battle with illusion* because it blinds us to reality: 'Religions, as consolations and relaxations, are dangerous: man believes he has a right to take his ease'.[310] 'A therapeutic *error*: instead of fighting weakness with a fortifying diet, we give it a sort of justification, moralization, that is to say, interpretation'.[311] The force of which Nietzsche speaks is merely the (problematic) response to the frustrating nature of reality. His project: 'My innovations: ... critique of morality, disintegration of the last consolation',[312] could in turn be merely negative. It none the less remains that he denounces morality as a consolation, a hiding place used to dispense with having to confront, modify or love reality. Consolation is obtained through the transfiguration, embellishment, denegation or ennobling of evil:

> Religion gives [ordinary man] an invaluable contentment with their nature and station, manifold peace of heart, an ennobling of obedience, one piece of joy and sorrow more to share with their fellows.[313]

> Christianity has been the richest treasure house of ingenious nostrums. Never have so many retoratives, palliatives, narcotics been gathered together in one place, never has so much been risked for that end, never has so much subtlety been employed in guessing what stimulants will relieve the deep depression, the leaden fatigue, the black melancholy of the physiologically incapacitated.[314]

Consolation consists in returning evil to a certain category – a projection of the primary process of the weak man's desire (the *Wünschbarkeit* constantly confronted by Nietzsche) – to a certain syntax applied to the world:

> In the inner psychic economy of the primitive man, fear of evil predominates. What is evil? Three things: chance, the uncertain,

the sudden. How does primitive man fight against evil? – He conceives it as reason, as power, even as a person. In this way he establishes the possibility of entering into a kind of treaty with it. ... Another expedient is to assert that its malice and harmfulness are merely appearance: one interprets the consequences of chance, of the uncertain and sudden as well meant, as meaningful. A third means; one interprets the bad above all as 'deserved': one justifies evil as punishment. *In summa one submits to it*: the whole religio-moral interpretation is only a form of submission to evil. – The faith that a good meaning lies in evil means to abandon the struggle against it. ... With the increase of culture, man can do without that *primitive* form of submission to ills (called religion or morality), that 'justification of evil'. Now he makes war on 'ills' – he abolishes them. ... Let us dwell a moment on this symptom of highest culture – I call it the pessimism of strength. Man no longer needs a 'justification of ills'; 'justification' is precisely what he abhors.[315]

This text clearly shows the link between consolation and justification. Nietzsche feels himself constrained to encapsulate his own conception, named 'a pessimism of force' within the genre of theodicy. This confirms how Nietzsche, though he may have gone astray, to some degree is still part of a classical problem which we call metaphysical: he says yes for the same reasons that made him say no, and so challenges the optimistic justifications of morality only through denegation:

This sort of person requires the belief in a 'free subject' able to choose indifferently, out of that instinct of self-preservation which notoriously justifies every kind of lie.[316]

[Religion gives] some transfiguration of the whole everydayness, the whole lowliness, the whole half-bestial poverty of souls.[317]

There are moralities which are intended to justify their authors before others; other moralities are intended to calm him and make him content with himself; with others he wants to crucify and humiliate himself; ... with others transfigure himself and set himself on high.[318]

Leave them their opinions and illusions with which they justify or hide from themselves their servile labour.[319]

The love of humanity[320] needs a justification – this justification is that *God ordained it.* It follows that every natural instinct in man (love, etc.) appears guilty in itself to him and recovers its rights only after it has been *denied* (*Verleugnung*), and then welcomed once more as obedience before God.[321]

Natural inclinations are satisfied all the same, but by adopting a new interpretation:[322] we interpret them, for example, as 'justification before God', the 'feeling of redemption through grace'. ... A general problem: what becomes of the man who blasphemes against nature, denies it (*verleugnet*) and neglects it in his practices? ... In order to control his desires, he appears to need to wipe them out (*vernichten*) or crucify them.[323]

One phrase was enough – 'evangelical freedom' – to enable every instinct that had reason to remain hidden to burst upon us like a pack of savage dogs, the most brutal needs to find the courage to affirm themselves and everything to appear justified. We avoided trying to understand the true nature of the freedom we wanted, we shut our eyes to ourselves. But shutting our eyes and moistening our lips with high-minded discourse did not prevent our hands from taking a secure hold wherever they could, or our bellies from becoming the god of the 'free Gospel' or all our vengeful and envious desires from satisfying themselves with an insatiable fury.[324]

The interpretation thanks to which the Christian sinner thinks he understands himself consists in trying to *justify* his lack of power and confidence. He prefers to think himself guilty rather than suffer for nothing; it is in itself a symptom of *décadence* to need such interpretations.[325]

C.   Since denegation (consolation and justification) creates an equivalence between the reality of drives and the way it is expressed 'through the language of morality', Nietzsche can now proceed to the opposite operation: *translation.*

Translation is the opposite of naming. The latter puts itself forward as a natural designation. Nietzsche, on the other hand, underlines the arbitrary nature of this operation (as opposed to the necessary nature of drives) and, at the same time, *re-establishes the semantic equivalences*, the value of words and morality that is derived from drives. He tries to relate moral vocabulary back to what determines its *structure* and even its *nature.* Far from insisting on the arbitrary nature of the sign (which has only an abstract worth), Nietzsche *joins* what morality tries to *separate* (in the event, nature and culture) on the basis of a principle of transformation that is itself generated by the logic of drives. Where superficial observations see only difference, Nietzsche pinpoints deep *grouping, genealogical* structures.

As a linguist working somewhere between deep and surface structures, Nietzsche is a genealogist strictly to the extent that he practises precisely what Chomsky will later call *generative* grammar: the procedure is identical – each tries to relate statements back to the deep processes that engendered them (the nature of the human spirit in Chomsky, the world of drives in Nietzsche, without either of them neglecting the importance of acquired 'cultural' factors). Nietzsche extols his own genealogical and philological abilities as a generative linguist when he writes: 'I have spelled ... out (the questions of *décadence*) forwards and backwards'.[326]

But the heterogeneity of drives and language once more emerges. Nietzsche does not translate from one language into a second language isomorphic to the first, he translates the language of morality, either into a language that is itself 'metaphysical', or into a 'language' that refers back to a heterogeneous referent: the 'language' of drives, 'physiology', the text of '*homo natura*'.[327] In addition to translation, which is a strictly linguistic operation, Nietzsche also has to have recourse to disciplines that try to relate language or language states to diachrony, history, etymological origins, as if relating a dialect to a dominant language and designating the structures and operations that governed the modifications of this dialect in relation to the language in question.[328] Nietzsche's language should therefore be a better constructed language, if that idea means anything, one more respectful of the text of reality,[329] while the words of morality 'become unusable'.[330] Nietzsche stresses this point: 'the terrible basic text of *homo natura* must again be discerned ... to translate man back into nature.'[331]

Therefore, we have a translation that is a transposition of one language into another 'language', but Nietzsche's translation *reworks* a moral translation *in reference to the text of reality*, without forgetting that the apparent isomorphism of the two languages does not prohibit the translation from being a *rereading*, a reinterpretation. To translate morality is to translate what it does not mean to say.

Therefore, in *The Antichrist*, Nietzsche begins with the principle that the priests have falsified the Jewish nation's past to their own profit: 'they translated their own national past *into religious terms*'

And he analyses from this point of view all the false denominations
on the part of the priests: 'the priest abuses the name of God: he
calls a state of society in which the priest determines the value of
things "the Kingdom of God". He calls the means by which such a
society is achieved or perpetuated "The will of God"'. Nietzsche
contrasts this with a *language* of reality: 'the *reality* displaced by this
pitiable lie'. By way of example of Nietzsche's line-by-line translation: 'to this end a "revelation" is required. In plain words: a great
literary forgery becomes necessary, a "sacred book" is discovered
... to *denaturalize* (life's natural events) – in his language to
"sanctify" them. ... Supreme law: "God forgives him who
repents" – in plain language: *who subjects himself to the priest'.*[332]

A punctilious philologist, Nietzsche never tired of correcting
incorrect expressions and translates them 'into a physiological
language'.[333] This is a retranslation into the *language* of reality ('*ins
Wirkliche übersetzt'*).[334] He tries to pass from an illusory language
(morality), not into reality, properly speaking, 'in itself' but into
another language, as is borne out by the use of inverted commas or
linguistic terms ('means', 'language', 'for', 'in terms', etc.). He
must 'translate man back *into terms* of nature and natural truth'[335]
and, conversely, 'if we want to formulate reality in morality' we
can translate in the opposite direction and 'translate into Christian,
Buddhist or Schopenhauerian'.[336]

> Read in cold blood, this means nothing more than 'We weak
> ones are, in fact, weak'. .... The subject, or in popular language
> the soul.[337]

> The egotism–altruism dichotomy takes possession of the human
> conscience; to use my own terms, it is the herd instinct that now
> asserts itself.[338]

> [He] feels his existence to be a state of distress (expressed in
> moral terms as a state of *injustice*).[339]

> The fact 'I am perishing' translated into the imperative 'you all
> *shall* perish'.[340]

> 'Christian' signifies raising to a principle the counterfeiting of
> psychological interpretations.[341]

> 'Innocence': that is their name for the ideal state of stupefaction;
> 'blessedness': the ideal state of sloth; the ideal state of the herd
> animal that no longer wants to have enemies.[342]

The 'other world', as it turns out from these facts, is *synonymous with non-being*, non-living, non-willing-to-live.[343]

[Christianity] is an absolutely arbitrary interpretation based on a scheme of *fundamentally different* needs: translated into the language of every *subterranean religion* already in existence.[344]

All this [Christian] *transformation* is a translation into the needs and on the level of comprehension of the age's *religious mass*.[345]

Instinct, or as the Christians call it 'faith', or as I call it 'the herd'.[346]

The Christian agitators known as the Fathers of the Church.[347]

For me to 'improve' means to tame, to weaken, to discourage, to effeminate, emasculate, sophisticate – in short, to 'make worse'.[348]

The 'real world' and the 'apparent world' – in plain terms: the *fabricated* world and reality.[349]

Pascal's maxim, 'We must stultify ourselves'. The result, in psychological and moral terms, is a self-abrogation, sanctification. In physiological terms, it is a hypnosis – the attempt to achieve for man something approximating the hibernation of certain animal species or the estivation of many plants in tropical climates.[350]

The concept 'unbeliever' (i.e. one who believes in *another* God).[351]

'Idealist' – (ideal-castrato).[352]

A faith (i.e. a self-deception, a madness).[353]

Recovery – in religious language: 'redemption'.[354]

The 'savage' (or, in moral terms, the evil man).[355]

To the extent that everything big and strong has been conserved by man as *superhuman, strange*, man has grown smaller. He has separated two faces from one another, one of them pitiful and weak, the other strong and astonishing, and created two distinct spheres, the first of which he calls 'man', the second 'God'. And he has continued with this, in the period of moral idiosyncrasy, he has not interpreted his elevated and sublime moral states as being 'willed', as the 'work' of his person. The Christian equally decomposes his own personality into one petty and feeble fiction which he names 'man' and another which he names 'God' (Saviour, Messiah).[356]

When it is trodden on a worm will curl up. That is prudent. It thereby reduces the chance of being trodden on again. In the language of morals: *humility*.[357]

L'art pour l'art means: 'the devil take morality!'.[358]

In Kantian terms, [these are] truths of *practical* reason. They know what they *have* to prove, they are practical in that – they recognize one another by their agreement over 'truths'. – 'Thou shalt not lie' – in plain words: *take care*, philosopher, not to tell the truth.[359]

Into the 'Beyond' – into *nothingness*.[360]

'Faith' means not *wanting* to know what is true. ... God (is) a word of the stupidist kind of accidental occurrence.[361]

'The truth exists': this means, wherever it is heard, *the priest is lying*.[362]

Christianized, that is to say *dirtied*.[363]

Revelation, that is the assertion that the reason for these laws is *not* of human origin, ... *tradition*, that is, the assertion that the law has already existed from time immemorial, that it is impious, a crime against the *ancestors*, to call it in question.[364]

The metaphysics of language – which is to say, of *reason*.[365]

Ignorance *in physiologis* – accursed 'idealism'.[366]

If we follow the well-ordered play of these equivalences, we can understand certain seemingly mysterious, posthumous texts, texts which form moral or linguistic compendia or glossaries of reality:

Are you saying that you believe religion is necessary? Be sincere! You believe only that the police are necessary.[367]

Pity, cruelty
Love, voluptuousness
Envy, ambition, emulation
Vengeance, justice
Ridiculous, original
Weakness, humility
Dissimulation, comedian
Murder, war
Rapine, cheating, merchant
Slave, soldier, public official

Madman, poet, saint
Wisdom, intelligence.[368]

What does this enterprise of systematic translation signify? That Nietzsche 'rebels against turning reality into a moral formula'. So saying, he sums up the meaning of his undertaking: 'This is why I am horrified by Christianity and vow it a mortal hatred, because it created sublime words and attitudes in order to cloak a terrifying reality with righteousness, virtue and divinity.'[369] He therefore uses philology as a weapon in order to retranslate (zurückübersetzen) morality into reality. However, Nietzsche does not intend to remain strictly on the level of language. 'Translation [is] a form of conquest':[370] to unveil the 'primitive text of *homo natura*' means to try to dis-cover reality in order to *recover* it. The states involve not just ways of speaking, but also ways of conducting oneself, *culture*, which the linguistic processes of translation allow us to understand better. Therefore, certain institutions are merely transpositions (Christianity, for example, in relation to more ancient religions) or euphemisms, terms, expressions, formulations, in short noble (denegatory) interpretations of drives and of reality in general:

Marriage: the authorized form of sexual satisfaction. War: the authorized form of the murder of your neighbour. School: the authorized form of education. Justice: the authorized form of revenge. Religion: the authorized form of a desire for knowledge ... what are all these excesses, if not the consequence of the fact that the *authorized forms* do not manage to satisfy all men? What is crime, if not being incapable or contemptuous of simulation, like a 'good' person?[371]

Translation would none the less remain purely 'conceptual' and would not achieve the 'active interpretation' required to find 'new goals'[372] – a new culture – if Nietzsche confined himself to linguistic equivalences. What Nietzsche aims to achieve through retranslation is less another 'proper' language (which is in any case problematic)[373] than what he calls reality:

What in fact guide the moralist are not moral instincts but the *instincts of décadence*, translated into the formulae of morality: he feels the growing uncertainty of instincts like a *corruption*.[374]

I try to show what instincts have been at work behind all these *pure* theoreticians – how all of them, subjugated by their instincts, have flung themselves on something that was *for them* 'truth', for them and them *alone*. The conflict of systems, including that of the theoretical systems of knowledge ... is a very precise conflict of instincts, such that the position of pure knowledge, or intellectual integrity is abandoned on the spot as soon as morality demands its own responses.[375]

But 'Has a *force* even been demonstrated? No, only *effects* translated into a completely foreign language'.[376] Thought and language merely '[translate] the "genius of the species" ... back into the perspective of the herd'.[377] And

> the species needs the weak, degenerate failures to perish. ... What is 'virtue', what is the 'love of humanity' in Christianity, if not this reciprocity of reservation, this solidarity among the weak, this obstacle to selection? What is Christian altruism, if not the collective egoism of the weak, which perceives that if everyone is concerned for the welfare of everyone else, each individual will be spared for longer?[378]

Philology, in the genealogical field, must therefore take account of society, drives, history – in brief of what, in language, is the expression of temporality: diachrony. This research into the 'natural *history* of morality' will be translated into analyses of the history of the language and the etymology.

D. The history of the language, etymology, diachronic linguistics. Genealogy consists in asking *from where an ideal comes*. Certain phrases express this question: 'Every conviction has its history and its primitive forms ... among these embryonic forms ... becomes a conviction ... what therefore brings about ... a history of intimate passion, at the origin of which we find deceit, its God'.[379] This enquiry must be led with the help of *physiology*. But, in accordance with the philological *a priori*, the genealogical and philological analysis must decode the origin from the linguistic point of view as a history of language and etymology. Nietzsche, when he tackles the genealogical question of origins, simultaneously invokes, in the *Genealogy of Morals*, both physiology *and* philology:

> The clue to the correct explanation was furnished me by the question 'What does the etymology of the terms for good in various languages tell us?' I discovered that all these terms lead us back to the same conceptual transformation. The basic concept is

always *noble* in the hierarchical, class sense, and from this has developed, by historical necessity, the concept *good* embracing nobility of mind, spiritual distinction. ... Here we have an important clue to the actual genealogy of morals; that it has not been hit upon earlier is due to the retarding influence which democratic prejudice has had upon all investigation of origins. This holds equally true with regard to the seemingly quite objective areas of natural science and physiology.[380]

Let us note, in the etymological remarks, the appearance of metaphors taken from genealogy in the primary sense: origin, filiation, engendering, heredity, growth, ground, fruits, etc. Etymology, the science of origins, evolution (*évolution*) and the history of language, establishes kinships and, like genealogy, insists on evolution, or becoming (*devenir*). *Like genealogy*, it therefore links words to their past and their bodily origin – the most commonly used words often having a 'bodily' origin:

> What separates us most radically from Platonism and Leibnizianism is that we no longer believe in eternal concepts. ... Philosophy, to the extent that it is scientific and not dogmatic, is for us merely the largest extension of the notion of 'history'. Etymology and the history of language have taught us to treat all concepts as having *become* so, and many of them as still in the process of becoming; in such a way that the most generous concepts, being *the most false* ones, must also be the most ancient. 'Being', 'substance', the 'absolute', 'identity', the 'thing' – thought at once and for all antiquity has invented these schemes which fundamentally contradict the world of becoming, but which seemed initially to correspond to it. ... It is only extremely slowly that we have come to recognize the multiplicity of different qualities in a single object; in the history of the human language, we still see a manifestation of the resistance to a multiplicity of epithets. ... The philosophers who have best reproduced in themselves the oldest instincts of humanity, its oldest anguishes and superstitions ... – in them we can speak of an atavism *par excellence* – have countersigned this confusion by teaching that it is precisely signs, or 'ideas' that are the true reality, an invariable and universally valid reality. ... The very words of the human language have for a long time seemed and still seem today to people not to be signs, but truths that are relative to the things they designate.[381]

It is indeed the genealogical and historical dimension (atavism, time, ancient, history) that Nietzsche underlines in this reference to etymology. For him, 'concepts and words are our inheritance from ages in which thinking was very modest and unclear'.[382] And morality is *par excellence* the legacy of ancient errors. However, etymology indicates the trace of affects to us in concepts: and it is in this way that words can provide a vehicle for a truth, not about things, but about the relationship between man and things. This must be the meaning of Nietzsche's recourse to etymology in the *Genealogy of Morals*. Nietzsche thus relates the word *sophos* back to *sapio*, being to *esse*, which he links with breathing,[383] traces *malus* back to μέλας (black), ἐσθλός (noble) back to ἐστὶν (is), *bonus* back to *duonus-duellum*,[384] and tries to show how words serving to designate values (good, bad, etc.) go back to terms designating *feelings*: which is the aim of genealogy.[385] 'We might classify human activities according to the number of words needed to define them; the more we need, the worse a sign it is for the activities.'[386]

It is certain instincts that lead us to inflate language and speak morally. When Nietzsche designates the whole range of morality, he uses the term *ideal*. When he defines this as 'untruthfulness in the face of necessity',[387] Nietzsche restates its kinship with language: '(it is) the penalty man pays for ... weariness [and] weakness'.[388] The ideal consists in 'transforming one's own Devil into one's own God'.[389] This is why 'it is where our deficiencies lie that we indulge in our enthusiasms'.[390]

Nietzsche has above all directed his criticisms against the Christian ideal, because it seemed to him to be typical of the way in which an ideal is formed and because it has been dominant in Western culture to the point of still determining modern ideals, even those that see themselves as challenging the Christian ideal.[391] But most of the commentaries on Nietzsche's critique of modern culture vie with one another in insisting on his critique of Christianity, accepting unquestioningly Nietzsche's definition of it and ignoring absolutely the texts, the history and so the true consequences of this critique for Nietzsche. His critique is applied, not just to 'Christianity', but above all to its avatars, which according to Nietzsche *are still Christian*: socialism, science, and the ideals allied to them. In view of the culture of Nietzsche's present readers, there is now a side-stepping attempt to deflect, not to say lead astray, Nietzsche's critique, and lead it towards what, from the point of view of *Kultur*, is a *caput mortuum*: Christianity. It is taken over by its updated equivalents: the vulgarized concepts of 'progressism' and the ideology of 'scientificity'. In showing that the kinship between the gregarious *décadent* and finalist rationality allows this ideal to persist in spite of its displacements, Nietzsche's critique confirms its untimely topicality.

Genealogical kinship is expressed philologically: it is a linguistically localizable isomorphism. From the genealogical point of view, the ideal, a rejection of the chaos of reality,[392] is a consolation. Fifty years later on, Freud confirms Nietzsche's genealogical intuition. The phrase: 'humanity as a whole has up until now never gone beyond the means of consolation'[393] finds an echo in 1930 in the ironic remark of a 'completely atheist Jew': 'I bow to their reproach that I can offer them no consolation: for at bottom that is what they are all demanding – the wildest revolutionaries no less passionately than the most virtuous believers'.[394]

We shall therefore find, in 'socialism' and 'science', the same statements (and in Nietzsche the same denunciations) from the idealist imagination, designed to justify and console:

> *More hidden forms of Christianity's worship of the moral ideal. The soft and weak idea of nature'* ... An attempt to decipher in nature itself this ideal of moral and Christian humanity, the Rousseauist idea of nature, as if nature were freedom, goodness, innocence, equity, justice, *idyll* – always, at bottom, the worship of Christian morality ... *the soft and weak idea of 'man'* as in Comte or Stuart Mill, pushed if possible to the point where it becomes an object of worship ... it is still the worship of Christian morality under a new name. .... *The soft and weak conception of 'art'*, a sympathy for everything that suffers and has been disinherited; ... it is still the worship of the Christian moral ideal. And finally the whole *socialist ideal*, a vulgar travesty of that Christian moral idea.[395]

Christianity was a disguise, and moral ideals are in their turn a disguised form of Christianity.

The weak want to have firm points: 'How much one needs a *faith* in order to flourish, how much that is "firm" and that one does not wish to be shaken because one *clings* to it, that is a measure of the degree of one's strength (or, to put the point more clearly, of one's weakness)'.[396] So,

how has the need for a fixed *point* become so great? Because we
have been taught to mistrust *ourselves*: that is to say because we
can no longer be passionate without having an uneasy conscience. It
is this defamation of our being that has given such strength to the
instinctive need for a certainty that is external to us: (1) the path of
religion; (2) the path of science; (3) abandoning ourselves to
money, princes, parties, Christian sects, etc.[397]

As the outcome of a need analagous to that which nourishes
religion and which is encouraged by religion, science is only aimed
for, through the will to truth, in so far as it can provide mooring
points useful to the masses: it is not the will to truth, but the herd's
need for a certainty. Therefore,

> Nothing could be more wrongheaded than to want to wait and
> see what science will one day determine once and for all
> concerning the first and last things. . . . The impulse to desire in
> this domain *nothing* of these certainties regarding the furthest
> horizon to live a full and excellent human life: just as the ant has
> no need of them to be a good ant.[398]

It is here that Nietzsche insists most strongly on *culture*. He
stresses that the search for goals, in contrast to what, as *the activities
of the man of the herd*, is merely its means (science, for example) can
only place on philosophy the onus to question the values of the
herd. From the second *Untimely Meditations* to *Ecce Homo*, this is an
unfailing idea, even in the period of *The Gay Science*.

> The *second* untimely essay (1874) brings to light what is
> dangerous, what gnaws at and poisons life, in our way of
> carrying on science – : life *sick* with this inhuman clockwork and
> mechanism, with the 'im-personality' of the worker. . . . The *goal*
> gets lost, culture – the means, the modern way of carrying on
> science, *barbarized*. . . . Two pictures of the sternest *selfishness*,
> *self-discipline* are erected against this as signposts to a *higher*
> concept of culture, to the restoration of the concept 'culture'. . . .
> Schopenhauer and Wagner, *or*, in one *word*, Nietzsche . . . [399]

Why? Because 'science can neither control nor indicate the path:
it has no *possibility* of being useful until one knows where to go'.[400]
For 'it is not truth, but the human being that finds itself known' (by
science).

Science merely pursues the process that established the essence of the species, a process that lends belief in certain things endemic and to eliminate incredulity by letting it wither away. . . . Mass instinct also rules over the realm of knowledge; the masses always want to know more about the conditions governing their existence, so they can live longer. Uniformity of feeling, which used to be sought by society or religion, is now sought by science: a *normal taste* in everything is established; knowledge rests on a belief in persistence and finds itself serving *the most common forms* of persistence (masses, people, humanity) . . . it works against *individualization*.[401]

All of Nietzsche's malice here aims to contradict the idea (which comes from morality) that science is capable, by itself, of proposing goals, when it creates nothing, and serves the will to conservation.

In comparison with a genius, that is to say with a being which either *begets* or *bears*, . . . the scholar . . . always has something of the old maid about him. . . . What is the man of science? An ignoble species of man for a start.[402]

The *ideal* scholar is certainly one of the most precious instruments there are: but he belongs in the hand of one who is mightier. He is only an instrument, let us say a *mirror* – he is not an 'end in himself'. And the objective man is in fact a mirror: accustomed to submitting to whatever wants to be known, lacking any other pleasure than that provided by knowledge, by 'mirroring' – he waits until something comes along[403] . . . his perilous unconcernedness over Yes and No. . . . His mirroring soul, for ever polishing itself, no longer knows how to afirm or how to deny. . . . The objective man is an instrument, a precious, easily damaged and tarnished measuring instrument and reflecting apparatus. . . . Consequently nothing for women either, *in parenthesis*.[404]

This gives us the leitmotif of Nietzsche's critique, analogous to his position with regard to morality: 'I insist that philosophical labourers and men of science in general should once and for all cease to be confused with philosophers'.[405]

To reassure us in the face of an enigma, science wishes to bring the enigma down to something *common*.[406] 'The so-called (*angeblich*) instinct for causality is merely *fear of the strange* (*ungewohnt*) and the attempt to discover something known in it'.[407] Nietzsche demystifies *language* in science by deciphering the gregarious role of grammar in it. The non-existence of the object, the invention, negation or twisting of reality ('as if'), the substitution of a causalist grammar for the play of forces and a formula for reality, the confusion of signs with the in-itself, the mythology, the concepts put in inverted commas: all this is destined in science, as in morality, to bring reality back to the self, to identity, and to the speaking herd.

> 'Cause' and 'effect' are a psychological belief given expression in the word, the active and the passive, the doing and the enduring. . . . It is still our representation of the self that leads us to interpret becoming as an act, thanks to a mythology that creates a being corresponding to the 'I'.[408]

> 'Cause' does not exist; in the few cases where it seemed given to us and where we have projected it from ourselves onto the facts *in order to understand them*, it is demonstrated that we created an illusion for ourselves. . . . *There are neither causes nor effects.* We cannot free ourselves of this through language. . . . Ultimately, *a fact is neither caused nor causing.* Cause is a *faculty of acting* that is invented and added to the phenomenon.[409]

> The invariable succession of certain phenomena does not confirm a 'law', but a power-relation between two or several forces. . . . The distinction between 'to do' and 'doing', between the 'fact' and the person who sets off that fact, between the process and what is not the process but a durable *substance*, a thing, a body, a soul . . ., this old mythology consolidated belief in 'cause' and 'effect', after this belief had already found a form in the grammatical functions of language.[410]

> 'Regularity' in succession is merely an imaged expression, it suggests that everything takes place *as if there were* a rule, it does not start *de facto*. The same goes for its conformity to 'law'. We find a formula to express a sort of succession that always returns; we have not in this way discovered a 'law', even less a force that would be the cause for the return of this succession. The fact that a thing always happens in such and such a way is interpreted as if there were a being who would always act in such and such a way.[411]

In brief, science is the erroneous interpretation, through language, of a reality which it reduces. In other words, it is a morality: 'it is an illusion that something is *known* when we possess a mathematical formula for an event: it is only designated, described; nothing more!'.[412] Thus Nietzsche can say, without playing on words: 'I beware of speaking of chemical *"laws"*: that savours of morality'.[413]

Nietzsche is therefore consistent when he affirms[414] that science is 'the most recent manifestation of the aescetic ideal', because it also rests on a 'faith': faith in the 'truth' and faith in a truth abstracted ascetically from *life*. Thus, to conclude, Nietzsche puts 'modern science' in inverted commas, as he does with German philosophy and the vocabulary of morality. This presentation brings science back to supposedly neutral language ('Objectivity' versus perspectivism), falsifying language ('as if'), and the language of the herd (obedience, instrument), and has the goal of offering a reassuring vision, which Nietzsche continually criticized, from *Human, All Too Human* onwards.[415] One phrase from this work sums up his position: 'there is no pre-established harmony between the furtherance of truth and the well-being of mankind'.[416] It is for having thought the opposite that our idealist culture can note, a little late, what Nietzsche suspected as early as 1880: 'An age of barbarism is beginning, the sciences will place themselves in its service'.[417] Nietzsche certainly does not mean what it is customary to have him mean (something, according to him, that 'women' and weak spirits want):[418] that he should renounce knowledge, and privilege any old ineffable 'value' as a counterweight to a scientific critique. He stresses that, in science itself, because of a *non-scientifically justifiable* faith in the value of truth, what precisely are swallowed up are morality and metaphysics which, under the name of 'scientificity' (*Wissenschaftlichkeit*) dominate culture in the name ʼof values that are founded on weakness. Nietzsche challenges the morality *of* science, the scientific ideal of objectivity which, for want of a scientific foundation or secularized religions, perpetuate the 'Christian' ideal. Since it is objective, science cannot pass for a value, but the objectivity it sets itself is a value. Scientific research, as such, is founded, through its choices and its goals, on an ideal that escapes it: the will to truth. As Nietzsche reproaches Socrates, science, as such, places itself 'at the service of barbarism'.[419]

Contrary to what the political theologians of the left and the right would like to have us believe, Nietzsche's vision of socialism has many nuances. The greatest paradox is that Nietzsche, who himself represents sociologically a reactionary *petit-bourgeois* class, on the basis of a misunderstanding of the historical, political and economic significance of the socialism and arnarchism of his day,[420] can utter statements that are not (unfortunately?) devoid of pertinence in view of the recent orator, of what he understood by the term 'socialism' and which it is now the custom to call 'Stalinism', something that has the advantage of annoying no-one.[421] It is an elementary precaution to show what corresponds in our time, from the *genealogical* point of view (the only one to interest Nietzsche), to what he designates as *will* in the 'socialism' of his day, and what does not correspond exactly to what it is today the custom to call by that term. Any reader of Nietzsche can know that morality is the art of mixing. Any bias would risk disappearing if we realized that Nietzsche is little concerned to define a historical concept of socialism – witness the way he confused it with anarchism[422] – but, sticking to a genealogical definition, neglects the essence of socialism in order to bring out its typology. He aims to show what drives it translates.[423] In fact, to exonerate socialism of Nietzsche's charges is to suppose that the 'truth' lies in an an-historical essence and so to confirm Nietzsche's critique which sees socialism as an extratemporal, unreal ideal. Many 'socialist' counter-attacks, like those of 'Christians' (the term constitutes an abuse) generally serve merely to reinforce his analyses: they are founded on the conviction that the ideal is something other than the history of the will that is masked by it, and so on an idealizing denegation and subsequently on resentment and slander.[424]

Nietzsche reproaches socialism for not having created a new ideal[425] and for being merely a copy, a supposedly atheist 'travesty of the Christian moral ideal'[426] – after the fashion of science – 'a denaturalized form of the morality of the herd'.[427] Socialism, which takes the herd as its end, can only repeat the identical: '*A fundamental error*: to place the ends in the herd and *not* in the isolated individuals. The herd is a means, *nothing more*. But at the moment one is trying to represent *the herd as an individual*, and to put it on a superior level to that of the individual – *A profound misunderstanding!*'[428] 'Modern socialism tends to create a form of secular Jesuitism: to make *all men* pure instruments. But so far they have not discovered the ends (*Zweck*), the reasons why (*Wozu*)'.[429] It is because it represents the drive to gregariousness that socialism, like 'Christianity', is *'nur ein Wort'*, nothing but a word, even though it tries, like an ideal, to become fixed in a 'true' idea.[430]

Just as there are no 'laws' of nature, so there is no socialism: it is just a *word* that translates drives, according to Nietzsche, who articulates this principle before history has even been able to incarnate socialism by siding too often with it (social-democracy, national-socialism, Christian-socialists, 'socialist' countries). Therefore, Nietzsche has to translate this word, after having put in inverted commas the concepts that depend on it: 'When the anarchist ... demands with righteous indignation "his rights", "justice", "equal rights", he is only acting under the influence of his want of culture'.[431] But these big words are signs:

> Wherever altruistic felings prevail, we find they represent the general instinct of people who know they have failed. A value-judgement, at bottom, means no more than 'I am worthless': this is the sound of exhaustion, impotence, and a lack of strong, bracing, affirmative feelings in the muscles, nerves and motor centres.[432]

The happiness 'of the greatest number',[433] 'progress',[434] 'perfection', 'the man of the future',[435] 'free society',[436], 'exploitation',[437] 'liberal',[438] 'justice', 'equal rights':[439] these are some of the 'big words' that Nietzsche puts in inverted commas. He detects, in a socialism that projects a feeling of fault, no longer on to itself, but also society, a denegation of reality,[440] an egoist search for power,[441] under the leadership of ascetic priests who stimulate dissatisfaction in order to make it serve their interests, an escape towards a historical beyond that is as unreal as the timeless beyond of 'Christianity'. Socialism, as Nietzsche sees it, following the example of Christianity and science, denies contradiction and chaos, challenges nature with a moral optimism and rejects the tragic dimension of life. There is no doubt that Nietzsche neglected to question his idea of the tragic with the aid of the conceptual tools of history, sociology and economics, or to wonder whether this idea of the tragic was not in part determined by his social grouping,[442] or that he wrongly transposed from the biological realm into the social domain the idea of assimilation in order to come up with the view of the vital fatality of exploitation.[443] The partiality of some of his views does not justify us to adopt the same Christian (in the

Nietzschean sense) attitude with regard to them, which is to justify oneself by amusing the other. It is a pity that the majority of 'socialist' responses to these conceptions of Nietzsche should corroborate such conceptions by adopting this kind of tactic.

It none the less remains that Nietzsche's genealogical and philological analyses – and his intuitions as a moralist and metaphysician, which pose the pertinent problem: that of reality and exploitation – take on after the event an explanatory value for certain 'socialist' phenomena of history subsequent to him: the hypertrophy of the State and bureaucracy, ideological conformism, moralism, a millenarism that hides oppression beneath the utopia, the inflation of empty slogans, the apology of 'the masses', the casting of accusations by way of justification, the institutionalization of guilt by the police, the idolatry of personality, dogma. It is worrying that criticisms of Nietzsche have put back Marxism itself in terms of the (infrastructural or genealogical) analysis of concepts or words relating to Revolution, State and Socialism, and constitute at least a sketch of what Marxism could not or would not undertake through its own concepts:[444] a critique of the evolution of historically revolutionary societies, called socialist, towards bureaucracy, the reconstitution of a dominant class, statism and vindictive terror, or even of what Marxism merely timidly undertook with Lenin in 1920: a critique of leftism. Finally, taking care not to confuse socialism with a simple discourse,[445] Nietzsche was able to have a preventative usefulness by questioning the temptation to *idealism*, which is always complicit with *real* oppression, that socialism can involve (though it is not alone in this), a socialism that, once it has become ideology, can only be its own negation. At the same time, Nietzsche showed the shortcomings of a new type of socialist culture and the hasty way in which it was elaborated: if one considers 'socialist' societies (the inverted commas are not pure philological pedantry, as is borne out by the grave ideological conflicts that contest them), we are forced to note the reactionary or at least conservative nature of their morality and their anthropology, and the empty verbosity of their conceptuality. If one refuses to confuse socialism, as a model of society, with the societies that lay claim to it, is it not once more threatened by idealism, as a projection, into the beyond, of a verbal imaginary that is always linked to the negation of present and real people?[446]

9
The Body and Metaphors

Nietzsche deprived himself of having recourse to language in order to express the truth it covers over: the body, reality. At most, he can acknowledge a 'phenomenality':

> I maintain the phenomenality of the inner world, too: everything of which we become conscious is arranged, simplified, schematized, interpreted through and through – the actual process of inner 'perception', the causal connection between thoughts, feelings, desires, between subject and object, are absolutely hidden from us – and are perhaps purely imaginary.[1]

Eugen Fink has shown remarkably where the problem lies for Nietzsche, then:

> What Nietzsche lacks even more decisively (for his work of destroying metaphysics) is a suitable language. What he wants, in fact, is something he cannot yet formulate. For language itself is metaphysical.[2]

The importance of this problem has not been felt and we have neglected to ask why Nietzsche's style should help us to understand the problem. And yet, the question of knowing whether Nietzsche could or could not 'go beyond' metaphysics, a theme in recent debates ever since works by Heidegger, Fink and Granier, an important question for us, even if it is only one aspect, and in reality a fairly exaggerated one, of the critique of morality and the search for a new culture, is crystallized in the question of language,[3] as for example in this text:

> Our oldest metaphysical foundation is the one we shall get rid of last, even supposing we ever get rid of it. This foundation has been incorporated into language and grammatical categories and has become so indispensable that we feel we should have to stop thinking, if we were to renounce such a metaphysics.[4]

Should we challenge language? Obviously no-one is obliged to think: 'I do not want to persuade anyone to philosophy'.[5] This is the 'most difficult "ideal"'.[6] But we risk depriving ourselves of 'freedom of spirit': 'being a hundred times superior to philosophers and other disciples of "truth" in severity towards oneself, in cleanliness and courage, in the unconditional will to say No where it is dangerous to say No'.[7] But this is something that, as Nietzsche opportunely reminds us during a period of 'scientificity', the scholar cannot have: 'knowledge does not make one a philosopher. A scholar is just a beast of burden on the kingdom of knowledge'.[8] The only recourse is to what can scarcely have been given any name other than philosopher. But we have to use language.

Just as metaphysics involves 'the populace',[9] so, too, does language: 'We have already grown beyond whatever we have words for. . . . Speech, it seems, was devised only for the average, medium, communicable. The speaker has already *vulgarized* himself by speaking'.[10] It is through language, therefore, that the priest dominates.[11]

On the other hand, 'linguistic means of expression are useless for expressing "becoming"'.[12] Language ignores a reality which it 'schematizes': 'At the point where our ignorance begins and beyond which we no longer see anything, we place a word'.[13] Language explains nothing, since it expresses only a relation, and an explanation is, in fact, merely a descriptive language.[14] 'Mere semiotics and nothing real',[15] a fiction,[16] a mythology.[17]

Language falsifies reality in terms of perspective, plurality,[18] the play of wills to power, becoming, chaos. It is the 'tartuffery of words'.[19] Nietzsche rarely fails to add a restrictive adverb to *Wort*, *Sprache*, *Grammatik*, etc. 'The "world" is only a word for the totality of these actions'.[20] A name is merely a skin, or cloak, or *trompe-l'oeil*, or rainbow.[21] Consequently, any phrase or formulation 'tyrannizes'.[22] For example: 'the Crucified [is] a formula for [life's] condemnation',[23] while by way of contrast Nietzsche approvingly indicates that '[Christ's faith] resists formulas'.[24] The same goes for Nietzsche, which reveals the difficulty of his position in relation to language: 'A long story! – You want a word for it? – If I were a moralist, who knows what I might call it? Perhaps self-overcoming. – But the philosopher has no love for moralists. Neither does he love pretty words'.[25] In order to write *Ecce Homo*, for example, did he not use words?

Nietzsche's principle is, therefore, not to take language (*die Worte*) 'at its word', or literally (*wörtlich*).[26] The entire dilemma of his undertaking can be measured in these two similar and opposite signifiers. How can Nietzsche '*say yes*' (*Ja SAGEN*) and be the spokesperson or advocate (*Für SPRECHER*)[27] of life? The words that define the taste of opposing the influence of morality themselves designate a task for language. If we have to 'suppress the word "Ideal"',[28] how can we speak of reality? Has he not revoked absolutely the idea of an adequate language? 'Linguistics helps to prove how man has entirely misunderstood and falsely named nature'.[29] As early as 1873, Nietzsche puts forward a thesis he will never revoke:[30] 'words are merely sounds for the relations which things have with themselves and with us, they never reach the absolute truth'.[31] The truth of language is perhaps the body. 'Thoughts and images are, like words, only signs of thoughts; the inexplicability of every action'.[32] But Nietzsche insists on affirming that 'words [are] in the service of physiological functions'.[33] The dilemma can be read in a text from *The Gay Science*, which is a veritable anthology of metaphors dealing with language (clothing, veil, appearance) and genealogy (origin):

> To realize that what things *are called* is incomparably more important than what they are. ... What at first was appearance becomes in the end almost invariably, the essence and is effective as such. ... But let us not forget this either: it is enough to create new names and estimations and probabilities in order to create in the long run new 'things'.[34]

The only solution would seem to be silence. And perhaps this is what Nietzsche ultimately 'chose', by merely drawing out, as it were, the blanks and dashes or dots (*Gedankenstriche*) which, in the work itself, indicate the eloquent silence or the resonance that must follow the words of an aphorism. Or has Nietzsche tried to write a new language in order to express reality and life? He committed himself to the path of *Versuch*: a metaphorical plurality in which language, he thinks, instead of simplifying, can try to regain a multiplicity of perspectives on life. Philological misology will be succeeded by metaphorics. It is the body which he must express. Nietzsche will, therefore, relativize language, and so philology, but, instead, as was expected, of moving the accent on to physiology, he will try to represent the world of drives by 'creating' a 'new language', a metaphorical one, and, following the logic of this concept, he will end up with a metaphor which acts like a principle to metaphors: the metaphorics of the text. Genealogy, if we think of culture philosophically, relates ideals back to the body as though to their hidden origin. Nietzsche must, therefore, state what should be understood by *body* and clarify the notion of *origin*. As discursive language is doomed to failure, Nietzsche attempts a metaphorical discourse.

It would all be simple if metaphor were represented by Nietzsche as being just something we encounter on this side of the concept. We could believe, as Nietzsche occasionally did, that metaphors of the body, which are predominant in his texts, have the job of giving an account of a preconceptual foundation, by virtue of their more obvious proximity to the empirical world. The body, in contrast to the evanescent Ideal, is apparently more real; the empirical phenomenon would be, in metaphor and in general, closer to reality, as the foundation for an Ideal that itself is immaterial and nebulous. Nietzsche lets this be understood when he speaks of the 'Königsberg' fog.[35] What is insinuated is the virtual reduction of reality to materiality, which inevitably leads to metaphysical dualism. This can be noted in the example of the (still metaphorical) implications of the image of foundations (*Grund*) or infrastructure (*Unterbau*) in Marx: in relation to this foundation, which is called material, consciousness is merely a *reflection*: a simple inversion of the dualism called Platonic which is incompatible with the explanation of matter by a concept. However, Nietzsche precisely states:

> Neither of the two explanations of organic life has yet succeeded: neither the one that proceeds from mechanics *nor the one* that proceeds from the spirit. I stress *this last point*. The split is more superficial than we think. The organism is governed in such a way that the mechanical world, *as well as* the spiritual world, can provide only a symbolical explanation.[36]

The term 'symbolical' (*symbolisch*) contrasts with the concept or the theory. Through this term, Nietzsche tries to challenge spiritualist idealism just as much as mechanics (or biologism). In the first, the body is spirited away, while in the second, it is realized and conceptualized or objectivized. Nietzsche wishes to contest these with, on the one hand, the primacy of the body and, on the other hand, a non-empiricist conception. One can no longer relate ideals back to the body by reabsorbing the former into the latter, nor can one fall back any more into dualism. Nietzsche's *monism* will therefore rest on a union and separation which exists between the ideal and the body, and operates according to a modality that metaphor will have the job of specifying: in .order to reject mechanist 'materialism' as much as idealist spiritualism, this monism will not be assimilated for all that to the Spinozist doctrine of correspondence, in which the unity of substance dualistically separates out extension and thought into attributes that are almost deceptively seen to derive from a single substance.[37] The union and separation existing between the ideal and the body will be spelt out as metaphor and through metaphor according to the axis of interpretation. Nietzsche's metaphors on physiology are therefore not tangible images: they lead instead to the philological notion of interpretation. And it is in this way that these metaphors will not only constitute the *style* of *Nietzsche's* descriptive metalanguage, but also the interpretative status *of his object* itself; the body.

If Nietzsche contests the duality of body and spirit, does he none the less reduce man (and consequently culture) to the body, and spirit and consciousness to the organism?

§ 14 of *The Antichrist* indicates one possible solution. Nietzsche begins by challenging the spirit: 'We have become more modest in every respect. We no longer trace the origin of man in the "spirit", in the "divinity", we have placed him back among the animals'.[38] As man is an animal, he is a body. But there is no symmetrical physiologism here: man is not the most perfect animal, some sort of '*Übertier*' evoking a naturist image of the 'blond beast', but a lost and failed animal. Nietzsche thus contrasts his conception as much to the anthropological vision of Genesis as to the finalist ideological implications of Darwin's theory of evolution. For a certain Christian Platonic tradition, man was a noble being by virtue of his spirit and afflicted by a flaw; his body. For Nietzsche, it is man's animality, his sureness of instinct, that is weakened by the precariousness of conscious thought: 'man is, relatively speaking, the most unsuccessful animal, the sickliest, the one most dangerously strayed from its instincts – with all that, to be sure, the most *interesting*!'.[39] The idea of failure not only serves to contest a proud vision of man, or an anthropocentrism:[40] in relation to the monism involving a reduction to animality, it introduces into man an interval to which certain phenomena testify, phenomena called (wrongly, in Nietzsche's view) 'will', 'spirit', 'consciousness', 'free will', and which are 'a symptom of a relative imperfection of the organism, as an attempting, fumbling, blundering, as a toiling'.[41] Moreover, Nietzsche describes these phenomena as a multiplicity: spirit and body constitute one unit, but it is a plural unity. '[Will is] a resultant, a kind of individual reaction which necessarily follows a host of partly contradictory, partly congruous stimuli'.[42]

But if consciousness and the spirit are therefore modes of the body, in what sense can one say that man is 'body entirely, and nothing beside'?[43] With the notion of interpretation, consciousness seems to be surreptitiously reintroduced into this body. What use is reference to the body, if it is thus virtually spiritualized? In what sense can the body remain the *foundation* or *origin*? The question is thus put once more: what is the body as fundamental interpretation?

The body is a series of instincts (*Instinkte*) or drives (*Triebe*) that constitute reality as they interpret it. The short circuit between reality and spirit is replaced by a detour via the body, which *interposes itself* [44] between 'the world' and the conscious spirit. There are two consequences: (a) a constitution (for example a categorical constitution) is replaced by an interpretation based on the body and drives; (b) the conscious spirit and intellect becomes the *instrument* of an unconscious interpreting body. Therefore, the former dualism is not simply overturned. There is an *interpretation (a detour)* and *a change of order.*

Nietzsche's metaphors regarding the founding nature of the body will, therefore, not be simple metaphors of foundation. Nietzsche does not reduce culture to the body: he tries to express this philosophical proposition: 'everything begins through the body.'

The world, as brute nature, is chaotic: '*Chaos sive natura*';[45] 'the world is not an organism at all, but chaos';[46] 'the beautiful chaos of existence'.[47] Prior to the body, there is no order or relation or text, and the world is the greatest possible multiplicity. A text comes into existence only through (or for) drives, which reduce this 'absolute' multiplicity.[48] But this reduction is not, like that of the intellect, the introduction of unity: if the body interprets, it does so as affects, and if affects *interpret*, they institute a certain simplicity only in order to pluralize it, the affects constituting the unstable points of view of a *game* in which they exist only in the plural. Nietzsche's detour via the body is a detour through the plurality of drives. 'Who interprets? (*Wer legt aus?*) – Our affects'.[49] This is why 'there are no facts, there are only interpretations'.[50] Nietzsche contrasts the intellect to the drives in terms of the difference between singular and plural:

> Science – this has been hitherto a way of putting an end to the complete confusion in which things exist, by hypotheses that 'explain' everything – so it has come from the intellect's dislike of chaos. – This same dislike seizes me when I consider myself: I should like to form an image of the inner world, too, by means of some schema, and thus triumph over intellectual confusion. Morality has been a simplification of this kind: it taught that men were known, familiar. – Now we have destroyed morality – we have again become completely obscure to ourselves! I know that I know nothing of myself.[51]

Culture begins as plurality and interpretation, as both simplification and plurality.

> 'Essence', the 'essential nature', is something perspective and already presupposes a multiplicity. At the bottom of it there always lies 'what is that for *me*?' (for us, for all that lives, etc.).[52]

> The origin of 'things' is wholly the work of that which imagines, thinks, wills, feels. The concept of 'thing' itself just as much as all its qualities. – Even 'the subject' is such a created entity, a 'thing' like all others: a simplication with the object of defining the force which posits, invents, thinks, as distinct from all individual positing, inventing, thinking as such.[53]

The body is therefore an intermediary space between the absolute plural of the world's chaos and the absolute simplification of intellect. If chaos and humanity begin with the body as interpretation, a model of this unity and plurality, a schema of the will to power. If the body comes first, it does so as a model of the *mixed*. If multiplicity comes first, the body as the play of affects will come first (as multiplicity) *in relation to the intellect* conceived of as unifying and simplifying, while it will come second *in relation to the chaos of the world*. Nietzsche, therefore, intends not to reduce the intellect to the body, but, in presenting the *body* as a 'plurality of intellects', to reveal the radical nature of *plurality*.

Consciousness, the spirit or 'little reason'[54] come second because they represent only a tiny ('modest') part whose subordination can be measured by their incapacity to perceive multiplicity. Nietzsche, apparently Spinozist in his opposition to a Platonic or Cartesian form of dualism, instead takes up Leibniz's intuitions once more when he affirms that the body thinks *in its entirety* and that consciousness is merely an *accident*:

> First, Leibniz's incomparable insight that has been vindicated not only against Descartes but against everybody who had philosophized before him – that consciousness is merely an *accidens* of experience and *not* its necessary and essential attribute; that, in other words, what we call consciousness constitutes only one state of our spiritual and psychic world (perhaps a pathological state) and *not by any means the whole of it.*[55]

Nietzsche holds to this idea:

> Man, like every living being, thinks continually without knowing it; the thinking that rises to *consciousness* is only the smallest part of all this – the most superficial and worst part – for only this conscious thinking *takes the form of words, which is to say signs of communication.*[56]

This has several consequences of a Leibnizian type:
— The body in its entirety is thought:[57] 'the soul always thinks'.[58]
— Conscious thought is merely a part, an accident or, as Leibniz would say, a *relatio* rather than a *res*. Nietzsche uses the term *perspective*.[59]
— The reality of the body is more the movement and relation between forces than a substance or a thing: this is what is indicated by the idea of the will to power as an ontological fixing.[60]
— The distance between the body as thought and conscious thought is more a distance between multiple and simple than between consciousness and unconsciousness, such that while preserving Leibniz's schema, Nietzsche inverts it:

> Since only the last scenes of reconciliation and the final accounting at the end of this long process rise to our consciousness, we suppose that *intelligere* must be something conciliatory, just and good – something that stands essentially opposed to the instincts,

while it is actually nothing but a *certain behaviour of the instincts toward one another*. For the longest time, conscious thought was considered thought itself. Only now does the truth dawn on us that by far the greatest part of our spirit's activity remains unconscious and unfelt.[61]

According to Leibniz's terminology, conscious thought is an incomplete knowledge, which is therefore obscure and inadequate, indeed blind or symbolical.[62] But confused perception is synonymous with passion and action goes hand in hand with clear perception.[63] For Nietzsche also, it is the confusion of conscious perception that implies the passivity of conscious thought. For him, the body is therefore the *totality* of perceptions ('little' perceptions) whose consciousness represents only a *part*, and thus a confused perception.

Nietzsche's metaphors regarding the primacy of the body are nothing original. The very metaphor of foundations could lead one to think that Nietzsche takes up an inverted form of the metaphorical function of the concept of foundations (*Grund*, *Unterbau*, base, substance, subject, ὑποκείμενον, etc.). The body is indeed for him 'an underworld of organs'.[64] Nietzsche always speaks of the soul's *Unterwelt*,[65] which designates the most secret aspects of the body.

The *Unterwelt*, the underworld of unconscious drives is less a cause or a nature than an invisible force, recognized as such because it is undecipherable for an interpretative thinking process that is concerned less with true foundations than with reading, looking for a way to balance what is fixed and what is unstable, the πέρας and the ἄπειρον. Therefore, Nietzsche does not intend, like Marx in *The German Ideology*,[66] to take up once more the image of Plato's cave in order to show that the ontological relation of eminence as well as the systemological relation of causality should be turned upside down.[67] The underground body does not replace the sun as the cause and true reality of appearances (shadows), as if, for Nietzsche, the shadow should be, contrary to Plato, the ultimate reason for the deceptive light (of the conscious). In this case, Nietzsche would merely repeat Schopenhauer's philosophy of the in-itself, reversed as a result of the effect of a conception of the will to live as being the deep reality of illusions, even when many texts can be invoked in this metaphysical sense:

Actions are *never* what they appear to us to be! We have expended so much labour on learning that external things are not as they appear to us to be – very well! the case is the same with the inner world![68]

Most often, Nietzsche defines this darkness of the body as that philological enigma of plurality rather than as a hidden foundation,[69] as the opposition of simple visibility and readability to the darkness of multiplicity, in this sense acting more as a philological interpreter of meaning than a physiologist researching foundations and causes.

> However far a man may go in self-knowledge, nothing however can be more incomplete than his image of the totality of *drives* which constitute his being. He can scarcely name even the cruder ones: their number and strength, their ebb and flood, their play and counterplay among one another, and above all the laws of their *nutriment* remain wholly unknown to him.[70]

This definition is attested to by: (a) the constant use of terms indicating an association between multiplicity and darkness (resulting for example in its replacement by the image of the labyrinth); (b) by images indicating, not the establishment of a ground, but on the contrary destruction, crumbling, and erosion, the pluralization of foundations; (c) the ultimate recourse to the metaphor of readability as the reason behind visibility: Nietzsche's genealogical concerns aim not to exhume a hidden in–itself that is the foundation for ideals, but to fix an interpretative thinking process.[71]

(a) Plurality

'The body is a great intelligence, a multiplicity with one sense, a war and a peace, a herd and a herdsman.'[72] 'The thing that marks out this "conscious" which we normally imagine to be unique, the intellect, is precisely that it remains protected and excluded from the innumerable and diverse (*unzählig vielfach*) aspects of the experience of these diverse consciousnesses: it is a consciousness of a superior level, a reigning collectivity (*eine regierende Vielheit*).'[73] 'A tremendous multiplicity which is none the less the opposite of chaos.'[74] 'A multiple complexity.'[75]

Since knowledge is impossible, the spirit can only 'schematize, and impose on chaos enough regularity and forms in order to satisfy our practical needs'.[76] 'It is presented with only one choice (*Auswahl*) of experiences, simplified experiences, which are easy to oversee and therefore false'.[77] This is why 'the intellect is merely an *instrument*, but in which hands? Certainly in the hands of affects; and the latter are a plurality behind which there is no need to postulate a unity'.[78] The intellect must content itself with 'simplifying, equalizing': 'There is no reason to attribute to the spirit the particular ability to organize and systematize'.[79] 'Our intellect is absolutely incapable of grasping, let alone producing the complexity of a collective operation (*Zusammenspiel*) as subtlely intelligent as, for example, digestion. There we find the collective functioning of *a very great number of intellects*.'[80]

This creates a devaluation of the intellect, in this numerical relation of forces: 'Feelings and things are extremely rare and minor things in comparison with the innumerable facts that fill the last moments'.[81] 'What we used to call the 'body' and 'flesh' is so much more rich! All the rest is a puny appendage to it.'[82] The body is 'a multiform process' (*tausendfältiger Prozess*)[83] and is therefore 'obscure' to the conscious spirit, which does not oversee its continual plurality. This is the reason why Nietzsche compares the non-conscious body as a whole to the internal processes of the digestive tract.[84] If it is obscure or dark, it is not in the sense of being a base that is deprived of light and cannot be seen, but in the sense that its plurality cannot be grasped. Nietzsche's gastroenterological comparisons, especially in *The Genealogy of Morals*, take up once more Schopenhauer's metaphorical suggestions, but Nietzsche changes their meaning. He writes:

> What we experience and digest psychologically does not, in the stage of digestion, emerge into consciousness any more than what we ingest physically does.[85]

Schopenhauer had written:

> Our internal process of thought is in reality not so simple as the theory of it; for here it is involved in many ways. ... It is in the obscure depths of the mind that the rumination of the materials received from without takes place, through which they are worked up into thoughts; and it goes on almost as unconsciously as the conversion of nourishment into the humours and substance of the body. Hence it is that we can often give no account of the origin of our deepest thoughts. They are the birth of our mysterious inner life. Judgments, thoughts, purposes, rise from

out that deep unexpectedly and to our own surprise. .... Consciousness is the mere surface of our mind, of which, as of the earth, we do not know the inside, but only the crust.[86]

Schopenhauer's goal was to demonstrate that it is will that acts as substratum in itself and as the unconscious cause of our thoughts. It is this in-itself as cause that Nietzsche challenges by insisting on arbitrariness and plurality.

(b)   The pluralization of 'foundations'
This is borne out by many of Nietzsche's images:

Whoever looks into himself as into vast space and carries galaxies in himself, also knows how irregular all galaxies are; they lead into the chaos and labyrinth.[87]

Following another metaphor, Nietzsche continues:

Our experiences are ... all in this sense means of nourishment, but the nourishment is scattered indiscriminately without distinguishing between the hungry and those already possessing a superfluity. .... These inventions ... are interpretations of nervous stimuli we receive while we are asleep, *very free*, very arbitrary interpretations of the motions of the blood and intestines.[88]

It is the notion of interpretation that is grafted on to the metaphor of intuition, by means of the notion of arbitrary and fortuitous circumstances. From this point on, the interpreter (Nietzsche) of these fundamental bodily interpretations is not only an underground being, who would descend more deeply into the substratum in itself of things, albeit one equipped with Schopenhauerian intuition, in order to reach the ground of reality:

Order of rank. – There are, first of all, superficial thinkers; secondly, deep thinkers – those who go down into the depths of a thing; thirdly, thorough thinkers, who thoroughly explore the grounds of a thing – which is worth very much more than merely going down into its depths! – finally, those who stick their heads into the swamp; which ought not to be a sign either of depth or of thoroughness! They are the dear departed underground.[89]

As an underground thinker, Nietzsche claims not to reach the foundations (*Grund*), but to undermine them from beneath (*untergründlich*). It is in this sense that Nietzsche presents himself in the preface to *Daybreak* as an underground being (*unterirdisch*):

In this book you will discover a 'subterranean man' at work, one who tunnels and mines and undermines. You will see him – presupposing you have eyes capable of seeing this work in the depths – going forward slowly, cautiously, gently inexorable, without betraying very much of the distress which any protracted deprivation of light and air must entail ... Does it not seem as though ... he perhaps desires this prolonged obscurity, desires to be incomprehensible, concealed, enigmatic.[90]

Calling himself a 'trophonios, an underground being, a mole', Nietzsche presents his task as being the labour of destruction,[91] and not the work of hollowing out designed to find solid foundations:

I descended into the depths, I tunnelled into the foundations, I commenced an investigation and digging out of an ancient *faith*, one upon which we philosophers have for a couple of millennia been accustomed to build as if upon the firmest of all foundations.[92]

He undermines not only morality,[93] but even the foundations, which he breaks up and desubstantializes. Nietzsche speaks almost always of HINTER*grund* or UNTER*grund*, of a ground's underground, when he evokes the metaphor concept of foundations (*Grund*),[94] for him there is always a comparative element in any foundation: 'the world is deep: and deeper than day'.[95] The metaphor of depth does not lead to the solidity of a foundation, but instead transposes the infinite plurality of perspectives, which is undecipherable and obscure to figurative meaning![96] Therefore, we must not speak of the spirit as a foundation, but of the body as a plurality and of 'the soul as a plurality of subjects' and the 'soul as a social edifice of drives and affects'.[97]

(c)   Visibility, readability
The body as a 'foundation' is opaque or dark. The metaphor of depth therefore shifts towards the concepts of differentiation, restriction and pluralization, invisibility, and then unreadability:

We must show to what extent everything that is conscious remains on the suface; to what extent action and the image of action are different (*verschieden*), how *little* (*wenig*) we know of what *pre*-cedes (*vorhergeht*) an action . . .; to what extent thoughts are merely images,[98] to what extent words are merely (*nur*) signs (*Zeichen*) of thoughts, the impenetrable nature (*Unergründlichkeit*) of any action.[99]

'The motives for our actions remain in the dark'.[100] The dark depths no longer designate the concealment of foundations, but the difficulty involved in understanding meaning: 'The most visible actions are particularly insignificant'.[101] In this way we tackle the epistemological question of interpretation.

This creates the appearance of terms like 'instrument' and 'toy', preceded by a restrictive '*nur*', and the transposition of these images into philological terms: interpretation, sign, image, variation and commentary. 'Our intellect is only the blind instrument of *another drive*'.[102] The 'only' (*nur*) marks the abbreviation of the sign in relation to the plurality which it bears in spite of itself (creating the words 'instrument' and 'toy'), without being *by itself* a reference to what it signifies. Alienated, the sign is the evident site of a frequently invisible plurality that makes the sign a servant and bearer of *what does not depend upon it*. In relating the conscious or spirit, as a sign, back to the deep foundation, Nietzsche wants to say once more that nothing evident is not a sign: the world is deep because everything in it is a sign, the body being *the* principal agency in which the chaos of the world is first reduced by each drive and then pluralized once again: the body, as a unity and plurality, is the site of the interpretation that establishes the chaos of the world in plural units, or signs.

We now have a better understanding of the transposition of the world or culture into text. This text has an infinitely plural outside which prohibits the text from turning in on itself, and to which the text is subordinate. If, as Fink writes, 'a game is characterized by a lack of regard for the ludic material, by a sense of licence',[103] the text, like man in relation to the gods in Plato,[104] is, like the sign, subjected in a ludic way to a plural transcendence which deepens it.

It is in order to clarify this '*nur*' belonging to the sign that Nietzsche employs the metaphors of the toy (a pluralizable singularity) and the instrument (subordination), both designed to contest 'overestimating what is conscious'.[105] This overestimation confuses

the unification and simplification of the sign represented by consciousness with the unification of chaos by the body, by shortcircuiting the body as a game of the unity and pluralization of
drives. Overestimating what is conscious involves taking the sign
to be a thing-in-itself. 'Where a certain unity exists in the grouping,
we have always put forward the *spirit* as being the cause of this
coordination, without the slightest reason. . . . The nervous system
has a much wider domain: the world of consciousness can only be
added to it'.[106] Nietzsche therefore replaces consciousness back
within the body's invisible *plurality*: 'Consciousness is an organ,
like the stomach',[107] and makes it seem subject to the body: 'Our
intellect is only (*nur*) the blind instrument (*das blinde Werkzeug*) of
another drive'.[108] 'We shall perceive a *multiple complexity* to be a
unity, in such a way that we introduce an invented causality into it
wherever any cause behind a movement or a modification remains
invisible to us.'[109]

'Your little intelligence, my brother, which you call "spirit", is
also an instrument of your body, a little instrument and toy of your
great intelligence.'[110] Consciousness, as a toy, is a polysemic
object. Conversely, to scorn the body is to belittle the world,
turning it into a series of objects, instead of playing with it through
interpretation:

> When we observe only internal phenomena, we are like deaf and
> dumb people who guess at the words they cannot hear by
> watching someone's lips. What inner meaning sees is used by us
> to deduce visible and different phenomena, which we should see
> if our means of observation were sufficient.[111]

Consciousness is merely the site in which plurality is expressed
singularly, 'a reflection captured in a mirror' (*Spiegelbild*), a coded
language to designate something essentially other (*wesentlich
Anderes*)',[112] a 'puny appendage (*ein kleines Zubehör*)'.[113]

> Instead of understanding the conscious state as an instrument, a
> detail of life as a whole, we think of it as a criterion, as the state of
> supreme value in life: in brief, it is the mistaken perspective of
> part for whole (*des a parte ad totum*).[114]

> There are no immediate facts; the same goes for sensations and
> thoughts; as soon as I am *conscious* of them, I abstract, simplify
> and attempt to construct; this is what we call *being conscious* of

things, it is a very *active* way of arranging them. ... A thought or sensation are the *signs* of certain phenomena: if I consider them in the absolute (*absolut*), if I put them forward as being necessarily *univocal* (*eindeutig*), I also presuppose that all men are intellectually similar – this is a temporarily permissible *simplification* of the true state of the facts.[115]

Consciousness is merely an abbreviation of a plurality: that of the body as text.

> That our moral judgments and evaluations too are only images and fantasies based on a physiological process unknown to us, a kind of acquired language for designating certain nervous stimuli? that all our so-called consciousness is a more or less fantastic commentary on an unknown, perhaps unknowable, but felt text?[116]

Therefore the relationship between man and the world as chaos is more of the order of an interpreting imagination than of a concept because man is thrown into the midst of the labyrinthine efflorescence of a world of signs:

> In the meantime all possible drives would have *had time* to imagine the experience and to comment on it. – What then are our experiences? Much *more* that which we put into them than that which they already contain! Or must we go so far as to say: in themselves they contain nothing? To experience is to invent?[117]

This is no longer an in–itself, but signs: 'we falsify the real state of affairs, but it would be impossible to know it unless we falsified it'.[118] Nietzsche sums this up: 'Like speech, thought is merely a sign: there can be no question of an identity between thought and reality. Reality is a particular movement of instincts.'[119] Chaos becomes a world only through the body.

Asking what the body is means asking what interpretation is. But the description of an interpreting body relies on metaphors that become entangled with one another: a gastroenterological metaphor, a political metaphor, a philological metaphor. 'The intellect is merely an instrument ... in the hands of affects which are a plurality (which) needs to be considered only as a regency council.'[120]

> The *body*: one never ceases to marvel at the idea that ... this

extraordinary collectivity of living bodies, all of them dependent and subordinate, but in another sense dominant and endowed with voluntary activity, can live and grow as a whole. . . . In this 'miracle of miracles', consciousness is merely an 'instrument', nothing more, – in the same sense in which the stomach is an instrument of the same miracle. . . . What makes this 'conscious element', which we normally imagine to be unique, stand out . . . is that it is the consciousness of a higher level, a reigning collectivity, an aristocracy. . . . Each of these voluntary acts presupposes a choice made by a dictator. But what offers this choice to our intellect, what has first simplified, levelled out, and interpreted (*ausgelegt*) these experiences, is certainly not this same intellect. . . . At every level . . . (there is a repetition of) this same choice, this same presentation of experiences, this same method of abstracting and grouping, this will, this translation (*Zurückübersetzung*) of a still vague will into a definitive activity. Led by the guiding thread of the body, as I said, we learn that our lives are possible thanks only to the play (*Zusammenspiel*) of a number of intelligences of very unequal value, thanks, therefore, to a perpetual swapping around of obedience and commandment in innumerable forms.[121]

The relationship between unity and plurality is attested to *a contrario*: 'And it is not a simple *addition* we are dealing with here. Our arithmetic is very crude for this kind of relation, it is merely an individual arithmetic'.[122] 'This whole phenomenon of the "body" is, from the intellectual point of view, as superior to our consciousness, our "spirit", our conscious ways of thinking, feeling and willing, as algebra is superior to multiplication tables.'[123] To take account of this non-arithmetic relation, Nietzsche uses metaphorical schemas. But the metaphors link up. Do they establish a semiological system that is closed in on itself? They are schemas used to think through the unity of plurality and the plurality of the interpreting body's singularity: what is therefore their relationship: (a) to the body as interpretation?; (b) to Nietzsche's discourse as a discourse – or interpretation – on the body?

Nietzsche's thought proceeds by way of transference, and perhaps in a circle. The meta-phorical movement of metaphors illustrates by its form what its imaginary content proposes to explain: the relation between unity and plurality, the meta-phorical relation of carrying something over. The metaphors of the body run into a body as meta-phor, an interpretative unity and plurality, in such a way that the body, used metaphorically in order to think of interpretation, is interpreted as interpretation.

The *gastric* metaphor rests on the idea of *assimilation* and functional dependence. The stomach reduces several things to one by assimilation (*ad simile*):

> This inferior being assimilates (*assimiliert*) whatever lies in its immediate vicinity, and appropriates it (property initially being food (*Nahrung*) and provision for food), it seeks to assimilate (*einverleiben*) as many things as it can and not only to compensate itself for loss: this being is greedy (*habsüchtig*).[124]

But this assimilation presupposes a relation between forces that are opposed and resist or give in to one another, and so a *struggle* that runs up against a state of power of wills. The gastric metaphor, therefore, refers back to a *political* metaphor: the body is a more or less regulated collectivity, in which such and such an agency 'reigns' or assumes power, and so 'excludes, dismisses or chooses',[125] simplifies, equalizes, translates and so *interprets*. The *philological* metaphor of interpretation, consisting in 'using signs to become the master'[126] of the plurality involved in the struggle takes over from the political metaphor.

> What is commonly attributed to the *spirit* seems to me to make up *the essence of organic life*. In the spirit's highest functions, I find only sublimated organic functions (*eine sublime Art*) (assimilation, discrimination, secretion, etc.).[127]

This note reveals clearly the different uses of metaphors. For Nietzsche, it is not a question of describing the body physiologically: the spirit is reduced to one unduly privileged aspect of the organism, while on the other hand the organism sees a spiritual (*geistlich*) function being attributed to it which can extend to cover everything. There is, therefore, a spirit in the general sense: the body. To describe this spirit and body, Nietzsche turns to images from gastroenterological physiology, which have no descriptive physiological value, but which, in a circular sort of way, serve as a metaphor for interpretation. The body is therefore led back to the interpretation which is its principle. Moreover, if, ontologically, Nietzsche maintains the body as a first reality, on the other hand, from the epistemological point of view (the only one he can support by virtue of challenging the in-itself), the ultimate principle is not the body, but interpretation, the 'body' being merely the metaphor of interpretation, the human means of interpreting it. This leads Nietzsche, where we might expect a physiological reductionism, to deploy epistemologically a metaphysics of interpretation, whose 'physiological' discourse in reality is merely *metaphor*. Nietzsche's apparently biologizing texts, far from reducing the ideal to the body, are merely attempts to bring culture (conceived of *as* a body) back to the fundamental interpretation, the physiological body being one case of interpretation among others.[128]

This general approach allows us first of all to explain the anthropomorphism of Nietzsche's organic metaphors (the body chooses, sorts out, refuses), and why physiology is described in terms that are psychological, then political and finally philological. Conversely, culture as an interpreting body and spirit, as a collection of evaluations and ideals (corporal and spiritual), will be presented by the *not medical, but interpretative* metaphor of the stomach.

From this point on, culture (which is like a body) and the body (which is an interpretative system) are phenomena of Interpretation – one might almost say: of being as interpretation – or modes of Interpreting. For Nietzsche, interpretation is a quasi-ontological principle, whose life, body, intuition and reproduction are merely 'derivative' (*abgeleitet*),[129] 'special cases' (*Einzelfall*)[130] of the will to power,[131] 'simple consequences of insatiable appropriation by the will to power'.[132] The will to power is interpretation to which everything 'is led back'.[133] The images of physiology provide not a foundation for a materialism, but a metaphysics of the will to power as interpretation: 'We must not ask; "Who is interpreting?"', on the contrary, interpreting itself (*das Interpretieren selbst*) as a form (*Form*) of the will to power, has existence (*Dasein*) (not, however, as "being" (*Sein*), but as process (*Prozess*) and *becoming*), as an affect'.[134]

The questions: what is the body (spirit)? what is culture? what is the will to power? therefore come back to: what is interpreting? 'The spirit is more like a stomach than anything else.'[135]

(a)   The gastroenterological metaphor
How does the metaphorical digestive system of Interpretation work?

First of all it assimilates: it absorbs what is foreign, tries to reduce to its own uniqueness and identity (which eventually becomes multiple) the diverse and plural material. 'To assimilate is already to make a foreign thing *similar* to oneself, to *tryannize* it – *cruelty*.'[136] In protoplasm, an example chosen by Nietzsche, nutrition consists in overpowering a being that resists, appropriating it (*aneignen*) and incorporating it (*einverleiben*).[137] Here, metaphorics juxtapose and treat as equivalents the terms 'digest, live, absorb, and incorporate (*verdauen, erleben, hineinnehmen, einverleiben*)'.[138]

This is a secret, underground labour that is dark and repugnant. To see the entrails would be to see a true reality, and Nietzsche is thinking of haruspices, but an internal reality that is both threatening and sickening, a mixture of *pudendum* and *horrendum*: as if the real chaotic plurality initially caused fear, as much to consciousness as to morality.

> What offends aesthetic meaning in inner man – beneath the skin: bloody masses, full intestines, viscera, all those sucking, pumping monsters – formless or ugly or grotesque, and unpleasant to smell on top of that! *Therefore suppression through thought*, whatever, in spite of that, appears outside awakens shame (faecal matter, urine, saliva, sperm). Women do not like to talk about digestion. Byron could not bear to see a woman eat. . . . The body hidden beneath its skin which has to be ashamed of itself! The clothing that covers the parts where its intimate nature comes out! (Even though he is not an external form, man represents an object of disgust to himself, – he does everything in his power *not to think about it*).[139]

> When we love a woman, we easily conceive a hatred for nature on account of all the repulsive natural functions to which every woman is subject. . . . 'The human being under the skin' is for all lovers a horror and unthinkable, a blasphemy against God and love.[140]

It is in order to contrast an abominable truth to the surface of the ideal that Nietzsche speaks of entrails: 'With this book (St Augustine's *Confessions*) we see the entrails of Christianity: reading it, I experience the curiosity of a doctor and a physiologist'.[141] Entrails in reality come from a body that incorporates and assimilates plurality. They must reduce excess. The stomach must, like culture and interpretation, refuse, on pain of not functioning.

The Epicurean selects the situation, the persons, and even the events that suit his extremely irritable, intellectual constitution; he gives up all others, which means almost everything, because they would be too strong and heavy for him to digest. The Stoic, on the other hand, trains himself to swallow stones and worms, slivers of glass and scorpions without nausea; he wants his stomach to become ultimately indifferent to whatever the accidents of existence might pour into it.[142]

The ability to absorb can be a criterion of power:

The strong man, mighty in the instincts of a powerful health, digests his deeds in just the same way as he digests his meals; he can cope even with heavy food: in the main, however, he is led by a faultless and severe instinct into doing nothing that disagrees with him, just as he eats nothing he does not enjoy.[143]

This trouble with absorption and assimilation can take several forms, which Nietzsche evokes in great detail: the spirit wishes to create 'the will to simplicity' 'out of simplicity', revealing 'a strong inclination to assimilate the new to the old, to simplify the complex, to overlook or repel what is wholly contradictory'. Its intention is 'the incorporation of new "experiences", ... all this being necessary according to the degree of its power to appropriate, its "digestive power", to speak in a metaphor'.[144] Nietzsche extends the metaphor of the 'spirit' to the phenomena of culture:

More ponderous spirits than we may have done with what in our case is confined to a few hours and is then over only after a longer period: one takes half a year, another half a life, according to the speed and power with which he digests it and of his 'metabolism'.[145]

The ability to assimilate confirms the power: therefore, the racist argument, still much used, in which a society has a threshold beyond which it cannot tolerate absorbing any more foreign elements, is turned back by Nietzsche on the Germans. The supposedly great race is in reality dyspeptic:

That Germany has an ample *sufficiency* of Jews, that the German stomach, German blood has difficulty (and will continue to have difficulty for a long time to come) in absorbing even this quantum of 'Jew' – as the Italians, the French, the English have absorbed them through possessing a stronger digestion – : this is the clear declaration and language of a universal instinct.[146]

The German *drags* his soul, he drags everything he experiences. He digests his events badly, he is never 'done' with them; German profundity is often only a sluggish 'digestion'. And just as all chronic invalids, all dyspeptics, have an inclination for comfort, so the German loves 'openness' and 'uprightness'.[147]

The German nation growing ever more sluggish and poor in instinct in spiritual matters, ever more *honourable*, which with an enviable appetite continues to nourish itself with opposites and knows how to gulp down 'faith' as well as scientificality, 'Christian love' as well as anti–Semitism, will to power (to 'the Reich') as well as the *évangile des humbles*, without having any trouble digesting them. ... This lack of party in choosing between opposites! This ventral neutrality and 'selflessness'! This fairness of German *taste*, which accords everything equal rights – which finds everything tasty.[148]

Bulimia results in dyspepsia. We have 'a society that no longer has the strength to *excrete*',[149] and 'the morbid indigestion of repentance', resulting from the fact that man 'has not got over some worry, some scruple, some self-criticism'.[150]

When one has not been able to show prophylactic discernment and frugality, the solution consists in facilitating excretion:

> Every body endlessly *eliminates*, it rejects what is unassimilable in the absorbed being; what man scorns, what he is disgusted with, what he calls bad, is excretia. ... When he 'shares' with others, when he is 'disinterested' – he is perhaps simply eliminating *unusable faecal matter* which he must reject if he is not to suffer. ... He makes a virtue of his 'liberality'.[151]

Under the auspices of morality, the cycle of carbon can be followed: 'constantly rejected excretia continue to reproduce among themselves'.[152]

> We all live this way! We greedily devour things with our insatiable eyes, and then just as greedily empty them of whatever flatters our task or might be useful to us – and then leave the bits our teeth and our appetite could not finish off to others and to nature, especially the bits we could not digest: our excrement. This means we are not greedy at all, we are inexhaustibly

generous: we bestow on humanity's *dungpile* what our spirit and our experiences found indigestible.[153]

The danger is one of loss: too rapid an excretion is a symptom of weakness: 'do not be too prodigious: only dogs shit all the time!'[154]

He who has been young in our times has lived through too many things. ... Most do not have the stomach for it: consequently they are not aware either of how this stomach is necessary in order to 'finish off' (*fertig werden*) lived experience, the greatest novelties pass right through (*fallen durch sie hindurch*). The rest of us, in our youth, have had to swallow many heavy, spicy dishes: and when we taste a rare and extraordinary dish ..., we experience true digestion, living, absorption and incorporation almost solely as a torture.[155]

Assimilation must be located between bulimia (the threat of dyspepsia, ingestion and waste) and diarrhoea, the *Durchfall*:

If anyone is unable to get rid of a psychological pain, the fault lies not in his 'psyche' but, more likely, in his belly. ... The strong, healthy person digests his experience [including every deed and misdeed] as he does his meals, even though he may have swallowed a tough morsel. If he can't get rid of an experience, then this kind of digestion is every bit as physical as the other, and often, in fact, merely one of the consequences of the other. Let me add that one may hold such notions and yet be an enemy of all materialism.[156]

Applying this schema to culture and interpretation, Nietzsche establishes their end as being a '*fertig werden*': absorbing in order to grow without losing anything but without losing oneself. Nietzsche denounces 'alimentary' excess, or 'voraciousness', which he contrasts with choice, the *slowness* of *physiological* operations, which, in the isomorphic field of the *philology of interpretation*, are discernment, subtlety and *lento*.

The nourishment of modern man. – Modern man understands how to digest many things, indeed almost everything – it is his kind of ambition: but he would be of a higher order if he did *not* understand it: *homo pamphagus* is not the finest of species. We live between a past which had a more perverse and stubborn taste than we and a future which will perhaps have a more dicriminating one – we live too much in the middle.[157]

The goal is not expenditure, but a certain form of economy. It is normal for a human being who has turned out badly, for example, to have associated 'with more spiritual company than he can digest'.[159] He is incapable of 'ruminating', as the Preface to *The Genealogy of Morals* demands, and would have to learn how to resist excitement. To be ill is not just to digest something badly, it also involves swallowing everything, eliminating badly: a morbid, dyspepsic culture is one which interprets badly, just as a weak intepretation swallows everything and lets everything in a text pass right through without ruminating on it.

> Truly, I dislike also those who call everything good and this world the best of all. I call such people the all-contented. All-contentedness that knows how to taste everything: that is not the best taste! I honour the obstinate, fastidious tongues and stomachs that have learned to say 'I' and 'Yes' and 'No'. But to chew and digest everything – that is to have a really swinish nature! Always to say *Ye-a* – only the ass and those like him have learned that.[159]

Nietzsche's 'taste' can be translated by warnings, an insistence on digestive problems and dietary advice.

> Then there arose that mendaciousness and spuriousness in German culture ... which on account of its furred tongue and congested stomach in the end no longer knows what it likes and what it finds boring. – Blessed are those who possess taste, even though it be bad taste![160]

> Not be an observer of it while still *in the midst* of it. For that would disturb the absorption of the experience: instead of a piece of wisdom one would acquire from it indigestion.[161]

> One speaks of being sick of man only when one can no longer digest him and yet has one's stomach full of him. Misanthropy comes of an all too greedy love of man and 'cannibalism'; but who asked you to swallow men like oysters, Prince Hamlet?[162] The art of association with people depends essentially on an aptitude (requiring long practice) for accepting and eating a meal in whose cuisine one has no confidence. If you come to the table ravenously hungry, it is all very easy ... but one does not have this ravenous hunger when one needs it. How hard it is to digest one's fellow men! First principle: to summon one's courage as in misfortune, to fall to boldly, to admire oneself in the process, to

grit one's teeth on one's repugnance, and to swallow one's nausea.[163]

If problems with digestion can come from excess, they are sometimes due to 'laziness of the bowels',[164] the result of a bad diet. One remedy offered might be to chew on your food. But the best way to prevent these problems is to put the body through movements that encourage intestinal activity: this appeal to something outside the spirit or stomach is typical of Nietzsche.

> Our first questions about the value of a book, of a human being, or a musical composition are: Can they walk? Even more, can they dance? . . . How quickly we guess how someone has come by his ideas; whether it was while sitting in front of his inkwell, with a pinched belly, his head bowed low over the paper – in which case we are quickly finished with his book, too! Cramped intestines betray themselves – you can bet on that – no less than closet air, closet ceiling, closet narrowness.[165]

This accounts for the importance of the theme of walking in Nietzsche: it helps the digestion, it symbolizes exteriority and an opposition to a bookish culture:

> All prejudices come from the intestines. – Assiduity – I have said it once before[166] – the actual *sin* against the holy spirit.[167]

> A never so infinitesimal sluggishness of the intestines grown into a bad habit completely suffices to transform a genius into something mediocre, something 'German'; the German climate alone is enough to discourage strong and even heroic intestines. The *tempo* of the metabolism stands in an exact relationship to the mobility or lameness of the *feet* of the spirit; the 'spirit' itself is indeed only a species of this metabolism.[168]

> [Move] freely about. . . . One has to *know* the size of one's stomach. . . . Each has here his own degree, often between the narrowest and most delicate limits. . . . With me the spirit moves over the water. . . . A big meal is easier to digest than one too small.[169]

Here are examples of the precepts which Nietzsche calls *morality*. Conversely, Nietzsche proposes a diet for the spirit:

> 'My man's fare, my succulent and strengthening discourse, is effective; and truly, I did not feed them with distending

vegetables! But with warrior's food, with conquerors' food: I awakened new desires. . . . To be sure, such food may not be for children, or for the fond little women, old or young. Their stomachs are persuaded otherwise.'[170]

On the other hand, faith spoils the digestion:

They sit together on long evenings and say: 'Let us again become as little children and say Dear God!' – ruined in mouth and stomach by the pious confectioners. . . . Or they listen to an old, roving, whistling tramp who . . . preaches distress in distressful tones.[171]

And it is the willing beggar who says to Zarathustra:

'If we do not alter and become as cows, we shall not enter into the kingdom of heaven. For there is one thing we should learn from them: rumination. And truly, if a man should gain the whole world and not learn this one thing, rumination: what would it profit him! He would not be free from his affliction.' . . .

Zarathustra, however, silently shook his head. 'You do violence to yourself, mountain sermonizer, when you use such stern words. Neither your mouth nor your eyes were made for such sternness. Nor your stomach either, as I think: *that* opposes all such raging and hating and over-frothing. Your stomach wants gentler things: you are no butcher.' . . .

'You have divined me well,' answered the voluntary beggar with lightened heart. . . . 'To be sure, these cows have attained the greatest proficiency in it: they have devised rumination and lying in the sun. And they abstain from all heavy thoughts that inflate the heart.'[172]

Nietzsche, on the one hand, proposes to apply physiological metaphors to culture – we might call him 'the culture doctor' – and, on the other hand, he describes the stomach morally. On the metaphorical plane, we remain in the closed circle of interpretation and spirit, versus stomach and digestion.[173] And because the second group is 'described morally'[174], Nietzsche then has to have recourse – since his object is culture, the interpretation of the body, and not the body of medicine – to the metaphors of politics and philology. It is therefore an interpretation which has to be spelled out. If there is a descriptive circle, it is because there is a monism:

the body is not, as such, what the spirit and culture have to be brought back to; instead, it is the metaphor of its principle: interpretation – a philosophical problem.

'We speak of stomach complaints by which we mean people who suffer from indigestion – as if the stomach were the only thing that digests!'[175] And yet Nietzsche hesitates. He declares that psychic assimilation is just as physiological as gastric assimilation, then he makes the first a 'consequence' of the second, but hastily challenges the materialism of such a proposition.[176] He goes so far as to say: 'depression results from lack of food or defective digestion and determines the ideal'[177] – a purely ideological materialism.

In vain Nietzsche multiplies certain shock phrases designed to reduce things to the physiological, for others carry the opposite meaning, one in which the psychic has a causal effect on the physiological.

Today we should treat that religious ecstasy with a purgative[179]

Now I know how to refute Germans: not with arguments, but with rhubarb. .... We can now see who my victims are, forceful geese of both sexes, the supposedly sensitive souls, idealists, in other words. ... I know the art of writing *crude* letters to supposed 'friends', to have a guaranteed purgative effect.[179]

The mere presence of a German hinders my digestion.[180]

Any infirmity of soul excludes one from them once and for all, any dyspepsia, even, does so: one must have no nerves, one must have a joyful belly. Not only does the poverty, the hole-and-corner air of a soul exclude it from them – cowardice, uncleanliness, secret revengefulness in the entrails does so far more: a word from me drives all bad instincts into the face.[181]

Nothing burns up one quicker than the affects of *ressentiment*. Vexation, morbid susceptibility, incapacity for revenge, the desire, the thirst for revenge, poison-brewing in any sense – for one who is exhausted this is certainly the most disadvantageous kind of reaction: it causes a rapid expenditure of nervous energy, a morbid accretion of excretions, for example of gall into the stomach.[182]

Here we note less the reduction to the physiological than the metaphorical unity: each of the two terms acts as a metaphor for the other. Thus:

Swallowing down necessarily produces a bad character – it even ruins the stomach.[183]

The so-called 'good conscience', a physiological condition some-times so like a sound digestion as to be mistaken for it.[184]

Intestines play a role in the emotion.[186]

But the very ideal can be a remedy for a bowel infection:

The wealthy class in England has need of its Christianity in order to endure its indigestion and headaches.[186]

Nietzsche presents himself as 'medicynisch'[187] (*medicynical*), but he is much more *zynisch* (*cynical*) than *medizinisch* (*medical*) in his insistence on the body, even when he speaks of the physiological cause for the ideal:

The reason why these individuals have different feelings and tastes is usually to be found in some oddity of their life style, nutrition, or digestion, perhaps a deficit or excess of inorganic salts in their blood and brain; in brief, in their *physis* ... Their aesthetic and moral judgments are among these 'subtlest nuances' of the *physis*.[188]

Not that Nietzsche wishes to reabsorb the psychical into the chemical: he enlarges the spirit to the dimensions of the thing of which it is merely a part. His 'medicynicism' is scarcely more than the reverse of the idealism that is a moral denegation of the psychosomatic totality of the body and spirit: 'they have enlarged the domain of *pudenda* to such a degree that a conversation about digestion, or even about toothbrushes, is felt to be in bad taste. Consequently sensitive people do not *reflect* on these matters.'[189]

The impact of numerous 'medicynical' phrases is less physiological than burlesque, with Nietzsche using and abusing a paradoxical or socially incongruous comparison or identification between a (noble) 'superior' level and a prosaic or repugnant inferior one – a comical procedure used by Aristophanes, Lucretius, Luther, Sterne, Schopenhauer, Heine, etc.:

When for example Kant says: 'Two things remain eternally venerable' – nowadays we say instead: 'Digestion is more respectable'.[190]

Many dishes equally contain revelations on the state from which we come. How much mystery there is, for example, in the relation between German dumplings and the 'childlike soul' of Germany! Once we have these dumplings in our stomachs, the soul begins to be moved: we start to 'get mysterious feelings'! ... What a long way this is from the 'reason of reasoners'![191]

What a lot of beer we find in Protestant Christendom![192]

Destiny and the stomach. – One slice of bread and butter more or fewer in the stomach of a jockey can occasionally decide the outcome of the race and the betting and thus affect the fortunes and misfortunes of thousands. – So long as the destiny of nations continue to depend on the diplomats, the diplomats' stomachs will continue to be the object of patriotic anxiety. *Quousque tandem.*[193]

The physiology we were expecting, therefore, does not go beyond the comic paradoxes of the cynical tradition, from Diogenes to Heine, via Montaigne or Swift, without ever attaining the scatological heights gloriously scaled by Nietzsche's precursors.[194]

The metaphors of digestion are, therefore, a scheme with which to interpret culture as interpretation: '"modernity" under the symbol of food and digestion', which is applied as follows:

A sensibility that is unspeakably more excitable ..., the *cosmopolitanism* of food, meals, literatures, newspapers, forms, tastes, even landscapes, etc. The *tempo* of this flood a *prestissimo* ...; we instinctively stop ourselves from absorbing something *deeply*, from 'digesting' it – a resultant *weakening* of the digestive system's capacity. A sort of *adaptation* of this accumulation of impressions intervenes: man ... uses his powers to *appropriate*.[195]

Culture is 'incorporation' (*Einverleibung*).[196] Nietzsche outlines the danger of 'dyspepsia':

Writing ought always to advertise a victory – an overcoming of *oneself*, but there are dyspeptic authors who write only when they cannot digest something, indeed when it is still stuck in their teeth.[197]

'I am not fond of myself', someone said in explanation of his love of society. 'Society's stomach is stronger than mine, it can digest me.'[198]

I equally want to *renaturalize asceticism*; in place of intending negation, to intend *reinforcement*: a gymnastics of will; an abstinence and periods of fasting interspersed in every domain, including intellectuality (Dinner *chez Magny*: all sorts of intellectual gourmets with upset stomachs).[199]

There will be deeps 'rumblings' in the stomach of the next century, and the Paris commune . . . was perhaps no more than a minor indigestion compared to what is coming.[200]

(b)   Political metaphors

But Nietzsche is constrained, in view of spelling out the body as interpretation, to refer to another metaphorical domain: politics. Culture as 'digestion' and interpretation, is comparable to a political body. The link-reference is clearly perceptible in this phrase: 'Assimilating means already making a foreign thing *similar to oneself*, tyrannizing it'.[201] Nietzsche follows up his description of the play of drives with the following terminology:

It subordinates itself . . . slavery is necessary for the formation of a higher organism, the same goes for castes . . . obedience is a constraint . . . the power to swallow others a function to be used . . . reigns . . . subordinates in turn have subordinates . . . perpetual struggle . . . adversaries . . . fighting . . . colonies . . . etc.[202]

And he clarifies his metaphorical analysis of the body:

L'effet, c'est moi: what happens here is what happens in every well-constructed and happy commonwealth: the ruling class identifies itself with the successes of the commonwealth. In all willing it is absolutely a question of commanding and obeying, on the basis, as I have said already, of a social structure composed of many 'souls'.[203]

The body is described as follows:

[An] extraordinary collectivity of living beings, all of them dependent and subordinate, but in another sense dominant and endowed with voluntary activity. . . . In this 'miracle of miracles', consciousness is merely an 'instrument', nothing more, – in the same sense in which the stomach is an instrument of the same miracle.[204]

The linking up of political metaphors with those of enterology must allow Nietzsche to interpret the latter and understand the game of assimilation as a relation beween forces, just as in turn philological metaphors will interpret the rules of these relations between forces being the game of interpretation, and 'the forever floating delimitation of power'.[205]

> If we follow the guiding thread of the body (*am Leitfaden des Leibes*), we recognize in man a plurality of living beings which, struggling or collaborating among themselves, or submitting themselves to one another, affirm their individual being and so involuntarily affirm the whole. Among these living beings, there are some which are more masters than subalterns; among these masters there is once again struggle and victory.[206]

From the beginning, Nietzsche insists on the image of a collective game (*Zusammenspiel*): drives, like individuals in a social group, should display a certain form of intelligence, consciousness and spontaneity. He applies this scheme to digestion, which he metaphorizes politically:

> A collective game as subtly intelligent as, for example, digestion. Here we have the collective game of a great number of intellects. Wherever I discover life, I perceive this collective game. And among these many intellects, there is also a leader.[207]

He can develop the political metaphor:

> The splendid cohesion (*Zusammenbindung*) of the most multiple (*vielfachst*) living creatures, the way in which superior and inferior activities adjust to one another and integrate one another, this multiform (*tausendfältig*) obedience, which is not blind, let alone mechanical, but is critical, prudent, careful, even rebellious (*widerstrebend*).[208]

This consciousness is not the privilege of the conscious intellect:[209] 'moral thought *follows* our conduct, it does not direct it'.[210] In this organicist political conception of what we might well call a political *body*, it is multiplicity that dominates:

> To begin with the *body* and physiology: why? – In this way we get an exact representation of the nature of our subjective unity, created from a group of leaders at the head of a collectivity . . .; we understand how these leaders depend on those they rule over, and how the conditions for a hierarchy and a division of labour create the possible existence of bitty beings and the whole . . .;

how struggle is expressed even in the swapping around of commandment and obedience and how a forever floating delimitation of power (*fliessendes Machtgrenzenbestimmen*) is necessary for life.[211]

The novelty here is the nature of the relation between the conscious intellect and the rest of the body, or more exactly between the groups of drives themselves: it is not causal either in a spiritualist sense (the spirit is a toy), or in a physiological or mechanist sense. The body is not a machine, but a political organization based on relations between forces that are unstable and not univocally regulated by conscious causal logic: there is no submissive obedience or function that is harmoniously regulated by laws. What is the rule of composition of these forces? Nietzsche considers the mechanism as only being 'symbolical' of the organism and the physical world. It is excluded by the representation of vital phenomena as conflicts.

It is a *basic error* to believe in concord (*Eintracht*) and the absence of conflict – that would be death! Wherever there is life, there is corporative training (*genossenschaftliche Bildung*) in which companions struggle for their food, and argue over space, and in which the weakest submit, live for a shorter time and have fewer descendants; diversity (*Verschiedenheit*) reigns in the smallest things . . . – identity is a great illusion. . . . Centralization is far from being as perfect –, and *the claim made by reason to be* at the centre of centralization is surely the gravest defect of this perfection.[212]

Imperceptibly, like Freud,[213] Nietzsche personifies his description in order to reveal fluctuations and the way in which they differ from a strictly mechanistic relation:

The relations between origins already demands that every *virtue* be put into practice: obedience, assiduousness, mutual aid, vigilance – organic life, which is autonomous, excludes any automatic nature.[214]

A mechanical system would result in a death-like state, while the *Will to Power* assumes a floating. Nietzsche above all stresses the impossibility of reaching a *single* meaning. Kinetics prohibits not only equilibrium, or the mutual cancelling-out of forces, but also concord. If 'the centre of the system is constantly displaced',[215] if the domination of a group or unity is precarious, it is because plurality is constantly emerging; Nietzsche attributes domination to 'regency councils' and 'aristocracies'. Life is the instability of power-relations, there is no domination, only a struggle *for* domination, *Wille ZUR Macht*: 'Many drives struggle to predominate within me (*Kämpfen in mir um die Oberherrschaft*). In this I am the image of everything living and I explain this to myself'.[216]

Man is 'a plurality of "wills to power"'.[217]

A plurality of hierarchized forces, such that there are leaders, but that the leader must procure from the subordinates everything that helps their subsistence; he is therefore conditioned by their existence. All these living beings have to be members of the same species, without which they would not know how to serve and obey one another; the masters must in some sense be subalterns in turn, and in more subtle cases they must temporarily swap roles; the person who normally commands must occasionally obey. . . . The centre of gravity is variable; the continual *production of cells*, etc. causes a perpetual change in the number of these beings. And this is not just a simple matter of *addition*.[218]

Conflict prohibits 'harmony'.

The plurality (*Vielheit*) and incoherence of impulses, and the absence of a system between them produces a 'weak will'; the coordination of these impulses under the predominance of one of them produces a 'strong will'; in the first case, there is oscillation and the lack of a centre of gravity; in the second case, there is precision and a clear direction.[219]

Direction, and not state of equilibrium. The body's drives are therefore 'beings that grow, struggle, become larger or wither, to such a degree that their number changes perpetually and our lives, like all life, involve a perpetual death'.[220] The body and spirit represents a contradictory disequilibrium. And that is why 'struggle is expressed even in the changing around of commandment and obedience'.[221]

A hierarchy is established to the benefit of a 'group of leaders' that forms 'the head of a collectivity'.[222] This is 'the aristocracy within the body, the plurality of masters',[223] such that 'the subject is a multiplicity'.[224] But is this unstable composition, lying between unity and plurality, not also equally the status of interpretation? The metaphorical logic of politics in Nietzsche and the problematics of his interpretation of texts appear to be isomorphic.

'If we were a unity, this conflict could not in itself exist. In fact, we are a multiplicity *that has constructed an imaginary unity for itself.*'[225] It seems that the text would be understood, and not something to interpret, if it were a unity. Just as in the domination of the conscious, struggle is not abolished, but persists in the form of a tense compromise between affects, so the interpretation of a text is a unity that does not reabsorb its plurality: there is no single interpretation, nor unity of interpretation of a text. 'Affects are a plurality behind which there is no need to postulate a unity: it is enough to consider them as a regency council.'[226] Just as it is not possible to attribute *one* meaning to a text, according to Nietzsche, for the body

> It is not necessary to admit that there is *only a single subject*: who knows if it would not be just as permissible to admit a multiplicity of subjects whose cooperation and struggle would form the basis of our thought and of all conscious life? A sort of *aristrocracy* of 'cells' in which authority lies? A group of equals who are used to governing together and who know how to command?[227]

Conversely, consciousness, a multiple unity that tries to impose itself like a 'monarch',[228] takes on the role of an interpretation in relation to the text as a whole.

(c)   The philological metaphor of interpretation

The philological metaphor is articulated on the political metaphor: the body functions according to a schema of interpretation. To interpret, is, when faced with a plurality, to choose possible meanings from a sign or set of polysemic signs. It is both to hand the sign over to its plurivocity, *and* necessarily to abridge this plurivocity: it involves *freeing* and *dominating*, becoming the master by debarment.

The domination of consciousness rests in reality and ignorance, a mode of interpretation:

> In man there are as many 'consciousnesses' as there are beings (at each moment of his existence) which make up his body. What makes this 'conscious' element, or intellect, which we normally

imagine to be unique, stand out, is precisely that it remains protected and excluded (*geschützt und abgeschlossen*) from the innumerable and diverse elements in the experience of these diverse consciousnesses; it is the consciousness of a higher level, a reigning collectivity (*eine regierende Vielheit*), an aristocracy, and for this reason we present it with merely a *choice* of experiences and simplified experiences, that are easy to oversee and grasp and are therefore *false* – in order for it to persist for its part in its work of simplification and clarification, and so of falsification, and to prepare what is commonly called a 'will'; – each of these voluntary acts presupposes in some sense a choice made by a dictator. But what offers this choice to our intellect, what has first simplified, levelled out and interpreted these experiences, is certainly not this same intellect, any more than it is the person who executes the will.[229]

According to the metaphor's themes, consciousness is a 'dictator', a 'monarch', a 'general', but its power rests on the element of simplification in an interpretative act: 'A certain ignorance in which the monarch is kept regarding the detail of operations, and even the troubles arising out of the collectivity, is part of the conditions that allow the monarch to reign'.[230] Just as a general desires and must remain in ignorance of a great number of facts, so as not to compromise his overall view, so there must necessarily be in consciousness a drive that *excludes*, *disperses* and chooses, and only lets *certain facts* be exposed.'[231]

What, though, should we understand by the term ignorance (*Nichtwissen*)? Nietzsche presents it as 'a certain way of seeing things in a general, overall manner, of simplifying and falsifying, according to one's perspective',[232] like the effect of a 'translation' (*Zurückübersetzung*), a 'collective game', in which experiences are 'simplified', 'levelled out' and 'interpreted'.[234] But these are the operations of interpretation, which is a condition for vital perspectivism:

> It is necessary for you to understand that without this special sort of ignorance life itself would be impossible, and that it is a condition without which the living person would not know how to preserve himself or prosper; you need around you a solid belljar of ignorance.[235]

It is by way of signs, simplifying abbreviations, that consciousness interprets and dominates:

> There are no immediate facts; the same goes for sensations and thoughts; as soon as I am conscious of them, I abstract, simplify and attempt to construct; this is what we call *being conscious* of things, it is a very *active* way of arranging them . . . a thought or sensation are the *signs* of certain phenomena. . . . This is a temporarily permissible *simplification* of the true state of the facts.[235]

Consciousness exists within a situation of interpretation. Therefore, 'inner experience' becomes conscious only after having found an *intelligible* language for the individual, that is to say a way of translating a state of consciousness into states that are more familiar to him'.[236] To interpret is 'to become master via signs of an enormous mass of facts'.[237] Such is the 'intellect''s ability. To say that consciousness is a simplifying sign is therefore to attribute to it the same status as that of interpretation, which presupposes that the body itself is comparable to a text:

> An idea is an invention to which nothing corresponds exactly, even though many things correspond to it more or less. . . . But this imaginary world is for man a means of using signs to grasp a huge mass of facts and to etch them into his memory. This system of signs constitutes his superiority, precisely because he is working away from the factual details. The reduction of experiences to *signs*, and the growing mass of things that let themselves be grasped in this way, constitute his *supreme power.*[238]

The ability to signify is an 'extraordinary faculty of abbreviation placed at the service of commandment'.[239]

All the same, the progression of metaphors finds itself blocked. By a sort of circular movement, Nietzsche refers the philological metaphors of interpretation back to the preceding metaphors. To clarify the former, Nietzsche has recourse to images of *assimilation* and *compromise*, which stem from the metaphors of digestion and politics:

> Thought consists in falsifying through transformation, sensation consists in falsifying through transformation, will consists in falsifying through transformation; everywhere, it is the craft of

assimilation (*die Kraft der Assimilation*) that is at work, and it assumes the will to make external things resemble us (*gleich zu machen*). This is no desire for 'objectivity', but a sort of incorporation (*Einverleibung*) and adaptation (*Anpassung*) in order to provide nutrition (*Ernährung*).[240]

Someone created an idea out of the body, however inexact – of the many systems that collaborate in it, of everything produced by mutual solidarity or hostility, of the extreme subtlety of the compromises (*Ausgleichung*) established.[241]

Nietzsche sometimes goes so far as to slide one metaphor into another:

This attitude towards the primary material which is provided by the senses . . . is not dictated by a plan to find the truth, but by a sort of will to dominate, assimilate and be nourished. Our constant functions are absolutely egoistical, machiavellian, astute and unscrupulous: commandment and obedience are pushed by them to the extreme.[242]

In every case, compromise and assimilation, like interpretation, constitute 'a momentary equilibrium of force between all our constitutive drives'.[243]

All we can conclude, as far as the body is concerned, is what is suggested by the notions of compromise, assimilation and interpretation: Nietzsche establishes the supposed *facts* as *signs*.[244] 'The series and apparent successions of sensations, thoughts, etc., are *symptoms* of true links. . . . The following thought is a sign (*Zeichen*) of the way in which the situation of forces as a whole has become modified in the meantime.'[245]

What we call 'life' is a multiplicity of forces linked by the phenomenon of nutrition which is common to them. This phenomenon of nutrition includes, as its means of fulfilment, everything we call sensation, representation, thought, that is to say: (1) resistance (*Widerstreben*) to every other force; (2) an arrangement (*Zurechtmachen*) of these forces on the basis of a certain form and rhythm; (3) an estimation (*Abschätzung*) of their assimilation or elimination.[246]

Growing personalization reinforces the link with the art of interpreting. Living is indeed 'directing the lived',[247] but in the sense that interpreting correctly means 'ruminating'. What we have, therefore, is less an attempt to fix the organic body than an attempt to clarify the concept of interpretation, or to avoid having to think it, as if it were not a concept:

> It is our needs *which interpret (auslegen) the universe*; our drives are their *pro* and *contra*. Every drive is a sort of ambition to dominate, each one has its own perspective which it tries to impose as the norm on all the other drives.[248]

Therefore: 'all meaning (*Sinn*) is a will to power'.[249] Culture is an interpretation of the will to power of drives: 'To what extent are interpretations of the world symptoms of a dominant drive?'[250] But this question is circular: as a domination and interpretation, 'all morality is ultimately merely a refined form of the measures taken by all organic life to *adapt (anpassen)* and yet to *feed itself (ernähren)* and *gain power (Macht gewinnen)*'.[251]

The body, as a *relation of forces* of the *assimilated* signs is an *interpretative* space.

> The will to power *interprets (interpretiert)* (– the formation of an organ is the result of an interpretation): it limits and fixes degrees of power, and the differences between them. Simple differences can only be felt as such; we need a thing that wants to grow, and which interprets on the basis of its own value every other thing that wants to grow. . . . – In truth, interpreting a fact is already a way to become a master. The organic process presupposes a *continuous activity of interpretation (fortwährend Interpretieren)*.[252]

But how do we define interpretation?

10
Philosophy: The Genealogical Analysis of Culture

The genealogy of culture leads to an interpretative form of thought. We have only interpretations or interpretative metaphors of interpretation: this is neither a semiological system, nor a conceptual structure. Does this weaken thought? Perhaps the circular process is necessary.

At the same time, the question of the status of discourse in Nietzsche is posed: it is an interpretative discourse on interpretation. Metaphor assumes two rules: an epistemological role, concerning Nietzsche's interpretation of interpretation, and an ontological role, concerning interpretation as body and the body as interpretation. What can be the value of discourse in Nietzsche if, as interpretation, it is based, in the last resort, on metaphor? Should we not question the impossibility of discourse in Nietzsche, its inability to give itself a conceptual grounding? Is it not as a body thinking [la pensée du corps] that Nietzsche's thought makes it impossible to have a strictly conceptual foundation? There is no doubt a place to determine where this thought is located. Taking 'the body as a guiding thread', this interpretative thought based on a multiplicity of drives can have recourse only to metaphoricity as a scheme of body thinking that allows us to imagine the imaginative link between unity and plurality. Metaphor would then be an imaginary, and not a speculative, synthesis, making it possible to have a body thinking, that is, both a body that thinks and an interpretative thinking that thinks about the body.

This attempt at a body thinking obliges us to direct inquiries away from a concept towards a scheme, from a transcendental foundation towards a schematic imaginary production. The gap between Schopenhauer and Nietzsche on the one hand, and Kant on the other, corresponds perhaps to our taking account of imagination as a 'fundamental faculty' and the origin of the synthesis of intuition and thought, as Heidegger shows in his study of the first edition of Kant's *Critique of Pure Reason*.[1] Schopenhauer and Nietzsche, integrating both the body and will to thought, return in a sense to early Kant. The question that Kant puts: 'To institute a tribunal which will assure to reason its lawful claims',[2] is criticized by Nietzsche, but he does not so much criticize its legitimacy as move the question in the direction of something prior to reason:

> It is almost comic that our philosophers demand that philosophy should begin with a critique of the *faculty of knowing*: how plausibly can the organ of knowledge offer its own 'critique', if we are forced to mistrust the previous results of knowledge? To *reduce* philosophy to the 'will to find a theory of knowledge' is comic.[3]

> A tool cannot *criticize* its own practical value; intelligence cannot fix its own limit, or determine whether or not it is well constructed.[4]

> How should a tool be able to criticize itself when it can use only itself for the critique? It cannot even define itself![5]

What is 'absurd' and 'peculiar' in the demand made 'of an instrument that it should criticize its own usefulness and suitability',[6] is that one is asking an instrument to provide its own foundations, when it is something that is used, such that the question of 'the examination of foundations' is a *symptom* of subjection, a *false question* of instruments or toys, that has to do with their subordinate status. Founding something is a moral question.[7] 'Trust in reason – why not mistrust?'[8] Founding is merely an interpretation, and it is interpretation that has to be schematized, not founding.

The word 'interpret', in its largest sense, translates the terms used by Nietzsche which all refer to the philological practice of texts: *auslegen* (which is applied first of all to the exegesis of biblical texts), *erklären* (which Nietzsche contrasts, as explanation, with interpretative commentary), *interpretieren* (in the very general sense of commentary) and *(aus)deuten* (which consists in isolating a meaning in an enigmatic text, for example as in prophecy or dreams). In using the word 'interpretation' we shall confine ourselves to the philological category outlined in the German terms.[9]

Nietzsche applies the idea of interpretation metaphorically to the body, because:

(a) The text, composed from signs, does not immediately offer up its meanings, but assumes one or several codes which condition access to it. But the text can be distinguished from a discursive body inasmuch as it does not master or contain the code or codes that regulate understanding it, while the limits of a corpus consist in creating a coincidence between the discursive whole and the rules of a code: this is what Plato showed in the *Phaedo*[10] in presenting the text as an orphan deprived of its father's help. The text, on the other hand, can be submitted to a *multiplicity* of codes. An interpretation consists in *imposing* a code on the text. Nietzsche says: 'Interpretation is itself a means of becoming master of something'.[11] This means we limit the potential plurality of meanings. But it also means that we *pluralize* the text, in relation to the finite set of signs which it constitutes, by attributing meanings to it that it does not have *in itself*. For interpretation is a situation in which the text's in-itself is unknowable, due to the exteriority of the code or codes in relation to the text. There is no legitimate in-itself for the sign, which refers to that which lies outside it and therefore to a multiplicity which it does not master. As such, a text is therefore *subject* to an external plurality, if it does not contain in itself its own constituting rule.[12] As a result, the status of the interpretation of the text is in opposition as much to thingist explanations, for which the text signifies something in itself, as to structural conceptions, which decide to close the text in on its in-itself, creating a situation in which meaning is replaced by differential *value*.

(b) Every interpretation is *perspectivist*. Is this the 'nihilism' of 'Everything lacks meaning'?[13] Perspectivism implies, not the negation of meaning, but more insistence on speech than on the body and the impossibility of a totalization of meaning. Every interpretation is *in fact* limited: (1) to the enactment via speech of one or several codes on offer in a particular time and place; (2) to those who, in addition, are compatible with the particular set of signs of a given text. To speak of relativism, on the basis of the arbitrary nature of the sign, would be meaningful only if, when *an* interpreter and *a* text are specified, we could stage a confrontation between the common ground or their specific qualities and the system of the totality of possible codes. Moreover, prespectivism means that, *necessarily*, the distinctive nature (which is conceived of only in relation to a *thought* universality) of the interpreter must enter into relation with the distinctiveness of the speech act represented by the text (which is distinctive in relation to the timeless universality of the system of language). For Nietzsche, pulling oneself up to the level of a totalization involves going beyond in an abstract way, which implies a denegation of singularity of the body, the text's perspectivist reality and the interpreter. For Nietzsche, as for Kierkegaard, singularity, the only mode of reality, can be supervised only *in an abstract way*. Every perspective is therefore an absolute that can appear to be relative only to a thinking that abstracts and cuts itself off from perspective.

This is why Nietzsche replaces a system or abstract totality with the *Versuch,* or successive addition of perspectives. If interpreting constitutes the action of becoming master of a text, by assimilating it to one's own perspective, the interpreter cannot ignore the fact that other perspectives are possible. Interpretation is therefore located between a real perspectivist singularity and the denegatory abstraction of a generalizing concept. But the thing that singularizes perspective is the body, which is always located somewhere.[14] To interpret is to have a *body*, and to be a perspective. And the totalization of perspectives by a scientific concept can only be achieved at the price of a denegation of the body in the interpreter and in the text.

Perspectivism is a Spinozism from which all thought of the substance unifying the different modes is excluded, or a Leibnizism lacking in divine thought. With perspectives, there are only modes or monads, which can articulate or represent being only from a *finite* perspective, unless they inflate the '*Froschperspektive*'[15] until it is as big as the ox of infinite substance. Nietzsche therefore speaks only in the conditional tense about characterizing the essence of a thing as a totalization of perspectives:

A thing would be characterized only when every being would have asked: 'What is that? and would have had a reply. If a single being's relations and perspectives to things were still to be supplied, then the thing would still not be 'defined'. In short, the essence of a thing is basically just an *opinion* about that thing.[16]

Is this an absolute empirical idealism of the Berkeleyan type? The idea of perspective does not reduce the text to what can be perceived of it (*esse est percipi*), nor does it reduce reality to what is empirically perceived in each perspective. On the contrary, the image of perspective apparently involves: (a) the subsistence of the text in relation to perspectives, which are *points* of *view*, and not, as Berkeley believes, *visions*; (b) the creation of a relation between the empirical reality conditioning the perspective and the reality of the text; (c) the necessity of a *passage* from one perspective to another, since the idea of perspective insists simultaneously on the *located* reality of a point of view and a *relativity* in relation to others. How does this passage and the going beyond of a perspective operate, if it is not to fall into a denegatory abstraction? If a perspective thinking [*la pensée* ... *de la perspective*] in Nietzsche is a finitude thinking [*une pensée de la finitude*], how can finitude be expressed in *Selbstüberwindung,* which goes beyond *self* and *Same*?

If, for Nietzsche, a concept cuts itself off from perspectivism by a totalizing generalization which *denies* its perspectivist relation to a living reality, metaphor, on the other hand: (1) constitutes a *passage* from one perspective to another, as its etymology (displacement: μεταφόρα) indicates; (2) is the overlapping of two or more perspectives and therefore does not constitute an abstraction of perspectivism, but on the contrary affirms itself as a limited perspective; (3) appears as a perspectivist reference back to another perspective and, as a result of the immediate contradiction which this provokes, simultaneously constitutes an affirmation of perspective and an opportunity to go beyond it; (4) in this sense, is the principle of life as interpretation in which the singularity of perspective as a necessary relation to the world and the plurality of other perspectives are set out.

Therefore, *metaphor affirms and questions the world,* interpreting it as a play of perspectives and a contradiction of these perspectives without any hope of a totalizing reconciliation. In questioning the world (the other perspectives), it goes beyond itself. It also goes beyond the world of a perspectivist succession in life, without denying this world, by moving beyond it in an inappropriate way. In contrast to a concept, which is fixed as a single perspective once it totalizes perspectives from which it cuts itself off, metaphor is life or the world interpreting itself, an irreducible conflict of perspectives which, in their opposition of singularities, pluralize the world, whose metaphorical imaginary reveals that it is something more than its concept and something other than its perspectives: it consists of correspondences, and a conceptual non-totality. This non-totality is a rich non-pertinence, but only to the extent that, like a Kantian scheme, it joins the tangible to the intelligible and the plural to the singular. This is a tangible pluralization of tangible singularity, like Marxian praxis,[17] and it testifies simultaneously to man's presence and non-appropriateness in his *Dasein*.

Interpretation occurs only where the object and the status of investigation impose *lack of knowledge,* the first through its plurality, the second through its perspectivist nature. Metaphor interprets and is there to be interpreted, as a rich mistranslation (*false meaning: faux sens*), and is *displaced* in relation to what it signifies: by failing to be appropriate to the thing it aims at, it is displaced *by spilling over onto something else* while participating in the same movement of trans-ference (μετα-φόρα) and uniting the two parts in order to create a new plural unity. More than a discourse, it is therefore a movement, the movement of *Wille zur Macht.* This defines its truth as being *partial,* a condition of one truth associated with metaphor as *passage.*

If, in this sense, metaphor is the interpretative model and the structure of the *Wille zur Macht* as domination–passage–lack of knowledge, the interpretative truth of the world is more a question of interpretation than concept, evoking schematism. The 'transcendental' constitution of the interpreted world, instead of being based on the originally synthetic unity of aperception, rests on the body, which stands as the power of imagination and the place where metaphor is produced. In turn, a concept appears as a fixed perspective. Perhaps metaphor is that non-place where the world, far from being able to establish itself in an object, is subject to interpretation and becomes a metaphorical term. It is through interpretation that the world becomes infinite and interpretation becomes interminable: it is because of imagination as metaphor that the world is not what it is, and becomes what it is not and what it is. If metaphor is radical, then, the world, through metaphor, is not what it is in itself, nor is it any more what we make of it. It transcends itself because it does not contain its code, and it is imagination that constitutes the immanent transcendence of the world.

It was tempting, in the wake of Bachelard, to reveal the 'coherence' of Nietzsche's metaphors and to assemble them into a semiological structure that allowed us to extrapolate a concept of interpretation. But this is what is prohibited by a *deferring link* or *meta-phorical transference.* What is the nature of the interpretative logic of this succession of metaphors and what is its relation to the definition of metaphor as a paradigm of interpretation? That is what we must clarify now, by taking up once more what Paul Ricoeur established in the last chapter, and in particular its fourth paragraph, of *La métaphore vive*.[18]

For Ricoeur:

> The particular intention that animates the system of language put to work by a metaphorical utterance includes the requirement to elucidate, which can only be answered by offering the semantic possibilities of this discourse another space in which to express themselves, that of speculative discourse.[19]

But in Nietzsche, all this takes place as if 'the requirement in concept'[20] failed and were answered only in part by means of another metaphor. In Nietzsche, '"like" remains inferior to "same"'[21] and tries to overcome this defect by means of another 'like', without a conceptual unity managing to close this unstable succession. As is borne out by the circular movement between the body (digestion) and interpretation (philology), this metaphorical opening cannot be gone beyond and herein lies the fundamentality of the body and life. To have a body is to have access only to the 'as if', which precariously establishes the singularity of a plural and at the same time the plurality of a singular. In Nietzsche, metaphor is 'like a world made dynamic by a play of attraction and repulsion that continually creates interaction and intersection among different movements whose organizational centres are decentred in relation to one another, without this play ever coming to rest in an absolute knowledge that would reabsorb all the tensions'.[22] Through the body, which is the site of metaphorical imagination, the world, that ceases to be conceived of as a closed totality that contains its own codes of understanding, becomes a text, an object of interpretation, *Selbstüberwindung*.

The body is thus that part of the world through which the world is revealed to be something other than what it is. The body is living in so far as it is the place in which different perspectives confront one another. Metaphor is the mode in which a living passage from one perspective to another take place. But the body itself: (1) can only be designated metaphorically; (2) acts as a metaphor for the metaphorical interpretation that the body is said to establish.

The world is an enigma, and always presents itself with the

necessary singularity of a perspective that, in order to establish a life, is linked to the other perspectives only via a metaphorical relation. Metaphor does not create a synthesis, but frees 'the power that certain fictions have of redescribing reality'[23]: and if the metaphor is fundamental, if we are to define our relation to the world, the world exists for us only as something interpreted. The text of the world is a play of forces that releases only signs. If a text exists only through metaphor, it is because, in its singularity, it points outside of itself towards *the* meanings that, like metaphor, it declares to be plural. But the body is, as a location for perspectives that is always *singular*, the place where the text is joined to its other outside of discourse and the place where it is pluralized metaphorically. The body, as a metaphorical location, is thus the principle of the imaginary transcendence of the world. As opposed to a structural scientific analysis, Nietzsche's conception of interpretation implies the necessity of each perspective in diachrony and the impossibility of closing the text back in on its synchrony by reason of its necessary link to perspectivist diachrony.

'The will to power interprets';[24] 'every meaning (*Sinn*) is a will to power'.[25] In each perspective in which the text is *related back* to its other and reinterpreted, it is *overcome*. It is with its other that it makes sense, becoming through meaning the master of the alterity to which it refers in its ignorance. This is how Nietzsche breaks with a science of the world and the body and with metaphysics as a discourse, both of which are conceptual, univocal and closed. For him, the truth of the world is its meaning or meanings; the reality of the world is its non-coincidence. For there would be no concept of the world if not for a totalizing God and substance: but, in declaring that 'God is dead', Nietzsche also seems to want to indicate that, in relation to this meta-phorical life, 'God is dead'.

For the interpreter of culture, the world, which is a blossoming of images, glides along on endless metaphorical correspondences: for the imaginary, finitude, with its own inner perspectivist singularity, is infinite, since it is its own metaphor. Nietzsche's metaphors of the body and of interpretation do not constitute a semiological system or set of archetypes, but put forward the reality of the world and culture as an open game of metaphor. Nietzsche's metaphors of philological reading and interpretation therefore appear to be less a metaphor among others than an index of a 'transcendental' metaphoricity, that is obviously more regulatory than constitutive, in the sense that, if the world is properly speaking unknowable it is because, through us and for us, it is merely a metaphor.

This does not mean that metaphor has a debased status in relation to a discourse that could articulate the world's total truth. Nietzsche's textual practice shows that conceptual discourse, with regard to life, seems limited, while metaphor has the advantage of being able to transform its perspectivist singularity into a pluralized interrogation. It always leaves a 'residue',[26] therefore. This residue, in common with Kant's in-itself, cannot be fixed.[27] But, if we can speak, by way of analogy, of a 'metaphorical transcendental', as opposed to the Kantian transcendental, metaphor unveils a text that is regulatory and non-constitutive. The body, as an interpreting plurality that is perspectivist and metaphorizing, replaces the originally synthetic unity of aperception. In Nietzsche, the in-itself of life is displaced by perspectives and the play of metaphor: it is not, as in Kant, the hidden face of a relative universality. Nietzsche, with metaphor, insists on the *irreducibility of the singular* and, allowing a synthesis to occur only by way of a partial and inappropriate meta–phorical transference, stresses at the same time that the world can be covered only by an *interrogative pluralization*. The fact that Nietzsche thus comes up against the irreducibility of the relationship between thought and life is a homage he pays to his *Selbstüberwindung*. And it is in this way that metaphor institutes the world, or rather life. It is no longer nature, but culture, a culture in which life is metaphorically both more and less than itself – more, since it is an interpretation, less, since it consists of perspectives.

To speak of culture, then, is to speak of philosophy. This leads us to examine the nature and status that Nietzsche attributes to philosophy, not so much in his discourse as through his textual practice. For Nietzsche, the object of philosophy is culture, and when we isolate the labour and forms of Nietzsche's texts on culture, we in fact isolate the forms of Nietzsche's philosophy or philosophizing as a genealogy, that is to say an attempt to display a body playing (*le jeu du corps*) in the text of culture *and* in his own text. This philosophical discourse is impossible in the sense that it is based on metaphor in order to integrate life into it, but can do this only by undermining what could act as its foundation. This 'impossible' philosophical discourse, then, is presented by Nietzsche in the form of a text that would like to present itself to life as a

'*Ja-Sagen*'. But as life is a perspective reality that cannot be fathomed in its totality, Nietzsche's philosophy can only be an unstable discourse – a *text*. It cannot be denied that Nietzsche maintains a discourse. But Nietzsche knows that maintaining this discourse means getting trapped in a closed ('metaphysical' or 'moral') concept of life and so of culture. He must therefore unsay or retract what he says.[28] It remains to be seen how he plays this double game which seems to involve metaphorical 'partiality'.

Nietzsche's discourse on culture, in his philosophy, is the discourse of a *moraliste*,[29] in the sense the French term gives to *Menschenprüfer*.[30] It is perhaps a cause for regret that French studies, whether pursuing an idealist line, or reducing the problem to one of metaphysics, in the wake of Heidegger, have not seen the thing that places Nietzsche in a tradition which he has continually claimed for himself, as much by criticizing it as by continuing it. Yet, if the *Untimely Meditations* and *The Gay Science* were not sufficient proof, the works of the final period would testify to the constant nature of Nietzsche's moral concerns. One consequence of this, his predilection for maxims, never waned, and is present not only in *Twilight of the Idols,* but also within the larger paragraphs of *The Antichrist, Ecce Homo* or *The Case of Wagner.*[31] Nietzsche introduces or reintroduces terms, concepts or *ideas* that are designed to present an analysis of *culture* and tie him to the *moraliste* tradition of nihilism, *décadence,* genealogy, history, origin, mores, selection, training, race, morality, duty, power, weakness, virtue, will, life, heart, etc. But his very philosophical object and his philosophical method (or style) put him increasingly out of line with the discourse that he maintains, such that he finds himself in a position analogous to that of Sterne, 'the most liberated writer', in *Assorted Opinions and Maxims:*[32] 'An artistic style in which the fixed form is constantly being broken up, displaced, transposed back into indefiniteness, so that it signifies one thing and at the same time another'.[33] And the following remark on Sterne could be applied to Nietzsche: 'The reader who demands to know exactly what Sterne really thinks of a thing . . . must be given up for lost'.

For a long period, right up until *The Gay Science*, Nietzsche maintains this *moraliste* discourse without any sense of ambiguity. But, from *Beyond Good and Evil* and *Zarathustra* onwards, this discourse finds itself in an unstable situation. Conscious of this instability, Nietzsche plays with inverted commas, placing a received signifier within the double system of propriety and lexical impropriety. His use of parody is merely a special case of this double game, through which Nietzsche wishes to join any perspective, in an imaginary link, to other perspectives. Saying yes to life means expressing the singularity of perspective, but also questioning it with plurality. This is, in Nietzsche's philosophical text, the truth of the *untimely*:

> What does a philosopher demand of himself first and last? To overcome his time in himself, to become 'timeless'. With what must he therefore engage in the hardest combat? With whatever marks him as the child of his time. Well, then! I am, no less than Wagner, a child of this time; that is a *décadent*: but I comprehended this. I resisted it. The philosopher in me resisted.[34]

As an example of how Nietzsche's discourse gets to *work* on concepts, let us take first of all the term *genealogy*. Even if we agree to differentiate between this notion and that of Kantian criticism and psychophysiological causality, the definition still raises problems. Gilles Deleuze senses this difficulty and proceeds carefully:

> Genealogy means both the value of origin and the origin of values. Genealogy is as opposed to absolute values as it is to relative or utilitarian ones. Genealogy signifies the differential element of values from which their value itself, derives. Genealogy thus means origin or birth, but also difference or distance in the origin. Genealogy means nobility and baseness, nobility and vulgarity, nobility and decadence in the origin.[35]

In order to avoid terms relating to foundation and genesis, J.Granier has to resort to philology:

> The quest for an origin is only an authentic genealogy to the extent that this origin is no longer hypostasized as a *foundation beyond experience*. ... Existing things are therefore merely phenomena that demand to be deciphered according to the roles of what Nietzsche rightly calls a correct *philology* – 'phenomena' being synonyms of signs or, even better, 'symptoms'[36].

To define this 'quest for an origin', Granier evokes the 'stages of a constitution', and 'becoming' or evolution, and concludes, in the absence of a definition from Nietzsche, by comparing him to Marx and 'the Marxist critique of idealogies'.[37]

But, from the beginning of the Preface to *The Genealogy of Morals*, Nietzsche himself speaks of an 'origin' or 'provenance', and even, if not of 'foundations', at least of a 'ground':[38] 'my ideas about the provenance of our moral prejudices';[39] 'under what conditions did man construct value judgements *good* and *evil*?'[40] Why does Nietzsche, in order to designate what up until then he had called '*Naturgeschichte*', 'the natural history of morals',[41] use the even more metaphorical term of 'genealogy'?

We must begin with the deviation Nietzsche inflicts on the word. Properly speaking, it designates a discourse on ancestry (γενεά). Γενεαλογεῖν means to show how one individual (especially one considered noble) is descended from another. Hesiod's *Theogony* is a genealogy of the gods. Nietzsche's genealogy bears on morality and, more generally, on culture as a set of evaluations: the impropriety involves applying to abstract sets something that goes only for humans or, at most, for animals,[42] but it does generate a host of pertinent questions. Genealogy, in the proper sense, is *research,* 'very special, a marginal issue, (for someone who) learns how to ask questions'.[43] This is why Nietzsche says: 'we knowers are unknown to ourselves'.[44] This research therefore bears not only upon origins, but also upon the factors that allow *grouping* to take place while themselves remaining *hidden*. It bears not only upon a genesis, but also upon a *generation*:

> Our thoughts should grow out of our values with the same necessity as the fruit out of the tree. Our yeas and nays, our ifs and buts should all be intimately related and bear testimony to one will, one health, one soil, one sun.

Genealogy is, then, the 'need to know the conditions from which those values have sprung'.[45]

But, as indicated by the reply that Nietzsche liked to give from the age of thirty on to the question of the origins of evil; '[I made God] the father of evil',[46] genealogy questions a bodily and more precisely sexual origin, with the difference that it questions the causes or speculative foundations of ideas (for example in an *a priori*).[47] The body as a sexual cause then reveals itself to be the thing that produces a being that, in questioning its own origins, questions its *identity, evolution* and grouping habits. Moreover, the body, as an invisible anterior *origin* is what produces us as beings who question things because we are necessarily enigmatic to ourselves.[48] This is indicated in the myth of Oedipus, who replies to the Sphinx's riddle, an *enigma* regarding man's identity and origins, after he has unconsciously killed his father and before he marries his mother. Sexuality presents us as beings that are unconcious of their origins and question themselves over the question of origins: the question of identity is that of origins, of asking oneself who I am, of seeking to know where and who I come from. As a genealogical being, man merely manifests his position as a being separated, by his corporeity, from his truth.[49]

Research, grouping, dissimulation, generation, sexuality, identity, history, evolution, the origin of the species and natural history: these are the related connotations that make the notion of genealogy work within the imaginary, a genealogy understood as a knowledge of the conditions from which values have sprung.[50] In this way Nietzsche replies to the demands made by a philosophy[51] that wants to be 'a living thinking (*une pensée de la vie*). Not a thinking that makes life its object, but a living thinking that wants to inscribe in its own concepts the efforts through which life tries, through the I, to appropriate the world unto itself'.[52] Through this textual labour, Nietzsche's philosophy and genealogy present themselves simultaneously as concept and affect, inasmuch as an affect, a way in which *life* is apprehended via the body, is the imaginary non-totalizable linking of perspectives.

This labour, which operates under the term 'genealogy', a *philosophical* concept joined to the plurality of perspectives and connotations which it links up, is exemplary of Nietzsche's conception and practice of philosophy as being a genealogy of culture. It is the text that, disseminating conceptual discourse, allows a concept and life to be joined. This confirms the necessity, for Nietzsche's approach, of replacing a system with reading. A philosophical idea conceives of life only by turning it into a value through the plurality and singularity of the imaginary, a scheme of the world, or rule for conceiving of units of life as concept and value.

Reading Nietzsche so as to attempt to reconstitute a discursive conceptual structure is therefore an abstract business. Through its labours, the slightest text by Nietzsche, provided one tries to read it with some sense of continuity, overflows the conceptual limits without really contradicting them. In Nietzsche, the essence of a philosophical living thinking is played out other than in the concept.

This valorial work by the imagination on discourse could be illustrated by other examples. Thus it is that certain interpreters have not failed to note the difficulties implied in the use of terms such as 'strong' and 'weak', 'nihilism', 'will to power', 'morality', 'virtue', 'being', 'truth', etc.[53]

Let us take the idea of *décadence*. No doubt it is indispensable to isolate the concept from its biologizing coating. But it is none the less important to show how Nietzsche makes it signify a type of culture.

At the onset, if we stick to conceptuality, the term *décadence* ought to designate, within the framework of a fairly fanciful medical typology, the influence of a physical malady on value judgements: as if Nietzsche were in a position to prove the link between physiological impotence, asthenia and degeneracy or deterioration[54] and the corresponding psychic, intellectual and moral defects, the first being seen as causing the second. In certain fragments, Nietzsche was able to sketch this sort of pseudo-medical analysis.[55] But in this case it necessarily comes up against two objections: first, the impossibility of defining the body or the physico-chemical nature of its 'degeneracy'; second, the fact that, as the assumed location of this notion testifies, *décadence* designates more a loss of *psychic* 'power', 'energy' and 'vitality', something that cannot be delimited, than a properly somatic state of asthenia. According to the logic of this apparent 'concept', which joins the analyses of Burckhardt[56] to the medical 'theories' of the day on 'degeneracy', it is in fact the 'lack of soul' that weakens the body, which in turn produces 'decadent' ideals. If the medical notion of *décadence* could be consequent, it would have to result in a strict materialism, which cannot be discovered in Burckhardt and which the theories of degeneracy carefully aim to avoid! Nietzsche, while declaring himself to be an anti-materialist, on the other hand insisted in *Ecce Homo* on the material conditions (climate, hygiene, diet, etc.) that 'condition' or avoid *décadence* as a psychic illness resulting from a certain physiological state. But how can we believe in the materialism of this 'medicynicism' which is more polemical than scientific, when Nietzsche writes that 'the *décadent* as such always chooses the means harmful to him',[57] revealing, for a 'physiologist', a fairly curious voluntarism: 'I took myself in hand'?[58] In fact, Nietzsche borrows this term in order to turn it into a philosophical idea, that aims to interpret in a valorial way a cultural attitude that condemns life in which the body–spirit takes part as an interpretation of the world, and not as the 'moral' or 'physiological' cause of an 'illness'.

In French, from which Nietzsche borrows the term *'décadence'* more out of coquettishness than a 'European' spirit, the term *décadence* conforms to its Latin etymology in designating above all the physical[59] falling of buildings, bodies and, in the figurative sense, the falling or, rather, decline or decay (an interesting doublet reserved for the biological body) of institutions and civilizations.[60] In preference to *Verfall* (decline), the German equivalent, Nietzsche therefore adopts *décadence* in order to designate the decline of a culture as a set of evaluative bodies–spirits, but notes as he does so the *bodily* aspect of the weakness of groups of individals when faced with a life which they confront and interpret. *Décadence* is a weak *vital interpretation,* in which the organism moves towards its fall and its end.[61] Curiously, it is a historic notion, without any precise physiological connotation, which is used to present an idea of cultural degradation that rests on an illness in the instincts. Nietzsche, adopting a term that is used abstractedly, gives it life and a body via the imaginary,[62] and this is what distinguishes it from a concept like corruption or depravation (the progressive postponement of perfection, a downward trend) such as one finds in Rousseau. The term *décadence* is from the beginning improper, and recants or unsays the first meaning of a morbid physiological state that conditions 'weak'[63] moral evaluations: 'The moral weakening and hysteria of a weak, inbred, disoriented and sick population'.[64] Before all else, the idea of fall seems to designate a contraction or collapse in the body–spirit, as opposed to 'elevation, advance, strengthening'.[65] *Décadence,* like decease, is opposed to upward-moving life: 'Christianity . . . has waged a *war to the death* against this *higher* type of man [and] taken the side of everything weak, base, ill-constituted'.[66]

From this point on, *décadence* is inscribed within a opposition between high and low, which are represented as moral regions: *höherwertig, höher,* and *Erhöhung* versus *missraten, niedrig,* and *schwach,*[67] together with the valorial attitudes that are divided between life and death:

What is good? – All that heightens the feeling of power, the will to power, power itself in man. What is bad? – All that proceeds from weakness. What is happiness? – The feeling that power *increases* – that a resistance is overcome.[68]

This opposition between rising up and decomposition is displaced on to the opposition between domination and submission,[69] which engenders the paradox (unsustainable if *décadence* consisted only of physical weakness) that what is *low* is *dominant*:

> I consider life itself instinct for growth, for continuance, for accumulation of forces, for *power*: where the will to power is lacking there is decline. My assertion is that this will is *lacking* in all the supreme values of mankind – that values of decline, *nihilistic* values hold sway under the holiest names.[70]

> A long reflection on the subject of physiological exhaustion has obliged me to ask to what point the judgements of the weak have impregnated the world of values. My results have been as surprising as possible, even for me, someone who has already acclimatized himself to many strange regions; I found that all the higher values, all those that dominate humanity, or at least domesticated humanity, can be traced back to the judgements of debilitated men.[71]

This overturns the inversion resulting from 'the slave revolt in morals'[72] that Nietzsche calls *Umwertung*. *Décadence* is therefore the lack that lies within dominant values: 'where the will to power is lacking there is decline. My assertion is that this will is *lacking* in all the supreme values of mankind'.[73] This is why Nietzsche associates *décadence* with nihilism: 'values of decline, *nihilistic* values'.[74] 'Pity . . . is one of the chief instruments for the advancement of *décadence* – pity persuades to *nothingness*!'[75]

Thus worked, the idea of *décadence* becomes the philosophical and moral idea of an attitude that tends towards decomposition at the very heart of domination.[76] It is an interpretation to be metaphorized. The concept has become a philosophical idea which is found, for example, in Nietzsche's presentation of Socrates:[77] the dialogue on death in the *Phaedo*, dialectic as negation, Socrates' low birth, the monstrosity of decomposition, the play between reality and appearance, cold light and the darkness of the abyss, sickness and death, the morning[78] or evening twilight, end and defeat.

Nietzsche's concepts are therefore worked in a way that releases an imaginary polysemy – ideas – provided one agrees to ruminate.

An example of what Nietzsche means by the reading-rumination of aphorisms is: '*The disappointed man speaks.* – I sought great human beings, I never found anything but the *apes* of their ideal'.[79]

The discourse is clear, if we decode the metaphor of current usage: greatness, represented as being independent and creative, is just a servile imitation; there is no greatness in someone who shrinks in the face of an ideal; just as a monkey imitates man, the 'great man' imitates the ideal of a great man, which is in comic contrast to greatness.

But this maxim, which offers a foreboding of the neurotic role assigned by Freud to the superego, would be merely a neo-classical imitation of a *moraliste*'s maxim on affectation, vanity or conformism if it did not introduce another perspective that is properly genealogical: here, by way of allusion to Darwin,[80] man, and above all the great man, is descended from the ape. Man's relation to the ape is no longer just one of illusion to truth, but one of 'filiation'. Just as man, paleontologically, is descended from the ape, so a great man is merely (*nur*) the gregarious animal reality of an ape-like imitation, and vulgar Darwinism is used to provide a scheme for the notions of imitation, derivation, the paradoxical relations between ideal and animal, the relation between truth and appearance, man and animality, and ideal, history and nature, which genealogy embraces.

But working on the concept most often occurs within a textual *movement* in which Nietzsche's thought exceeds discourse. Let us therefore read a text in which *décadence*, genealogy, Socrates and Nietzsche are implicated in a labour and a movement which, in order to express life, shifts the text's weight on to the sound (*Klang*), the image of the genealogical reference.[81]

From the beginning, within the discourse itself, the text escapes towards the imaginary deferring link, which presents the idea of genealogy.

From the discursive point of view the text is solidly architectured:

I   *Observation*
   1. Universal proposition: every sage of every age belittles life.
   2. Particular confirmation: the example of Socrates (*selbst Sokrates*).

II   *Interpretation*
   1. Ancient interpretation (*ehemals*): universality = truth about the *object* (*beweisen*).

2. Nietzsche's new interpretation (*heute*): universality indicates (*weist auf*) a state or morbid typology on the part of the *subjects* of these judgements.

In the next paragraph, Nietzsche can then challenge the possibility of judging the object and show that only a genealogical judgement of the authors of judgement is pertinent.

But this discourse is played with by the text. First of all in reading this text we *also* read other texts. The first phase is a quotation from Goethe (*A Coptic Song*) which will be repeated later, and this text takes up again certain phrases from paragraph 110 of *Human, All Too Human,* which itself quotes Goethe's poem and comments: *consensus sapientum.* Here, then, we have a repetition, and the text's autonomy is thwarted (*déjouée*). Moreover, *Human, All Too Human* was already using the genealogical metaphor of the (more or less dubious) resemblance of children to their mother in order to illustrate the grouping of distinct phenomena (philosophies and religions). The '*gleich geurteilt*' of the *Twilight of the Idols* therefore suggests a universal sense of kinship. Nietzsche here speaks not of identical opinion, as he spoke in *Human, All Too Human* of identity of view, but of '*denselben Klan*', which corresponds to the earlier text's 'harmony'. The thing that here alerts the ear is less the tenor of the judgement than its resonance: it is a question of humour or desires. The charge carried by the word is accentuated by its repetition and the precision brought to it by '*Zweifel*', '*Schwermut*', '*Müdigkeit*', and '*Widerstand*', where a gradation moves from the theoretical and subjective '*Zweifel*' up to the physical attitude of opposition in '*Widerstand*' via intermediary states that psychological ('*Schwermut*') and psychomatic and physiological ('*Müdigkeit*').

It is via Socrates that Nietzsche brings about a declaration of the genealogical truth which the text tends towards. This Socrates is caught at the moment of his *death* (σῶμα-σῆμα): what Nietzsche has Socrates hear by subjectivizing the value of a statement through the slow transformation of the universal and totalizing '*das Leben*' into the existential and subjective '*leben*', is that he experiences *his* own life as a sickness, which *provokes* a judgement of universal appearance. 'I am sick' leads to 'life is worthless'. The question is no longer 'what is life?' but 'what [sick] body, what way of living judges life?' Nietzsche's interpretation[82], put into the mouth of Socrates, precedes the citation of Socrates' mysterious remark (118a) *in articulo mortis* in the *Phaedo*. This leads to the vigorous nature of the almost vulgar phrase: '*Selbst Sokrates hatte es satt*, which corresponds, in order of subjective psychology, to the scornful truth of the initial '*es taugt nichts*'.

It is then that the text overbalances: from '*Weisesten*', the guardians of '*Weiheit*' (*wisdom*), which is taken to be *absolute*, we pass to a truth that shifts towards something else. The phonic play on '*Weise*', '*beweisen*' and '*weisen auf*' demonstrates the move from an absolute truth to a relative truth: '*beweisen*' and '*weisen*' destroy the autonomy of '*weisen*' and point to something that goes beyond them as symptoms. The question therefore shifts from demonstration ('*beweisen*') to referral or genealogical *reference* ('*WEISEN auf*') and divides itself between '*ehemals*' and '*heute*'. From the question 'what does that say?' we move to '*who* is saying that?' or '*what* made them say that?'. The previous discourse, which was demonstrative by *petitio principii*, is presented as an affirmation, while the new affirmation, moving from 'true' (*wahr*) to 'sick' (*krank*), presents itself as a reply to a question. This is why the problem of the respective legitimacy of these questions ('*werden wir so reden? DÜRFEN WIR das?*') is raised, a legitimacy other than that of closed logical discourse, since the new discourse discovers its truth only upon *leaving* the circle of discourse and approaching the *body*: '*Man sollte sie sich erst aus der Nähe ansehn*'. What we must see is no longer the truth of discourse, but the Sages in flesh and blood (the word '*ansehn*' being very concrete).

Then comes the surprise, which turns back on the sages the contempt of the '*es taugt nichts*': life takes its revenge. Here the imaginary logic says it all: the image of the legs is a very *concrete* one of upstanding ('*wider-STAND*'): the legs offer support, a sub-'stance on a ground of truth. It is the bearers of truth that collapse.[83] Why? Because of senile weakness ('*spät*') and morbid fragility ('*wackelig*'). These two physiological motivations are interpretations of the imaginary charge of the word '*décadent*'.[84] In its turn *décadence* itself is linked to that of decomposition ('*Auflösung*') developed in §2, through which Nietzsche gathers together everything implied in the genealogical idea of *décadence*: the chemical evocation of a (hidden) body through the stench ('*Geruch*'), the foul taste of rottenness and death. But Nietzsche adds further resonances: wisdom is no longer the owl of Minerva taking flight in the evening,[85] but a bird of death attracted by what Nietzsche calls in

Ecce Homo, in connection with the pessimistic Schopenhauer, a
'*Leichenbitter-Parfüm*'.[86] The '*Geist*' of the sages is now scarcely
more than an enthusiasm (*begeistert*) provoked by the approach of
death and the eternal night. Finally, the carcass evokes a poem by
Nietzsche, entitled precisely '*Melancholie*' which contains, like the
present text, reminiscences of Baudelaire ('*Recueillement*') whose
'*La Charogne*' (here '*Aas*' or carrion) Nietzsche had no doubt read
and whom he considers to be precisely a *décadent*. It is not
impossible that Nietzsche, thinking here of the philosophers but
also of Christianity, which he conceives of as the divinization of
death under the symbol of the Cross, remembers a passage on the
last judgement from the Gospel According to Saint Matthew:
'wherever the body is, there the eagles will be gathered together'.[87]
Décadence is a life that, on earth, has already decided in favour of
death, which it pangs after like a food, as with Socrates and
Christianity, the related origins of Western culture.

If genealogy is the *discourse* that consists in relating cultural
phenomena back to the body, it only really achieves this as a result
of a *textual* labour and movement, which are irreducible to the
systematic unity of discourse. In this sense, the movement and
labour of Nietzsche's text constitute a *Ja-Sagen* to life and the text
is, to use Nietzsche's neat phrase, '*Verführer zum Leben*'.[88] It
certainly involves a gap. Genealogical philosophy is dangerous
(*verführerisch*), while 'the sense for truth ... is really the sense for
security'.[89] Philosophy does not depart from discourse, but turns
discourse back on itself through an imaginary game. In this way, it
is a *Fürsprecher des Lebens*',[90] neither a purely conceptual discourse,
nor an extra–discursive poetic work. It would be as inappropriate to
exhibit discursively such and such a metaphorical statement in
order to create a metaphysical semiological system as it would be to
consider metaphors as simple ornaments of discourse.

These two tendencies in Nietzsche's thought, discourse and idea,
intertwine in the movement and labour of the text in a relation of
saying and unsaying, just as in Nietzsche truth and appearance
contrast with one another in an infinite game:

> There is no antagonism here between a true world and an
> apparent one: there is only one world, and that world is false,
> cruel, contradictory, misleading and seductive (*verführerisch*),
> deprived of meaning ... such a world is the true world. *We need*

deceit in order to conquer this reality or 'truth', that is, in order *to live*. The fact that deceit is necessary in order to live still has to do with the terrible and problematic nature of existence. . . . 'Life *must* inspire confidence': thus defined, the task is enormous. To resolve it man must already be by nature a liar, and above all else, an *artist*. . . . And in fact he is: metaphysics, religion, morality and science are merely offshoots of his will to art, to deceit, to flight in the face of 'truth', and to the *denegation* of 'truth'. This faculty by which *he rapes reality with deceit,* this essentially artistic faculty in man, is something he has in common with everything that exists. . . . The fact that the nature of existence is not known (*verkannt*) is the deepest and highest secret intention on the part of knowledge, piety and artistic ability. Never to see a lot, but to see a lot falsely, to see a lot more.[91]

For philosophical thought to give an *idea* of life, one has to have lived a lot:

My writings speak only of experiences which I have lived personally – happily, I have lived a lot –: I give myself up to it body and soul.[92]

To know how to join images together into a plural interpretative unity, one also requires a great deal of art:

Art, and nothing but art. It is the great creator of possibilities (*Ermöglicherin*), the great seductor that leads one astray in life (*Verführerin zum Leben*), the great stimulant in life (*Stimulans zum Leben*).[93]

The thing that is above all necessary is life: style must *live*. Style must show that we *believe* in our thoughts, that we do not just think them, but also *experience* them.[94]

It is in this sense and under these conditions that Nietzsche's thinking is a living thinking (*une pensée de la vie*) and can be simultaneously read and lived.

Notes

INTRODUCTION

1 *Mus.*, XX, p. 226 (Fragments for the *Dithyrambs of Dionysus*, no. 26).
2 *BGE*, §1, 'Life itself has become a problem. . . . It is love for a woman that we doubt' (*NEW*, Epilogue, §1). On life as woman, enigma and Sphinx, see E. Blondel, 'Nietzsche: la vie et la métaphore', *Revue philosophique* (1971), no. 3.
3 *BGE*, §1. On Oedipus and the Sphinx as genealogical myth, see my 'Oedipus bei Nietzsche', *Perspektiven der Philosophie*, (1975), Band 1.
4 *BT*, §9. This perhaps accounts for the consequence: 'the time has forever gone when the public and I could have maintained relations without getting the knives out' (*Lettres choisies*, tr. Alexandre Vialatte, 5th edn (Paris: Gallimard, 1950), p. 292, 14 September 1888).
5 *EH*, 'Why I Write Such Excellent Books'.
6 *BGE*, §1.
7 *EH*, 'Why I Am a Destiny', §1. This would explain Walter Kaufmann's remark: 'All sorts of men, including some crackpots, have written about Nietzsche'. But he adds: 'but among those who have contributed to the literature are Thomas Mann and Camus, Jaspers and Heidegger, and leading poets as well as renowned scholars' (*Nietzsche: Philosopher, Psychologist, Antichrist* (Princeton: New Jersey, Princeton University Press, 1968), Preface to the 3rd edition, p. vi).
8 Stendhal, *Oeuvres romanesques*, 2 vols, Paris, Gallimard, Pléiade, p. 919 (*Lucien Leuwen*, tr. H.L.R. Edwards (Woodbridge: Boydell Press, 1984), p. 184). In *BGE*, §39, Nietzsche quotes the *Mélanges de littérature*.
9 *AOM*, §119: a good introduction to any reading of Nietzsche!
10 Immanuel Kant, 'D'un ton grand seigneur adopté naguère en philosophie' in *Première introduction à la critique du jugement*, tr. Louis Guillermit (Paris: Vrin, 1968), p. 90.
11 Herman Broch, Letter, 17 February 1948.
12 Cf. above all *KGW*, VIII, 2, 9 (165) = *WP*, §79. See also *WP*, §§77, 78 and 80.
13 *UM*, 3, §7.
14 *BGE*, §40.

15 *Selected Letters of F. Nietzsche*, edited and translated by Christopher Middleton (Chicago and London: University of Chicago Press, 1969), p. 227.

16 *LC*, no. 74, à Paul Gast, 24 November 1880, p. 166.

17 The word genealogy does not figure among the 'five capital terms in Nietzsche's thought' analysed by Heidegger in *Nietzsche*. This is not the place to discuss Heidegger's arguments (on this subject see J. Granier, *Le problème de la vérité dans la philosophie de Nietzsche* (Paris: Seuil, 1966), Appendix, pp. 611–28). Suffice it to add that Heidegger never questions his right to reconstitute, on the basis of a few grand concepts – and why those rather than others? – a metaphysical system proper to Nietzsche, as one might do for Plato, Kant or Schopenhauer.

18 Jaspers speaks of 'concepts replacing transcendence' (*Nietzsche, Introduction à sa philosophie* (Paris, Gallimard, 1950), p. 434).

19 J. Granier, *Le problème de la vérité dans la Philosophie de Nietzsche* (Paris, Seuil, 1966), p. 603.

20 *Le problème de la vérité dans la Philosophie de Nietzsche*, pp. 606–8.

21 See Curt Paul Janz, *Die Briefe Friedrich Nietzsche*, p. 150: 'In this way, he [Nietzsche] is closer to Plato. ... In Plato equally "doctrine" is never systematically constructed in the work'.

22 It is Nietzsche, in *Untimely Meditations*, who quotes Schopenhauer's phrase: 'a philosopher must be very honest not to call poetry or rhetoric to his aid' (p. 135). Speaking of the dogmatic philosopher and of his 'literary' opposition to critical philosophy, Kant, in this respect typifying the philosopher's discursive demands, writes: 'The crude *barbarous* language of critical philosophy displeases him, while it is precisely the intrusion of *literary* style into philosophy that we ought to consider barbarous' (*Annonce de le proche conclusion* ..., tr. Louis Guillermit, p. 122). See also Thomas Mann's letter to W. Schmitz, 30 July 1948).

23 See E. Blondel, 'Vom Nutzen und Nachteil der Sprache für das Verständnis Nietzsches', *Nietzsche Studien* (1981–2), 10–11, pp. 518–64.

24. *KGW*, VIII, 2, 11 (297). The definition of Plato is to be found in *TI*, 'What I Owe to the Ancients', §2.

25 By way of support for our analysis so far we can note the strange absence of Bachelard in all the recent semiological analyses of Nietzsche, which instead rely more on Freud but without managing to avoid the dualism we have already mentioned.

26 Gaston Bachelard, *L'Air et les songes*, ch. 5.

27 *L'Air et les songes*, ch. 4, p. 133.

28 This idealist substantialism, which relies on images, is all the more unexpected since it contrasts with the basic principles of epistemology and the history of Bachelardian sciences which, in their own field, condemn such substantialism as 'fetishism'. For the scientific Bachelard the image must be eliminated; when he rediscovers it instead in poetry, he is forced to regard the latter as being not true.

29 *TI*, 'Morality as Anti-Nature', §1.

1   READING NIETZSCHE

1 See Groupe M, *Rhétorique générale*, ch. 1, 2, 1, pp. 36–7.

2 *K*, XIV, Part One, §81 = *VP*, p. 63, §92.

3 *K*, XI, Part Two, §65 = *VP*, I, p. 69, §111.

4 Roman Jakobson, *Selected Writings II: Word and Language* (The Hague and Paris: Mouton, 1971), pp. 239–59.

5 J. Granier, *Le problème de la vérité dans la Philosophie de Nietzsche* (Paris, Seuil, 1966), p. 30.

6 *Le problème de la vérité dans la Philosophie de Nietzsche.*

7 Pierre Fontanier, *Les figures du discours*, p. 64.

8 See J. Lyons, *Introduction to Theoretical Linguistics*, 6. 6, pp. 247–9.

9 See E. Blondel 'Nietzsche: la vie et la métaphore', *Revue philosophique* (1971), no. 73, and Nicole Malet, 'L'homme et la femme dans la philosophie de Nietzsche', *Revue de métaphysique et de morale* (1977), no. 1.

10 'This thesis, made hard and cutting under the hammer-blows of historical intuition . . . might one day . . . be used as an axe to bare the very roots of man's "metaphysical needs"'(*HATH*, §37).

11 Here once again we perhaps detect an allusion to Moses (Exodus, 32:19).

12 *TI*, 'The Hammer Speaks'.

13 *TI*, Foreword.

14 An 'inspection' hammer can also be used to inspect a metal's flaws or ascertain its properties, see *TI*, Foreword, and '"Götzen aus horchen": Versuch einer Genealogie der Genealogie. Nietzsches philologisches Apriori und die christliche Kritik des Christentums', *Perspektiven der Philosophie* (1981), Band 7. See also my translation and commentary of *TI* (Paris: Hatier, 1983).

15 Only P. Valadier has noted some of the overdeterminations of metaphors in *Essais sur la modernité. Nietzsche et Marx*, ch. 5, p. 111.

16 See E. Bertram, *Nietzsche: essai de mythologie*, pp. 83–4.

17 If we wanted to suggest the metaphorical nature of this compound in French, we would have to come up with concoctions like 'ultra-man' or 'beyond-man', which are obviously unusable. In this English translation Kaufmann substitutes 'overman' for 'superman'. In *EH*, 'Why I Write Such Excellent Books', §1, Nietzsche adds a few restrictive touches to the word's polysemic nature. See also *GK*, §143.

18 See Gilles Deleuze, *Nietzsche and Philosophy*, tr. Hugh Tomlinson (London, 1983), pp. 2–3; and J. Granier, *Le problème de la vérité dans la Philosophie de Nietzsche*, pp. 149–56.

19 Deleuze notes that 'Hesiod is such a philosopher' (*Nietzsche et la philosophie*, p. 2).

20 *BGE*, §295.
21 *BGE*, §227.
22 *TSZ*, Prologue, §9, etc.
23 *CW*, 2nd postscriptum, p. 185.
24 *TSZ*, Part Three, 'Of Old and New Law-Tables', §28.
25 *TSZ*, Part One, 'Of the Bestowing Virtue', §1; 'Of Old and New Law-Tables', §30, *BGE*, §§39 and 59 offer up anthologies of paronomasia which use the German particle '*ver*' as in '*verdünnt, versüsst, verdumpft, verfälscht*'; '*verfälscht, verdünnt, verjenseitigt, vergöttlicht*'.
26 *TI*, 'Maximus and Arrows', §17 [bread and Circe in place of bread and circuses (panem et circenses) – tr.].
27 *TI*, 'Reason in Philosophy', §1.
28 *CW*, 2nd postscriptum, p. 186. See *EH*, 'Why I Am So Wise', §3: *abgründlich*.
29 *KGW*, VIII, 2, 9 (156) = *WZM*, §296.
30 *TSZ*, Part Two, 'Of the Tarantulas' [Tarantellas].
31 *TSZ*, Part Four, 'The Awakening', §§1 and 2.
32 *TSZ*, Part Two, 'Of the Virtuous'.
33 *EH*, 'Why I Write Such Excellent Books'.
34 On the other hand Kant writes in the *Critique of Pure Reason*: 'Fashioning new words is a way of legislating in language, and as a claim it rarely succeeds'. And in the *Critique of Practical Reason* we find a similar remark: 'it is a silly and pointless way of standing out from the crowd'.
35 On this point, see R. Roos, 'Règles pour une lecture philologique de Nietzsche' in *Nietzsche aujourd'hui?*, II, pp. 308–9.
36 Roos even speaks of *Kitsch* in Zarathustra. The work written for the millenia has difficulty in lasting beyond the age of Wilhelm.
37 *TI*, 'What I Owe to the Ancients', §2.
38 *EH*, 'Why I Write Such Excellent Books', §4.
39 This holds for the published work as much as for the posthumous fragments. During the period of *Jenseits (KGW*, VIII, I) Nietzsche dreamed of giving one of his works the title 'mes Gedankenstriche' (*KGW*, VIII, I, 3 (2)) and pondered philosophically on this typographical procedure (see *KGW*, VIII, I, 1 (232); 2 (41); 2 (43)). The dash refers to 'the psychologist's reservations'.'
40 P. Köster, (*Der sterbliche Gott*, p. 75) has thus noted that *GS*, §125, comprising barely 2 pages, contains 31 question-marks.
41 Examples of the second kind include '*Faitalismus*' and '*Monotonotheismus*'.
42 *TSZ*, Part Two, 'Of Poets'.
43 *TSZ*, Part Two, 'On the Blissful Islands'.
44 'To Goethe' in the *Songs of Prince Vogelfrei*, collected in *GS*.
45 Goethe, *Faust*, II, Act V.

46 *TSZ*, Part Four.

47 *EH*, 'Why I Write Such Excellent Books', §2. See also *GM*, Third Essay, §22, where this time Nietzsche puts himself forward as an admirer of the Old Testament and noisily proclaims his contempt for the style of the New Testament.

48 For example, the texts from *TSZ* in *EH*.

49 This procedure is reminiscent of what Freud terms '*Nachträglichkeit*'.

50 See *Philosophy in the Age of Greek Tragedy*, wherein Heraclitus is simultaneously Nietzsche, Schopenhauer and perhaps even Wagner; *EH*, 'The Birth of Tragedy', §3; and C. Andler, *Nietzsche, sa vie et sa pensée*, t. II, p. 84.

51 *EH*, 'The Birth of Tragedy', §4: 'in all the psychologically decisive passages I am the only person referred to – one may ruthlessly insert my name or the word "Zarathutra" wherever the text gives the word Wagner'. See Andler, *Nietzsche, sa vie et sa pensée* t. II, p. 211; 'a portrait where we recognize Nietzsche in person'. Above all see the unpublished variant of *NCW* (Paris: Gallimard), p. 588: 'The 4th "Inactuel" is entitled "Richard Wagner at Bayreuth" for which read Nietzsche–Zarathustra and the Festival of the Future, the *grand midi*'.

52 See Andler, *Nietzsche, sa vie et sa pensée* t. II, pp. 103 and 107; *EH*, 'The Untimely Essays', §3: 'in "Schopenhauer as Educator" it is my innermost history, my *evolution* that is inscribed'. The same variant quoted above from *NCW* states: 'for "Schopenhauer as educator" read Nietzsche as educator'. In *EH*, 'The Untimely Essays', §1, Nietzsche confirms this: 'untimely types *par excellence*, full of sovereign contempt for all that around them which was called "Reich", "culture", "Christianity", "Bismark", "success" – Schopenhauer and Wagner or, in one word, Nietzsche.' No doubt *EH* follows the example of *NCW* and is even more profoundly a rewriting of the pieces of Nietzsche's life in which we can trace a certain amount of bad faith. But ten years earlier Nietzsche was already writing: 'In everything that once moved Zoroaster, Moses, Muhammad, Jesus, Plato, Brutus, Spinoza, Mirabeau, I am already to be found thriving' (*OP*, §20) and 'When I speak of Plato, Pascal, Spinoza and Goethe, I know that their blood flows in mine' (*OP*, §21).

53 See also the famous letter of 1859: 'Every name in history is me', and *EH*, 'Why I am So Wise', §3 (a new text restored in *KGW*); 'Julius Caesar could be my father – or else Alexander, who is Dionysus made flesh'.

54 C.P. Janz has given some fine analyses of these in his work *Die Briefe Friedrich Nietzsches*, notably in ch. 8.

2 *DISCOURSE AND TEXT: NIETZSCHE'S STRATEGIES*

1 'Der Stil soll *leben*', *KBW*, VII, 1, I (109).
2 The reflection on culture places Nietzsche at the crossroads of philosophy, history, sociology, psychology, aesthetics. This is what explains the necessity of his encounters (and conflicts) with thinkers who weighed and evaluated things, like Jean-Jacques Rousseau, historians like Thucydides or Burckhardt, or poets and thinkers who were a symbol of their age, like, for example, Goethe or Voltaire and, above all, with all the moralists, notably those ancient and French.
3 *An*, §3.
4 For Hume, seeking refuge in 'day-to-day life' is just another form, in this case a vulgar one, of the scepticism that moves us from a 'false reason' to 'none at all' (*A Treatise of Human Nature*, Book I, Part IV, Section 7).
5 Cf. Henri Burgelin, *La société allemande (1871–1968)*, p. 80. The author indicates that Marx addressed this kind of reproach to the bourgeoisie in 1848.
6 The use of this word by Nietzsche is significant: it is overdetermined by its Schopenhauerian and Kantian meanings.
7 *LPh*, 'Le dernier philosophe', §37, pp. 53–5 (modified translation).
8 Cf. especially 'On a Grand Tone Formerly Adopted in Philosophy' and the 'Reply to Eberhard'.
9 'Illusion' is the term that Kant employs in the *Critique of Pure Reason* specifically to characterize a transcendental appearance (*Schein*).
10 In other words, between a pre-critical dogmatism and Hume.
11 *LPh*, 'Le dernier philosophe', §61, pp. 77–9.
12 *LPh*, 'On truth and deceit in the extramoral sense', §184, p. 213 (modified translation).
13 Attested by the phrase: 'We must create a concept here'.
14 *LPh*, §177, p. 209. One notes the Schopenhauerian expressions.
15 *LPh*, §184, p. 213.
16 *TSZ*, Part Two, 'Of Poets'.
17 *LPh*, 'Le dernier philosophe', §118, p. 116.
18 *KGW*, VIII, 1, 5 (22) = *WP*, §522 (1886–7).
19 *KGW*, VIII, 3, 36 (25) = *WP*, I, p. 253, §173. Cf. *KGW*, VII, 2, 27 (27) = *K*, XIII, §389 = *VP*, I, p. 258, §192.
20 I have developed this analysis in my article, 'Nietzsche: la vie et la métaphore', *Revue philosophique*. (1971), no. 3.
21 *KGW*, VIII, 1, 2 (148). Nietzsche adds: 'The organic process continually presupposes *interpretation* (*das Interpretieren*)'.
22 *An*, §26: 'Reality is. . . .' Nietzsche contrasts moral language, which he puts in inverted commas, with his own language of reality: 'or,

as I would put it in my language'. In this domain, Nietzsche is a translator.

23 *KGW*, VIII, 1, 5 (22) = *WP*, §522.

24 *KGW*, VIII, 2, 11 (73) – *WP*, §715: note the inverted commas which place the term 'evolution' back in the metaphysical field of language. But any discourse here would have to be put in inverted commas, given the metadiscursive plane on which Nietzsche places himself.

25 *KGW*, VIII, 3, 14 (79) = *WP*, §634. Nietzsche adds: 'Mechanistic theory as a theory of motion is already a translation into the sense language of man'. Conversely (*KGW*, VIII, 3, 14 and *WP*, §635), Nietzsche has recourse to the Greek term *pathos*, in contrast to being and becoming, to express the will to power.

26 Note, alongside a first determiner, a number of unusual verbal creations that form a hapax and indicate the text's uniqueness.

27 *KGW*, VIII, 2, 9 (91) = *WP*, §552 [modified translation – tr.].

28 *UM*, 2, §10.

29 Cf. *KGW*, VII, 3, 38 (12) = *WP*, §1067: 'Do you want a *name* for this world? . . . *This world is the will to power*'.

30 It is already so by virtue of being culture, that is to say a means of mastering life.

31 *KGW*, VIII, 3, 24 (170) = *WP*, §811. Cf. *EH*, 'Why I am a Destiny', §1: 'I am not a man, I am dynamite'.

32 Our analysis of Nietzsche's text here tallies with the principles governing the reading of Heraclitus carried out by J. Bollack and H. Wismann: cf. *Heraclitus or Separation* (Paris: 1972), esp. pp. 11–56, and our review in *Revue philosophique* (1974), no. 1. Cf. also Pierre Bourdieu, 'La critique du discours lettré' in *Actes de la recherche en sciences sociales*, nos. 5–6, pp. 4–8.

33 On the blank spaces in and between Nietzsche's texts, see our remarks in *Nietzsche aujourd'hui?* vol. II, p. 182, and H. Wismann, 'Nietzsche et la philologie', *ibid.*, pp. 325–44.

34 From the point of view of *method*, nothing distinguishes either of these approaches from an annexionist type of 'interpretation', such as the one used by certain Nazi ideologues, which consists in fabricating or extracting certain discursive signifieds from a text that recants them.

35 On this nihilist dilettantism, cf. H. Wismann, 'Le métier de philologie, II', *Critique*, (1970), pp. 279–80.

36 But which must be deciphered.

37 Nietzsche's discourse and discourse on Nietzsche encounter a problem similar to the one outlined by Kant in relation to what he calls transcendental logic as opposed to general logic. An abstract, general discourse on Nietzsche is idealist and fetishist: it lacks philology.

38 *EH*, 'Why I Am So Clever', §8.

39 In the writings subsequent to *HATH*, this word tends to constitute a

doublet for genealogical analysis. This is how Nietzsche indicates that he is a 'psychologist' genealogist, evoking his own genealogy in a light-hearted way in the original text of *EH*, 'Why I Am So Wise', §3 (restored in *KGW*); 'Julius Caesar could have been my *father*. . . . I am a terrible *atavism*' (my emphasis).

40 For example, *BGE*, Preface.

41 *BGE*, §203, which speaks of needing leaders, offered many temptations in this respect, and there are some who have indeed succumbed. It is true that, according to Nietzsche, it is precisely a sign of 'unspirituality' and 'vulgarity' not to be able to resist succumbing to temptation: 'one *has* to react, one obeys every impulse. In many instances, such a compulsion is already morbidity, decline, a symptom of exhaustion' (*TI*, 'What the Germans Lack', §6).

42 *EH*, 'The Wagner Case', §4.

43 We should have to be able to quote the whole of the three texts in which Nietzsche compiles a register of the articles from *Bund* and *Kreuzzeitung* that relate to some of his books and comments on how his works were greated: *TI*, 'Expeditions . . .', §37; *EH*, 'Why I Write Such Excellent Books', §1; and above all a projected Preface to *TI*, a real masterpiece of maliciousness, which can be found in the Kröner edition, vol. 8, XIV, pp. 415–17, and in *KGW*, VIII, 3, 19 (1) to 19 (7).

44 *WS*, §33, for example, declares that words are 'pockets; into which you stuff things and, in the case of the use of the term 'vengeance', shows, on the other hand, the large number of its real applications. Cf. also *TI*, '"Reason" in Philosophy', §5: 'error has . . . our language as a perpetual advocate. Language belongs in its origin to the age of the most rudimentary form of psychology'.

45 *WP*, §810 = *KGW*, VIII, 2, 10 (60): 'Words make the uncommon common'. The idea is developed in *TI*, 'Expeditions . . .', §26: 'Speech . . . was devised only for the average, medium, communicable. The speaker has already *vulgarized* himself by speaking. – From a moral code for deaf-mutes and other philosophers'. Cf. *TSZ*, Part One, 'Of Joys and Passions'.

46 *BGE*, §43.

47 *BGE*, §268, modified translation. Cf. *TI*, 'Expeditions . . .', §26: 'We have already grown beyond whatever we have words for. In all talking there lies a grain of contempt'. This is why 'education consists in rebaptizing differently' (*GS*, 11 (159), Gallimard edition) and new philosophers are 'unnamers' (cf. *GS*, §§261 and 58).

48 *TI*, '"Reason" in Philosophy', §5.

49 *WP*, §810 = *KGW*, VIII, 2, 10 (60).

50 *WP*, §479 = *KGW*, VIII, 3, 15 (90).

51 *TI*, 'What the Germans Lack', §7.

52 *TI*, 'Maxims and Arrows', §34.

53 *WP*, §809 = *KGW*, VIII, 3, 14 (119).

54 But we already note the first stages of textual subversion: the use of Schopenhauer is secretly contested by references to Goethe, Hölderlin, the Greeks, and an already fluctuating use of Schopenhauerian concepts that herald a genealogical analysis (*Wollen, Irrtum, Genie, das Persönliche*, etc.). One often commits the error of assimilating this move out of critical rationalism to the movement of going beyond metaphysics.

55 pp. 375–6.

56 Cf. P. Ricoeur, *La métaphore vive*, p. 376.

57 *La métaphore vive*, p. 368.

58 Cf. *La métaphore vive*, p. 118.

59 We made a first approach to this difficult problem posed by the reading of Nietzsche in our 'Nietzsche: la vie et la métaphore', *Revue philosophique* (1971), no. 3.

60 They are helped along by the collages, with which readers have become familiar, published in collected form under the apocryphal title of *The Will to Power*, which knits together fragments dating from 1873 and 1888. In particular, the French edition, *La volonté de puissance* translated from Würzbach's *Das Vermächtnis F. Nietzsches* by G. Bianquis (who has added two more texts to the German edition) is not *Der Wille zur Macht*.

61 Cf. O.Reboul, *Nietzsche critique de Kant*, pp. 158–9: 'Ultimately hyper-criticism tips over into a pre-critical dogmatism'.

62 One occasionally presents Nietzsche's thought from the period of *The Gay Science* as being the period of his *Aufklärung*, or enlightenment. But it is followed by *The Twilight of the Idols*!

63 *HATH*, §517 and the corresponding fragment 23 (82).

64 The title of Book Five of *GS*.

65 Cf. *GS*, Preface, §3.

66 *GS*, Preface.

67 *GS*, Preface.

68 The German title is followed by a subtitle in inverted commas and in Italian, 'la gaya scienza'. It is perhaps an illusion to Vico. But Nietzsche often uses the Provençal expression, 'gay saber' (*BGE*, §§260 and 293), alongside *gaya scienza* (*CW*, §10). The gay science is enriched by evoking Rabelais, in a manner that is nothing less than scientific (Preface and ch. 13 of *Gargantua*) and, with the help of games, by evoking Mürger (*Scenes from the life of Boheme*, Preface).

69 Cf. E. Blondel, 'Les guillemets de Nietzsche', pp. 163–5.

70 This ambiguity is also to be found in *GS*, §366, which deals with scholars.

71 '*Fröhliche Wissenschaft*', as opposed to '*frohe Botschaft*', therefore also signifies the gospel through knowledge, 'év-epistéme', as it were. Cf. *An*, §49: 'The priest knows only *one* great danger: that is science'.

72 *An*, §39: 'bad tidings, a *dysangel*'. Cf. *GS*, §373. This leads to the book's monotonous insistence on '*wir*', that is to say on a new polemical solidarity.

73 We must acknowledge here what our analysis owes to the reading principles established in J. Bollack and H. Wismann, *Héraclite ou la séparation*: 'The value of a statement is to be measured by the force of the negation it harbours.' Cf. pp. 274, 138, 69, 328–9 of this work.

74 *K*, X, p. 370, §150.

75 A certain Nietzsche incontestably provides arguments in favour of this attitude, a voluntarist, reminiscent of Descartes. Cf. *Discours de la méthode*,I and VI: 'In place of the speculative philosophy taught in school'.

76 Cultural Marxism, but also the Marxism of some of Marx's texts, has helped greatly to sharpen this antithesis of action and speculation. This is confirmed by the way a certain Marxist tradition takes away available opportunity to quote 'Feuerbach's eleventh thesis' only to offer a simplistic interpretation of it. Cf. on the other hand, the subtle commentary provided on this thesis by J. Granier in *Penser la praxis*.

77 *TSZ*, Part One, 'Of the bestowing Virtue', §3 (a text reproduced in the Preface to *EH*). Cf. also on this attitude on the part of Nietzsche, *GS*, §§106, 297, 319, and *EH*, 'Why I Am a Destiny', §1. On the shortcomings of education and the sterility of philologers, cf. *HATH*, 19 (1) to 19 (6).

78 This opposition is put forward as a problem, and left unresolved, by Nietzsche when he writes: 'one must want to *live* great problems through the body and the spirit' (*VP*, I, p. 34, §18 = *KGW*, 1, 5 (29)).

79 David Hume, *A Treatise of Human Nature*, Book One, Part Four, Section 7, pp. 254–5. In Plato's *Meno*, the theory of reminiscence also aims to offer philosophical justification for choosing philosophy rather than the sophist's frivolity. This choice, even in Socrates' view, is in fact based only on an extra-rational kind of decision choosing reason as opposed to the irrational is not rational (*Meno*, 81 (d–e: ὦἐγὼ πιστεύω ν ἀληθεῖ . . .).

80 *GS*, 23 (101), Gallimard edition = *KGW*, VII, 1, 1 (2).

81 Examples of unfinished phrases: *BGE*, §§194 and 227; *GS*, §372. The *Gedankenstrich*, a dash that is the equivalent of our row of dots, plays the same role of a break that produces a resonance. For *BGE*, Nietzsche thought of one subtitle: *Gedanken und Gedankenstriche (KGW*, VIII, 1, 3 (2)). He often raises this question: cf. *KGW*, VIII, 1 (232); 2 (41); 2 (43).

82 Cf. J. Blacking, *Le sens musical*, tr. E and M. Blondel (Paris, 1980).

83 Nietzsche's work on style, which we can deduce by comparing a draft with the definitive text, concentrates essentially on these three points. Cf. C.P. Janz, *Die Briefe Friedrich Nietzsches*, especially pp. 24–32. Reading Nietzsche, one recalls Leibniz's definition of music, quoted by

Schopenhauer in *The World as Will and Idea*, ch. 52, p. 327: '*exercitum arithmeticae occultum nescientis se numerare animi*'. Nietzsche, for his part, can (and should) be read aloud.

84 *WP*, §810 = *KGW*, VIII, 2, 10 (60).

85 *GS*, §372.

86 Letter to Georg Brandes, 27 March 1888. Nietzsche used the expression again in *TI*, 'Maxims and Arrows', §33.

87 Letter to Gast, 27 December 1888. O. Reboul is therefore absolutely right when he writes *Nietzsche critique de Kant*, p. 15: 'Instead of looking for the secret of Nietzsche's craft in the spatial nature of his metaphors, we should look for it in the musicality of his style'. Cf. *ibid.*, pp. 15–16, and C.P. Janz, *Die Briefe Friedrich Nietzsches* ch. 10, pp. 113–42.

88 Cf. *AOM*, Preface, §3: '*Cave musicam*', as well as, obviously, all the writings on Wagner and the texts on composers in *WS*, §149–69.

89 *WP*, §840 = *KGW*, VIII, 3, 14 (42). In *The World as Will and Idea*, supplement to Book Three, ch. 34, on the other hand, Schopenhauer writes: 'What is Life? This question ... is also answered by music, and the answer it provides is deeper than any other, for in a language that is immediately intelligible, if untranslatable into the language of reason, it expresses the intimate essence of all life and all existences' (pp. 1138–9). The principal text on music is to be found in ch. 52 of Book Four. Schopenhauer saw that 'music is a reproduction of will and the different forms of human desire' (*ibid.*, pp. 329, 332 *et passim*): he therefore expresses in his own particular language an intuition that will be maintained in the deepest realms of the thought of Nietzsche, for whom the text's musicality is a *Ja-Sagen* to life and an affirmative – or negative – will to power.

90 Cf. *WP*, §839 = *KGW*, VIII, 2, 10 (155): 'Come si *dorme* con questa musica'.

91 *TI*, 'What the Germans Lack', §2.

92 *NEW*, 'Where 1 Object'. (modified translation). Cf. also *CW*, §1: 'a disagreeable sweat'; §5: 'sick music'; 'Wagner is a neurosis'; §7: 'a psychological defect'; §8: 'not ... enough to chew on'; the Postscript: 'one does not refute a sickness; and the Second Postscript: 'Rhinoxera'.

93 H. Broch, letter to N. Maier, 5 December 1948.

94 *WP*, Preface, §1 = *KGW*, VIII, 2, 11 (411). One of the most beautiful examples of an innocent and cynical evocation of Nietzsche is to be found in Thomas Mann's 'Travels with Don Quixote', an essay, collected in *Nobility of Spirit*, which evokes the character of Sils as a double image of the Knight and Zarathustra.

3 THE PROBLEM OF CULTURE IN NIETZSCHE'S THOUGHT

1 *WP*, §462 = *KGW*, VIII, 2, 10 (28).
2 Cf. Hans Martin Klinkenberg, 'Der Kulturbegriff Nietzsches', *Historische Forschungen (1961)*, 4, p. 313: 'If the concept of *Kultur* is already weak and vague, every theory founded on it is from the beginning problematical. Imagination is given free reign'.
3 On these classical problems in linguistics, cf. Roman Jakobson, *Essais de linguistique générale*, ch. 4, and J. Lyons, *An Introduction to Theoretical Linguistics*, §§9.4.4 to 9.4.8.
4 This point holds for both English and French.
5 For example in Hegel: *The Phenomenology of Mind*, VI, 'The Spirit', B.
6 On the evolution of this notion in classical German literature, from the *Aufklärung* to Burckhardt, cf. Bernard Kopp, *Beiträge zur Kulturphilosophie der deutschen Klassik. Eine Untersuchung im Zusammenhang mit dem Bedeutungswandel des Wortes Kultur* (Meisenheim am Glan: Hain, 1974).
7 Cf. *KGW*, VIII, 3, 16 (10) = *WP*, §121. Cf. also *KGW*, VIII, 3, 15 (67) = *WP*, §122 = *VP*, II, p. 31, §54.
8 These days *Bildung* means 'individual culture'; up until the late eighteenth century *cultura* was translated as *Kultur*, and when this latter term took on an objective meaning, one specified '*subjektive Kultur*' before rapidly replacing the term with *Bildung* (cf. Kopp, *Beiträge zur Kulturphilosophie*, p. 6).
9 Cf. Hegel, *Phenomenology of Mind*, VI.
10 However, Nietzsche contrasts *Natur* with *Bildung*, *Züchtung*, *Moral*, etc., as elements that are always present in a *Kultur*. Cf., for example, *TI*, 'Morality as Anti-Nature'; *BGE*, §230; *EH*, 'Why I Am a Destiny', §§7 and 8; *An*, §49; *WP*, §120 = *KGW*, VIII, 2, 10 (53), etc.
11 Cf. for example the remarks by W. Jaeger, in *Paideia*: 'The suggestive comparison made between education and agriculture . . . goes back to a more ancient source (Plutarch). Translated into Latin, this source penetrated European thought and allowed it to create the new metaphor of the *cultura animi*: man's culture (*culture*) is a spiritual cultivation (*culture*) just as the cultivation of the earth is agri*culture*. The modern term *culture* is an obvious relic of the original metaphor. . . . This striking comparison between education and agriculture explains the universal value of the new Greek concept of paideia – the most noble application of the general rule establishes the possibility of perfecting natural gifts through human will and reason'.
These thoughts by Jaeger are based on the semantic status of the German word *Bildung*: 'In this way the image of plasticity (εὔπλαστον) of the young man's soul stems perhaps from Plato and the beautiful

idea of an art that compensates for natural deficiency appears in Aristotle'. On the basis of a non-explicit metaphor of culture as the forming of the formless, the words *Bildung* and 'culture' coincide in meaning, beyond the etymological correspondence of 'culture' and *Kultur*. On this point, cf. B. Kopp, *Beiträge zur Kulturphilosophie*, p. 6.

Certain aspects of the problem of culture in Nietzsche, during a certain period, allow us to confirm the importance assumed by the original determination of the concept by the metaphor, with a number of Epicurean observations. Cf. *D*, §560: 'One can dispose of one's drives like a gardener'; *D*, 7 (30) and 7 (211); *GS*, §4: 'the farmers of the spirit'; *GS* (2) and 11 (170), Gallimard edition. It is not impossible, as we shall see later, for this metaphor to rediscover, subterraneanly – if we can say that! – with the help of the traditions of German romanticism, the much more widely known metaphor of the *Earth*.

12 The Littré dictionary, my emphasis. The figurative meaning is not yet noted by Littré (nor, according to B. Kopp, *Beiträge zur Kulturphilosophie*, p. 8, by the 1929 Larousse).

13 This was the case first of all for *Kultur*, and in this sense *Bildung* took over from *Kultur*.

14 Cf. Cicero, *Tusculanes*, II, 13: 'Ut agri non omnes frugiferi sunt qui coluntur, . . . sic animi non omnes culti fructum ferunt. Atque, ut in eodem simili verser, ut ager quamuis fertilis sine cultura fructuosus esse non potest, sic sine doctrina animus; ita est utraque res sine altera debilis. Cultura autem animi philosophia est; haec extrahit uitia radicitus et praeparat animus ad satus accipiendos eaque mandat iis et, ut ita dicam, serit, quae adulta fructus uberrimos ferant'. Cf. also Kopp, *Beiträge zur Kulturphilosophie*, pp. 2–4.

15 Lucretius, *De rerum natura*, V, 195–9:
    'hoc tamen ex ipsis caeli rationibus ausim/confirmare aliisque ex rebus reddere multis,/nequaquam divinitus esse paratam,/naturam rerum: tanta stat praedita culpa'. Such a view demolishes the eclectic finalism of a Cicero, or by implication 'his' conception of culture as the 'fulfilment' of nature.

16 Spinoza, *Ethics*, III, Preface.

17 In his *Speculations on the Origins of Human History* (1786), Kant still presents *Kultur* as being an activity, a creative realization of a disposition. For him, *Kultur* means the *'physische Kultur der Geschicklichkeit'*, *'pragmatische Zivilisierung, Moralisierung'*, a practical aptitude to society. Later, evidently, it would be the realm of ends which, in opposition to nature, would correspond to the notion here being discussed (cf. Kopp, *Beiträge zur Kulturphilosophie* pp. 30–40). But one notes that Kant makes culture grow out of nature's 'conflicts', which corresponds to what we later call a 'gap' in nature with respect to itself.

18 Cf. Spinoza, *Ethics*, IV, Preface, especially: 'This is why we see men

usually call natural things perfect or imperfect' (which comes down to separating fact from norm, the given from the ideal) 'more because of prejudice than a true knowledge of things'.

19 This is a view systematized in politics, by Hobbes, among others, but already implicit in the widespread view Cicero puts forward *Tusculanes,* II, 13.

20 As if the given were, in itself, a bad or false nature, an artificial 'second nature', placed on top of the 'true nature' by history, society, and men: it is this 'as if' that Nietzsche will claim to see in Rousseau and then denounce as the idealist illusion of a 'good human nature'. Let us note here in passing that the sophists' *paideia* was already trying to base itself on two opposing views of nature and its relationship to culture. Either, like Protagoras, nature (φύσις) should be viewed as a formless and savage given, which culture has the job of improving, forming, 'civilizing', and amending (the myth of Prometheus), a view echoed faintly in the popularizer Cicero: or else, as in Hippias, nature constituted what one should restore and free from the convention of law (νόμος), something in relation to which culture was therefore constrained (βία): Callicles illustrates the ultimate consequences of this latter view (cf. H. Joly, *Le renversement platonicien*, pp. 282–91). The artefact of the Hobbesian Leviathan and the civil society of Rousseau's social contract (that wishes to give back to nature its advantages as a civil plane) represents the modern political equivalent of this view taken from Greek sophists, in terms of a theory of culture.

21 'The Joust in Homer', in *Ecrits posthumes 1870–1873*, tr. 'Jean-Louis Backès, Michel Haar and Marc. B. de Launay (Paris: Gallimard, 1975), p. 192. Note the image of botanical growth, reserved this time for an action that is proper to nature.

22 *WP*, §343 = *VP*, 1, p. 138, §299.

23 Sigmund Freud, 'Delusions and Dreams in Jensen's *Gradiva*' (1907 [1906]), Standard Edition, *IX*, 3–93, p. 36.

24 *D*, 5 (25).

25 *D*, 6 (150).

26 *D*, 6 (136). Like Spinoza, Nietzsche identifies end with necessity.

27 Cf. *GS*, §301: 'Nature is always value-less, but has been *given* value'.

28 *D*, 6 (140).

29 *D*, 5 (27).

30 *GS*, Preface, §3.

31 This is why genealogy is presented first of all as 'the natural science of morals' (*BGE*).

32 *BGE*, §230.

33 *D*, 5 (25).

34 *HATH*, §514. Although Nietzsche's project of 'translating man back into nature' rests on a very different view of nature, it sems to evoke the

task of the human sciences as defined, for example, by Lévi-Strauss in *The Savage Mind*: 'the ultimate goal of the human sciences is not to constitute man, but to dissolve him ...: to reintegrate culture into nature' (pp. 326–7). The corollary is therefore: 'The opposition between nature and culture, on which we have hitherto insisted, today seems above all to be of methodological value' (*ibid.*). To dissolve man is certainly Nietzsche's project, but he contrasts man with the super-human, whose appropriateness – in the Spinozist sense – to nature does not seem to be assimilable to the kind proposed by Lévi-Strauss the anthropologist, because *nature* and *life* are not reabsorbed, in Nietzsche, into 'the set of (their) physico–chemical conditions' (Lévi-Strauss, *The Savage Mind*). Beyond the necessary diminution of human narcissism necessitated by their respective projects, as is also the case with Freud (cf. 'A difficulty in psychoanalysis', in *Essays in Applied Psychoanalysis*, where Freud evokes the three great decisive blows successively dealt to man's narcissism and 'vanity' (Nietzsche) by Copernicus, Darwin and psychoanalysis; cf. also Ernest Jones, *The Life and Work of Sigmund Freud*, vol. II), intentions and concepts differ: is nature the linear necessity of physico–chemical determinism, or the innocence of be-coming, the will to power or *amor fati*, life as enigma, the growth of desire, the necessity of lack, but also the *lack of necessity*?

35 *Amor fati* is for Nietzsche a way of putting this problem, that correlates to the 'innocence of becoming' and above all to the 'eternal return'. The ambiguity of this last notion perhaps 'turns round' the question of choosing between these two views of nature and affirms the necessity of desire more than that of determination: it converts the lack of necessity into a necessity.

36 Cf. Hegel, *Phenomenology of Mind*, IV, A, 'Independence and dependence of self-consciousness'.

37 Freud, *The Future of an Illusion*. The translation of *Kultur* as 'civilization' or 'cultural' follows the practice of the standard edition. See the editor's introductory note to *The Future of an Illusion*.

38 Freud, *Civilization and its Discontents*.

39 In this realm of ideas, *Kultur* and *Bildung* contrast with '*chaos sive natura*' (*GS*, 11 (330), Gallimard edition).

40 *D*, §130: 'the great cosmic stupidity [that] strikes some treasured purpose of ours dead'.

41 *D*, §130: 'Those iron hands of necessity which shake the dice-box of chance play their game for an infinite length of time: so that there *have* to be throws which exactly resemble purposiveness and rationality of every degree'.

42 *D*, 3 (82).

43 *GS*, 11 (307) (Gallimard edition).

44 *D*, 7 (71).

45 *EH*, 'Why I am So Clever', §10.

46 Meaning in this sense would be equally absent in psychoanalysis, to be replaced perhaps by neurological medicine; and in Marx's notion of revolutionary action, if economic determinism were direct.

47 *GS*, Preface, §2. One may note that these terms are borrowed from sciences or disciplines that 'interpret' in the largest sense of the term (medicine, psychology, theological exegesis, philology).

48 *GS*, Preface, §2.

49 J.-J. Rousseau, *Discours sur l'origine et les fondements de l'inégalité* . . . , Part One, (Paris: Gallimard, 1964) Pléiade, vol. III, p. 162.

50 This gap, in Nietzsche, is that of the will to power.

51 C. Lévi-Strauss, *Race et Histoire*, ch. 10, p. 84.

52 S. Freud, *Civilization and its Discontents*, conclusion.

53 Cf. our 'Nietzsche: la vie et la métaphore', *Revue philosophique* (1971), no. 3, where we had tried to refer this gap, in Nietzsche's thought, back to his conception of 'bad conscience'.

54 The term 'value' used by Nietzsche could lend support to the hypothesis of this reduction. In reality, Nietzsche moves it from the domain of morality – conceived *stricto sensu* as a universal system of values designed to direct individual behaviour – to the domain of culture. The 'shop where they manufacture ideals' (*GM*, First Essay, 14) is, as the syntax of this text indicates ('they'), a *collective* undertaking.

55 In the Nietzschean sense, culture is the 'morality' of a given collective entity. In this sense, the two terms are almost synonymous. Morality *per se* is the precise culture that Nietzsche ascribes to Platonic Christianity.

56 Coming back to etymology, Rousseau had already raised this question in his political philosophy when he insisted on the role of mores and their important function in inculcating respect for the law. Cf. R. Derathé, *Jean-Jacques Rousseau et la science politique de son temps*.

57 We used to say 'civilization', a term that encompassed fulfilled aspirations as well as a mentality. Influenced by the German word *Kultur*, the two terms gradually became synonymous, but 'culture' suddenly became confined to ideological concerns.

58 According to this 'logic', 'civilized' or 'cultivated' are only used to define someone who displays or possesses a good knowledge of the ideological traits or monuments of a given 'civilization', at the expense of a knowledge of its 'infrastructures'.

59 Only recently have we stopped speaking of 'savages' who are presumed to have no means of 'spiritual' expression or even intellect and to be a people 'without any culture', when in fact we are designating societies whose 'culture' is different from the one to which the speaker belongs. Nietzsche was aware of this: 'the European imagines that the growth of culture happens only in Europe and considers himself to be a sort of

summary of a world process; or . . . a Christian centres all existence in general around the notion of "saving one's soul"' (*KGW*, VIII, 2, 11 (285)). Cf. Lévi-Strauss, *Race et histoire*, ch. III: 'L'ethnocentrisme'.

60 It is this meaning that Sartre wishes to correct when he defines, less partially, culture as being 'the perpetually evolving consciousness that man has of himself and of the world in which he lives, works and struggles' (*Critique of Dialectical Reason*, vol. 1, p. 66).

61 Describing a manual labour, that is to say certain practices, in an idyllic or 'ecological' way so as to appreciate their worth once more always amounts to no more than the negative mask worn by an idealist refusal on the part of a culture to take account of the potential in its material conditions.

62 *UM*, 2, §4. Cf. *EH*, 'Why I am So Clever', §1: 'Only the perfect worthlessness of our German education – its "idealism" – can to some extent explain to me why on precisely this point I was backward to the point of holiness. This "education" which from the first teaches one to lose sight of *realities* so as to hunt after altogether problematic, so-called "ideal" objectives, "classical education" for example. . . . Until my very maturest years I did in fact eat *badly*'. The theme of digestion, raised in 1873 and 1888, continues to evoke the resistance on the part of the body and praxis to their being 'forgotten' by the Ideal.

63 This is the translation proposed by Y. Brès, in *La Psychologie de Platon*, for καλὸς κἀγάθος.

64 Cf. Y. Brès, *La Psychologie de Platon* and W. Jaeger, *Paideia*. Speaking of culture, Nietzsche recalls the Greek παιδεία. However, even if he intensely criticized a purely intellectual view of culture, that is the corollary of a Platonic–Christian idealism, Nietzsche the philologist, a cultivated bourgeois who mirrors his own age, while remaining an ancient Greek in his 'political' views, remains trapped in this dominant idea of the 'cultivated' man as an intellectual. In this respect, his critiques scarcely transcend the level of commonroom wit.

4 PROBLEMATICS IN NIETZSCHE AND ITS PRECEDENTS

1 More exactly, literature on Nietzsche is divided between axiological works, that are often idealizing in the way they forget genealogy, and others that totally neglect to evoke this formative point of view, through fear of falling back into a 'moral' trap: the ideology of the *Übermensch* versus the nihilism of the 'last man'.

2 Cf. J. Droz (ed.), *Le romantisme politique en Allemagne*. The romantic desire to renew onself and become pure again through a so-called 'return to the source' and the roots of one's national soil – the themes of a politically reactionary German romanticism – can still be read in the doctrinarians of Nazism and, as we know, in Wagner, who became the musical symbol of Germanness between 1933 and 1945.

3 Many of the irrational overdeterminations of infatuation for Nietzsche credit this impassioned reader and ardent plagiarist with ideas that the author of *The World as Will and Representation* regretted to see were still being ignored. A funny path for a celebrity to take!

4 Cf., for example, *UM*, 3: 'What is being in general worth?', but also, in 1886, in the 'Attempt at Self-Criticism', §1, p. 2: 'the great question concerning the value of existence'. Cf. J. Granier, *Le Désir du Moi*, Introduction, pp. 9–16.

5 *UM*, p. 137.

6 We can therefore suspect, like Nietzsche, that Kant challenged the whole of reason's genealogy when he declared that he regarded as secondary the question: 'How is the actual power to think possible?' (*UM*, Preface to the First edition). Without playing on words, one can none the less believe that the challenge Kant makes to a 'genealogy' or a 'physiology of human understanding', such as that of which Locke offers an example, in Kant's own terms, shows up, in the face of Nietzschean accusations of idealism, the risk that a 'genealogy', in the Nietzschean sense, can get bogged down in the empiricism of 'vulgar common experience'.

7 *TI*, Foreword.

8 *TI*, 'The Problem of Socrates', §2.

9 *UM*, 3, §4: 'A series of curious questions . . .'

10 The question is then raised of knowing in what name a life can judge, evaluate and challenge another life, or a culture, that is to say, living conditions.

11 *UM*, III, §2. Nietzsche adds later: 'Never have moral educators been more needed, and never has it seemed less likely they would be found' (p. 133).

12 *UM*, III §4, pp. 154–55. Cf. also, §4, pp. 148–49.

13 *D*, 3 (158) = *VP*, II, p. 99, §298.

14 Nietzsche, who in *Ecce Homo* claims to have the finest sense of smell to be found, could never stomach Zola: 'Zola: or "delight in stinking"'. (*TI*, 'Expeditions . . .', §1); 'A man's ridiculture the intellectual dessert for many: GorgonZola – in the grotto of his nymph *soir Egeria*' (*Aigrégérie* = aigre and égrérie) (*GS*, 12 (231), Gallimard edition = *KGW*, V, 2, 12 (2)).

15 *WP*, §79 = *KGW*, VIII, 2, 9 (165).

16 Cf. *UM*, 3, §45, p. 153: 'But there is a kind of denying and destroying that is the discharge of that mighty longing for sanctification and salvation and as the first philosophical teacher of which Schopenhauer came among us desantified and truly secularized men. All that exists that can be denied deserves to be denied'.

17 *Homer's Wettkampf*, *Mus.*, II, p. 369. One translator has translated *Weichlichen* as 'effeminate' (*weiblichen*).

18 Cf. in particular the works of E.R. Dodds, W. Jaegar and Y. Brès.

19 Cf. Y. Brès, *La Psychologie de Platon*, chs One to Four.

20 Plato, *Laws*, II, 671c. Cf. *Republic*, II, 377b; in which Plato insists on the necessity of educating the young man: 'It is in fact at that moment that the thing is malleable (πλάττεται) and takes on the form (τύπος) that in each case one would have wished to imprint upon it (ἐνσημύνασθαι)'.

21 Cf. the metaphor of 'anthropoculture' (*GS*, 11 (170)); *D*, 7 (211), 7 (30) and 7 (96). It condenses data relating to *Bildung* as *cultura animi* and images doubtless of Epicurean origin that persist right up to our classic literature: e.g. 'The Scythian Philosopher' in La Fontaine (*Fables*, 12, 20).

22 *Conversations with Eckermann*: 'He who claims to make something great must have pushed his education so high that he is able, like the Greeks, to raise the humble reality of nature to the heights of his spirit and achieve something that, in natural phenomena, through inherent weakness or because of external impediment, remained in an intentional state'.

23 Cf. *TI*, 'Expeditions . . .', §49 to 51, and *ibid.*, 'Why I Owe to the Ancients'. 'Goethe did not understand the Greeks': *ibid.*, §4.

24 *Mus.*, VI, p. 340 (preparatory work for the second of the *Untimely Meditations*).

25 *WS*, §125 (*Mus.*, IX, p. 253). Nietzsche classes the *Conversations with Eckermann* among the few books that survive into the nineteenth century and surpass it (*K*, XIV, Part One, p. 349).

26 *Mus.*, III, p. 246, §§84 and 85 ('Reflections on *tragedy and free spirits* . . .').

27 This is borne out, notably in the *Conversations* . . . , by generalizations such as 'the French', 'the English', etc.

28 *Wilhelm Meister, the Journey Years*, Book II, chs I and II.
29 On Goethe as a 'precursor' of Nietzsche, cf. Andler, *Nietzsche, sa vie et sa pensée*, vol. 1, ch. 1.
30 Preparatory work for the second of the *Untimely Meditations*, Mus., VI, p. 340.
31 Hölderlin, *Hyperion*. The theme of the critique of the State, 'the coldest of all the cold monsters', will be taken up later by Nietzsche. Cf., for example, 'Every philosophy which believes that the problem of existence is touched on, not to say solved, by a political event is a joke – and pseudo-philosophy (*Spass-und Afterphilosophie*)' (*UM*, 3, §4, pp. 147–8).
32 Hölderlin, *Hyperion*. Text quoted by Andler, *Nietzsche, sa vie et sa pensée*, vol. 1, p. 51.
33 Cf. The relationship between Schopenhauer's philosophy and a German culture, in *Ecrits posthumes 1870–1873*, p. 188 et seq.
34 *UM*, 3, §3.
35 Hölderlin, *Hyperion*. One cannot help thinking that it is Kant that is in mind here, and beyond his philosophy, the rationalism of the whole of the Enlightenment.
36 'It is true that Kant did not arrive at the knowledge that the phenomenon is the world as representation and that the thing-in-itself is the will.' (Arthur Schopenhauer, *The World as Will and Representation*, vol. 2, p. 421.)
37 Gueroult writes that Hegel constructed 'a philosophy that overcame this duality [in Kant] and achieved a reconciliation between the ideal and reality at the heart of the concrete substantiality of the universal spirit'. But Gueroult shows that the price paid by Hegel is 'a distorting and systematically vicious interpretation' of Kantianism. Cf. Gueroult, 'Les "déplacements" de la conscience morale Kantienne selon Hegel' in *Hommage a Jean Hyppolite* (Paris: 1971).
38 Kant, *Critique of the Faculty of Judgement*, Introduction, §IV.
39 Kant, *Critique of the Faculty of Judgement*, §83.
40 On the other hand, one could accuse Kant of *petitio principii*, contrary to the very limits he assigns metaphysics, in accepting without question that fulfilling one's duty is the absolute goal of human existence, and that Reason, like practical Reason, is a determining factor in grasping human essence.
41 Cf. Leibniz, 'On the ultimate origination of things', in *Philosophical Writings* (London: Dent, 1934), pp. 32–41.
42 Kant, *The Philosophy of History*, Idea of the universal history, 3rd proposition.
43 Leibniz, *Philosophical Writings*, p. 34.
44 Leibniz, *Philosophical Writings*, p. 33.
45 The very image of sight here necessarily evokes Leibniz's famous

comparison between the world as an infinite finality and a painting of which the eye sees only a part (Leibniz, *Philosophical Writings*), p. 39.

46 Kant, *The Philosophy of History*, 2nd proposition.

47 Leibniz, *Philosophical Writings*, p. 41.

48 Kant, *The Philosophy of History*.

49 Kant, *The Philosophy of History*, 'It seems that nature . . .' 'as if it wanted man to. . . .' Cf. Gottfried Martin, *Kant's Metaphysics and Theory of Science*, II, ch. 2, and Eric Weil, *Problèmes kantiens*, ch. 2.

50 *LPh*, I, §46.

51 'In this sense metaphysics goes beyond the phenomenon, i.e., nature, to what is concealed in or behind it (τὸ μετὰ τὸ φυσικόν). . . . According to the definition of metaphysics repeated also by Kant, it is neither a science of mere concepts nor a system of inferences and deductions. . . . It is a rational knowledge (*Wissen*) drawn from perception of the external actual world. . . . I admit entirely Kant's doctrine . . .; but I add that, precisely as phenomenal appearance, it is the manifestation of that which appears, and with him I call that which appears the thing–in–itself.' (Arthur Schopenhauer, *The World as Will and Representation*, vol. 2, p. 183). There is no will without ends: this explains the importance of teleology for Schopenhauer (see in particular *The World as Will and Representation*, pp. 327–41).

52 In the section following on from this text, Nietzsche is obviously already challenging Hegel and the need to give world history a goal. The person who upholds the innocence of becoming none the less develops the (Schopenhauerian) idea that the production of geniuses is the real if unconscious goal of history.

53 Nietzsche, 'The State according to the Greeks' in *Ecrits posthumes 1870–1873*, p. 186.

54 Cf. in particular Schopenhauer, *The World as Will and Representation*, ch. 28.

55 *The World as Will and Representation*, ch. 29.

56 To put it crudely, one could say that perhaps Nietzsche's *impossibility* comes from the fact that, in many respects, he is this monster: a Godless Leibniz, a *contradictio* – if we may put it thus – *in adjecto*.

57 Cf. especially the 'Attempt at Self–Criticism'. You will say that, since Nietzsche denounces metaphysics as a system, we cannot denounce his position in the name of such a metaphysics. But we must still prove that the will to overcome metaphysics is not, as is the case with a number of his professional destroyers, the expression of a will to vengeance, that weakly unifies different elements under a vague concept. To overcome is slavish when it results only in over-turning, and the hallmark of weakness, like neurosis, is to think it has overcome something when it has merely set it back. This goes for Nietzsche: the suspicion can be created that he freed himself

only by falling into the void, to use a metaphor from the Königsberg 'metaphysician'.

58 This type of text is not absent in Nietzsche and it would be as facile as it would be malicious to conceal the author's name and have them pass as idealist exhortations that naturally any convinced, that is to say, believing, 'Nietzschean' would rashly stigmatize as reactionary. And why should we be afraid of him being so? For example, *UM*, 3, §2.

59 *EH*, 'Why I Am a Destiny', §7.

60 But it is not by chance that only a very few twentieth-century thinkers have paid attention to his writings on culture: in order to do so, one has to abandon the dogma of immaculate scientificity and the reflex action of assimilating philosophy into ideology.

61 Why is it that the term 'culture', so frequently used by Lévi-Strauss in his book *Race et histoire*, is never given a definition, something we are committed to do to uphold any scientific discourse that claims to have detached itself from all philosophy?

5 NIETZSCHE'S QUESTIONING AND ITS STAGES

1 Plato, *Gorgias*, 500c, and 492d.

2 Theodor Adorno, *In Search of Wagner* (London, 1981). See also in particular chs 9 and 10. On the other hand, Adorno will show how Gustav Mahler is the first composer to have refused to mark or resolve these contradictions in his music. Perhaps Nietzsche would have called him the first tragic musician. See Adorno's book on Mahler.

3 History is contemptuous: as we know, it was Bismarck's State that was to set this *Kulturkampf* in motion, to different ends.

4 *UM*, 3, §3.

5 *UM*, 3, §4.

6 *UM*, 3, §4. Note the idealist Schopenhauerian or Platonic tone of this text and its closing allusion to Goethe.

7 *EH*, 'Twilight of the Idols', §2.

8 This duality can be found at the lexical level: *Kultur* has a descriptive value at the same time as having a normative one. Cf. the remarks by R.E. McGinn, 'Culture as Prophylactic: Nietzsche's Birth of Tragedy as Culture Criticism', *Nietzsche Studien* (1975), 4, pp. 75–138, especially p. 77: 'Kultur is used both descriptively and prescriptively in German'.

9 The word 'revolution' could be questioned in the same way. Is revolution determined or determining with respect to history? Is it simply the expression of a contradiction followed by a solution to the contradiction: a 'good' contradiction? Surely the word which promises resolution in re-volution, affirmation in and through negation, still expresses the problem even as it claims to be resolving it? Does it not stem from the same ambiguity as the one pinpointed here by Nietzsche? Cf. J. Ellul, *Autopsie de la révolution*.

10 *BT*, 'Attempt at Self-Criticism', §2.

11 'Attempt at Self-Criticism', §2. Repeated twice in the same paragraph.

12 'Attempt at Self-Criticism', §2.

13 Cf. Plato, *Republic*, 7, 539b–c: 'The youth, like puppies, enjoying themselves tearing and gnawing with their arguments'; cf. also *Philebus*, 15c; *Phaedo*, 90c and above all *Gorgias*, 484b–486d.

14 Cf. *HATH*, §17: 'The young person values metaphysical explanations because they reveal to him something in the highest degree significant in things he found unpleasant or contemptible; and if he is discontented with himself this feeling is alleviated when he comes to recognize the innermost enigma or misery of the universe in that which he so much condemns in himself'.

15 *GM*, Third Essay, §20. A slightly different version is to be found in *KGW*, III, 2, 10 (78): 'Beware of your first movement; it is almost always generous'.

16 *BT*, 'Attempt at Self-Criticism', §7.

17 'Attempt at Self-Criticism', §3.

18 This is the period of Wagner and Malwida von Meysenbug, a period that was soon to see a spiritualist revival, prior to Rolland and Bergson. It is here, in our opinion, that Nietzsche comes closest to certain themes to be found in twentieth-century reactionary thinking, from Maurras to the 'national revolution' of Petainism.

19 *UM*, 3, §4: 'In becoming, everything is hollow, deceptive, shallow and worthy of our contempt; ... to destroy all that is becoming ... he measures the distance between himself and his lofty goal and seems to see behind and beneath him only an insignificant heap of dross'.

20 Nietzsche is not yet questioning clearly the status and origin of the ideal of culture, an ideal apparently maintained as a metaphysical entity that transcends becoming, an 'idea' in the Schopenhauerian sense. Nor does he question the reason for the diversity of ideals and we do not know where they come from. Cf. his phrase: 'the various cultures are various spiritual climates' (*WS*, §188: cf. also *HATH*, §236), which certainly comes from Herder's *Outline of a Philosophy of the History of Man*, Part Two, Book Seven. Cf. Kant's *Philosophy of History*.

21 This is borne out by the way he questions the *value* of values.

22 In this respect, in terms of the hagiography common to Marx, Nietzsche and Freud, the last two, from the point of view of the drives at work within veneration, play a compensatory role: lost in Marxism or Marxist structures, the individual prefers to rediscover himself in Freud and Nietzsche. The latter also has the 'advantage' of offering the added bonus of poetry, something which the other two offer only sparingly.

23 Cf. Rousseau's political writings (in particular his *Projet de constitution pour la Corse* and *Considérations sur le gouvernement de Pologne*). On moralists as precursors of genealogy and the difference between them and Nietzsche, cf. *KGW*, VIII, 2, 11 (54).

24 Conversely, the economic system of drives is described by Nietzsche in terms of political metaphor.

25 Nietzsche's object, culture, therefore seems to be located somewhere between the problems outlined in Freud, which at first are strictly individual but are subsequently viewed as collective (which explains Nietzsche's greater affinity to Freud than to Marx), and a Marxian socio-economic analysis.

26 Cf. E. Durkheim, *Les règles de la méthode sociologique* (Paris: PUF, 1960), pp. 27–8.

27 It is perhaps on the question of the interpretation of the Eternal Return of the Same that these difficulties crystallize most visibly: the very idea perhaps aims simply to simulate mythically a harmony operating between the ideal norm (selection) and necessity, between freedom and

determinism. Is this wish fulfilment or a solution? Note that the adjective 'unzeitgemäss' (untimely) bears witness, throughout the whole of his work, to the continuity of an attitude whose goal is ethical. The goal is justified initially in terms of the gap between being and becoming, and then in terms of the genealogical gap between the tragic truth of drives and the 'moral ideal': 'What does a philosopher demand of himself first and last? To overcome his time in himself, to become "timeless". With what must he therefore engage in the hardest combat? With whatever marks him as the child of his time'. (*CW*, Preface). 'Timeless', echoes 'untimely'.

28 *EH*, 'Human All Too Human', §1. Cf. *HATH*, 1886 Preface, §3.

29 As if Nietzsche went back from Schopenhauer to Kant: one might ask if Nietzsche's third stage, in particular the idea of genealogy, would not have come from a sort of composition located somewhere between Schopenhauer and Kant: genealogy is the Kantian 'critique' of Nietzsche applied to the will to life of the Schopenhauerian body.

30 Cf. *HATH*, 1886 Preface, §1.

31 In *BT*, especially §6.

32 Individualities (Homer, Handel, Luther, Mozart, J. -S. Bach, Racine, Claude Lorrain, Beethoven, Rossini, to choose, for example, from hundreds: cf. *AOM* §171) are invoked only as being characteristic or symbolic of a 'spirit', age or culture.

33 We note the most common expression in *HATH*, *D* and *GS*: 'some people', 'the ages', 'there are people', 'usually', 'young men', 'women', 'idealists', 'unbelievers' – which characterize an attempt on the part of Nietzsche the moralist to place himself on the collective level of an entity whose worth must be judged. Cf. the 'chapter' headings of *HATH*, or the aphorisms in *GS* and *D*; for example: highbrow and lowbrow characters; Women and Child; the religious life; on the soul of artists and writers; the State; socialism, etc.

34 The expression 'natural history', which anticipates genealogy, is already to be found in *D*, (e.g. §112) and is stated to be 'a history of moral feelings' in *HATH*, ch. 2. It finds its way into the title of Part Five of *BGE*, before assuming its definitive name in the subsequent work. The three moments (or periods) of Nietzsche's thought are successively: questions and experiments; followed by 'natural history'; and then 'genealogy'.

35 It is very noticeable, if one compares Nietzsche to Hegel, that in the former it is not philosophy that determines and presents its ends to culture, but culture that now determines philosophy. Nietzsche, however, seeks to escape from this by authorizing the new philosopher to evaluate culture.

36 *TI*, 'The "Improvers" of Mankind', §1: *Zeichenrede* (sign-language); cf. *BGE*, §187: 'in short, moralities too are only a *sign-language of the emotions*'.

37 *TI*, 'The "Improvers" of Mankind', §1.
38 *TI*, 'The "Improvers" of Mankind', §1.
39 *TI*, 'The Four Great Errors', §1 and 2.
40 *Ibid.*, 'The Four Great Errors', §3.
41 Corporeity and typology therefore play, *mutatis mutandis*, a role that is equivalent to that of the originally synthetic unity of apperception, 'constituting' the transcendental object, within· the framework of a Kantian critique.
42 *UM*, 4 §4. Nietzsche had already sensed this unity without being able to designate its precise status when he wrote on several occasions in *UM*: 'Culture is, above all, unity of style in all the expressions of the life of a people'. (*UM*, 1, §1 and §2; 2, §4).
43 Any revolution has a history, unless it is merely the illusory mythology of something new created *ex nihilo*. The *Umwertung* and the overtuning achieved by genealogy have antecedents.
44 *BGE*, §42, §211. Likewise, Kant, setting up reason as a tribunal in which philosophy appears, contrasts 'critical' or 'transcendental' philosophy with ('dogmatic') 'metaphysics'. When Nietzsche presents himself as a (new) philosopher, his object becomes 'metaphysics' or 'morality'. On the other hand, it is the *new* psychologist, genealogist or philosopher who can judge and evaluate philosophy.
45 We borrow this word from Freud in order to designate more easily what Nietzsche is driving at in speaking of a play of forces, a hierarchy of drives that present themselves on each occasion within a specific typology. 'Typology' is the scholarly term for this play, and Nietzsche has no precise word to designate the set of evaluations.
46 *BGE*, §230.
47 *EH*, 'Twilight of the Idols', §2. The author of the phrase is P. Gast. Cf. the Gallimard edition, p. 334, note 1. Cf. *EH*, 'Why I Am a Destiny', especially §§1 and 8.
48 *EH*, 'Why I Am a Destiny', §8.
49 Letter from Nietzsche to Gast, 30 October 1888; *KGW*, VIII, 3, 25 (5).
50 *EH*, 'Twilight of the Idols', §2 and *EH*, 'Why I Am a Destiny', §8.
51 *EH*, 'Why I Am a Destiny', §8: 'he breaks the history of mankind into two parts'.
52 *BGE*, §61.
53 *BGE*, §211.
54 Cf. *WP*, §409: 'philosophers ... must no longer accept concepts as a gift, nor merely purify and polish them, but first *make* and *create* them' (= *KGW*, VIII, 3, 34 (195)).
55 *EH*, 'Why I Am a Destiny', §1.
56 *TI*, 'Expeditions ...', §47: 'one must not mistake the method involved here: a mere disciplining of thoughts and feelings is virtually nothing (— here lies the great mistake of German culture, which is totally

illusory): one first has to convince the *body*. .... It is decisive for the fortune of nations and of mankind that one should inaugurate culture in the *right place* – *not* in the "soul" (as has been the fateful superstition of priests and quasi-priests): the right place is the body, demeanour, diet, physiology: the *rest* follows'. Cf. a variant in *EH*, 'The Wagner Case', §4: 'Now I know how one refutes Germans: not with arguments, but with rhubarb' (Gallimard edition, p. 568).

57 *Mus.*, XIV, p. 39 (*Einzelbemerkungen aus der Zeit des Zarathustra*).

58 Letter to Schmeitzner, 14 February 1883.

59 Heidegger's view that the Historical determines human action is one of the post-Niezschean forms of the choice that raises this ambiguity.

60 *WP*, §256, *Mus.*, XVIII, p. 190.

61 *WP*, §257.

62 *Mus.*, VI, p. 9.

63 *TSZ*, Part Two, 'Of the Famous Philosophers'.

64 *WP*, §458 (*Mus.*, XVIII, pp. 325–6) = *KGW*, VIII, 3, 14 (107) = *VP*, I, p. 48, §56.

65 Cf. our article, 'Wohin? Wozu? Ein Kulturproblem: Wahrheit und Leben bei Hume und Nietzsche', *Perspektiven der Philosophie* (1980), 16.

66 *Mus.*, XI, p. 306.

67 *KGW*, V, 2, 13 (20).

68 *KGW*, V, 2, 13 (18).

69 *KGW*, V, 2, 13 (17).

70 *Mus.*, XI, pp. 234–5 (*KGW*, V, 2, 11 (258) and 13 (20); cf. the Gallimard edition, 11 (207) and 18 (24).

71 *Mus.*, XI, p. 143.

72 For example, *WP*, §254; *D*, §42; etc.

73 *Mus.*, XXI, p. 81 (Kritische persönliche Bemerkungen, 1880–1881, Zeit der *Morgenröthe*). Cf. variants of *EH* (Gallimard edition, p. 545).

74 *Mus.*, XXI. Cf. *KGW*, VIII, 2, 10 (68): the new morality of 'corporal and spiritual discipline'.

75 'You are acquainted with these things as thoughts, but your thoughts are not lived experiences, merely the echo of those lived by others' (*KGW*, VIII, 2, 10 (68)).

76 *KGW*, V, 2, 11 (262) (*Mus.*, XI, p. 310).

77 Cf. *WP*, §552 (*Mus.*, XIX, p. 53) = *KGW*, VIII, 2, 9 (91), §D.

78 A frequent word in Nietzsche's texts: for example, *GM*, Second Essay, §1.

79 One cannot help thinking that the Eternal Return is a substitute for the infinity of the soul's immortality (cf. Kant, *Critique of Practical Reason*, Book Two, ch. 2, §IV).

80 Eugen Fink has notably stressed this problem in *La philosophie de Nietzsche* (Paris, 1965), ch. 3, Section 6.

81 *Mus.*, XI, p. 184 (Aus der Zeit der Fröhlichen Wissenschaft, III: die

ewige Wiederkunft) = *KGW*, V, 2, 11 (143), French edition: 11 (226).

82 Sigmund Freud, 'Fragment of an Analysis of a Case of Hysteria', Standard Edition, 7, 3.

83 *An*, §3. Cf. *GM*, Second Essay, §16.

6 NIETZSCHE AND THE GENEALOGY OF CULTURE: THE 'VERSUCH'

1 Cf. Peter Heller, *Studies on Nietzsche*, p. 13: 'Nietzsche therefore appears to aid and abet that false sense of sophistication displayed by literary sophists who will cheerfully assert that there are no correct or incorrect interpretations of linguistic communications, but will never marvel at, say, airline schedules and the widespread argument as to whether a person or machine is or is not on time'.
2 Cf. Plato, *Meno*, 79a: μή καταγνύαι μηδὲ κερματίζειν.
3 Gaston Bachelard, *L'engagement rationaliste*, 'the philosophical dialectic of the Notions of Relativity', p. 120. Bachelard is referring to *UM*, 2 §10. Cf. *TSZ*, Part Three, 'Of Old and New Law-Tables', §25.
4 *TI*, 'Maxims and Arrows', §34.
5 *CW*, §1.
6 Cf. J. Granier, *Le discours du monde*, ch. 10.
7 'All fish talk like that,' you said: 'what *they* cannot fathom is unfathomable.' (*TSZ*, Part Two, 'The Dance Song').
8 *TSZ*, Part Two, 'The Dance Song'.
9 *WP*, §481 = *KGW*, VIII, 1, 7 (60).
10 Thomas Mann, *Tonio Kröger*, ch. 4: 'Erkenntnisekel'.
11 Thomas Mann, *Tonio Kröger*, chs 4 and 5: *'ein verirrter Bürger'*. Cf. J. Granier, *Le discours du monde*, ch. 10, §84. On this point we also recall Hegel's unsurpassable critique in the Introduction to the *Phenomenology of Mind*: 'Living substance ... is the mediation between one's own *becoming* – other and oneself'. Obviously, Nietzsche's dilemma challenges the possibility of such a mediation. It is Adorno who accuses a certain ontologist phenomenology of lived experience or invocation of remaining untouched by the thought of having forgotten the lessons of Hegel and Nietzsche: 'Hegel perceived that the obsessional rigidity of the invocation of being resembled the formal clickety-click of the prayer wheel. He understood what got falsified and lost in the process, in spite of all the chatter about the concrete: it was precisely the magic of the indeterminate concrete whose only content was its own aura. ... He rejected, as did the Nietzsche of *The Twilight of the Idols* no doubt only in the wake of Hegel, the assimilation of the philosophical content of truth to the highest abstraction. ... The said, which aims to rise above the dialectic by using words that are original and innate, is only ever something the dialectic turns into a mouthful, an abstraction, which expands until it reaches being in-itself and for-itself, and then founders in a total lack of content, in tautology, in being that performs only the same old refrain of being' (Theodor W. Adorno, 'Drei Studien zu Hegel' in *Gesammelte Schriften*, Rolf Tiedemann (ed.) (Frankfurt am Main, Suhrkamp, 1971), vol. 5, pp. 247–382).

12 *NEW*, Epilogue (cf. *GS*, Preface).

13 Freud and Marx, as thinkers concerned with domination by the unspoken forces of the libido and labour in culture, might also seem to be imprisoned in the same dilemma. Their discourses, by their very discursive nature, are metaphysical in relation to their object: speaking is not labouring and unconscious affect is not discourse, as every proletariat and neurotic knows. The latter are also caught between idealism (science, theory) and thingism, as is subsequently borne out by the history of Marxism and psychoanalysis ('Stalinist' dogmatism, materialist realism, the science of dreams, the theory of praxis, the thingism of oniric symbolism ...). Only the psychoanalytic session and revolutionary practice can, as perspectivist reference points, reestablish some interpretative movement in these disciplines.

14 One sign of this: according to Nietzsche, the philologist, who is always seated, is a victim of nihilist assiduity (*TI*, 'Maxims and Arrows', §34). He does not live, and denies life because he consults too many books: 'Early in the morning at the break of day, in all the freshness and dawn of one's strength, to read a *book* – I call that vicious! ...' (*EH*, 'Why I am So Clever', §8). Nietzsche continues to insist on this point, even if he does not always express himself with the perfunctory anti-intellectualism of a roughneck: 'The philologist of the future, sceptical as regards our entire culture and for that very reason also denying the state of philologist' (*K*, X, p. 356).

15 Cf. H. Wismann, 'Nietzsche et la philologie' in *Nietzsche aujourd'hui?*, II, pp. 325–44.

16 Cf. *TI*, and *CW*. Prefaces.

17 Most of these occurrences are noted by W.A. Kaufmann in *Nietzsche, Philosopher, Psychologist, Antichrist* (p. 85, n. 4). To this list we can add: a posthumous fragment (*K*, XII, p. 410) quoted twice by Heidegger (*Nietzsche*, I, p. 28); *EH*, 'Thus Spoke Zarathustra', §2; and above all *WP*, §§424 and 1041 (*KGW*, VII, 35 (31) and (32); VIII, 3, 16 (32), which we shall consider shortly.

18 Heidegger, *Nietzsche, I*, p. 28.

19 *D*, §547.

20 Or some kind of authority: 'The best we can do in this interregnum is to be as far as possible our own *reges* and found little *experimental states*. We are experiments: let us also want to be them!' (*D*, §453).

21 *Mus.*, XIV, p. 22 = *K*, XII, p. 259 = *KGW*, VII, 1, 4 (55).

22 'But we, we others who thirst after reason, are determined to scrutinize our experiences as severely as a scientific experiment – hour after hour, day after day. We ourselves wish to be our experiments and guinea pigs.' (*GS*, §319.

23 *D*, Preface, §1.

24 '*Truthfulness.* – I favour any *skepsis* to which I may reply: "Let us try it!" But I no longer wish to hear anything of all those things and questions that do not permit any experiment. This is the limit of my "truthfulness"; for there courage has lost its rights.' (*GS*, §51). 'The philosophers of the future . . . will certainly be experimenters. Through the name with which I have ventured to baptize them I have already expressly emphasized experiment and the delight in experiment' (*BGE*, §210).

25 The image of *discovery* occurs frequently: cf. *GS*, §343. The new is always contrasted by Nietzsche to the '*bisher*' (hitherto): cf. *BGE*, where the word returns time and time again, from the beginning of the Preface, as Kaufmann notes in the commentary to his own translation (New York: Vintage Books, 1973, p. 2, n. 1).

26 'We have reconquered our courage for error, for experimentation, for accepting provisionally' (*D*, §501). 'The moral earth, too, is round. The moral earth, too, has its antipodes. The antipodes, too, have the right to exist. There is yet another world to be discovered – and more than one. Embark, philosophers!' (*GS*, §289). 'The great liberator came to me: the idea that life could be an experiment of the seeker for knowledge – and not a duty, not a calamity, not trickery. . . . For me [knowledge] is a world of dangers and victories' (*GS*, §324). 'A strange, seductive, dangerous ideal' (*EH*, 'Thus Spoke Zarathustra', §2, repeating *GS*, §382).

27 Martin Heidegger, *Nietzsche*, tr. David Krell (London, 1981), I, p. 28.

28 *D*, §187.

29 *BGE*, §42.

30 *BGE*, §205.

31 Heidegger, *Nietzsche I*, p. 28.

32 Kaufmann, *Nietzsche, Philosopher, Psychologist, Antichrist*, p. 85.

33 *GS*, §7. Nietzsche has not forgotten his idea: he will develop his philosophy of nutrition in *EH*, 'Why I am So Clever', especially §1. In this sense, he will insist on what he calls the 'problems of life', as opposed to 'problems for philosophers' (*KGW*, VIII, 3, 14 (227)).

34 Cf. *GM*, Preface, §6; *BGE*, Preface: 'what is the suspicion . . .'; *D*, §93; *TI*, 'Maxims and Arrows', §1. Cf. the remarks by R. Roos in *Nietzsche aujourd'hui?* II, p. 300.

35 *BGE*, §1.

36 This leads to Nietzsche's repeated affirmation: 'the strength of a spirit could be measured by how much "truth" it could take, more clearly, to what degree it *needed* it attenuated, veiled, sweetened, blunted, and falsified'. (*BGE*, §39). Cf. *ibid.*, §59.

37 *GS*, 18 (13) = *KGW*, V, 2, 13 (12).

38 *EH*, Foreword, §3.

39 *BGE*, §39.

40 *K*, XII, p. 410 = *Mus.*, XIV, p. 188. Heidegger quotes this text twice. Here we can add that the analytic session, which aims to lay bare conflicts, generates resistance and brings unconscious forces into play is in this respect a sort of *Versuch*: it needs must imply the same danger for the patient and the same defensive neutrality for the analyst (even if the patient dies of it!).

41 *WP*, §493 = *KGW*, VII, 3, 34 (253). Compare this to the mechanisms of defence in psychoanalysis, notably the resistances.

42 *WP*, §483 = *KGW*, VII, 3, 38 (3).

43 *GS*, 13 (910), Gallimard edition = *KGW*, V, 2, 15 (10) = *Mus.*, XI, p. 164.

44 *GS*, 11 (261) = *KGW*, V, 2, 11 (229). Cf. *GS*, 11 (279) = *KGW*, V, 2, 11 (171): 'I recognize something true to be merely the opposite of a really living non-truth: in this way truth enters the world stripped of power, as a concept, and it must first *fortify itself by merging with living errors!* This is why we must let these errors live on'. This is expressed even more clearly in *BGE*, §11: 'for the purpose of preserving beings such as ourselves, such judgements must be *believed* to be true; although they might of course still be *false* judgements!' From the biographical point of view, Nietzsche expresses his idea of *Versuch* thus: 'the human paths diverge at this point: if you want to find pleasure and peace of soul, then believe; if you want to devote yourself to truth, then seek' (Letter to his sister, 11 February 1865).

45 *D*, §90.

46 *KGW*, VIII, 3, 15 (46). Cf. *WP*, §552 = *KGW*, 2, 9 (91).

47 *GS*, §110.

48 *BGE*, §43. Cf. *ibid.*, §268 and §284.

49 One can read countless examples of this type of analysis: in particular in *KGW* 1, VIII, 1, 15 (46) cf. *TI*, 'Morality as Anti-Nature', §3); *KGW, ibid.*, 15 (58). Nietzsche writes: 'in itself to demand that one speak only the "truth" would be to suppose that one, possessed the truth; but if this means only that we say only what we hold to be true, there are cases where it is *important* to say it in such a way that *others* also *hold* it to be true: in order that it affect them. . . . We live out *lies* and *falsifications* – the ruling classes have always lied' (*KGW*, VIII, 3, 15 (57)).

50 Cf. *KGW*, VIII, 1, 1 (232); 2 (41); 2 (43); 3 (2).

51 Cf. *TI*, 'Morality as Anti–Nature', §3. The series of 'ors' ends with a 'who knows? perhaps . . .', etc.

52 αἴνιγμα stems from αἰνός.

53 *BGE*, §296. It is *also* in this sense that we can read expressions such as the following: 'Every philosophy is a foreground philosophy – that is a hermit's judgement: "there is something arbitrary in the fact that *he* stopped, looked back, poked around here, that he stopped digging and laid his spade aside *here* – there is also something suspicious about it".

Every philosophy also *conceals* a philosophy; every opinion is also a hiding-place, every word also a mask'. (*BGE*, §289). And also: 'Every profound thinker is more afraid of being understood than of being misunderstood' (*BGE*, §290). The text that translates this basic problem into Nietzsche's style in the most revelatory way is the very fine paragraph in which Nietzsche discusses the author of *Tristram Shandy*, turning the description, as he often did, into a self-portrait: *AOM*, §113.

54 This certainly does not mean that genealogy is merely a simple textual game, since it puts itself forward only on the basis of a supposed referent outside the text. But the problem consists in the fact that it is located both within the text (which it is) and outside the text, and is therefore a labour that disrupts the systematic stability of discourse.

55 *EH*, 'Why I Write Such Excellent Books', §5. Cf. also *K*, X, p. 370, §150 = *Mus.*, VII, p. 173.

7 NIETZSCHE AND GENEALOGICAL PHILOLOGY

1 *GS*, Gallimard edition, 23 (95).
2 *EH*, 'Why I am So Clever', §2: 'Naumburg, Schulpforta, Thuringia in general, Leipzig, Basel, Venice – so many ill-fated places for my physiology. . . . Ignorance *in physiologis* – accursed "idealism" – is the real fatality in my life, the superfluous and stupid in it, something out of which nothing good grows, for which there is no compensation, no counter-reckoning. It is as a consequence of this "idealism" that I elucidate to myself all the blunders, all the great deviations of instinct and "modesties" which led me away from the *task* of my life, that I became a philologist for example – why not at least a physician or something else that opens the eyes?'
3 *KGW*, VIII, 3, 25 (90), 15 (82), 15 (91); *An*, § 52.
4 *BGE*, §22: 'You must pardon me as an old philologist'.
5 *GS*, Preface, §2: 'But let us leave Herr Nietzsche: what is it to us that Herr Nietzsche has become well again?'
6 *GM*, Preface, §8. (Cf. *EH*, 'Why I Write Such Excellent Books', §4 and 5).
7 *GS*, §102: 'Philology presupposes a noble faith – that for the sake of a very few human beings, who always "will come" but are never there, a very large amount of fastidious and even dirty work needs to be done first'.
8 *BGE*, §426.
9 *HATH*, 2 47 (7), Gallimard edition.
10 *Mus.*, II, p. 29, §§19, 20.
11 *EH*, 'Why I am So Wise', §1.
12 Plato, *Republic*, VII, 537c.
13 *D*, Preface, §5.
14 This is why 'every profound thinker is more afraid of being understood than of being misunderstood' (*BGE*, §290).
15 *HATH*, 1, 23 (22).
16 *K*, X, p. 370, §150.
17 *An*, §26: 'the reality is . . .'.
18 *GM*, Preface, §8.
19 This is why we *also* need a touch of *décadence* or dyspepsia, to be someone who 'can't be done with anything' (*GM*, Second Essay, §1). But, on the other hand, cf. *D*. Preface, §5.
20 *HATH*, 1, 19 (1).
21 *BGE*, §22.
22 *KGW*, VIII, 3, 15 (82). Not that we need to give a text an essential meaning by reducing interpretations, since there is no reading of a text without interpretation. Nietzsche means that interpretation (which is

always perspectivist) should not be elevated into an exclusive understanding of the semantic 'essence' of an unassignable text, forgetting that interpretation is (just) interpretation (one perspective among many possible ones), and substituting itself for the text as a plurality of potential interpretations: the text is life, it offers itself up only through interpretation, but is not to be confused with any single interpretation.

23 *HATH*, 23 (108), Gallimard edition. Cf. *D*, §84.

24 *HATH*, 31 (5).

25 *BGE*, §22.

26 *BGE*, §38.

27 J. Granier's expression 'philological integrity' is falsely attributed to Nietzsche. The letter speaks of philological 'dishonesty', 'falsification' (*An*, §26) or 'inadequacy' (*KGW*, VIII, 3, 15 (82) and (91)).

28 The proof is that it is above all 'Christians' and theologians whom Nietzsche accuses of philological dishonesty. Moreover, morality's triumph over itself (*Selbstaufhebung der Moral*), which is evoked so often by Nietzsche, is presented as being an effect of this philological integrity, an integrity which is a legacy of Christianity and which turns back on it. Cf. *GS*, §357, which is reiterated in *GM*, Third Essay, §27: 'What is it, in truth, that has triumphed over the Christian god? . . . The Christian ethics with its key notion, ever more strictly applied, of truthfulness; the caustic finesse of the Christian conscience, translated and sublimated into the scholarly conscience, into intellectual integrity to be maintained at all costs'. Cf. *D*, §§84 and 86.

29 Plato, *Phaedrus*, 275e.

30 *HATH*, §270, Gallimard edition.

31 *HATH*, 19 (3) compares philologists to road-sweepers.

32 *An*, §26.

33 *An, §38*.

34 *An*, §47.

35 *An*, §47.

36 *An*, §44.

37 *An*, §52. Cf. *D*, §84. This also holds for the metaphysician: 'He who explains a passage in an author "more deeply" than the passage was meant has not explained the author but *obscured* him. This is how our metaphysicians stand in regard to the text of nature; indeed, they stand much worse. For in order to apply their deep explanations, they frequently first adjust the text in a way that will facilitate it: in order words, they *spoil it*. As a curious example of the spoiling of a text and the observing of its author let us here consider Schopenhauer's thoughts on the pregnancy of women. . . . Schopenhauer [prepares] the text for himself so as to harmonize it with the "explanation" he is about to bring forward'. (*WS*, §17).

38 *UM*, 2, Foreword.

39 *KGW*, VIII, 3, 14 (60).

40 *KGW*, VIII, 3, 14 (57) = *WP*, §171 = *VP*, I, p. 190, §415.

41 For example, *BGE*, §47 and *KGW*, VIII, 3, 15 (82).

42 *KWG*, VIII, 3, 14 (151) = *WP*, §394 = VP, p. 191, §417.

43 *KGW*, VIII, 2, 10 (184).

44 Cf. *KGW*, VIII, 2, 10 (184): 'One must distinguish . . .' (*unterscheiden*).

45 'Do not confuse' is the remark of a philologist who is a hermeneut, grammarian and linguist. Nietzsche often uses it: 'What I am careful to remember: do not confuse *décadent* instincts with "humanity": do not confuse the dissolving means of civilization, *which necessarily push us towards décadence*, with culture: do not confuse libertinage, the principle of *laisser aller* with the will to power (which is its *contrary* principle)' (*KGW*, VIII, 3, 15 (67)). From the genealogical point of view, we shall see that *Verwechslung* (confusion) is the linguistic version of the psychological *Verfälschung* which corresponds fairly closely in behaviour to the Freudian *Entstellung*. Nietzsche replaces *error*, which metaphysicians speak of, and which presupposes a truth beyond appearance, with confusion, which enters into an energetic play of forces such as *Falschmünzerei* and *Verfälschung*, or the art of the 'as if'. Cf. *WP*, §453 = *KGW*, VIII, 3, 15 (91): 'The causes of error lie just as much in the good will [as in the will] of man − : in a thousand cases he conceals reality from himself, he falsifies it, so as not to suffer from his good [or ill] will. E.g., God as the director of human destiny: or the interpretation of his own petty destiny as if everything were contrived and sent with a view to the salvation of his soul − this lack of "philology", which to a more subtle intellect would have to count as uncleanliness and counterfeiting is, on the average, performed under the inspiration of good will'.

46 *KGW*, VIII, 3, 15 (90).

47 *KGW*, VIII, 3, 15 (82).

48 Plato said equally that the good dialectician is someone who knows how to respect the distinctions (*Phaedrus*, 265e–266c).

49 *KGW*, VIII, 14 (57): *sic!* R. Roos (*Nietzsche aujourd'hui?*, p. 285) writes: 'The minute and methodical examination of texts, free of all annexionist aims or restrictions, is what we call philology'. From this point on, Nietzsche the philologist *can only be a repressive Nietzsche*: at least a Nietzsche who tries to invoke *the material reality of the text* in the face of interpretative falsifications and its semantic hollowing-out.

50 *HATH*, 19 (2) to 19 (6).

51 *GS*, §358.

52 *KGW*, VIII, 2, 11 (302) = *WP*, §242.

53 *KGW*, VIII, 2, 11 (319) = *WP*, §241.

54 *KGW*, VIII, 2, 10 (911) = *WP*, §888. 'To grin', is Kaufmann's translation of *ochsen* (in French, *bûcher*), which means to swot or cram,

or labour like a beast (French equivalents would be *bosser* or *chiader*). The image of grinding recalls the description of scholars, especially philologists, in *TSZ*, Part Two, 'Of Scholars', who 'know how to grind corn small and make white dust of it'.

55 One cannot meddle with biblical philology if one does not know Hebrew (cf. *An*, §45) or what the dogma of the immaculate conception is (cf. *An*, §34).

56 *EH*, 'Why I am So Clever', §2.

57 Or *philological* overturning: this is no longer what lies outside the text translating itself into the text, this is the philologist reading what lies outside the text, this non-text, *as a text*.

58 *BGE*, §246. Cf. our article, '"Götzen aushorchen": Versuch einer Genealogie der Genealogie. Nietzsches philologisches Apriori und die christliche Kritik des Christentums', *Perspektiven der Philosophie*, (1981), 7. Cf. also Thomas Reik, *Listening with the Third Ear* (New York, 1948).

59 *TI*, Foreword.

60 We then have a better understanding of why Nietzsche wants to destroy or 'unmask' (*entdecken*) morality in favour of the body, while Schopenhauer proposes a morality based on pity and the negation of will.

61 *D*, §119.

62 In the absence of 'dedication', we may ask if this transcendental subject is not in reality empirically, that is to say biographically and historically, determined by Nietzsche the philologist.

63 It is a short step from metabole to metabolism in Nietzsche: he therefore asks for good readers to know how to 'ruminate' (*wiederkäuen*). Nietzsche reads organic dyspepsia as a text, but reading, for him, also involves assimilating (*einverleiben*), digesting and ruminating.

64 Cf. *Critique of Pure Reason*, Transcendental Dialectic, The Antimony of Pure Reason, Section 6; *ibid.*, Paralogisms of Pure Reason, Paralogism of Ideality; *Prolegomena*, First Part of the Major Question, Third Remark.

65 Cf. *Critique of Pure Reason*, Transcendental Dialectic, Paralogisms of Pure Reason, Paralogism of Ideality.

66 'The realist in the transcendental meaning of this term, treats these modifications of our sensibility as self-subsistent things, that is, treats *mere representations* as things in themselves' (*Critique of Pure Reason*, The Antimony of Pure Reason, Section 6).

67 But the 'critical' undertaking is also quite advanced here: not content with 'criticizing' language and 'separating' true language from deceptive (ideal) language, Nietzsche 'nonsuits' all language, considering it to be essentially metaphysical. He therefore ceases to be a pure philologist and declares himself to be a physiologist.

68 *TI*, Foreword. Listening so that something which would like to stay silent has to speak: Freud would not reject this as a basic definition of psychoanalysis, in which an exchange takes place between listening and a monologue. Moreover the German *still*, translated as 'silent', also means 'calm', as opposed to what Freud calls the 'seething boiler of the Id'.

69 *BGE*, §10.

70 *BGE*, §54. Freud uses similar expressions in 'The Question of Lay Analysis', Standard Edition XX, pp. 179–258.

71 Cf. *EH*, Foreword, §4: 'Such things as this reach only the most select; it is an incomparable privilege to be a listener here; no one is free to have ears for Zarathustra'.

72 Cf. *EH*, 'Why I Write Such Excellent Books', §1 and *TI*, 'Expeditions . . .', §26.

73 *CW*, Postscript.

74 A musician who hears like a megalomaniac but is primarily a performer. Nietzsche was a pianist, and is also a masterful player of the instrument 'man' – who does not remember Hamlet?: 'Let the instrument be what it will, let it be as out of tune as only the instrument "man" can become out of tune – I should have to be ill not to succeed in getting out of it something listenable. And how often have I heard from the "instruments" themselves that they had never heard themselves sound so well' (*EH*, 'Why I am So wise', §4).

75 Nietzsche parodies, in *TSZ*, Part Three, 'Of the Apostates', the biblical phrase: 'Let those who have ears to hear, hear' (Matthew 11:15).

76 This is why 'ears today offer such truths – *our* truths – no ready welcome' (*BGE*, §202): philosophers are deaf, while the ordinary man is even more deaf, since he *does not want* to hear. But Nietzsche claims that his 'voice reaches even the hard-of-hearing' (*An*, §50). Cf. *TI*, 'Maxims and Arrows', §15.

77 *BGE*, §246. Compare with *GS*, §104: 'Of the sound of the German language'. It is significant that this text follows a section on German music.

78 *TI*, Foreword.

79 *BGE*, §247.

80 *EH*, Foreword, §4. Note the musicological terms, the same as those used by Nietzsche to describe the rhythmical reading of the philologist.

81 *TSZ*, Part Four, 'The Sign'.

82 *TSZ*, Part Four, 'The Intoxicated Song', §§3 and 4 (cf. also §§2, 8, 12).

83 *TSZ*, 'Expeditions . . .', §26.

85 *Mus.*, XVI, pp. 190–1 = VP, I, p. 46, §52.

86 *TSZ*, Part Two, 'The Stillest Hour'.

87 *TSZ*, Part Two, 'Of Great Events'.

88 *TSZ*, Part One, 'Of the Bestowing Virtue', §2. We shall see that the wind brings almost inaudible sounds, but also fragrances.

89 *GM*, Preface, §1.

90 *EH*, 'Why I Write Such Excellent Books', §1. Further on: 'He into whose ear I whispered he ought to look around rather for a Cesare Borgia than for a Parsifal did not believe his ears'.

91 *GS*, Foreword, §4.

92 *KGW*, VIII, 2, 11 (411) = *WP*, Preface, §2.

93 *BGE*, §10.

94 *GM*, First Essay, §14.

95 *GM*, First Essay, §14.

96 *TSZ*, Part Two, 'Of the Virtuous'; Part Four, 'The Awakening', §2 and 'The Ass Festival'.

97 *Mus.*, XVI, p. 242.

98 The analogy with Freud is striking: among many examples, one thinks of 'S.P. – (W) Espe'. See Standard Edition, XVII, p. 94. Cf. Serge Leclaire, *Psychoanalyser*, I, 'De quelle oreille il convient d'écouter' and IV, 'Le corps de la lettre'.

99 *EH*, 'Twilight of the Idols', §2.

100 *WS*, §110.

101 'Men are only beginning to notice that music is the figurative language of the passions. And later on they will learn to discern a musician's collective instincts through his music. Such a musician certainly didn't think he would *betray himself in that way*' (*KGW*, VII, 1, 7 (62) = *VP*, I, p. 46, §52 = *Mus.*, XVI, p. 190).

102 In German, *Klangfarbe* or *Tonfarbe*: 'der Klang', writes Nietzsche, is heard 'in a loud voice: that is to say, with all the crescendos, inflections, variations of tone and changes of tempo' (*BGE*, §247).

103 *BGE*, §246. Cf. *KGW*, VIII, 2, 11 (285) = *WP*, §917: 'Colours and tones oppress (the philosopher); to say nothing of the dim desires – that which others call "the ideal"'.

104 *TI*, Foreword and *EH*, 'Why I am So Clever', §10.

105 *KGW*, VII, 7, 1 (125) = *Mus.*, XVI, pp. 199–200.

106 Nietzsche's model in this respect, Moses, did not even require a hammer to break the Tablets of the Law (Exodus 32:19–20).

107 For example, *BGE*, §203; §211; §225: 'in man there is also creator, sculptor, the hardness of the hammer'; *EH*, 'Thus Spoke Zarathustra', §8; *EH*, 'Human, All Too Human', §6: 'This proposition, at some future time ... serves as the axe which is laid at the root of the "metaphysical need" of man' (= *HATH*, §37); *TSZ*, Part Two, 'On the Blissful Islands'; 'Of the Famous Philosophers'; *WP*, §1054; §1055. Cf. Kaufmann, *Nietzsche, Philosopher, Psychologist, Antichrist*, p. 112, and Heidegger, *Nietzsche*, I, pp. 66, 325.

108 *TI*, Foreword.

109 *LPh*, III, 'On Truth and Falsehood . . .', §1.
110 Cf. *TI*, Foreword: '*eternal* idols which are here touched with the hammer as with a tuning fork (*Stimmgabel*)'. Nietzsche's metaphor rests on a confusion. He means *Stimmhammer*, not *Stimmgabel*: the latter resonates itself, rather than making something else resonate.
111 Nietzsche is perhaps thinking of this in *GM*, Third Essay, §14: 'For we cannot withhold a certain admiration for the counterfeiter's skill with which they imitate the coinage of virtue, even its golden ring'. The metaphor of counterfeiting for the ideal is almost a nervous tick with Nietzsche.
112 The 'drum skin' to which Nietzsche alludes in mentioning the 'famous hollow sound which speaks of inflated bowels' is a classic symptom of malnutrition or of certain intestinal disorders: the skin of the belly is stretched and gives off a 'hollow' sound when tapped, all the more so when the belly is full of air.
113 *Aushorchen*: to sound out, but also to surprise or spy on.
114 For example Leviticus 19:4; 26:1; Isaiah 2:20; I Corinthians 10:19. In his book, *Martin Luther: Un destin*, L. Febvre notes how the Lutheran translation of the Bible persistently uses the metaphors of hearing and smelling. The same is true of Nietzsche.
115 Cf. Habbakuk 2:18–19; I Corinthians 12:2 (in which Paul quotes the preceding text); Psalms 115:4–7; Isaiah 41:29; Jeremiah 51:17–18. We have developed this comparison in our article, 'Götzen aushorchen'.
116 For Freud also, who possesses a 'floating', 'second hearing', silence is eloquent.
117 *EH*, 'Why I am So Wise', §5.
118 *An*, Foreword.
119 Nietzsche likes to present himself as someone who 'tests the kidneys and the heart' (for example Jeremiah 17:10): cf. *EH*, 'The Wagner Case', §4: 'The first thing in which I "test the kidneys" of a person', or *KGW*, VIII, 2, 9 (18): 'a psychologist who tests the kidneys'.
120 *TI*, Foreword.
121 We are not far here from the 'resounding brass and clashing cymbals' (I Corinthians 13:1–3) that are a sign of the nothingness of *agape*.
122 *GS*, §359. Cf. ibid., §375.
123 *GM*, Third Essay, §14.
124 *WS*, §88.
125 *WS*, §89.
126 *KGW*, VII, 1, 1 (109) = *GS*, Gallimard edition, 23 (32).
127 *BGE*, §28.
128 'One test of the amount of *classical taste* someone possesses is the way that person reacts to the New Testament (cf. Tacitus): whoever is not revolted by it, does not openly and strongly register a *foeda superstitio*, something one tries not to soil one's hands on, does not know what is

classical. One must register the 'cross' like Goethe' (*KGW*, VIII, 2, 10 (181)).

129 *EH*, 'Why I am so Clever', §4.

130 Cf. naturally *CW*, *NCW*, and *KGW*, VIII, 3, 16 (49): 'A musician's greatness cannot be measured by the fine sentiments he arouses: that is what women believe. Greatness is measured in terms of the tension in his willpower, the sureness with which chaos obeys his artistic command and becomes a form, and the necessity that his hand bestows on a succession of forms. A musician's greatness, in a word, is measured in terms of his ability to capture the grand style'.

131 *GS*, §290.

132 *WS*, §131.

133 *WS*, §87.

134 *WS*, §96.

135 Cf. Heidegger, *Nietzsche*.

136 *KGW*, VIII, 2, 11 (3). Cf. *KGW*, VIII, 3, 18 (6), and *VP*, II, p. 313, §344: 'It is by manner and style that we must be distinguished!'. The index of the Musarion edition notes dozens of references to the word *Stil*.

137 *CW*, §7. Cf. *KGW*, VIII, 3, 16 (29).

138 *KGW*, VIII, 3, 15, (118), Gallimard edition, p. 231.

139 *KGW*, VIII, 3, 14 (61) = *WP*, §842. Cf. the quotation from Stendhal in *BGE*, §39: Stendhal is often praised by Nietzsche for being a moralist and above all a stylist – we know the value the French writer placed on mathematics and the *Code civil* in the matter of style!

140 *D*, 4 (260).

141 *WS*, §217. Cf. *HATH*, 2, 41 (34).

142 *NCW*, 'Where I Admire'. Cf. the long text in which Nietzsche develops the observation that Wagner 'employs music for something other than music' (*WP*, §838 = *KGW*, VIII, 3, 16 (29). In *KGW*, VIII, 3, 14 (61), Nietzsche is brutal: 'Is modern music not already *décadence*?'. He analyses Sainte-Beuve in the same way in *KGW*, VIII, 2, 11 (9).

143 *NCW*, 'Where I have Something to Say Again'. This text takes up and completes *GS*, §368.

144 *K*, XIV, p. 155: early sketches for *CW*, (*Mus.*, XVII, p. 326).

145 'Whether behind the antithesis classic and romantic there does not lie hidden the antithesis active and reactive?' *KGW*, VIII, 2 9 (112) = *WP*, §847). CF. *WP*, §848 = *KGW*, VIII, 2, 9 (166), which develops this hypothesis, and *KGW*, VIII, 1, 2 (112).

146 One of the most amusing examples of this collaboration: *KGW*, VIII, 2, 10 (116): Nietzsche, analysing modern music, speaks of heaviness and constipation.

147 *TI*, 'Expeditions . . .', §11.

148 *TI*, 'Expeditions . . .', §11.

149 *KGW*, VIII, 3, 14 (117) = *WP*, §800. Cf. *KGW*, VIII, 2, 9 (166) = *WP*, §848.

150 *KGW* VIII, 2, 11 (312) = *WP*, §849. Cf. *WP*, §826.

151 *BGE*, §188. Cf. *WS*, §140, as well as Kaufmann, *Nietzsche, Philosopher, Psychologist, Antichrist*, p. 155; M. Bindschedler, *Nietzsche und die poetische Lüge*, pp. 78–9. One already finds in *BT*, 5 (45) remarks that are moving in this direction.

152 This is why Nietzsche can say that 'Goethe is a culture' (*WS*, §125), both a text and a body, and therefore a style. Cf. *WS*, §§131, 132, 136.

153 *EH*, 'Why I am so Wise', §10.

154 As a moralist and psychologist, Nietzsche is inspired by Chamfort, anatomist (and doctor) of the soul, a soul compared to a body masked by its skin (the 'virtues'): 'Just as the bones, flesh, intestines and blood vessels are enclosed in a skin that makes the sight of man endurable, so the agitations and passions of the soul are enveloped in vanity: it is the skin of the soul' (*HATH*, §82). Cf. Chamfort, *Maximes et pensées*, §48, and Andler, *Nietzsche, sa vie et sa pensée*, pp. 146 et seq.

155 We have sketched this analysis in our article, 'Nietzsche: la vie et la métaphore'. (Clairvoyance, voyeurism, appearance, reality, phenomenon). But Nietzsche, in a same text (*KGW*, VIII, 2, 11 (54)) says that his 'tractatus is not for the *ears* of anyone' and that it uncovers new things, 'provided one has eyes to see hidden things'.

156 *TSZ*, Part Four, 'The Intoxicated Song', §12.

157 *WS*, §119.

158 *TSZ*, Part Three, 'Of the Apostates', §2.

159 *GM*, Third Essay, §14.

160 *TSZ*, Part Two, 'Of Immaculate Perception'.

161 Cf. *HATH*, §82.

162 *TSZ*, Part Two 'Of Immaculate Perception'.

163 *WS*, §119.

164 *TSZ*, Part Two, 'Of Immaculate Perception'.

165 *EH*, 'The Birth of Tragedy', §2: '*Er riecht die Verwesung*'. As concerns Schopenhauer, Nietzsche has just smelled his cadaverous perfumer (*ibid*, §1).

166 *TSZ*, Part Two, 'Of Scholars'.

167 *TSZ*, Part Three, 'Of Old and New Law-Tables', §16.

168 *TSZ*, Part Three, 'The Home-Coming'.

169 *KGW*, VIII, 2, 11 (118) = *WP*, §390. Speaking of his adversaries, Nietzsche writes in a variant of *EH*: 'It is flattering even to speak of venom – it was something else and it smelt bad' (Gallimard edition, p. 560).

170 *TSZ*, Part Two, 'Of the Rabble'. We should therefore aerate and generate a draught: 'And like a wind will I one day blow among them and with my spirit take away the breath from their spirit: thus my

future will have it. Truly, Zarathustra is a strong wind to all flatlands; and he offers this advice to his enemies and to all that spews and spits: "Take care not to spit *against* the wind!"'. Similarly, in *TSZ* Part Two, 'Of Scholars': 'I love freedom and the air over fresh soil; . . . I have to get into the open air and away from all dusty rooms'. And in *TSZ*, Part Three, 'Of Old and New Law-Tables', §16: 'Zarathustra comes as a fresh, blustering wind to all the way-weary; he will yet make many noses sneeze! My liberal breath blows even through walls and into prisons and imprisoned spirits!'

171 *BGE*, §30. Cf. *BGE*, §198: 'great and little artifices and acts of prudence to which there clings the nook-and-cranny odour of ancient household remedies and old-woman wisdom': and *An*, §52: the 'stuffing of their existence'.
172 *GM*, First Essay, §14.
173 *BGE*, §48.
174 *BGE*, §52.
175 *EH*, 'Why I am so Wise', §8. Cf. *GS*, §379: 'we cannot persuade our nose to give up its prejudice against the proximity of a human being' (*GS*, §379).
176 *EH*, 'The Wagner Case', §3.
177 *EH*, 'Why I Am a Destiny', §1. Cf. 'Why I am So Wise', §8.
178 *BGE*, §45.
179 *EH*, 'Untimely Meditations', §3.
180 *GM*, First Essay, §14.
181 *GM*, First Essay, §12. Cf. *EH*, 'The Wagner Case', §3.
182 *CW*, §5. The 'More air!' is undoubtedly a parody on Goethe's famous dying words, 'more light!'.
183 *TSZ*, Part Four, 'Of Science'.
184 Letter to K. Hillebrand, mid-April 1878. Nitrogen is odourless. Nietzsche is no doubt thinking of ammonia or else mentions nitrogen because, unlike oxygen, it cannot be breathed.
185 *TSZ*, Part One, 'Of the New Idol'.
186 *TSZ*, Part One, 'Of the Flies of the Market-Place'. Cf. *TSZ*, Part One, 'Of Reading and Writing': 'Another century of readers – and spirit itself will stink', and Nietzsche's call for 'air thin and pure'.
187 *TSZ*, Part Two, 'Of the Priests'.
188 *An*. §38.
189 *EH*, 'The Birth of Tragedy', §1.
190 *AOM*, §205.
191 To the Mistral, in *GS*, 'Songs of Prince Vogelfrei' (*Vogelfrei*: free as a bird and the pure air!).
192 *An*, §1.
193 *TSZ*, Part Two, 'Of the Rabble'.
194 *EH*, Foreword, §3.

195   *TI*, Foreword.

196   *KGW*, VIII, 3, 16 (32).

197   Nietzsche, who has ears behind his ears, none the less wants to remain deaf to the clamour of the ideal, to the braying ass, the animal that says 'Ye-a' (hee-haw) to every form of servitude: 'We all know, some even know from experience, what a longears is. Very well, I dare to assert that I possess the smallest ears' (*EH*, 'Why I Write Such Excellent Books', §2). The ass uses its big ears to hear and obey, whereas Nietzsche uses his not to acquiesce in the ideal, but to decipher its ulterior motives.

198   *CW*, Postscript.

199   *EH*, 'Human, All Too Human', §1: 'One error after another is calmly laid on ice, the ideal is not refuted – *it freezes*. . . . Here for example "the genius" freezes; on the next corner "the saint" freezes; "the hero" freezes into a thick icicle; at last "faith", so called "conviction", freezes; "pity" also grows considerably cooler – almost everywhere "the thing in itself" freezes'.

200   *EH*, 'Twilight of the Idols', §2.

201   We recall that breath is for Nietzsche what is heard in style and *tempo*. These can be picked up by the philologist, who is an acoustics expert (cf. *BGE*, §§27, 247 and *CW*, §5.

202   *KGW*, VIII, 2, 10 (114).

203   *Ibid.*, (117).

204   *KGW*, VIII, 3, 15 (39).

205   *GM*, Third Essay, §26; *TSZ*, Part Three, 'Of the Spirit of Gravity', §2; 'Of the Three Evil Things', §2, and Matthew 23:27. In *GM*, Third Essay, §22, Nietzsche denounces the 'nuzzling and pawing of God!'.

206   *KGW*, VIII, 3, 21 (8). In this fragment and in the preceding one, Nietzsche opposes those things 'against which, at bottom, not only task, but even smell protests, antisemites for example' and speaks of a Jewish scholar who 'has always given me a deep impression of beauty, of cleanliness in the sense in which I understand it'. We know how the metaphor of 'cleanliness' has been abused by every racist ideology: contrary to what one might think, Nietzsche avoids this charge by calling on moral rigour in order to define health and cleanliness.

207   Plato, *Republic*, VIII, 533d.

208   *TI*, '"Reason" in Philosophy', §3.

209   *TSZ*, Part One, 'Of the Despisers of the Body'.

210   See further on Nietzsche's analysis of gastroenterology, the necessary correlative to a physiological genealogy.

211   Gaston Bachelard, *L'air et les songes* (Paris, 1943), V, p. 146: 'their proper destiny'. Cf. p. 164: 'material and dynamic coherence'; p. 166: 'perfect coherence'.

212   Cf. especially the important §119 of *Daybreak*.

213 Gaston Bachelard, *L'air et les songes*, pp. 157–8, 160.
214 *EH*. 'Why I am So Clever', §1. Cf. *BGE*, §244.
215 *TSZ*, Part Four, 'The Song of Melancholy', §1. The same idea occurs in *TSZ*, Part Four, 'Of Science', closing remark.
216 *TSZ*, Part Four, 'Among the Daughters of the Desert'.
217 *TSZ*, Part Four, 'The Awakening', §1. In §2, it is Zarathustra's nose that tells him his guests are praying and adoring the ass (*'seine Nase roch einen wohlriechenden Qualm und Weihrauch'*) and his ear which is startled (*'plötzlich aber erschrak das Ohr Zarathustras'*).
218 *TSZ*, Part Four, 'The Ass Festival'.
219 *EH*, 'Why I am So Clever', §2. The dry Paris air: a fairly metaphysical geography!
220 *EH*, 'Why I am So Clever', §2. Cf. the variant in the Gallimard edition, p. 535.
221 *EH*, 'Why I am So Clever', §2.
222 *EH*, 'Why I am So Clever', §2.
223 *EH*, Foreword, §4.
224 *EH*, 'Human, All Too Human', §3.
225 *EH*, Foreword, §4.
226 In the text: *'décadent zugleich und Anfang'*, *'Aufgang und Niedergang'*, (*EH*, 'Why I am So Wise', §1).
227 *EH*, 'Why I am So Clever', §1: 'No eating between meals, no coffee: coffee makes gloomy. *Tea* beneficial only in the morning. Little, but strong ... In a very *agaçant* climate it is inadvisable to start with tea: one should start an hour earlier with a cup of thick oil-free cocoa. – *Sit as little as possible*; credit no thought not born in the open air and while moving freely about – in which the muscles too do not hold a festival. All prejudices come from the intestines. – Assiduity – I have said it once before – the actual *sin* against the holy spirit.' The invention of a process to make oil-free cocoa dates from 1820 and since the seventeenth century coffee has had revolutionary images of ideology and myth associated with it. Cf. W. Schivelbusch, *Das Paradiese, der Geschmack und die Vernunft* (*Le goût des stimulants*).
228 For example, the 'theory' that apes Marx in seeing existence and praxis only in the text, the 'Bücherwurm's' books. Nietzsche had already replied in *EH*, 'Why I am So Clever', §8: 'The scholar expends his entire strength in affirmation and denial, in criticizing what has already been thought – he himself no longer thinks ... the scholar – a *décadent'*.
229 *EH*, 'Why I am So Clever', §10.
230 This applies equally to the interpretation of Marx: but it is not certain that 'theoretical practice' is any more rigorous a praxis-type thought than this vague reference to lived experience. It smacks too much of the intellectual who transforms the world into texts, books, and the phenomenology of spirit.

231 *BGE* §187. Cf. *K*, XIII, §362 = *Mus.*, XVI, p. 190.

232 *HATH*, Preface, §1. Cf. *D*, Preface, §4.

233 *Mus.*, XVI, p. 190 = *KGW*, VII, 7 (62).

234 See our study, '"Les guillemets de Nietzsche", I, Volonté de puissance et dénomination', pp. 158–62.

235 *KGW*, VII, 7 (60) = *Mus.*, XVI, p. 190.

236 *KGW*, VII, 7 (126) = *Mus.*, XVI, p. 201: '*Das Geistige ist als Zeichensprache des* Leibes *festzuhalten*'.

237 Nietzsche prides himself on having 'un-covered' morality: *EH*, 'Why I Am a Destiny', §8. *Entdecken* in this case means two things: to attain what is hidden, to divine and clarify (*aufklären*), to recognize, but also to demystify, expose, publish, uncover, in the strong sense, what *wishes* to remain hidden, to denounce, expose, surprise, lay open, and even thwart.

238 *D*, Preface, §15.

239 *KGW*, VIII, 3, 26 (31) = *WP*, §320. Cf. '*Ich lernte Alles, was bisher philosophirt hat*, anders ansehn', *ibid.*, 16 (32).

240 *KGW*, VIII, 3, 16 (32).

241 *KGW*, VIII, 3, 16 (32).

242 *KGW*, VII, 1, 7 (77) = *Mus.*, XVI, p. 193.

243 *KGW*, VII, 1, 4 (205) = *Mus.*, XVI, p. 211.

244 *KGW*, VII, 1, 7 (87) = *Mus.*, XVI, p. 211.

245 *KGW*, VII, 1, 7 (87).

246 *KGW*, VII, 1, 7 (154).

247 *An*, §50. Nietzsche's draft has 'critique' instead of 'psychology'. Note the appeal made to voice and hearing.

248 '*Zeichen*-sprache' indicates the transcendental distance between the linguistic phenomenon and the bodily thing-in-itself. Nietzsche's phenomenality is that of a world of signs: such are its limits.

249 Immanuel Kant, *Critique of Pure Reason* (Macmillan, 1929), p. 346.

250 Cf. for example *NCW*, 'We the Antipodes'.

251 Kant, *Critique of Pure Reason*, p. 286.

252 *Critique of Pure Reason*, p. 287.

253 *KGW*, VII, 7 (60) = *Mus.*, XVI, p. 190.

254 Cf. *KGW* VII, 7 (62) = *Mus.*, XVI, p. 191: '*Moral* literature and *religious* literature are the most *untruthful* (*verlogenste*) sort.'

255 *KGW*, VII, 7 (62).

256 *KGW*, VII, 7 (62).

257 Nietzsche can therefore describe play and a hierarchy of drives only in a metaphorical way.

258 *KGW*, VII, 7 (149) = *Mus.*, XVI, p. 196.

259 *KGW, VII, 7 (125)* = *Mus.*, XVI, pp. 199–200.

260 *KGW*, VII, 7 (173) = *Mus.*, XVI, p. 214.

261 *TI*, 'The "Improvers" of Mankind'.

262 *An*, §32.

263 *'Ordo et connexio rerum idem ac ordo et connexio idearum'*: Spinoza, *Ethics*, II, Proposition 7. Cf. Nietzsche's Letter to Overbeck, 30 July 1881.

264 *TI* Foreword, or *KGW*, VIII, 3, 14 (96) = *WP*, §226.

265 *KGW*, VII, 7 (126) = *Mus.*, XVI, p. 201.

266 *EH*, Foreword, §2.

267 *GM*, First Essay, §11.

268 This is why Nietzsche challenges any idea of a 'practical *reason*' and the correlative postulate of a 'noumenal freedom': freedom is for him only a *word*, while the body is a hierarchy of drives, in its psychological *reality*. He therefore *inverts* the Kantian relationship between a phenomenal determination and a noumenal freedom: cf. *TI*, 'The Four Great Errors', §§7 and 8.

269 *KGW*, VII, 1, 7 (115). Nietzsche adds: 'so do moralists'.

270 *Mus.*, XVI, p. 207: 'It hides evaluations in all the activities of the senses. It hides evaluations in all the functions of the organic'.

271 Cf. *TSZ*, Part Two.

272 *TSZ*, Part Two, 'The Dance Song'.

273 *EH*, Foreword, §4.

274 *VP*, I, p. 287, §290 = *Mus.*, XVI, pp. 64–5. It is because the body is absence and dissimilation that it gives rise to 'misunderstanding' in the Ideal.

275 *TI*, 'The Problem of Socrates', §1.

8 *THE CRITIQUE OF METAPHYSICAL DISCOURSE: PHILOLOGICAL GENEALOGY AND MISOLOGY*

1 *KGW*, VIII, 1, 5 (22) = *WP*, §522 = *VP*, I, p. 67, §102.
2 But Nietzsche's 'transcendental' is sometimes presented by him as being sociolinguistic and historical: there is a genesis to this *a priori*, an origin to ideas in language and a history of language, which can account for the wide range in types of thought and philosophies. Cf. *BGE*, §20, and also §§16, 17 and 19.
3 Cf. *Critique of Pure Reason*, Preface to Second Edition: 'If he is to know anything with *a priori* certainty he must not ascribe to the figure anything save what necessarily follows from what he has himself set into it in accordance with his concept'; Introduction: 'space . . . cannot be removed'; 'we cannot take away that property through which the object is thought as substance'; 'the necessity with which this concept of substance forces itself upon us'. Instead of *a priori* forms or concepts, Nietzsche uses the term 'schema'. Cf. *KGW*, VIII, 3, 14 (152): 'Do not "know", schematize. . . . In the construction of reason, logic, categories, one need has been determining: the need, not to "know", but to organize, to schematize, in order to understand and calculate. . . . Categories are "truths" only in the sense that they condition our lives'. Similarly *KGW*, VIII, 3, 15 (90): 'Our "outside world" . . . is indissolubly linked to the old causal error, we interpret it thanks to the schematism of the "thing", etc. "Inner" experience becomes conscious only when we have found a language that is intelligible to the individual, that is to say a way to translate a state of consciousness into states that are familiar to the individual: "to understand" becomes reduced naively to the ability to express a new thing in the language of something old and familiar'. Cf. *BGE*, §24. These texts are transcendental in style.
4 Examples: 'It is completely impossible to demonstrate that the in-itself of things behaves according to this formula for a model administrator' (*K*, XIII, §138). 'We cannot establish any fact "in itself"': perhaps it is folly to want to do such a thing' (*KGW*, VIII, 1, 7 (60) = *WP*, §481). Note the negative formulation.
5 There is a lot of negative 'theology' in Nietzsche.
6 'Wir Philologen', *Mus.*, VII, p. 152. Nietzsche explains this opposition in terms of past (dead) and present (lived). Cf. *ibid.*, the opposition he establishes between Greeks and philologists.
7 'Philology is to be understood here in a very wide sense as the art of reading well – of being able to read off a fact *without* falsifying it by interpretation, *without* losing caution, patience, subtlety in the desire for understanding. Philology as *ephexis* [indecisiveness] in interpretation'. (*An*, §52).

8 Andler, *Nietzsche, sa vie et sa pensée*, II, p. 191 and note 1.

9 *Nietzsche, sa vie et sa pensée.*

10 Cf. H. Wismann, 'Nietzsche et la philologie', in *Nietzsche aujourd'hui?* II, pp. 325–44. Cf. E. Blondel, 'Struttura, filologia, filosofia . . .', in *Nietzsche contemporaneo o inattuale?* (Brescia, 1980), and 'Lectures de Nietzsche. Philologie', *Perspektiven der Philosophie* (1976), 2, pp. 347–53.

11 Cf. *EH*, 'Why I am So Clever', §2: 'a philologist . . . why not at least a physician?'; *An*, §47: 'the physician says "incurable", the philologist "fraud"'.

12 *GM*, First Essay, Concluding Note. Note also that, according to Nietzsche, this question 'deserves the attention' of philosophers as well as philologists, and he proposes it to 'the philosophy department of some leading university'. This is a peculiar move back to Basel.

13 *GM*, Preface, §16.

14 *GM*, Preface, §7.

15 In the same way, in Kant, in spite of the impossibility of applying the category of causality outside of tangible experience, the transcendental object is regarded as the cause of phenomena. Cf. *KGW*, VIII, 1, 5 (4): 'Kant did not have the right to distinguish between the "phenomenon" and the "thing-in-itself"; he deprived himself of the right to insist on this former distinction since he regarded as illicit the conclusion that goes back from the phenomenon to the *cause* of the phenomenon, in accordance with his conception of the idea of causality to which he attributed a strictly *intra-phenomenal* ('*entdecken*', *GM*, Preface, §7) a referent, the body.

16 *KGW* VIII, 3, 16 (31) = *WP*, §320.

17 *KGW*, VIII, 1, 5 (22) = *WP*, §522. Cf. *BGE*, §47, conclusion: '[psychology hitherto] *diese Gegensätze in den Text und Tatbestand hineinsah, hinein las, hinein deutete*'. Cf. Kant: '*Was wir selbst in sie legen*'.

18 Cf. *KGW*, VIII, 3, 15 (82): 'The shortcoming in philology: we forever confuse the explanation with the text – and what an "explanation"!' and 15 (90): 'This is what I call the "lack of philology": to be able to read a text as a text, without slipping in an interpretation, is the final form of "inner experience" – perhaps a form that is scarcely possible'.

19 *BGE*, §22.

20 Cf. *NCW*, Epilogue: 'life has become a problem'.

21 *EH*, 'Why I am so Wise', §1.

22 *An*, §47.

23 A quasi-technical term from philology.

24 *An*, §44.

25 *HATH*, 23 (22).

26 *HATH*, 23 (24).

27 *D*, §103.

28 *D*, 3 (170).
29 *BGE*, §20. Cf. also *WP*, §254, and *GM*, First Essay, Concluding Note.
30 *GM*, First Essay, §4. This is the reason for Nietzsche's long etymological and genealogical ruminations on 'the words and roots' of morality in *GM*, First Essay.
31 *GM*, First Essay, §14.
32 *GM*, Third Essay, §§1, 2, 5. '[Wagner] now became an oracle, a priest, or more than a priest – a kind of mouthpiece of the absolute, a telephone line of Transcendence. God's ventriloquist, he would talk not only music but metaphysics. Small wonder, then, that one day he should talk ascetic ideals.'
33 *TI*, 'The "Improvers" of Mankind', §1. Cf. *ibid.*, §2 (*heissen, nennen*) and *GM*, First Essay, §2 and §10 (*sagen, Namen ausprägen*).
34 *KGW*, VIII, 3, 14 (142) = *WP*, §423.
35 *WP*, §1074 (*Mus.*, XIX, p. 380), quoted by Kaufmann in the note to §440 of his translation of *WP*.
36 *WP*, §270 = *KGW*, VIII, 2, 10 (121).
37 *WP*, §258 = *KGW*, VIII, 1, 2 (165).
38 *WP*, §254.
39 *WP*, §479 = *VP*, I, §245, p. 272.
40 *WP*, §481 = *VP*, I, §133, p. 239.
41 *WP*, §590 + 003 *VP*, I, §134, p. 239.
42 *WP*, §482 = *KGW*, VIII, 1, 5 (3).
43 *WP*, §643 = *VP*, I, p. 239, §130. Note already that the *organic* process is itself an interpretation and that *in itself there is no signification*. Signification is the phenomenon structured by the philological *a priori*.
44 *HATH*, 22 (20).
45 For example, *An*, §52; *WP*, §201 = VP, I, p. 188, §409 = *KGW*, VIII, 2, 10 (204): 'the unchecked impudence [of] the least qualified'.
46 *An*, §25. Cf. §26, which accumulates terms such as *übersetzen, Interpretation, Sprache, missbrauchen, literarische Fälschung, auf Deutsch*, etc.
47 *D*, 4 (235).
48 *An*, §59.
49 *GS*, §58.
50 Cf. *D*, §3: 'When man gave all things a sex he thought, not that he was playing, but that he had gained a profound insight. . . . In the same way man has ascribed to all that exists a connection with morality and laid an *ethical significance* on the world's back. One day this will have as much value, and no more, as the belief in the masculinity or femininity of the sun has today.'
51 Cf. J. Figl, *Interpretation als philosophisches Prinzip*, (Berlin, 1982).
52 *KGW*, VIII, 1, 2 (78): '*Ausdeutung, nicht Erklärung . . . Sinn hineinlegen*'.
53 Cf. *Critique of Pure Reason*.
54 *An*, §52.

55 *GM*, Preface, §8.

56 *D*, Preface, §5, already quoted: 'a teacher of slow reading', 'friends of *lento*', 'to become slow', etc. Note some fifteen references to slowness and its opposite. In *An*, §52, Nietzsche also speaks in the same vein about 'patience' (*Geduld*).

57 For Nietzsche, there is no closure to a text.

58 *GM*, Preface, §8, and *An*, §52 (*eine Kunst der Auslegung, die Kunst, gut zu lesen*).

59 *BGE*, §22.

60 Cf. Kant, *Critique of Pure Reason*: 'the use or transcendent abuse of categories' (p. 453), '*Missbrauch*' (*pp. 252 and 467*), '*confusion (verwechseln)*' (p. 317, 2nd edition).

61 *BGE*, §21. The in-itself of nature ('science') is for Nietzsche 'mythological' (what Kant calls dialectical); cf. *KGW*, VIII, 1, 2 (78).

62 It is the text's, and therefore the reader's will to power that is the *a priori* form of textual interpretation in Nietzsche. Interpretation can provide only reflexive judgements, not determining ones (cf. Kant, *Critique of Judgement*, Introduction, IV).

63 Kant, *Critique of Pure Reason*, Analytic of Principles, The Ground of the Distinction of all Objects in general into Phenomena and Noumena: '*bloss auf Erscheinungen*', '*nur durch die empirische Anshauung*', etc.

64 *Ibid.*, The Antinomy of Pure Reason, III, Solution of the Cosmological Idea.

65 In Nietzsche, there is not metaphysical exposition or transcendental deduction of the interpretative *a priori* of the will to power. What takes its place 'is merely an interpretation'. In the Kantian world, Nietzsche therefore falls into the dialectic.

66 *BGE*, §230.

67 *An*, §15.

68 Examples: the title of *Twilight of the Idols*; *TI*, 'Expeditions . . .', §46 (Goethe); *EH*, 'Why I Write Such Excellent Books', §2: 'Hier stehe ich . . .' (Luther), as well as in *TSZ*, Part Four, §16 and in *GM*, Third Essay, §§22, with inverted commas.

69 *KGW*, VIII, 2, 10 (174).

70 *BGE*, §17.

71 *CW*, Epilogue.

72 *VP*, I, p. 123, §256 = *K*, XIII, §350.

73 *KGW*, VIII, 3, 16 (87) + 003 *WP*, §158.

74 *GM*, Third Essay, §2.

75 *KGW*, VIII, 3, 14 (182) = *WP*, §864. Cf. *TI*, 'Expeditions . . .', §38: 'Liberalism: in plain words, *reduction to the herd animal*. . . .'

76 *KGW*, VII, 2, 25 (211) = *WP*, §862.

77 *WP*, §335 = *VP*, I, p. 41, §33.

78 *TI*, 'The Problem of Socrates', §4. Cf. *ibid.*, 'The "Improvers" of

Mankind', §2: 'improve', 'morality', 'Christian', translated by Nietzsche in terms of castration.

79 *EH*, 'Why I am So Clever', §10.
80 *KGW*, VIII, 2, 11 (8).
81 *KGW*, VIII, 1, 5 (22) = *WP*, §522.
82 *WP*, §265.
83 *WP*, §627.
84 *WP*, §482 = *VP*, I, p. 68, §105.
85 *BGE*, §16.
86 *BGE*, §34.
87 *WS*, §11.
88 *WS*, §11.
89 *WS*, §55. That is indeed what it says: *each* word. Cf. §251.
89 *TI*, '"Reason" in Philosophy', §5.
90 *TI*, 'Expeditions . . .', §26. Cf. *WP*, §810 (= *KGW*, VIII, 2, 10 (60): a text in which Nietzsche most approaches a sort of mysticism about life, allying himself consequently with Schopenhauer, who is also very suspicious with regard to language.
91 *VP*, I, §286, p. 285.
92 *BGE*, §47. Cf. *WP*, §462.
93 *WP*, §552 = *KGW*, VIII, 2, 9 (91) = *VP*, I, p. 287, §291.
94 *KGW*, VII, 38 (12). On the impossibility of making judgements about the world and its global worth, cf. *TI*, 'The problem of Socrates', §2, and 'Morality as Anti-Nature', §5.
95 *KGW*, VIII, 2, 11 (72).
96 *KGW*, VII, 38 (12) = *WP*, §1067.
97 *KGW*, VIII, 2, 11 (73). Cf. *WP*, §461, in which Nietzsche uses italics to indicate this shift.
98 *EH*, 'Twilight of the Idols', §1.
99 *EH*, 'Twilight of the Idols', §2. Cf. another example in *EH*, 'Why I Am a Destiny', §5: 'When mendaciousness at any price appropriates the word "truth" for its perspective, what is actually veracious must. . . .'
100 *TI*, 'Expeditions . . .', §48. Nietzsche could have saved himself the effort to return in this distinctive manner by reading Rousseau, in particular this passage: 'But human nature never regresses and one never returns to a time of innocence and equality once it has been left . . . So one's object could not be to bring various peoples or great status back to their first simplicity' (*Rousseau juge de Jean-Jacques*, Third Dialogue (Paris: Gallimard (Pléiade), 1959), vol. I, p. 935.
101 *TI*, 'The "improvers" of Mankind', §1.
102 Plato, *Cratylus*, 383a.
103 *Cratylus*, 422d.
104 *Cratylus*, 433e.

105 'Vom Ursprung der Sprache' (1864–1870), *Mus.*, V, p. 469 = *K*, XIX, p. 386.

106 Since morality is dominant, everyone speaks 'ill'. But one can link this deviation to certain overall conditions: Nietzsche will show that the defects in language stem from certain historical and physiological conditions that lie outside the text. If moral man speaks ill, it is because he is ill, a victim of the priestly ideal. To speak today of 'virtues', 'values', or 'sharing' or 'revolution' is still to indicate that one belongs to some religion or other.

107 Cf. *TI*, 'The Four Great Errors', §6.

108 Cf. *D*, 4 (149).

109 *D*, §103.

110 *VP*, I, pp. 183–4, §400 = *WP*, §228 = *KGW*, VII, 44 (6).

111 *VP*, I, p. 182, §395 = *WP*, §685 = *KGW*, VIII, 3, 14 (123).

112 *VP*, I, p. 191, §417 = *WP*, §394 = *KGW*, VIII, 3, 14 (151).

113 *VP*, I, p. 142, §306, al. V = *KGW*, VIII, 3, 23 (5) = *Mus.*, XVII, pp. 267–8.

114 *VP*, p. 190, §415 = *KGW*, VIII, 3, 14 (57).

115 *VP*, pp. 64–5, §96 = *WP*, §477 = *KGW*, VIII, 2, 11 (113).

116 *VP*, p. 86, §159 = *WP*, §552 = *KGW*, VIII, 2, 9 (91).

117 *VP*, p. 90, §169 = *WP*, §574 = *KGW*, VII, 1, 8 (25).

118 *VP*, p. 91, §170 = *K*, XIV, Part One, §59.

119 *VP*, p. 108, §213, al. C = *WP*, 586 = *KGW*, VIII, 3, 14 (168).

120 *VP*, pp. 311–12, §374 = *WP*, §634 = *KGW*, VIII, 3, 14 (79).

121 *KGW*, VIII, 2, 10 (57) = *WP*, §786. This text is an anthology of the point of view where we place ourselves. Cf. *WP*, §711 = *KGW*, VIII, 2, 11 (74).

122 *D*, 6 (7).

123 *EH*, 'Why I am So Clever', §10.

124 *BGE*, §202. The most complete text on philological 'correction' is *BGE*, §22.

125 *WP*, §639 = *KGW*, VIII, 2, 10 (138).

126 *TI*, 'How the "Real World" . . .', §1. Cf. *ibid.*, 'What I Owe', §2, on Plato: 'higher swindle', 'Plato mixes all forms of style', 'Plato is boring', in contrast to Sallust (*ibid.*, §1) and Thucydides (§2).

127 *CW*, Second Postscript.

128 *TSZ*, 'Of the Bestowing Virtue', §1.

129 *An*, §7. Cf. §§9 and 24: rhetoric borders on deliberate misunderstanding here: '*umgekehrt*', '*umdrehen*'.

130 *An*, §23.

131 *GM*, First Essay, §11.

132 *VP*, I, p. 240, §138 = *WP*, §311. Note the use of the particles *um-* and *ver-*.

133 *BGE*, §20.

134 *GS*, §14.
135 *WP*, §345 = *KGW*, VIII, 1, 2 (168).
136 *WP*, §206 = *KGW*, VIII, 2, 9 (88) = *VP*, I, p. 174, §375. Cf. also *WP*, §§310 and 311.
137 *VP*, I, pp. 175–6, §380 = *WP*, §202 = *KGW*, VIII, 2, 10 (201).
138 *GS*, §335.
139 *GS*, §360.
140 *TI*, 'What I owe to the Ancients', §1.
141 *KGW*, VIII, 2, 11 (135) = *VIP*, I, p. 166, §355.
142 *KGW*, VIII, 2, 11 (136). Cf. *ibid.* (143).
143 *Cf. VP*, I, pp. 173–7 (*WP*, §§175, 210, 206, 199, 186, 208, 182, 202, 197, 188, 181, 203, 180); *GM*, Third Essay, §§22; *An*, §§46, 28; *BGE*, §§52, 250, *CW*, Epilogue; *NCW*, 'A Music Without a Future'.
144 *NCW*, 'Wagner Considered a Danger'.
145 *KGW*, VIII, 3, 16 (80): 'The refutation of W. given in this book is not only aesthetic, it is above all physiological. Nietzsche considers Wagner to be an illness, a public danger'.
146 *VP*, I, p. 133, §287 = *WP*, §344 = *KGW*, VIII, 2, 11 (58).
147 *GS*, §138. Note the corrective inverted commas.
148 *VP*, I, p. 128, §276 = *WP*, §347 = *KGW*, VIII, 2, 9 (124). *Verführung* language: cf. *BGE*, §§16 and 17; *VP*, I, pp. 65–6, §98. Nietzsche will therefore base his 'critique of concepts', (*VP*, I, p. 66, §§99) on a critique of language. 'In this way the *word* used to pass for knowledge of the thing, and even today grammatical functions are the things in which one most believes and of which one cannot be too wary' (*ibid*, = *K*, XIV, Part One, §38).
149 *VP*, I, p. 138, §299 = *WP*, §343 = *KGW*, VIII, 1, 7 (6).
150 *KGW*, VIII, 2, 10 (184) = *VP*, I, p. 190, §416. Cf. *KGW*, *ibid.* (185).
151 *KGW*, VIII, 2, 10 (199).
152 *WP*, §179 = *KGW*, *ibid.* VIII, 2, 11 (240).
153 *VP*, I, p. 184, §400 = *WP*, §228.
154 *VP*, I, pp. 183–4.
155 *KGW*, VIII, 1, 1 (120).
156 *TI*, 'The "Improvers"', §1. Cf. *An*, §§15 and 55.
157 *TI*, 'The "Improvers"', §1.
158 *EH*, 'Why I am So Clever', §1.
150 *TI*, 'Maxims and Arrows', §23.
160 *VP*, I, p. 60, §82 = *WP*, §409.
161 *KGW*, VIII, 3, 16 (82). Cf. *An*, §40: 'everything is misunderstood'.
162 *KGW*, VIII, 3, 15 (13) = *WP*, §54. Cf. *An*, §26.
163 *KGW*, VIII, 3, 15 (70). Cf. *BGE*, §47, conclusion.
164 *TI*, 'Expeditions . . .', §41.
165 *KGW*, VIII, 2, 11 (148) = *WP*, §30.
166 *KGW*, VIII, 2, 11 (251).

167 *An*, §9. Cf. *An*, §25: 'Inverting the concepts "good" and "evil", "true" and "false" in a mortally dangerous and world-calmunating sense'.

168 *VP*, I, p. 285, §286 = *K*, XIV, Part One, §39.

169 *VP*, I, p. 81, §147 = *WP*, §484 = *KGW*, VIII, 2, 10 (158).

170 *VP*, I, p. 79, §141 = *K*, XIII, §123.

171 *VP*, I, p. 65, §97 = *K*, XIII, §117. Cf. *ibid.*, §98, and *BGE*, §54.

172 *TI*, '"Reason" in Philosophy', §5.

173 *GS*, §354.

174 *KGW*, VIII, 3, 14 (13).

175 *KGW*, VIII, 14 (125).

176 *D*, §133. Cf. *D*, 3 (66), and *BGE*, §149.

177 *VP*, I, p. 326, §419.

178 *KGW*, VIII, 3, 14 (134). Cf. *EH*, Foreword, §2.

179 *GS*, §355.

180 *GS*, §373.

181 *TI*, 'The Four Great Errors', §6. Cf. *ibid.*, 'Morality as Anti-Nature', §3, on 'peace of soul'.

182 *VP*, I, §322, §403 = *KGW*, VIII, 2, 11 (285).

183 *VP*, I, p. 184, §403 = *KGW*, VIII, 2, 9 (18).

184 *GM*, Third Essay, §17.

185 *D*, 4 (309). Cf. *KGW*, VIII, 2, 11 (8).

186 *KGW*, VIII, 3, 25 (6), §2.

187 *KGW*, VIII, §2 (draft of *EH*, 'Why I Am a Destiny', §1.

188 *KGW*, VIII, 25 (1).

189 *K*, XII, p. 81 = *OP*, §505.

190 *AOM*, §170.

191 *GS*, §359. Note the assonance: '*Gerechtigkeit, Weisheit, Heiligkeit*'.

192 *D*, 3 (72).

193 *TSZ*, Part Four, 'The Awakening', §2.

194 *TSZ*, Part Two, 'Of the Virtuous'.

195 *TSZ*, Part One, 'Of Reading and Writing'.

196 *TSZ*, Part Three, 'Of Old and New Law-Tables', §26, and Prologue, §9.

197 *EH*, 'The Wagner Case', §3.

198 *KGW*, VIII, 2, 9 (145).

199 *VP*, I, p. 327, §426.

200 *EH*, Foreword, §2.

201 *BGE*, §201.

202 *VP*, I, p. 139, §301 = *KGW*, VIII, 2, 9 (156).

203 *BGE*, §2.

204 *BGE*, §227.

205 *GS*, 11 (159), Gallimard edition = *VP*, I, p. 327, §422.

206 *BGE*, §11. Cf. *GS*, §14.

207 *GM*, Third Essay, §18. Cf. *VP*, I, p. 150, §318; p. 240, §138; p. 102, §209.

208 *An*, §27. Cf. Schopenhauer: 'an adventure that happened in Galilee' (*World . . . , p. 449*).

209 *KGW*, VII, 2, 9 (147). Cf. *WP*, §786, al. 4, to be compared to *VP*, I, p. 138, §299. Cf. also: *WP*, §95; *TSZ*, Part Three, 'Of the Spirit of Gravity', §2: Part Two, 'Of the Immediate Perception'; *VP*, I, p. 243, §248; p. 360, §524.

210 *VP*, I, p. 175, §379 = *KGW*, VIII, 2, 10 (79).

211 *VP*, I, p. 328, §430 = *KGW*, VIII, 2, 9 (145).

212 *VP*, I, p. 89, §165 = *KGW*, VIII, 2, 9 (58).

213 *VP*, I, p. 115, §230 = *KGW*, VIII, 2, 11 (100).

214 *KGW*, VIII, 2, 11 (55). Other interesting examples: *VP*, I, p. 48, §56; p. 64, §95; p. 85, §158; p. 137, §295; p. 195, §432; p. 370, §548; *BG*, §202, conclusion; *An*, §44: *KGW*, VIII, 2, 10 (195).

215 The 'floating' character stems much more, according to Nietzsche from the fluctuations of *history* and becoming than from the evanescence through nature of an inessential immateriality. *Fluctuat nec mergitur.*

216 Cf. E. Blondel, 'Vom Nutzen und Nachteil der Sprache für das Verständnis Nietzsches', *Nietzsche Studien*, (1981), 10–11. Cf. Benveniste, *Problèmes de linguistique générale*, chs 2, 4.

217 'Do you want a *name* for this world?' (*VP*, I, p. 216, §51 = *WP*, §1067, pr *K*, XVI, p. 515).

218 Nietzsche is one of a group of people who have been excluded from philosophical tradition, on the grounds that they are neither systematic nor conceptual: namely, moralists, those who analyse *mores*, which are a mixture of representations and lived actions.

219 *BGE*, the title of Part Five.

220 *BGE*, §16.

221 We have seen how the inverted commas also serve to mark the gap between common acceptance ('metaphysics') and the new acceptance of a word.

222 *BGE*, §268.

223 *D* §84. Cf. *An*, §52, and *VP*, I, p. 188, §409 = *WP*, §201.

224 *BGE*, §11.

225 *KGW*, VIII, 3, 15 (42).

226 *KGW*, VIII, 14 (133).

227 *KGW*, VIII, 15 (43).

228 *VP*, I, p. 196, §433.

229 *VP*, I, p. 49, §57. The title of the First Thesis of *GM* is 'Good and Evil', 'Good and Bad'.

230 *VP* I, §58.

231 *VP*, I, p. 193, §426. Cf. also *GS*, §377; *VP*, I, p. 133, §286; *D*, §501 (and P. Köster, *Der sterbliche Gott*, p. 109, n. 1); *TSZ*, Part One, 'Of

the Thousand and One Goals'; Part Four, 'Of Science'; The Song of Melancholy.

232 *An*, §4.

233 *An*, §49.

234 *An*, §38. Cf. §26 and §15. Compare with *EH*, 'Why I am a Destiny', §8.

235 *TI*, '"Reason" in Philosophy', §2. Cf. *ibid.*, §6, Fourth Proposition.

236 *VP*, I, pp. 148–9, §318.

237 For example, *EH*, 'Why I Am a Destiny', §8. 'The unmasking (*Entdeckung*) of Christian morality'. The idea can be found in other expressions: 'The curtain rises on a monstrous falsification' (*VP*, I, p. 150, §318), or again in the play of words on *Schleiermacher* to be found in *EH*, 'The Wagner Case', §3. To be a philologist involves not only interpreting but also unmasking. The importance of this task, though, must not make us forget its relative lack of effectiveness, which is once again due to the defect in the philologist: 'Having stripped off (*aufgedeckt*) all the defensive and protective measures used to preserve an ideal, have we refuted it?' (*VP*, I, p. 138, §299). The reply: 'Morality is the concern of those who *cannot* go beyond it; it is part of their "living conditions". We canot refute living conditions – we can only *have others* (*VP*, II, pp. 168–9, §543). Nietzsche's hesitation underlines the secondary nature of language and philology. It is worth nothing, since one often attributes to Nietzsche the erroneous idea that the inversion of values simply involving a subversion of language.

238 *VP*, I, p. 150, §318 = *WP*, §786.

239 *D*, 3 (30). Cf. *D*, §377.

240 *GS*, §359. Cf. *KGW*, VIII, 2, 9 (22): 'Powerful needs whose brutality urgently demanded a spiritual disguise'; *GM*, First Essay, §13: 'Quiet, virtuous resignations ... require the belief ... which notoriously justifies every kind of lie'.

241 *An*, §15.

242 *D*, 8 (78). Cf. *BGE*, §260: '"We who are truthful" – thus did the nobility of ancient Greece designate themselves'.

243 *GS*, 11 (144) = *KGW*, V, 2, 11 (95).

244 *GM*, First Essay, §14.

245 *VP*, I, p. 328, §430 (*WP*, §721), already cited for its use of '*als*'.

246 *GS*, §352, a veritable anthology of moral disguise. Cf. *D*, 3 (23); *GS*, 12 (136) and §282.

247 *GS*, §352.

248 *TI*, 'Expeditions ...', §49. Cf. *ibid.*, §44.

249 *An*, §9. Cf. §25.

250 *An*, §21.

251 'Pompous terms for something completely different – the opposite, indeed!' (*KGW*, §22).

252 *BGE*, §223.
253 *KGW*, VIII, 1, 2 (121) = *WP*, §78.
254 *BGE*, §230.
255 *KGW*, VIII, 2, 9 (165) = *WP*, §79.
256 Cf. *KGW*, VIII, 2, 9 (75) = *WP*, §1024: 'the old masquerade', 'moral checking-up', 'naked nature'. This is completely unlike the mask designed to make one feel the depth of a reality that, in all its richness, is never offered up naked to the eye.
257 *VP*, II, p. 129, §412 = *WP*, §327.
258 *VP*, II, p. 374, §560 = *K*, XII, Part Two, §682.
259 *BGE*, §208.
260 *D*, §186.
261 *OP*, §570. Cf. *WP*, §357.
262 *KGW*, VIII, 2, 10 (165) = *WP*, §916 = *VP*, II, p. 300, §288.
263 *BGW*, §33.
264 *TSZ*, Part Two, 'Of the Tarantulas'.
265 *KGW*, VIII, 2, 11 (150) = *WP*, §56.
266 *KGW*, VIII, 1, 7 (10) = *WP*, §81. Cf. *VP*, I, p. 46, §51.
267 *GS*, §365. Cf. §377.
268 *TI*, 'Expeditions . . .', §35. Cf. *NCW*, 'Where I Have Something to Say Again, Beginning'.
269 Variant of *TSZ*, Gallimard edition, p. 390. Cf. *TSZ*, Part Four, 'Of the Higher Man', §8; Part Two, 'Of the Land of Culture'; *WP*, §1024.
270 *BGE*, §295. Cf. *TSZ*, Part One, 'Of the Friend'; Part Two, 'Of Manly Prudence'; Part Three, 'Of Old and New Law-Tables', §2.
271 *TSZ*, Part Two, 'Of the Virtuous'. Cf. *D*, 6 (339).
272 *VP*, I, p. 46, §49 = *WP*, §447.
273 *VP*, I, p. 47, §52. Cf. *GM*, Preface, §3: '*Was bisher als Moral gefeiert worden ist.*'
274 *OP*, §640. Cf. *HATH*, §§45 and 99.
275 *An*, §17. Cf. *HATH*, §96.
276 *GM*, Third Essay, §20.
277 *GM*, Third Essay, §16.
278 *GM*, Third Essay, §17. Cf. *VP*, II, p. 362, §514 = *WP*, §1045.
279 *GM*, Third Essay, II, §11. Note the following: 'as if . . .'. Cf. *TSZ*, Part Two, 'Of Redemption'.
280 *GM*, Third Essay, §18. There is another list in *VP*, II, p. 83, §241 = *WP*, §62. Cf. *VP*, II, p. 59, §150.
281 *TSZ*, Part Two, 'The Child with the Mirror' (cf. Matthew 13:25). Cf. *ibid.*, 'Of the Priests'; 'Of the Famous Philosophers'; 'The Dame Song'; 'Of Marriage and Children'; 'Of Chastity'; 'Of the Flies of the Market-Place'; 'Of Redemption', etc.
282 *TSZ*, Part Three, 'The Home-Coming'.
283 *KGW*, VIII, 2, 10 (206) = *WP*, §385.

284 *An*, §62.

285 *VP*, I, p. 138, §299. Cf. *BGE*, §259; *VP*, I, p. 129, §277 (= *WP*, §351).

286 *KGW*, VIII, 3, 23 (4) = *VP*, I, p. 142, §306, alinea IV. Cf. *An*, §55, and *TI*, 'The "Improvers" of Mankind', §1.

287 *VP*, I, pp. 371–2, §552.

288 *BGE*, §39.

289 *GM*, First Essay, §11.

290 = *VP*, I, p. 184, §400.

291 Cf. *TI*, 'The Problem of Socrates', §11.

292 = *VP*, I, p. 184, §402.

293 *VP*, I, p. 286, §287 = K, XIV, Part One, §69.

294 Laplanche and Pontalis, *The Language of Psycho-analysis*, '(De) negation'.

295 *VP*, I, p. 172, §371 (= *WP*, §179). Cf. *VP*, I, ibid., §372 (*WP*, §185): '*Artifice*: to deny all natural *mobilia* and to transfer them to the spiritual realm beyond – to exploit virtue and its veneration entirely for one's own ends, step by step to deny virtue to everything non-Christian' (*ableugnen, umkehren, absprechen*).

296 *VP*, I, p. 328, §427 (*WP*, §375).

297 *WP*, §204 (= *KGW*, VIII, 2, 10 (157)). Cf. *KGW*, VIII, 2, 10 (192): '*Die moralische Werturteile sind Verurteilungen, Verneinungen, Moral ist die Abkehr vom Willen zum Dasein*'.

298 *WP*, §312 = *KGW*, VIII, 2, 10 (144). Cf. other examples in *An*, §§7 and 27.

299 *KGW*, VIII, 2, 10 (57) = *WP*, §786.

300 *An*, §55. Cf. *EH*, 'Why I Am a Destiny', §4. Nietzsche stresses the link between nihilism, negation and metaphysical nihilization in *KGW*, VIII, 2, 9 (62) = *WP*, §580.

301 Cf. our article 'Götzen auschorchen' and our *Nietzsche: le 'cinquième évangile'*?

302 *BGE*, §61: 'Perhaps nothing in Christianity and Buddhism is so venerable as their art of teaching even the lowliest to set themselves through piety in an apparently higher order of things and thus to preserve their contentment with the real order, within which they live hard enough lives – and necessarily have to!'

303 These expressions, which recall epithets applied to God in the Old Testament, or the term 'unfathomable', used to described life in *TSZ*, occur frequently in Nietzsche. For example: *WP*, §§1020, 1050, 1052 (cf. §§881, 1028); *TI*, '"Reason" in Philosophy', §6, Fourth Proposition; *NCW*, 'We the Antipodeans'; *KGW*, VIII, 3, 17 (3), §2 and 14 (14); *BT*, 'Attempt at a Self-Criticism', §2; *KGW*, VIII, 1, 2 (117) and 2 (114).

304 Nothing is stranger to Nietzsche than 'freedom' or the pleasure principle representing an ethical value or a metaphysical principle. Cf. *TI*, 'What the Germans Lack', §6: 'The essence of it is precisely *not* to

"will", the *ability* to defer decision. All unspirituality, all vulgarity, is due to the incapacity to resist a stimulus – one *has* to react, one obeys every impulse. . . . Almost everything which unphilosophical crudity designates by the name "vice" is merely this physiological incapacity *not* to react'. *Ibid.*, 'Morality as Anti-Nature', §2: 'weakness of will, more precisely the inability *not* to react to a stimulus, is itself merely another form of degeneration'. Note also that the idea of the obscenity of disguise and the 'moral' immorality of clothing merges with the presentation of Genesis, chs 2 and 3.

305 *D*, 3 (119).
306 A remark already given by Plato in the *Phaedo*, 77c: 'Socrates, you must argue us out of our fears – and yet, strictly speaking, they are not our fears, but there is a child within us to whom death is a sort of hobgoblin: him too we must persuade not to be afraid when he is alone in the dark' (*The Portable Plato*, Scott Buchanan (ed.) (Harmondsworth: Penguin, 1948), p. 221).
307 *D*, 3 (69).
308 *D*, 3 (82). Nietzsche adds: 'Science will perhaps one day destroy monsters but ultimately it will also have to destroy the forms of consolation that in the course of their long life have themselves become monsters'. In fact, 'to know is to understand anything to the best of our interest' (*VP*, I, p. 236, §122).
309 *D*, 4 (230).
310 *VP*, II, p. 336, §442 = *WP*, §958.
311 *VP*, II, p. 364, §533 = *KGW*, VIII, 3, 14 (65).
312 *KGW*, VII, 1, 24 (28) = *WP*, §417.
313 *BGE*, §61. Cf. *GS*, §359.
314 *GM*, Third Essay, §17. For Nietzsche, 'grace' equals consolation. Freud will not offer greater insight into religion and, more generally, into neurosis (a refusal that paralyses reality and a submission to an illusory absolute: the superego). Moreover, morality in Nietzsche and neurosis in Freud are both purely defensive or *negative* (denegation, denial, defence mechanism, repression). This creates convergence on *Verneinung* and every other process beginning with *ver-*, which tends to suggest that the common vision of a frightening reality that frustrates desire is the result not of an encounter, or of chance, but of one or several common sources: Greek tragedy, the Jewish thought of the Old Testament, and Shakespeare, not to mention Schopenhauer who ultimately epitomizes such a vision.
315 *KGW*, VIII, 2 10 (21) = *WP*, §1019.
316 *GM*, First Essay, §13.
317 *BGE*, §61.
318 *BGE*, §187. It is in this text, linking consolation to justification, Nietzsche concludes that morals are the '*sign-language of the emotions*'. It is language that permits these two operations.

320   *Nietzsche: The Body and Culture*

319 *OP*, p. 174, §768 (= *K*, XII, Part One, §439). Cf. *VP*, I, p. 146, §311.
320 Nietzsche recalls: 'One needs only to see what tendencies the "God of love" inspires in his believers: they ruin mankind for the sake of the "good"' (*WP*, §244 = *VP*, I, p. 135, §292). Note the inverted commas.
321 *VP*, I, p. 132, §284.
322 My emphasis: note the link made between denegation and interpretation, inverted commas and words in *ver-*. Cf. above the link established between 'justification, moralization, interpretation' (*VP*, I, p. 364, §533).
323 *VP*, I, p. 184, §400.
324 *VP*, I, p. 194, §428. As this text refers to the Reformation, we appreciate the ironic use of 'justification'. Cf. *ibid.*, p. 365, §534: 'noble interpretation.'
325 *VP*, I, p. 374, §557 = *KGW*, VIII, 3, 14 (29).
326 *EH*, 'Why I am So Wise', §1.
327 *BGE*, §230.
328 *TI*, 'The Four Great Errors', §6: 'In reality all these supposed explanations are *consequented* states and as it were translations of pleasurable and unpleasurable feelings into a false dialect'. Cf. *BGE*, §22, quoted above, pp. 199–200.
329 On the diversity of languages and the problem of translation, cf. *BGE*, §28; *D*, 4 (149): 'it is probably (in morality that we speak) with the least precision'; *GS*, §83.
330 *BGE*, §22.
331 *BGE*, §230. Cf. *WP*, §299. Note how, both here and later, Nietzsche insists on the *frightful* nature of this text and the intrepid character needed to decipher it.
332 *An*, §26.
333 *GM*, Third Essay, §17.
334 *CW*, §3: here it is the language of Wagner that is to be translated.
335 *HATH*, 2, 27 (20): examples in *WP*, §462. Cf. *EH*, 'Daybreak', §2 (*zurückübersetzt*) and *EH*, 'The Birth of Tragedy', §1 (*übersetzt*).
336 *KGW*, VIII, 3, 14 (123).
337 *GM*, First Essay, §13.
338 *GM*, First Essay, §2.
339 *TI*, 'Expeditions . . .', §40.
340 *EH*, 'Why I Am a Destiny', §7. Cf. §8.
341 *WP*, §147 = *KGW*, VIII, 2, 10 (193). Cf. above: 'Christian is a no to natural' (*Neinsagen*).
342 *VP*, I, p. 41, §33 = *WP*, §335.
343 *VP*, I, p. 108, §213, alinea *C*, = *KGW*, VIII, 3, 14 (168).
344 *KGW*, VIII, 2, 11 (294). Cf. *ibid.* (295): *umgesetzt*.
345 *KGW*, VIII, 2, 11, (295). Cf. *ibid.*, (281) and 10 (180).

346 *BGE*, §191. Cf. §186.

347 *GM*, Third Essay, §22. Translation here takes the form of a denunciation of designations that create a course effect as a result of an unforeseen equivalence. This is a well-known procedure to be found at the heart of Fielding's *Jonathan Wild*. The same applies to *GM*, Second Essay, §6: domestic animals means modern man meaning us.

348 *GM*, Third Essay, §21. Cf. *TI*, 'The "Improvers" . . .', §2.

349 *EH*, Foreword, §2. Cf. *GS*, Preface, §2: 'What was at stake in all philosophizing hitherto was not at all "truth" but something else – let us say health, future, growth, power, life'.

350 *GM*, Third Essay, §17.

351 *WP*, §140 = *KGW*, VIII, 3, 14 (189).

352 *WP*, §204, al. 2 = *KGW*, VIII, 2, 10 (157).

353 *WP*, §224 = *KGW*, VIII, 2, 111 (263). Cf. *WP*, §225 (= *KGW*, VIII, 2, 11 (365)).

354 *WP*, §229 = *KGW*, VIII, 3, 14 (179).

356 *WP*, §684 = *KGW*, VIII, 3, 14 (133).

357 *TI*, 'Maxims and Arrow', §31.

358 *TI*, 'Expeditions . . .', §24.

359 *TI*, 'Expeditions . . .', §42. Cf. *EH*, 'Twilight of the Idols', §1: 'That which is called *idol* on the title-page is quite simply that which has hitherto been called truth. *Twilight of the Idols* – in plain terms: the old truth is coming to an end'.

360 *An*, §43.

361 *An*, §52.

362 *An*, §55.

363 *An*, §56.

364 *An*, §57.

365 *TI* '"Reason" in Philosophy', §5.

366 *EH*, 'Why I am So Clever', §2. Cf. *ibid.*, 'Why I Write Such Excellent Books', §5: 'with the word vice I combat every sort of anti-nature or, if one likes beautiful words, idealism'.

367 *OP*, §173. Re-used in *TSZ*, Part Two, 'Of the Virtuous'. Cf. *OP*, §505 = *GS*, 12 (31).

368 *D*, 8 (3).

369 *KGW*, VIII, 3, 14 (123).

370 *GS*, §83.

371 *OP*, §637 = *GS*, 23 (25). In his search for a new culture, Musil will criticize 'modern culture' in a very Nietzschean way when he writes in *The Man Without Qualities*, ch. 48: 'it is only criminals who presume to damage other people nowadays without the aid of philosophy'. Cf. Nietzsche's remark: 'Virtue remains the costliest vice: it *must* remain so!' (*KGW*, VIII, 3, 15 (118)). On the relationship between culture, custom and fear, cf. *OP*, §453: 'To be moral means to be open, in

large part, to fear'. Freud, who was also a translator (cf. *The Birth of Psychoanalysis*, note 1) equally sought a different kind of culture (*Civilization and its Discontents*, *The Future of an Illusion*) and he frequently used the term *translation* to designate the relationship between the drives and the conscious when censorship is being overcome. Cf. *The Birth of Psychoanalysis*: 'It is the lack of translation that we call, clinically, *repression*'.

372 *WP*, §605 = *KGW*, VIII, 2, 9 (48).

373 'The demand for an *adequate means of expression* is senseless: it is in the nature of a language or means of expression to express only a simply relation' (*KGW*, VIII, 3, 14 (122)).

374 *KGW*, VIII, 3, 14 (142).

375 *KGW*, VIII, 3, 14 (142).

376 *WP*, §620 = *VP*, I, p. 294, §314.

377 *GS*, §354.

378 *KGW*, VIII, 3, 15 (110).

379 *KGW*, VIII, 3, 14 (159), *passim*.

380 *GM*, First Essay, §4. Cf. *HATH*, 1, 16 (23): 'Wagner's etymologies are authentically artistic even if they are not scientific: the former is the right relationship to nature'.

381 *VP*, I, pp. 69–70, §112 (*K*, XIII, §46).

382 *VP*, I, p. 60, §82 = *WP*, §409.

383 *NPh*, III, p. 38; XI, p. 73.

384 *GM*, First Essay, §5.

385 *GM*, First Essay, §10. Freud, who, like Nietzsche, enjoyed wordplay and linguistic links, from 1897 on began to make etymological and linguistic analyses of a genealogical nature. Cf. his letter to Fliess of 22 December 1897: An old fantasy of mine, which I would like to recommend to your linguistic sagacity, deals with the derivation of our verbs from such originally coproerotic terms. ... In the same way, everything related to birth, miscarriage, [menstrual] period goes back to the toilet via the word *Abort* [toilet] (*Abortus* [abortion]) *The Complete Letters of Sigmund Freud to Wilhelm Fliess, 1887–1904*, Jeffrey M. Masson (ed.) (Cambridge, Mass.: Harvard University Press, 1985), p. 288.

386 Robert Musil, *The Man Without Qualities*, Book One, ch. 61.

387 *EH*, 'Why I am So Clever', §10.

388 *WP*, §335.

389 *GS*, 23 (47).

390 *D*, §377. Cf. *D*, 3 (30); 6 (6); 3 (164); 7 (95); *GS*, 11 (59).

391 Cf. the works of P. Valadier and E. Blondel, *Nietzsche: le 'cinquième évangile'*? and '"Götzen aushorchen": Versuch einer Genealogie der Genealogie. Nietzsches philologisches Apriori und die christliche Kritik des Christentums', *Perspektiven der Philosophie* (1981), Band 7.

392 Cf. *WP*, §594 = *KGW*, VII, 1, 24 (18).

393 *D*, 3 (82).

394 *Sigmund Freud, Civilization and its Discontents*, (Harmondsworth: 1984, pp. 245–340; p. 339.

395 *VP*, I, p. 195, §432 = *KGW*, VIII, 2, 10 (170). Cf. *K*, X, p‹ 120, §40: 'The philosophies and theologies that have been abolished continue to operate today in the sciences' (*VP*, II, p. 203, §684).

396 *GS*, §347.

397 *D*, 7 (256). 'Support doubt and a sea-crossing rather than wanting to arrive too quickly at a certainty!'. Cf. *EH*, 'Why I am So Clever', §4: 'Is Hamlet *understood*? It is not doubt, it is *certainty* which makes mad'.

398 *WS*, §16.

399 *EH*, 'Untimely Meditations', §1.

400 *D*, 8 (98) = *OP*, p. 62, §98. Cf. *D*, 8 (63) and 7 (179); *GM*, Third Essay, §25, beginning.

401 *GS*, 11 (248).

402 *BGE*, §206. Cf. §248 and *VP*, I, p. 44, §42 (= *WP*, §444).

403 Note the critical genealogy of the theory of reflection, from which certain Marxists could eventually learn something.

404 *BGE*, §207. On this point, see A. Langaney, *Le sexe et l'innovation* (end).

405 *BGE*, §211. Cf. *K*, XIII, Part One, §31: the scholars are 'the camels of civilization'.

406 Cf. *WP*, §608 = *KGW*, VIII, 1, 5 (14).

407 *VP*, I, p. 85, §154.

408 *VP*, I, pp. 83–4, §153.

409 *VP*, I, p. 84, §154.

410 *VP*, I, p. 85, §156. Cf. *ibid.*, §157: 'mythology', 'facility', 'abbreviation'.

411 *Ibid.*, §158. Cf. *VP*, I, pp. 86–7, §159.

412 *KGW*, VIII, 1, 2 (89) = *WP*, §628.

413 *WP*, §630 = *KGW*, VII, 36 (18).

414 *GM*, Third Essay, §§23 to 25.

415 Cf. *HATH*, §§6 and 7.

416 *HATH*, §517. Cf. *HATH*, 23 (82).

417 *D*, 8 (61).

418 Cf. *D*, 6 (313): 'Women see in science a vampire of man'. Many remarks by Nietzsche point in the same direction (cf. *TI* 'Maxims and Arrows', especially), not in order to challenge science for the sake of a 'modesty' or mystery, but in order to confront this kind of critique addressed to science.

419 Let us be careful: Nietzsche said that science cannot found values and so cannot itself be barbarous: it can only 'be at the service' of barbarism. It *rests on* an ideal that it cannot itself *be*, and to which it can therefore only act as a *means*. It is only 'barbarized' when it is erected

into an ideal, since barbarism consists in taking *means* to be absolute *ends*, when there are not possible ends. Cf. the pertinent remarks of A. Langaney in *Le sexe et l'innovation*, on the transformation of 'science' into a value.

420 Cf. *D*, §206; *An*, §57; *D*, 7 (97); *WP*, §209 (= *VP*, I, p. 197, §435), as well as *AOM*, §§304 and 310; *WS*, §285; *WP*, §40; *HATH*, 21 (32); *D*, 6 (106). One also thinks of Nietzsche's hatred of Hugo and above all Zola, even before the Dreyfus affair.

421 Since no one called himself or herself a Stalinist, while many proclaimed themselves to be communists or socialists, in several different ways. It is amusing to speculate on how, if the fashion had facilitated it, lots of recriminations against Nietzsche could have been silenced by replacing every instance of the word 'socialism' in his texts with the word 'Stalinism': this simple shift onto a scapegoat would have been enough, not to answer his questions, but to create one voice from his very different interpreters. The guilty party is the other, that is to say no one: there is a localizable 'sin', so we are all good.

422 The same ignorance (voluntary or involuntary) is to be found in the strange mixture called 'collectivism' that tries to fuse socialisms as different if not contrary as those symbolized by Marx or Bakunin, Trotsky or Stalin, Jaurès or Tito, etc.

423 Cf. *HATH*, §§463 and 446.

424 Cf. *KGW*, VIII, 3, 15 (30); *TI*, 'Expeditions . . .', §34; *An*, §58.

425 *HATH*, 25 (1) 7.

426 *KGW*, VIII, 2, 10 (170) (= *VP*, I, p. 195, §432). Cf. 10 (2); 10 (5); 11 (226); *WP*, §209; *HATH*, 23 (25).

427 *KGW*, VIII, 2, 10 (7) = *VP*, I, p. 196, §434.

428 *KGW*, VIII, 1, 5 (108) = *VP*, I, p. 199, §442.

429 *KGW*, VII, 25 (263) = *VP*, I, p. 199, §443.

430 Cf. *WP*, §§753, 754, sqq.

431 *TI*, 'Expeditions . . .', §34. A draft of this text read: 'When the *socialist*' (Gallimard edition, p. 472).

432 *TI*, Gallimard edition, variants, pp. 472–3.

433 *BGE*, §203.

434 *An*, §4.

435 *BGE*, §203.

436 *GS*, §356; *BGE*, §§202 and 203.

437 *BGE*, §259.

438 *WP*, §864 = *KGW*, VIII, 3, 14 (182).

439 *WP*, §784 = *KGW*, VIII, 2, 10 (82); *TI*, 'Expeditions . . .', §34; *HATH*, §473.

440 *WP*, §40; *BGE*, §§259 and 202.

441 Cf. *KGW*, VIII, 2, 10 (82).

442 There is a large gap, as J. Granier remarks (*Concilium*, 164, p. 152),

separating heroic tragedy, the springboard for *Selbstüberwindung*, from tragedy as it usually manifests itself, which usually culminates in the pure and simple suppression of the *Mensch*, instead of permitting the *Übermensch*.

443 Cf. *BGE*, §259; *HATH*, §452.

444 Even the analyses of Trotsky, who wishes to present a Marxist critique of Stalinism as something that distorts Marx's analyses, remain verbal, that is to say non-Marxian ('bureaucracy' is a vague concept) and marked by the resentment that shifts the 'blame' inward, instead of searching for the eventual inner and material causes.

445 Can history show him his error?

446 Cf. our remarks in *Nietzsche, 'le cinquième évangile'?*, chs 2 and 3.

9   THE BODY AND METAPHORS

1 *VP*, I, p. 64, §96 (and §95) = *WP*, §477 (and §478).
2 E. Fink, *La philosophie de Nietzsche*, p. 181.
3 Cf. especially J. Granier, *Le problème de la vérité*, pp. 97–101; J. Simon, 'Grammatik und Wahrheit', *Nietzsche Studien* (1972), Band 1, pp. 1–26.
4 *VP*, I, p. 65, §97 = *K*, XIII, §117.
5 VP, I, p. 43, §36 = *WP*, §420.
6 *VP* I, §37 (*WP*, §421). Cf. *An*, §50: 'the service of truth is the hardest service'.
7 *VP*, I, p. 44, §41 (*WP*, §465).
8 *VP*, I, p. 43, §37. Cf. Kant, *Logique*: 'Without experience one will never become a philosopher, but by the same token experiences will never of themselves make one a philosopher'.
9 *EH*, Why I Am a Destiny, §1.
10 *TI*, 'Expeditions …', §26. Cf. *KGW*, VIII, 2, 10 (60): '*Macht das Ungemeine gemein*', and *VP*, I, p. 285, §286; p. 319, §395; *GS*, §354.
11 Cf. P. Valadier, *Nietzsche et la critique du christianisme*, p. 238.
12 *KGW*, VIII, 2, 11 (73) = *WP*, §715.
13 *VP*, I, p. 68, §105. Cf. *GM*, Third Essay, §16: 'a fat word taking the place of a vague [thin] question mark'.
14 *WP*, §628 = *KGW*, VIII, 1, 2 (89).
15 *WP*, §634 = *KGW*, VIII, 3, 14 (79).
16 *KGW*, VIII, 1, 2 (83) = *WP*, §627.
17 *KGW*, VIII, 1, 7 (14) = *WP*, §629; cf. *KGW*, ibid., 2 (139) = *WP*, §631, and *WS*, §11: 'Through words and concepts we are still continually misled into imagining things as being simpler than they are. … A philosophical mythology lies concealed in *language*'.
18 Cf. *D*, §502; *BGE*, §19; *WS*, §33.
19 *GM*, Third Essay, §19, etc. Cf. *BGE*, §249: 'Every people has its own tartuffery and calls it its virtues.
20 *VP*, I, p. 102, §208 (*WP*, §567). Cf. *WP*, §30 = *KGW*, VIII, 2, 11 (148).
21 *TSZ*, Part Four, 'The Shadow'; Part Three, 'The Convalescent'.
22 *WP*, §827 = *KGW*, VIII, 2, 10 (37).
23 *WP*, §1052 = *KGW*, VIII, 3, 14 (89).
24 *An*, §32. And, suddenly, logically, '[Christ] does not deny' (*ibid.*).
25 *CW*, Preface.
26 *An*, §32.
27 *KGW*, VIII, 3, 15 (44).
28 *VP*, I, p. 118, §243.
29 *HATH*, 1, 23 (24).
30 Cf. for example *WP*, §625 = *KGW*, VIII, 3, 14 (122), *in fine* (1888).
31 *NPH*, XI, p. 73.

32 *KGW*, VII, 1, 24 (16) = *VP*, I, p. 278, §261 = *WP*, §676 (where a mistake in the reading of the manuscript falsifies the text: *und* instead of *nur*).

33 *D*, 2 (55).

34 *GS*, §58 (my emphasis).

35 *TI*, 'How the "Real World" at Last Became a Myth', §3.

36 *VP*, I, p. 257, §188.

37 In the sense that there is an infinity of other attributes. Cf. *KGW*, VIII, 3, 14 (144) = *WP*, §523: 'Nothing is more erroneous than to make of psychical and physical phenomena the two faces, the two revelations of one and the same substance. Nothing is explained thereby: the concept "substance" is perfectly useless as an explanation'.

38 *An*, §14. Cf. 'We come to the phase in which the conscious becomes modest' (*VP*, I, p. 278, §261). Note this last word, which indicates less an ontological degradation that a lowering in a relation between forces.

39 *An*, §14.

40 As with Freud, who places his discovery of the predominance of the unconscious within the line of discoveries made by Copernicus and Darwin, each of which was a humilating blow to man's narcissism.

41 *An*, §14.

42 *An*, §14.

43 *TSZ*, Part One, 'Of the Despisers of the Body'.

44 Cf. *GM*, Second Essay, §1: 'so that, between the original determination and the actual performance of the thing willed, a whole world of new things, conditions, even volitional acts, can be interposed without snapping the long chain of the will. But how much all this presupposes!'. *OP*, p. 137, §322: 'Everything that enters consciousness represents the final link in a chain, an end, a term'.

45 *GS*, 11 (330) and 22 (3).

46 *VP*, I, p. 117, §240 = *WP*, §711.

47 *GS*, §277 and §322. Nietzsche adds, in this final paragraph, the metaphor of the labyrinth.

48 'Reality is a certain movement of instincts' (*OP*, p. 113, §263).

49 *VP*, I, p. 242, §146.

50 *VP*, I, p. 239, §133. Cf. *BGE*, §108, and *WP*, §556.

51 *WP*, §594 = *KGW*, VII, 1, 24 (18). Cf. *VP*, I, p. 267, §227: 'The *principal* great activity is unconscious'.

52 *WP*, §556 = *KGW*, VIII, 1, 2 (149).

53 *KGW*, VIII, 1, 2 (152) (= *WP*, §556).

54 *TSZ*, Part One, 'Of the Despisers of the Body'.

55 *GS*, §357.

56 *GS*, §354. In this text, Nietzsche expressly links consciousness to language, by virtue of their superficiality: 'the development of language and the development of consciousness . . . go hand in hand'.

57 *TSZ*, Part One, 'Of the Despisers of the Body'.
58 Leibniz, *New Essays*, II, 1 §12, and Preface.
59 *GS*, §354.
60 Cf. Leibniz, *New Essays*, Preface and II, I, §2; *GS*, §333: 'a certain behaviour of the instincts toward one another'.
61 *GS*, §333.
62 Cf. Leibniz, *Meditations*, and *New Essays*, II, XXIX.
63 *New Essays*, II, XXI, §72.
64 *GM*, Second Essay, §1. The term '*dienstbar*' introduces, as always, an extra metaphorical value, which is here political, to which we shall return.
65 For example, *BGE*, §295.
66 'Camera obscura' (sic) (*German Ideology*, I, A).
67 Cf. 'the Hades of half-conscious feeling' (*AOM*, §374).
68 *D*, §116. Cf. §115.
69 Nietzsche even explicitly condemns the idea that the affects can be a grounding (*Grund*): 'The affects are a construction of the intellect, the invention of causes which do not exist. Every bodily feeling that we do not understand is interpreted intellectually' (*KGW*, VII, 1, 24 (20)). The grounding is itself an interpretation.
70 *D*, §119. I emphasize '*incomplete*'.
71 This is what makes it possible to consider the metaphysics of the subject as a grammatical concept.
72 *TSA*, Part One, 'Of the Despisers of the Body'. Note from this point a shift towards metaphors of a 'political' type.
73 *VP*, I, p. 266, §226.
74 *EH*, 'Why I am So Clever', §9. Nietzsche thus contrasts his ego with a *nosce te ipsum* that would culminate in 'self-misunderstanding, self-diminution, self-narrowing'.
75 *KGW*, VIII, 3, 14 (145).
76 *KGW*, VIII, 3, 14 (152).
77 *VP*, I, p. 266, §226.
78 *VP*, I, p. 281, §270.
79 *KGW*, VIII, 3, 14 (144).
80 *VP*, I, pp. 280–1, §269.
81 *VP*, I, p. 278, §261.
82 *VP*, I, p. 276, §259.
83 *GM*, Second Essay, §1.
84 Cf. *GM*, Second Essay, §1; *VP*, I, pp. 280–1, §269.
85 *GM*, Second Essay, §1.
86 A. Schopenhauer, *The World as Will and Representation*, supplements to the First Book, ch. XIV.
87 *GS*, §322.
88 *D*, §119.

89 *D*, §446. Cf. *GS*, §231.
90 *D*, Preface, §1. Cf. *GS*, 'Joke, Cunning and Revenge', §3: '*Undaunted.*
   'Where you stand, dig deep and pry!/Down there is the well./Let the
   obscurantists cry:/"Down there's only – hell"'. Cf. also *KGW*, VIII,
   3, 20 (73).
91 'I am not a man, I am dynamite' (*EH*, 'Why I Am a Destiny', §1)
   stems from the same principle.
92 *D*, Preface, §2.
93 Cf. *GM*, Preface, §7 (*unterirdisch*). This subterranean labour designated
   genealogy as the uncoding of hieroglyphs.
94 Cf. note 90 above plus *TSZ*, Part Three, 'The Wanderer'.
95 *TSZ*, Part Three, 'Before Sunrise'; The Second Dance Song; Part
   Four, 'The Intoxicated Song'.
96 This is why the public easily confuses him who fishes in troubled
   waters (*im Trüben*) with him who plumbs the depths (*aus der Tiefe*)
   (*AOM*, §262).
97 *BGE*, §12.
98 *K* and *Mus. WP*, §676 here has '*und*' instead of '*nur*', which changes the
   whole meaning of the phrase. We follow the *KGW* text.
99 *KGW*, VII, 1, 24 (16).
100 *D*, 5 (44).
101 *VP*, II, p. 154, §491.
102 *D*, §109.
103 E. Fink, *Le jeu comme symbole du monde*, p. 176.
104 Plato, *Laws*, VII, 803c.
105 *KGW*, VIII, 3, 14 (146).
106 *KGW*, VIII, 3, 14 (144).
107 *VP*, I, p. 282, §276.
108 *D*, §109.
109 *KGW*, VIII, 3, 14 (145).
110 *TSZ*, Part One, 'Of the Despisers of the Body'.
111 *KGW*, VIII, 14 (144). Cf. *TI*, 'Expeditions . . .', §26.
112 *KGW*, VII, 1, 24 (16).
113 *KGW*, VIII, 2, 11 (83).
114 *KGW*, VIII, 2, 10 (137). This refers to morality as a causalist
    interpretation that restricts life. Cf. *TI*, 'Expeditions . . .', §34; 'The
    Four Great Errors', §8; 'The Problem of Socrates', §2.
115 *VP*, I, p. 271, §244. Cf. *ibid.*, p. 270, §236, to which we shall return.
116 *D*, §119.
117 *D*, §119. There is no reality that does not exist for us ('for me': cf.
    KGW, VIII, 1, 2 (149); *VP*, I, p. 239, §§133 and 134; *GS*, 13 (9); *GS*,
    11 (26)).
118 *GS*, 11 (30).
119 *OP*, p. 113, §263.

121 *VP*, I, p. 281, §270.

122 *VP*, I, pp. 266–7, §226.

123 *VP*, I, p. 259, §193.

124 *VP*, I, p. 266, §226.

125 *OP*, §522.

126 *VP*, I, p. 270, §236.

127 *VP*, I, p. 270, §236.

128 *VP*, I, p. 262, §210.

129 This leads to the non-pertinence of the apparent applications of Nietzsche in biosociological, that is to say racist, themes.

130 *WP*, §657 = *VP*, I, p. 213, §43. Cf. *WP*, §702 = *VP*, I, 317, §390.

131 *WP*, §689 = *KGW*, VIII, 3, 14 (82).

132 *WP*, §702 = *KGW*, VIII, 3, 14 (174). '*Nicht aus Hunger, sondern aus Willen zur Macht*'.

133 *WP*, §1077 = *VP*, I, p. 214, §45. Cf. *WP*, §658 (*VP*, ibid., §44).

134 *WP*, §651 = *KGW*, VIII, 2, 11 (121). Cf. *VP*, I, p. 222, §§673 et seq.

135 *KGW*, VIII, 1, 2 (151).

136 *BGE*, §230.

137 *VP*, I, p. 340, §460. Note that here like elsewhere the stomach as assimilator is compared to a biologically elementary being: it is not an organ, but an individuated being, a 'will'.

138 *VP*, I, p. 317, §390 = *WP*, §702.

139 *KGW*, VII, 2, 25 (8).

140 *OP*, §499 = *K*, XII, pp. 76–7, §148. Cf. *HATH*, 42 (29) and compare this to Freud's meditations on the relationship between smells and man's upright position (*Civilization and its Discontents*, Ch. 4, note 2).

141 *GS*, §59.

142 Letter to Overbeck, 31 March 1885.

143 *GS*, §306.

144 *KGW*, VIII, 1, 7 (28) = *WP*, §906. Cf. *GM*, Third Essay, §16.

145 *BGE*, §230.

146 *BGE*, §241. Cf. *GS*, 11 (52): '*Simplification* is the basic need of anything organic'.

147 *BGE*, §251.

148 *BGE*, §244.

149 *EH*, 'The Wagner Case', §1.

150 *KGW*, VIII, 3, 16 (53) = *WP*, §50.

151 *KGW*, VIII, 3, 14 (179) = *WP*, §229.

152 *VP*, I, pp. 340–1, §460.

153 *KGW*, VIII, 3, 14 (224).

154 *GS*, 14 (13).

155 *GS*, 19 (6).

156 *KGW*, VII, 2, 25 (8). '*Fallen durch sie hindurch*' obviously evokes *Durchfall* or diarrhoea: food flows through the body without

remaining and being turned 'to profit'. It is the opposite of '*fertig werden*'.

157 *GM*, Third Essay, §16. Cf. *WP*, §906, and *BGE*, §44: 'with teeth and stomach for the most indigestible'.

158 *D*, §171.

159 *GS*, §359.

160 *TSZ*, Part Three, 'Of the Spirit of Gravity', §2.

161 *AOM*, §170: 'Furred tongue' (*belegte Zunge*, together with *verschleimter Magen*) is an expression Nietzsche uses to characterize *décadence*. Thus, in *GM*, Second Essay, §7: 'On his way to becoming an "angel" man has acquired that chronic indigestion and coated tongue which makes not only the naive joy and innocence of the animal distasteful to him, but even life itself'.

162 *WS*, §297.

163 *GS*, §167.

164 *GS*, §364.

165 *EH*, 'Why I am So Clever', §2.

166 *GS*, §366.

167 *TI*, 'Maxims and Arrows', §34.

168 *EH*, 'Why I am So Clever', §1. Cf. *ibid.*, §8.

169 *EH*, 'Why I am So Clever', §2.

170 *EH*, 'Why I am So Clever', §1.

171 *TSZ*, Part Four, 'The Awakening', §1.

172 *TSZ*, Part Three, 'Of the Apostates', §2.

173 *TSZ*, Part Four, 'The Voluntary Beggar'.

174 A circle of which the Eternal Return is the nodal formulation and the apparent solution. Cf. our article 'Wohin? Wozu?', *loc. cit.*

175 *GS*, 12 (11).

176 *GS*, 11 (262).

177 *GM*, Third Essay, §16.

178 *GS*, 11 (173).

179 *D*, 4 (173).

180 Draft of *EH*, Gallimard edition, pp. 568–9.

181 *EH*, 'Why I am So Clever', §5. Nietzsche says that Germany spoils (*verdirbt*) culture (*die Kultur*). The same is said of digestion: *ibid.*, §3.

182 *EH*, 'Why I Write Such Excellent Books, §3.

183 *EH*, 'Why I am So Wise', §6. Cf. *HATH*, 2, 38 (1): '"Pessimists" are malicious people with ruined stomachs: they take vengeance with their heads for their bad digestion.'

184 *EH*, 'Why I am So Wise', §5.

185 *TI*, 'The Four Great Errors', §6.

186 *D*, 4 (218). For example: 'the morbidity and neurasthenia of priests of all periods' (*GM*, First Essay, §6).

187 *D*, §203.

188 *EH*, 'Why I Write Such Excellent Books', §5.

189 *GS*, §39.

190 *HATH*, 2, 42 (29). Cf. *OP*, §499.

191 *KGW*, VIII, 1, 7 (62). In Maupassant's story, 'Le Docteur Héraclius Gloss' (1877), we read: 'I believe in digestion'. This is a commonplace of the period.

192 *KGW*, VIII, 3, 14 (43).

193 *KGW*, VIII, 3, 14, (45).

194 *WS*, §291.

195 Nietzsche's 'medecine' concerns essentially the digestive tract (it is concerned with monopolizing, not giving), never sexuality, and it is astonishing prudish. In this respect, Nietzsche did not reach the heights of some Christians (like Luther!) whom he condemns for slandering the body. Nietzsche evokes Sterne above all in *AOM*, §113 (cf. the corresponding posthumous fragment in *Mus.*, IX, p. 447), but he treats only his literary style. He quotes Swift in *UM*, 2, §6; 3, §8, and in *HATH*, §§44 and 54. Within the metaphorical framework evoked here, he could have profited speculatively (and personally) from the following passage out of *Gulliver's Travels*: 'Another professor advised great statesmen to examine into the diet of all supsected persons; their times of eating; upon which side they lay in bed; with which hand they wiped their posteriors; to take a strict view of their excrements, and from the colour, the odour, the taste, the consistency, the crudeness, or maturity of digestion, form a judgement of their thoughts or designs: because, men are never so serious, thoughtful and intent, as when they are at stool; which he found by frequent experiment' (London: Dent, 1975), Part III, Ch. 6, p. 203). One would be hard pushed to find in Nietzsche any convincing echo of Lucretius, Rabelais or Heine, who are his precursors in 'medicynicism'.

196 *KGW*, VIII, 2, 10 (18).

197 *K*, XII, p. 425; *GS*, §§11 and 110. Cf. Heidegger's commentary, *Nietzsche*, tr. David Krell (London, 1981).

198 *AOM*, §152.

199 *WS*, §235. Cf. *WP*, §75: 'in our time when the state has an absurdly fat stomach'.

200 *KGW*, VIII, 2, 9 (93). Cf. *EH*, 'The Wagner Case', §1.

201 *VP*, I, p. 198, §439 = *WP*, §125.

202 *VP*, I, p. 340, §460.

203 *VP*, I, p. 340, §460.

204 *BGE*, §19.

205 *VP*, I, p. 266.

206 *VP*, I, p. 268, §230 = *WP*, §492 = *KGW*, VII, 40 (21).

207 *VP*, I, p. 258, §192.

208 *VP*, I, pp. 280–1, §269.

209 *VP*, I, p. 266, §226.
210 Cf. *VP*, I, p. 268, §230: 'Putting direct questions to the subject on the subject and the spirit's self-reflections is a procedure fraught with danger: it could be useful and important for its activity for the subject to give a *false* interpretation of itself'.
211 *VP*, I, p. 263, §216.
212 *VP*, I, p. 268, §230.
213 *VP*, I, p. 258, §189.
214 Freud employs the same metaphors of war and 'political geography': censorship, resistance, defence mechanisms, investment, repression, etc. Cf. *VP*, I, p. 259, §196.
215 *VP*, I, 259, §194.
216 *KGW*, VIII, 2, 9 (98) = *VP*, I, p. 254, §175.
217 *VP*, I, p. 258, §190.
218 *VP*, I, §191.
219 *VP*, p. 259, §193.
220 *KGW*, VIII, 3, 14 (219).
221 *VP*, I, p. 266, §226.
222 *KGW*, VII, 3, 40 (21).
223 *KGW*, VII, 3, 40 (21).
224 *KGW*, VIII, 1, 2, (76).
225 *KGW*, VII, 3, 40 (42).
226 *VP*, I, p. 255, §177.
227 *VP*, I, p. 281, §270.
228 *KGW*, VII, 3, 40 (42).
229 *KGW*, VII, 3, 40 (21).
230 *VP*, I, p. 266, §226.
231 *KGW*, VII, 3, 40 (21).
232 *VP*, I, p. 270, §236 = *Mus.*, XVI, p. 125.
233 *KGW*, VII, 3, 40 (21).
234 *VP*, I, pp. 266–7, §226.
235 *KGW*, VII, 2, 26 (294) = *VP*, I, p. 271, §239.
236 *VP*, I, p. 231, §244.
237 *KGW*, VIII, 3, 15 (90).
238 *VP*, I, p. 270, §236.
239 *VP*, I, p. 270, §236.
240 *VP*, I, p. 270 §236.
241 *VP*, I, p. 286, §§287 and 288. Cf. p. 289, §295.
242 *VP*, I, p. 269, §232.
243 *VP*, I, p. 280, §267.
244 *VP*, I, p. 273, §248.
245 *TI*, 'The "Improvers" of Mankind', §1.
246 *VP*, I, p. 273, §248.
247 *KGW*, VII, 1, 24 (14) = *VP*, I, p. 227, §90.

248 *VP*, I, p. 228, §97.
249 *KGW*, VIII, 1, 7 (60) = *VP*, I, p. 239, §133.
250 *KGW*, VIII, 1, 2 (77) = *VP*, I, p. 240, §134.
251 *KGW*, VIII, 1, 7 (3) = *VP*, I, p. 329, §431.
252 *VP*, I, p. 327, §425.
253 *KGW*, VIII, 1, 2 (148) = *VP*, I, p. 239, §130.

10 PHILOSOPHY: THE GENEALOGICAL ANALYSIS OF CULTURE

1 Heidegger, *Kant et le problème de la metaphysique*, §27 et seq.
2 Kant, *Critique of Pure Reason*, Preface to the First Edition.
3 *VP*, I, p. 93, §185.
4 *VP*, I, pp. 93–4, §186.
5 *KGW*, VIII, 1, 2 (87) = *VP*, I, p. 94, §188.
6 *D*, Preface, §3.
7 *D*, Preface, §3: 'all philosophers were building under the seduction of morality, even Kant – that they were apparently aiming at certainty, at "truth", but in reality at *"majestic moral structure"*'.
8 *KGW*, VIII, 2, 9 (160) + 003 *VP*, I, p. 93, §182.
9 The English term possesses other derived meanings which German expresses through words that are not related to interpretation in the philological sense. To translate: *übersetzen, verdolmetschen*; artistic stylization: *darstellen*; to play a role: *darstellen*, or execute a work: *spielen*; to order facts: *erklären*.
10 Plato, *Phaedrus*, 275 d–e. Compare with *BGE*, §296.
11 *KGW*, VIII, 1, 2 (148) = *WP*, §643.
12 It is by force that structuralism restrains a text's meaning (when it does not annul it in the process) to the play of its internal oppositions, while simply eliminating this problem by means of the metaphysical notion of the arbitrary nature of the sign. The sign is merely arbitrary *sub specie aeternitatis*, but is never so when language is put to work as speech (*parole*). Cf. E. Benveniste, *Problèmes de linguistique générale*, I, chs 2, 4.
13 *KGW*, VIII, 1, 2, (127) = *WP*, §1.
14 This is what J. Granier, in *Penser la praxis*, designates as '*étayage*' ('propping-up').
15 *BGE*, §2. Cf. *Mus.*, XVI, p. 59: 'To grasp everything means suppressing and outstripping (*aufheben*: [sublating]) every perspectivist relation'.
16 *KGW*, VIII, 1, 2 (149) and (150) + 003 *VP*, I, p. 100, §204.
17 Cf. J. Granier, *Penser la praxis*.
18 P. Ricoeur, *La métaphore vive*, pp. 374–84.
19 *La métaphore vive*, p. 375.
20 *La métaphore vive*, p. 376.
21 *La métaphore vive*, p. 376.
22 *La métaphore vive*, p. 382.
23 P. Ricoeur, *La métaphore vive*, p. 11.
24 *VP*, I, p. 239, §130.
25 *VP*, I, p. 240, §134.
26 Cf. *Le discours du monde*, pp. 198–202.
27 Contrary to Schopenhauer's will, which he takes over from, with the

difference that Nietzsche denies one can have a direct and global intuition.

28 Cf. B. Pautrat, *Versions du soleil*, p. 256 et seq., especially pp. 259–60.

29 Such is the definition of Nietzsche given at one of the first Wednesday psychoanalysis meetings taking place around Freud in Vienna (Minute no. 75 1 April 1908, quoted by P.-L. Assoun, *Freud et Nietzsche*, p. 14).

30 The Littré dictionary defines a *moraliste* as 'a writer who deals with *mores*'. B. Poirot-Delpech, *Le Monde* (6 October 1978, p. 21), wrote that 'by "moralisme", we understand not a tendency to redress wrongs or to preach, but a completely French tradition that, from Montaigne and La Rochefoucauld to the greatest novelists of the nineteenth century, maps a portrait of mores, that is often a primary reflection, onto the human condition in general'. Cf. also H.P. Balmer, *Freiheit statt Teleologie*, p. 103, note 13: 'Nietzsche uses the word "moraliste" in two senses: on the one hand positively, in order to designate the *Menschenprüfer* who remains above morality (cf. *AOM*, §5; *HATH*, §35 et seq.; *AOM*, §33 and 72; *WS*, §19, et seq.); on the other hand, the concept of *moralist* can equally be given a negative meaning, designating someone who is the prisoner of morality, and make it into an absolute value' (cf. for example *WP*, §422). Thus Nietzsche writes: 'A *moraliste* is the opposite of a moral preacher; he is a thinker who sees morality as something open to question, a problem. I regret to have to add that the *moraliste*, for this very reason, is himself open to suspicion' (*VP*, I, p. 113, §224).

31 For example, *TI*, Foreword: 'There are more idols in the world than there are realities'. *EH*, Foreword, §2: 'I am, for example, absolutely not a bogey-man, not a moral-monster – I am even an antithetical nature to the species of man hitherto honoured as virtuous'. *An*, §2: 'What is good? . . . What is bad? . . . What is happiness?' And one must not forget the titles of the first two chapters of *EH*. Here we come back to the very full work by H. P. Balmer, *Philosophie der menschlichen Dinge* (Berne and Munich, 1981), and his chapter on Nietzsche the moralist (pp. 162–81). Cf. R. Roos, 'Nietzsche et Epicure: L'idylle héroïque', *Revue d'Allemagne* (1980), 12, 4.

32 *AOM*, §113.

33 *AOM*, §113.

34 *CW*, Preface. Cf. J. Granier, *Penser la praxis*, Conclusion: 'Presence to the world is a loan, not a gift. . . . Of course, the demands of our age, as Kierkegaard already bemoaned, are that "our roars are world–historical and our crowing systematic", such that the philosopher who speaks of wisdom, initiation and meditation seems behind the times. But what do we ultimately scorn in this way if not *untimely* thought, that is to say thought that opens its ears to eternity? For the untimely is the way in which eternity calls out to us within history' (p. 333).

35 G. Deleuze, *Nietzsche and Philosophy*, p. 2. It is a pity that Deleuze does not insist on the idea of nobility: it is in order to justify the nobility of one's origins that one undertakes genealogical research. This is the case with morality: but its pretentions collapse when genealogy interrupts and Nietzsche likes to speak in the event of '*pudenda origo*'.

36 J. Granier, *Le problème de la vérité*, p. 152. But we find the concept of foundations later on: 'To establish the genealogy of a concept is to explain the meaning of this concept by uncovering the ground (*sol*) for its establishment' (p. 471).

37 *Le problème de la vérité*, p. 153 et seq. It is the relationship between superstructure and praxis that creates the difficulty. J. Granier will only really clarify this problem in *Penser la praxis* (1980).

38 Unlike a foundation (*fondement*), which is represented as a plinth that supports what depends on it (a strange metaphorical illogicality), a ground (*sol*) is seen as a nourishment that has invisible depths, moreover. The ground nourishes vegetation and is linked to sexed reproduction.

39 *GM*, Preface, §2.

40 *GM*, Preface, §3.

41 *BGE*, title of Part Five.

42 We see how close this is to Buffon's natural history project, which uses the word 'genealogy'.

43 *GM*, Preface, §6. *TI*, Foreword: '*Schwarzes Fragezeichen*', and *BGE*, §1.

44 *GM*, Preface, §1, beginning.

45 *GM*, Preface, §2 and §6.

46 *GM*, Preface, §3.

47 This as suggested by certain barbs from Nietzsche, such as the following from *BGE*: 'many a peacock hides his peacock tail from all eyes – and calls it his pride' (§73a); 'The belly is the reason man does not so easily take himself for a god' (§141); 'Science offends the modesty of all genuine women. They feel as if one were trying to look under their skin – or worse! under their clothes and finery'. (§127; cf. §204).

48 Cf. our article, 'Ödipus bei Nietzsche'.

49 The knowledge of an origin comes only when one becomes distanced from it (abandonment, the murder of the father for Oedipus).

50 *GM*, Preface, §6.

51 'Philosophy owes that fact that it remains alive only to the *failure* of its attempts to reduce metaphors to purely logical analogies' (J. Granier, *Le discours du monde*, §57, p. 199). Cf. Nietzsche: 'Every profound thinker is more afraid of being understood than of being misunderstood' (*BGE*, §290).

52 J. Granier, *Le discours du monde*, §50, p. 175.

53 'Nihilism': cf. J. Granier, *Le problème de la vérité dans la philosophie de*

Nietzsche, p. 235; Heidegger, *Nietzsche*, II, 'Décadence'' J. Granier, *op. cit.*, p. 209 et seq. 'Power': Heidegger, *op. cit.*, I.

54 In the sense that one can speak medically of degeneration (senile, for example) in tissue.

55 We find the equivalent in the thoughtless use of the notion of 'reflection' in social and material praxis in many a 'reader' of Marx.

56 Burckhardt, *Die Zeit Constantins des Grossen*, quoted by Andler, *Nietzsche, sa vie et sa pensée*, I, p. 219.

57 *EH*, 'Why I am So Wise', §2. Cf. *An*, §6: 'I call an animal, a species, an individual depraved when it loses its instincts, when it chooses, when it *prefers* what is harmful to it'.

58 *EH*, 'Why I am So Wise', §2. Cf. *WP*, §43, as well as §§40 to 46. Nietzsche here defines *décadence* as a weakness of will (§43) and criticizes this idea (§46).

59 As borne out for example by Descartes: 'The firmest buildings eventually fall into decay (*décadence*)'. A rare example of pleonasm in the author of the *Discours*.

60 The best-known example is Montesquieu.

61 The word operates in parallel with *Entartung* (degeneration) (for example, *TI*, 'Expeditions . . .', §45), *Niedergang* (*An*, §6), *Verdorbenheit* (*ibid.*), *Verfall*.

62 This leads to the corresponding invention of the term '*moralenfrei*' (*EH*, 'Why I am So Clever', §1; *An*, §§2 and 6), which links abstraction to pharmacy, and therefore to the body.

63 This is why by right it avoids being used in a biologizing way.

64 *VP*, I, p. 177, §385 = *KGW*, VIII, 2, 11 (380).

65 *An*, §4.

66 *An*, §5.

67 *An*, §§3–5, passim.

68 *An*, §2.

69 The term '*Übermensch*' rests on such a play: he does not dominate by physical force, but represents life in terms of growth and overcoming.

70 *An*, §6.

71 *VP*, II, pp. 157–8, §505.

72 *GM*, First Essay, §10. Cf. *ibid.*, §9: 'The lords are a thing of the past, and the ethics of the common man is completely triumphant. I don't deny that this triumph might be looked upon as a kind of blood poisoning, since it has resulted in a mingling of the races, but there can be no doubt that the intoxication has succeeded'. Cf. on the other hand the meditations on etymology in *GM*, First Essay, §5, notably the link established between ἐσθλός and ἐστίν.

73 *An*, §6.

74 *An*, §6.

75 *An*, §7.

76 *An*, §9: '*Der Wille zum Ende, der nihilistische Wille will zur Macht*'.

77 *TI*, 'The Problem of Socrates'.

78 *TI*, 'How the "Real World" at Last Became a Myth'.

79 *TI*, 'Maxims and Arrows', §39. Reprinted in *BGE*, §97, with 'actor' instead of 'ape'.

80 They are frequent in Nietzsche, such as this caustic remark, which completes the sentence evoked here: 'Apes are too debonair for man to have descended from them' (*K*, XIII, §669).

81 *TI*, 'The Problem of Socrates', §1.

82 Sketched in discursively in *GS*, §340: 'He said, "O Crito, I owe Asclepius a rooster". This ridiculous and terrible "last word": means for those who have ears: "O Crito, *life is a disease*". *Is it possible that a man like him . . . should have been a pessimist? . . . Socrates, Socrates suffered life*! And then he still revenged himself – with this veiled, gruesome, pious, and blasphemous saying'.

83 Note the contrast with the image of dance in Nietzsche, especially in *TSZ*. Nietzsche writes to Malwida von Meysenbug (letter dated February 1884): 'Let us be of good cheer, hale and hearty, and firm on our feet'. In *UM*, 3, §2: 'where are the physicians for modern mankind who themselves stand so firmly and soundly on their feet that they are able to support others and lead them by the hand?'

84 The same image – inability to stand on one's own two feet – occurs as early as *Daybreak*: cf. *D*, 3 (158).

85 Hegel, Preface to *The Philosophy of Right*.

86 *EH*, 'The Birth of Tragedy', §1. In §2, Nietzsche resumes: 'He who not only understands the word "dionysian", but understands *himself* in the word "dionysian" needs no refutation of Plato or of Christianity or of Schopenhauer – *he smells the decomposition*'.

87 Matthew 24:28; cf. Luke 17:37. An image taken up from the Old Testament: Isaiah 18:6, 34:15–16; Jeremiah 7:33, 12:9, 15:3; Ezekiel 39:17.

88 *KGW*, VIII, 2, 11 (415) = *WP*, §853. Cf. *TI*, 'Expeditions . . .', §24: art as '*Stimulans zum Leben*'.

89 *D*, §26.

90 *TSZ*, Part Three, 'The Convalescent', §1.

91 *KGW*, VIII, 2, 11 (415).

92 *KGW*, VIII, 1, 6 (4).

93 *KGW*, VIII, 2, 11 (415).

94 *KGW*, VII, 1 (109), alineas 1 and 7 (= *GS*, Gallimard edition, 23 (32)).

Glossary

The following German words recur in the text.

ablesen	to read
Auslegung	interpretation
bedeuten	to mean
Brecher	breaker, crusher
buchstabieren	to spell
Deutung	interpretation
einverleiben	to incorporate
erfinden	to invent
erklären	to explain
Erlebnis	lived experience
Erscheinung	appearance, phenomenon
Form	form, shape
fragwürdig	doubtful, dubious
frohe Botschaft	good news
Furchtlosigkeit	fearlessness
Gedankenstrich	dash
gemein	in common
gerecht	just, fair, upright
Götzen	idol
Grenze	border, frontier
Handeln	bargaining; behaviour; action
heiligen	to sanctify
heimsuchen	to strike, attack
heissen	to call, name
Ja-sagen	yea-saying (affirmation, agreement)
Kulturphilister	culture philistine

Laut	sound
leben	to live
leer	empty
Leib	body
lieben	to love
lügen	to lie, fib
Mache	structure
Naturgeschichte	natural history
negieren	to negate, deny
nennen	to call, name
reden	to talk, speak
richtig	right, correct
sagen	to say
Schaffen	creation
Schein	light
schrecklich	terrible, dreadful
seelisch	spiritual; mental, psychological; emotional
Selbstüberwindung	willpower
Stoffwechsel	metabolism
Trieb	drive (instinct)
Übermensch	overman (superman)
Unterwelt	underworld
Ursprung	origin
Verarbeitung	use; processing; digestion
Verbrecher	criminal
verführen	to seduce
Verführung	seduction
verleugnen	to deny
Verneinung	denial; negation
versagen	to refuse, deny (someone or something)
Versuch	attempt
verwechseln	to mix up, get muddled
vogelfrei	outlawed
Wille zum Tode	will to death
Wille zur Macht	will to power
Wille zur Wahrheit	will to truth

Zeichensprache	sign language
Ziel	destination; goal
Züchtung	breeding; growing; culture
Zweck	purpose

Bibliography

I WORKS BY NIETZSCHE

Abbreviations are given in parentheses after the work.

GERMAN EDITIONS

Nietzsche, Werke, Kritische Gesamtausgabe, herausgegeben von Giorgio Colli und Mazzino Montinari (Berlin/New York: Walter de Gruyter, 1967) (*KGW*).

Friedrich Nietzsche, Gesammelte Werke, Musarionausgabe (München: Musarionverlag, 1928) (*Mus*).

Nietzsche, Werke, Grossoktavausgabe, 19 vols (Stuttgart: Alfred Kröner Verlag, Auflage, 1921) (*K*) (abbreviated *GAK* in *KGW*).

ENGLISH EDITIONS

These translations are generally used, though in particular cases I have translated directly from the French edition.

The Antichrist, tr. R.J. Hollingdale (Harmondsworth: Penguin, 1968) (*An*).

Assorted Opinions and Maxims in *HATH*, (*AOM*).

Beyond Good and Evil, tr. R.J. Hollingdale (Harmondsworth: Penguin, 1973) (*BGE*).

The Birth of Tragedy, tr. W. Kaufmann (New York: Vintage Books, 1967) (*BT*).

The Case of Wagner in *BT*, (*CW*).

Daybreak, tr. R.J. Hollingdale (Cambridge: Cambridge University Press, 1982) (*D*).

Dithyrambs of Dionysus, tr. R.J. Hollingdale (London: Anvil Press, 1984) (*DD*).

Ecce Homo, tr. R.J. Hollingdale (Harmondsworth: Penguin, 1979) (*EH*).

The Genealogy of Morals, tr. F. Golffing (New York: Doubleday, 1956) (*GM*).

The Gay Science, tr. W. Kaufmann (New York: Vintage Books, 1974) (*GS*).

Human, All Too Human, tr. R.J. Hollingdale (Cambridge: Cambridge University Press, 1986) (*HATH*).

The Twilight of the Idols in *An*, (*TI*).

Thus Spoke Zarathustra, tr. R.J. Hollingdale (Harmondsworth: Penguin, 1961) (*TSZ*).

Untimely Meditations, tr. R.J. Hollingdale (Cambridge: Cambridge University Press, 1983) (*UM*).

The Will to Power, tr. W. Kaufmann (New York: Vintage Books, 1967) (*WP*).

The Wanderer and His Shadow in *HATH*, (*WS*).

Also available are:

The Complete Works of Friedrich Nietzsche, Oscar Levy (ed.), 18 vols (New York: Macmillan, 1909–11; reissued New York: Russell and Russell, 1964).

Philosophy in the Tragic Age of the Greeks, tr. M. Cowan (South Bend, Indiana: Gateway, 1962).

The Portable Nietzsche, tr. W. Kaufmann (New York: Viking Books, 1973).

A Nietzsche Reader, tr. R.J. Hollingdale (Harmondsworth: Penguin, 1977).

FRENCH EDITIONS

I have translated directly from the French, and retained the French title and different abbreviations in footnotes, where French editions do not correspond to an extant English translation, or where I have preferred my own version. This applies in particular to the following:

Lettres choisies, tr. A. Vialatte, 5th edn (Paris: Gallimard, 1950) (*LC*).

Le Livre du Philosophe, tr. A. Kremer-Marietti (Paris: Aubier-Flammarion, 1969) (*LPh*).

Oeuvres posthumes, tr. H.J. Boile (Paris: Mercure de France, 1934) (*OP*).

La volonté de puissance, tr. G. Bianquis, 32nd edn, 2 vols (Paris: Gallimard, 1947) (*VP*).

II WORKS ON NIETZSCHE

BOOKS CONSULTED AND QUOTED FROM

Andler, Charles, *Nietzsche, sa vie et sa pensée*, 3rd edn, 3 vols (Paris: Gallimard, 1958).

Assoun, Paul-Laurent, *Freud et Nietzsche* (Paris: PUF, 1980/1982).

Balmer, Hans Peter, *Freiheit statt Teleologie* (Freiburg-München: Alber, 1977).

Baroni, Christophe, *Nietzsche éducateur* (Paris: Buchet-Chastel, 1961).

Beaufret, Jean, *Dialogue avec Heidegger*, II, *Philosophie moderne* (Paris: Minuit, 1973).

Bindschedler, Maria, *Nietzsche und die poetische Lüge* (Basel: Verlag für Recht und Gesellschaft, 1954).

Blanchot, Maurice, *L'entretien infini* (Paris, Gallimard, 1969).

Blondel, Eric, *Nietzsche: le 'cinquième "évangile"'?* (Paris: Bergers et Mages, 1980).

Deleuze, Gilles, *Nietzsche and Philosophy*, tr. Hugh Tomlinson (London: Athlone, 1983).

Diet, Emmanuel, *Nietzsche et les métamorphoses du divin* (Paris: Cerf, 1972).

Figl, Johann, *Interpretation als philosophisches Prinzip* (Berlin/New York, Walter de Gruyter, 1982).

Fink, Eugen, *La philosophie de Nietzsche*, tr. H. Hillendbrand and A. Lindenberg (Paris: Minuit, 1965).

Granier, Jean, *Le problème de la vérité dans la philosophie de Nietzsche*, (Paris: Seuil, 1966).

Haar, Michel, *Nietzsche* in *Histoire de la philosophie* coll. de la Pléiade, t. III (Paris: Gallimard, 1974).

Halévy, Daniel, *Nietzsche* (Paris: Grasset, 1944; reissued by Librairie Générale Française, 1977).

Heidegger, Martin, *Nietzsche*, tr. David F. Krell, 2 vols (London: Routledge RKP, 1981).

Heidegger, Martin, *Chemins qui ne mènent nulle part*, tr. W. Brokmeier (Paris: Gallimard, 1962).

Heidegger, Martin, *Essais et conférences*, tr. A. Préau (Paris: Gallimard, 1958).

Heidegger, Martin, *Qu'appelle-t-on penser?*, tr. A. Becker and G. Granel (Paris: PUF, 1967).

Heller, Peter, *Studies on Nietzsche* (Bonn: Bouvoir, 1980).

Henke, Dieter, *Gott und Grammatik* (Pfüllingen: Neske, 1981).

Janz, Curt Paul, *Die Briefe Friedrich Nietzsches* (Zürich: Editor Academica, 1972).

Jaspers, Karl, *Nietzsche, Introduction à sa philosophie* (Paris, Gallimard, 1950).

Jaspers, Karl, *Nietzsche und das Christentum* (München, Piper: 1952).

Kaufmann, Walter, A., *Nietzsche, Philosopher, Psychologist, Antichrist*, 3rd edn (New York: Vintage Books, 1968).

Klossowski, Pierre, *Nietzsche et le cercle vicieux* (Paris: Mercure de France, 1969).

Köster, Peter, *Der sterbliche Gott*, (Meisenheim am Glan, 1972).

Kremer-Marietti, Angèle, *Thèmes et structures dans l'oeuvre de Nietzsche*, (Paris: Lettres modernes, 1957).

Kremer-Marietti, Angèle, *L'homme et ses labyrinthes* (Paris: UGE, 1972).

Marion, Jean-Luc, *L'idole et la distance* (Paris: Grasset, 1977).

Müller-Lauter, Wolfgang, *Nietzsche, Seine Philosophie der Gegensätze und die Gegensätze seiner Philosophie* (Berlin/New York: Walter de Gruyter, 1971).

Pautrat, Bernard, *Versions du soleil. Figures et système de Nietzsche*, (Paris: Seuil, 1971).

Peters, H.F., *Ma soeur, mon épouse*, tr. Léo Lock (Paris: Gallimard, 1967).

Peters, H.F., *Nietzsche et sa soeur Elisabeth*, tr. M. Poublan (Paris: Mercure de France, 1978).

Podach, E.F., *L'effondrement de Nietzsche*, tr. A. Vaillant and J. Kuckenburg (Paris: Gallimard, 1931).

Pütz, Heinz Peter, *Kunst und Künstlerexistenz bei Nietzsche und Thomas Mann* (Bonn: Bouvier, 1963).

Reboul, Olivier, *Nietzsche critique de Kant* (Paris: PUF, 1974).

Schaeffner, Pierre, Introduction *Lettres à Peter Gast* (Monaco: Editions du Rocher, 1957).

Schlechta, Karl, *Le cas Nietzsche*, tr. A. Coeuroy, (Paris: Gallimard, 1960).

Tiedemann, Rolf (ed.), Gesammelte Schriften (Frankfurt am Main, 1971).

Valadier, Paul, *Nietzsche et la critique du christianisme* (Paris: Cerf, 1974).

Valadier, Paul, *Essais sur la modernité. Nietzsche et Marx*, (Paris: Cerf-Desclée 1974).

Valadier, Paul, *Nietzsche, l'athée de rigueur* (Paris: Desclée de Brouwer, 1975).

Valadier, Paul, *Jésus-Christ ou Dionysos* (Paris: Desclée, 1979).

PERIODICALS AND COLLECTED ESSAYS

Nietzsche, Cahiers de Royaumont, 7th colloquium (Paris: Minuit, 1967).

Nietzsche aujourd'hui?, 2 vols (Paris: UGE, 1973).

Nietzsche contemporaneo o inattuale, (Quaderni di humanitas, Brescia: editrice Morcelliana, 1980).

The New Nietzsche, Contemporary Styles of Interpretation, David B. Allison (ed.) (New York: Delta Books, 1977).

Nietzsche Studien. Internationales Jahrbuch für die Nietzsche-Forschung, hersg. von M. Montinari, W. Müller-Lauter, H. Wenzel (Berlin/New York, vols 1–10/11, 1972–81/1982).

Perspektiven der Philosophie, Neues Jahrbuch, hersg. von R. Berlinger, E. Fink, Friedrich Kaulbach, Wiebke Schrader (Amsterdam: Rodopi-Hildesheim Gerstenberg, vols 1–7, 1975–81).

Revue philosophique de la France et de l'Etranger, 'Nietzsche' (Paris, PUF, July–September 1971).

Concilium, 'Nietzsche et le christianisme' (Paris, Beauchesne, 165 1981).

ARTICLES AND ESSAYS NOT INCLUDED IN THE ABOVE

Birault, Henri, 'Sur un texte de Nietzsche: "En quoi, nous aussi, nous sommes encore pieux" (GS, §344)', *Revue de métaphysique et de morale*, (January–March 1962).

Blondel, Eric, '"Götzen aus horchen": Versuch einer Genealogie der Genealogie. Nietzsches philologisches Aprior und die christliche Kritik des Christentums', *Perspektiven der Philosophie*, 1981, Band 7.

Blondel, Eric, 'Wohin? Wozu? Ein Kulturproblem: Wahrheit und Leben bei Hume und Nietzsche', *Perspektiven der Philosophie* (1980), 16.

Flécheux, André, 'La ligne brisée. Note sur la philologie nietzschéenne', *Annales de la Faculté des Lettres et Sciences humaines de Nice* (1973), 20.

Figl, Johann, 'Nietzsches philologisch-historische Kritik der theologischen Bibelinterpretation', *Studia Urbaniana*, (Brescia: Rome Urbaniana University Press, editrice, Paideia, 1981), 16.

Foucault, Michel, 'La pensée du dehors', *Critique*, (Paris, Minuit, June 1966), 229.

Gerhardt, Volker, 'Nietzsches ästhetische Revolution', *Die Kunst gibt zu denken. Schriften der Abteilung für Kunsterzieher* (Münster 1981), 7.

Granier, Jean, 'La pensée nietzschéenne du chaos', *Revue de métaphysique et de morale* (Paris: A. Colin, 1971), 2.

Klinkenberg, Hans Martin, 'Der Kulturbegriff Nietzsches', *Historische Forschungen*, Karl Erich Borne (ed.), (Wiesbaden: Fritz Steiner, 1961), 4.

Malet, Nicole, 'L'homme et la femme dans la philosophie de Nietzsche', *Revue de métaphysique et de morale* (Paris: A. Colin, 1977), 1.

Roos, Richard, 'Nietzsche et Epicure: L'idylle héroïque', *Revue d'Allemagne et des pays de langue allemande* (October–December 1980), XII, 4.

Simon J., 'Grammatik und Wahrheit', *Nietzsche Studien* (1972), Band 1.

Wismann, Heinz, 'Le métier de philologue', I, II, *Critique* (Paris: Minuit, 276 (May 1970) and 279–280 (August–September 1970)).

III   CLASSIC PHILOSOPHICAL TEXTS, HISTORY OF PHILOSOPHY, HISTORY, LITERARY WORKS

Adorno, Theodor W., *In Search of Wagner*, (London: Verso, 1981).

Adorno, Theodor W., *Mahler. Une physionomie musicale*, tr. J.-L. Leleu and Th. Leydenbach (Paris: Minuit, 1976).

Adorno, Theodor W., *Trois études sur Hegel*, tr. E. Blondel, O. Hansen-Løve, P. Joubert, M. de Launay, Th. Leydenbach, P. Pénisson (Paris: Payot, 1979).

Bachelard, Gaston, *L'air et les songes* (Paris: Corti, 1943).

Bachelard, Gaston, *L'engagement rationaliste* (Paris: PUF, 1972).

Balmer, Hans Peter, *Philosophie der menschlichen Dinge. Die europäische Moralistik*, (Bern und München: Franke, 1981).

Baudelaire, Charles, *Les fleurs du mal* in *Oeuvres complètes* (Paris: Gallimard, 1961).

348 *Nietzsche: The Body and Culture*

Bianquis, Geneviève, *Histoire de la littérature allemande*, 6th edn (Paris: A. Colin, 1969).

The Bible, Revised Standard Version (London: Collins, 1952).

Blacking, John, *How Musical is Man?* (Washington, 1973).

Blanchot, Maurice, *Le Livre à venir* (Paris: Gallimard, 1959).

Bollack, Jean and Wismann, Heinz, *Héraclite ou la séparation* (Paris: Minuit, 1972).

Brès, Yvon, *La Psychologie de Platon* (Paris: PUF, 1968).

Broch, Hermann, *Lettres*, tr. A. Kohn (Paris: Gallimard, 1961).

Broch, Hermann, *Création littéraire et connaissance*, tr. A. Kohn (Paris: Gallimard, 1966).

Broch, Hermann, *Le tentateur*, tr. A. Kohn (Paris: Gallimard, 1960).

Burgelin, Henri, *La société allemande, 1871–1968* (Paris: Arthaud, 1969).

Burgelin, Pierre, *La philosophie de l'existence de Jean-Jacques Rousseau*, 2nd edn (Paris, Vrin, 1973).

Cassirer, Ernst, *The Philosophy of the Enlightenment*, tr. F. Koelin and J. Pettegrove (Princeton, 1951).

Chamfort, H., *Maximes et Pensées* (Paris: Gallimard, 1982).

Cicero, *Tuscalan Disputations* (Havard, 1927).

Colli, Giorgio, *La naissance de la philosophie* (Paris: Ed. de l'Aire, 1981).

Daval, Roger, *Perspectives sur la métaphysique de Kant d'après la théorie du schématisme* (Paris: PUF, 1950).

Delbos, Victor, *La philosophie pratique de Kant*, 3rd edn (Paris: PUF, 1969).

Derathé, Robert, *Jean-Jacques Rousseau et la science politique de son temps*, 2nd edn (Paris: Vrin, 1974).

Descartes, René, *Oeuvres*, coll. de la Pléiade (Paris: Gallimard, 1953).

Descombes, Vincent, *L'inconscient malgré lui* (Paris, Minuit, 1977).

Descombes, Vincent, *Le Même et l'Autre* (Paris: Minuit, 1979).

Djurić, Mihailo, *Mythos, Wissenschaft, Ideologie* (Amsterdam: Rodopi, 1979).

Dodds, E.R., *Les Grecs et l'irrationnel*, tr. M. Gibson (Paris: Aubier, 1965).

Droz, Jacques (ed.), *Le romantisme politique en Allemagne* (Paris: A. Colin, 1963).

Dumas, André, *Nommer Dieu*, (Paris: Cerf, 1980).

Durkheim, Emile, *Les règles de la méthode sociologique*, 14th edn (Paris: PUF, 1960).

Ellul, Jacques, *Autopsie de la révolution* (Paris: Calmann-Lévy, 1969).

Febvre, Lucien, *Martin Luther, Un destin*, 4th edn (Paris: PUF, 1968).

Fink, Eugen, *Le jeu comme symbole du monde*, tr. H. Hildenbrand and A. Lindenburg (Paris: Minuit, 1966).

Fontanier, Pierre, *Les figures du discours* (Paris: Flammarion, 1968).

Freud, Sigmund, *Three Essays on the Theory of Sexuality* (1905) (London, 1962) Standard Edition, 7, 125; Penguin Freud Library, 7, 31.

Freud, Sigmund, *Five Lectures on Psycho Analysis* (1909), Standard Edition, 11, 3.

Freud, Sigmund, *The Future of an Illusion* (1927) (London, 1962) Standard Edition, 21, 3; Penguin Freud Library, 12, 179.

Freud, Sigmund, *Civilization and its Discontents* (1929), (New York and London, 1963) Standard Edition, 21, 59; Penguin Freud Library, 12, 243.

Girard, René, *Deceit, Desire and the Novel: Self and Other in Literary Structure*, tr. Y. Freccero, Baltimore, Johns Hopkins University Press, 1966.

Girard, René, *Violence and the Sacred*, tr. P. Gregory (Baltimore: Johns Hopkins, 1977).

Girard, René, *Des choses cachées depuis le commencement du monde* (Paris: Grasset, 1978).

Goethe, *Conversations avec Eckermann*, tr. J. Chuzeville 19e éd. (Paris: Gallimard, 1949).

Granier, Jean, *Le discours du monde* (Paris: Seuil, 1977).

Granier, Jean, *Penser la praxis*, 'Philosophie d'aujourd'hui' (Paris, PUF, 1980).

Groupe M (J. Dubois *et al.*), *Rhétorique générale* (Paris: Larousse, 1970).

Hegel, G.W., *Phenomenology of the Spirit*, tr. A.V. Miller and J.N. Findley, Oxford, OUP, 1977.

Hegel, G.W., *Philosophy of Right*, tr. T.M. Knox (Oxford: OUP, 1942).

Heidegger, Martin, *Kant et le problème de la métaphysique*, tr. A. de Waelhens and W. Biemel (Paris: Gallimard, 1953).

Herder, Johann G., *Traité sur l'origine de la langue*, tr. P. Pénisson (Paris: Aubier, 1977).

Hesse, Hermann, *The Glass Bead Game*, (Harmondsworth: Penguin, 1972).

Hölderlin, Friedrich, *Hypérion ou l'ermite de Grèce*, tr. R. Rovini (Paris: UGE, 1968).

Hobbes, Thomas, *Leviathan or the Matter, Forme and Power of a Commonwealth ecclesiastical and civil*, M. Oakeshott (ed.) (Oxford: Blackwell, 1960).

Hommage à Jean Hyppolite, (Paris: PUF, 1971).

Hume, D., *A Treatise of Human Nature*, 2 vols (London: Dent, 1964).

Jaeger, Werner, *Paideia: The Ideals of Greek Culture*, 3 vols (Oxford: OUP, 1943–5).

Jaeger, Werner, *A la naissance de la théologie* (Paris, Cerf, 1966).

Jakobson, Roman, *Essais de linguistique générale*, tr. N. Ruwet (Paris: Minuit, 1963).

Joly, Henri, *Le renversement platonicien. Logos, Epistémè, Polis* (Paris: Vrin, 1974).

Jones, Ernest, *The Life and Work of Sigmund Freud*, 3 vols (New York: Basic Books, 1953–7).

Kant, Immanuel, *Critique of Pure Reason*, tr. N. Kemp Smith (London, Macmillan: 1929).

Kant, Immanuel, *Critique of practical reason*, tr. Lewis W. Beck, (New York: Bobbs Merrill, 1956).

Kant, Immanuel, *The Critique of Judgement*, tr. J.C. Meredith (Oxford: Clarendon, 1952).

Kant, Immanuel, 'D'un ton grand seigneur adopté naguère en philosophie' in *Première introduction à la critique du jugement*, tr. Louis Guillermit (Paris: Vrin, 1968).

Kant, Immanuel, *Logique*, tr. L. Guillermit, 2e éd. (Paris, Vrin, 1970).

Kant, Immanuel, *On history*, tr. Lewis W. Beck (Bobbs Merrill, 1963).

Kopp, Bernhard, *Beiträge zur Kulturphilosophie der deutschen Klassik. Eine Untersuchung im Zusammenhang mit dem Bedeutungswandel des Wortes Kultur* (Meisenheim am Glan: A. Hain, 1974).

LaRochefoucauld, *Maximes* (Paris: Garnier, 1967).

La Fontaine, *Fables et contes* (Paris: Gellimard, 1948).

Langaney, André, *Le sexe et l'innovation* (Paris: Seuil, 1979).

Laplanche, J. and Pontalis, J.-B., *The Language of Psycho-Analysis* (London: Hogarth, 1973).

Leclaire, Serge, *Psychoanalyser* (Paris: Seuil, 1968).

Leclaire, Serge, *Démasquer le réel* (Paris: Seuil, 1971).

Leibniz, G.W., *New Essays on Human Understanding*, Peter Remnant and Jonathan Bennet (eds), (Cambridge: CUP, 1982).

Leibniz, G.W., *Opuscules philosophiques choisis*, tr. P. Schrecker (Paris: Vrin, 1966).

Lévi-Strauss, Claude, *Structural Anthropology*, tr. L. Jacobson and B. Grundfest, Schoepf (Harmondsworth: Penguin, 1968).

Lévi-Strauss, Claude, *The Savage Mind*, (London, 1966).

Lévi-Strauss, Claude, *Race et histoire* (Paris: Gonthier, 1961).

Löwith, Karl, *From Hegel to Nietzsche* (London: Constable, 1965).

Lucretius, *De rerum natura* (Oxford: OUP, 1922).

Lyons, John, *Introduction to Theoretical Linguistics* (Cambridge, CUP, 1968).

Mann, Thomas, *Gesammelte Werke in dreizehn Bänden*, 2e éd. (Frankfurt: Fischer, 1974).

Mann, Thomas, *Tonio Kröger* (Oxford: Basil Blackwell, 1968).

Mann, Thomas, *Noblesse de l'esprit*, tr. F. Delmas (Paris: A. Michel, 1960).

Mann, Thomas, *Les maîtres*, trs. L. Servicen and J. Naujac (Paris: Grasset, 1979).

Martin, Gottfried, *Kant's Metaphysics and Theory of Science*, tr. P.G. Lucas, (London: Greenwood, 1974).

Marty, Pierre, *Les mouvements individuels de vie et de mort. Essai d'économie psychosomatique*, t. I (Paris: Payot, 1976).

Marx, Karl, *German Ideology* (London: Lawrence and Wishart, 1974).

Maupassant, *Contes et nouvelles*, 2 vols, coll. de la Pléiade (Paris: Gallimard, 1974–7).

Mürger, *Scènes de la vie de Bohème* (Paris: Julliard, 1964).

Musil, Robert, *The Man Without Qualities*, 3 vols (London: Picador, 1968).

Plato, *Oeuvres complètes*, 2 vols, coll. de la Pléiade, (Paris: Gallimard, 1950).

Rabelais, *Oeuvres complétes*, coll. de la Pléiade (Paris: Gallimard, 1934).

Reik, Theodor, *Listening with the third ear. The inner experience of a psychoanalyst* (New York: Grove Press, 1948).

Ricoeur, Paul, *Freud and Philosophy: An Essay on Interpretation* (New Haven: Yale University Press, 1970).

Ricoeur, Paul, *The conflict of Interpretations: An essay on Hermeneutics* (North Western University Press, 1974).

Ricoeur, Paul, *La métaphore vive* (Paris, Seuil, 1975).

Rousseau, *Oeuvres complètes*, t. I–IV, coll. de la Pléiade (Paris: Gallimard 1959–69).

Ruwet, Nicholas, *Introduction à la grammaire générative* (Paris: Plon, 1967).

Sartre, Jean-Paul, *Critique de la raison dialectique*, t. I, (Paris, Gallimard, 1960).

Saussure, Ferdinand de, *Cours de linguistique générale*, nouv. éd., (Paris: Payot, 1972.

Schivelbusch, Wolfgang, *Das Paradiese, der Geschmack und die Vernunft* (*Le goût des stimulants*), tr, E. Blondel, O. Hansen-Løve, P. Pénisson, (Paris, unpublished.).

Schnerb, Robert, *Le XIXe siècle. L'apogée de l'expansion européenne (1815–1914)*, 3e éd., Paris: PUF, 1961).

Schopenhauer, Arthur, *The World as Will and Representation*, tr. E.F.J. Payne, 2 vols, (Indian Hills, Colorado: The Falcon's Wing Press, 1958).

Spenlé, Jean-Edouard, *La pensée allemande de Luther à Nietzsche* (Paris: Colin, 1967).

Spinoza, Baruch, *Oeuvres complètes*, tr. R. Caillois, M. Francès and R. Misrahi, coll. de la Pléiade (Paris: Gallimard, 1954).

Stendhal, H. *Oeuvres romanesques*, vol. 4, coll. de la Pléiade (Paris: Gallimard, 1952).

Sterne, Laurence, *The Life and Opinions of Tristram Shandy* (Harmondsworth: Penguin: 1975).

Swift, Jonathan, *Gulliver's Travels* (London: Dent, 1975).

Weil, Eric, *Problèmes kantiens*, 2nd edn (Paris: Vrin, 1970).

Index